GW00537669

CATAMARANS

The Complete Guide for Cruising Sailors

CATAMARANS

The Complete Guide for Cruising Sailors

GREGOR TARJAN

Foreword by

Charles K. Chiodi

Adlard Coles Nautical

London

page 2 Aerial shot of a large catamaran's aft deck shows the abundant room for water sports and socializing.

page 6 Mood lighting in the saloon of this 56' catamaran lures one to evening cocktails and a relaxing game of chess.

Published by Adlard Coles Nautical
an imprint of A & C Black Publishers Ltd
38 Soho Square, London W1D 3HB
www.adlardcoles.com

First published in the United States in 2006 by Aeroyacht Ltd and Chiodi Publishing Inc

This edition published in the United States in 2008 by International Marine, a division of the McGraw-Hill Companies

ISBN 978-1-4081-0073-8

A CIP catalogue record for this book is available from the British Library.

Text, illustrations and graphs: Gregor Tarjan, Aeroyacht Ltd
Photography: Gilles Martin-Raget, unless noted otherwise
Printed and bound in China

To my parents Shaque and Marcus,
who made my dreams possible, and to Flo,
who always stands beside me pursuing them.

TABLE OF CONTENTS

ACKNOWLEDGEMENTS

There are many individuals who contributed to "Catamarans." Most are mentioned below. However, there are countless people who, in one way or another, developed my sense for multihulls and the sea, either by having taken me out for a sail or sharing ideas that I would never have come across otherwise. Sailing is an art and it is the hands-on experience of these people and various mentors that gave this book its invaluable reference content. We must never forget that we all profit from their knowledge and understanding of catamarans, their design, and seamanship.

A very important role in my multihull-life was Charles Chiodi. During my years in Vienna, Austria I was one of the first subscribers to his magazine and I read it from cover to cover. In fact, I still do. "MULTIHULLS Magazine" was possibly one of the biggest catalysts that fueled my obsession, one that eventually led me to make the step from high-performance monohulls to catamarans. He was instrumental in showing me "the light" and the exciting alternative to conventional sailing yachts. Charles Chiodi did more for the multihull movement and the acceptance of these new types of craft, over the last 50 years, than anyone else. He wrote the "Foreword" and "History" chapters in this book and provided invaluable advice and encouragement throughout the sometimes arduous research and writing process. Charles, a big Thank You goes out to you.

If I mention Charles, the staff at MM cannot be left out. Here's a big hug for your editorial service and proofreading of all the chapters. Also, my gratitude goes to Eric, Rick and the entire production team, it would have been impossible without you.

There is a list of individuals I would like to mention, all of whom helped shape my opinions and know-how. There is Arthur Kalisiky – I sailed with him in the STAR North American Championships; the acclaimed Dennis Conner, whose presence on "Stars and Stripes" was a great motivation for the America's Cup; Paul Derecktor and his father Bob, who showed me the ropes in the tough US mega yacht-building and project-management industry; my friend Bruno Nicolletti, who demonstrated endless courage and seamanship during his "geriatric" Southern Ocean circumnavigation; Yves Parlier, who let me sail on the highly experimental "Hydraplaneur;" and Udo Gabbert, who sold me "Flo," a boat that taught me more about big boat solo sailing than any other vessel.

This book would not be complete without mentioning my friend Stephane Stolz. His invaluable technology competence and companionship, will never be forgotten. Also, thanks go to my other sailing buddy, Kirk Siemsen, whose 50' racing cat was often a test bed for new ideas and a wonderful platform upon which both our families spent unforgettable times.

Special thanks go out to all previous multihull authors and top industry professionals, such as: Jean-Jacques Costes of Blubay, and Chris White, Charles Kanter, Derek Harvey, Derek Kelsall, Phil Weld, Rob James, Dick Newick, Jim Brown Thomas Firth Jones, Dr. Gavin Le Sueur, James Wharram and many others who, in a sense, all contributed to this book. Of course, I cannot forget my many colleagues, including designers, manufacturers and yacht brokers, who submitted information and photographs of their catamarans to make this publication as objective and comprehensive as possible. In fact, the chapter on "Noteworthy Multihulls" would have been impossible without their help.

I am especially grateful to Hélène de Fontainieu and her assistant Peggy; Eric Bruneel and Jean Francois Fountaine, for providing material for this book. More than just credit should be given to the generosity of top marine photographer Gilles Martin-Raget, whose artistic talents are featured in this book. It is an honor to share the following pages with him. All anonymous photographers whose pictures have been included and have no specific photo credit, were contacted by our office on several occasions. I am more than appreciative for their contribution.

Further thanks go to all my many clients and crewmembers from around the world for their confidence and trust throughout business transactions, as well as companionship during many, sometimes rough, offshore trips we sailed together. Special appreciation goes to Robin Griffiths, Brian Nixon, Peter Crosbie, and Matthieu with whom I have crossed the Atlantic on different occasions. Ocean passages bond people in a very special way; we had tons of fun and I have learned a great deal from your various backgrounds and skills.

At last, I am deeply grateful to my parents Shaque (who also helped edit the book) and Marcus, and to my brother Miki, who shared my enthusiasm for the sea for over four decades, and always believed in my abilities to follow my ideas. Without you this book would not have been possible.

Most important, I want to thank my family: my two sons Philippe and Victor and, you Flo, for your critique, patience and understanding. We have shared so many thoughts as well as countless hours at sea together and you have always stood beside me, pursuing my dreams – a big hug and kiss to you all.

Gregor Tarjan

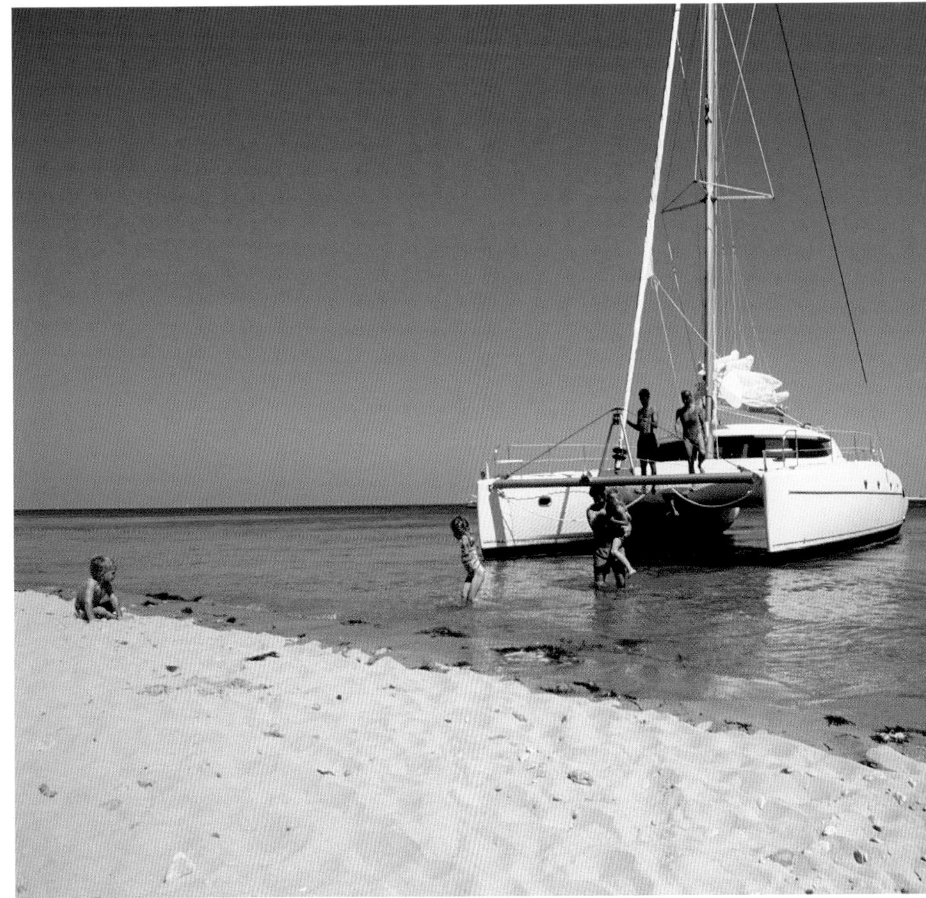

below There are few activities in life as rewarding as the adventures of exploring our world with our families on our own boat. Modern cruising catamarans have the amenities of waterfront condos – with the added benefit of relocation.

FOREWORD

In my 40-year career in multihulls – 31 in publishing a magazine by that title – I have seen three distinctive eras emerge from the heritage of the Micronesian outriggers. In the history of the modern multihulls first came the "I build my own" era by the die-hard believers, nearly fanatics of the multi-hulled sailing craft; followed by the quasi acceptance of the open-minded but skeptical sailors of our society, the "Will they capsize?" era; to what we have today: "What's the difference between mono and multihulls?" era. This is the most burning question I receive almost daily by our readers who span the globe geographically, and the entire spectrum demographically. From King Juan Carlos of Spain (who has a SuperCat) to a prisoner incarcerated for life (who can only dream of far horizons), the input I receive runs the gamut.

below This large L-shaped settee permits 6 people to enjoy dinners in comfort, while at the same time allowing one crew member to navigate at the chart table.

The "I build my own" era was necessitated by the fact that in the early days (the 1950s and '60s) there were very few, if any, production multihulls. If you wanted one, you had to buy plans from a multihull designer (see History Chapter, following) and build it, or have it built, for yourself. Those boats were mostly trimarans, "monohulls with training hulls," as the pundits called them, for there was no "catamaran culture," save the few Wharram and Choy cats.

The "Will they capsize?" era came on the heels of a few disasters at major transoceanic races when the greed-for-speed sailors pushed the envelope just a bit too far and upended their sailboats. The news media, ever-so-hungry for headlines, quickly trumpeted sensational accounts which, to the monohull salesmen's delight, slowed down the emerging threat of multihulls that started to cut into their business. The obvious advantages of the multihulls prompted a proliferation of builders and yards that started producing mostly catamarans, not unlike Detroit builds automobiles, albeit on a much smaller scale. The multitude of advantages of catamarans over their monohull sisters, however, became more and more undeniable.

The "What is the difference?" era is now! The most often asked questions are no longer "Are they going to capsize?" or "Are they really safe?" but "Why should I buy (or switch to) a catamaran?" and "Which catamaran is best for me?"

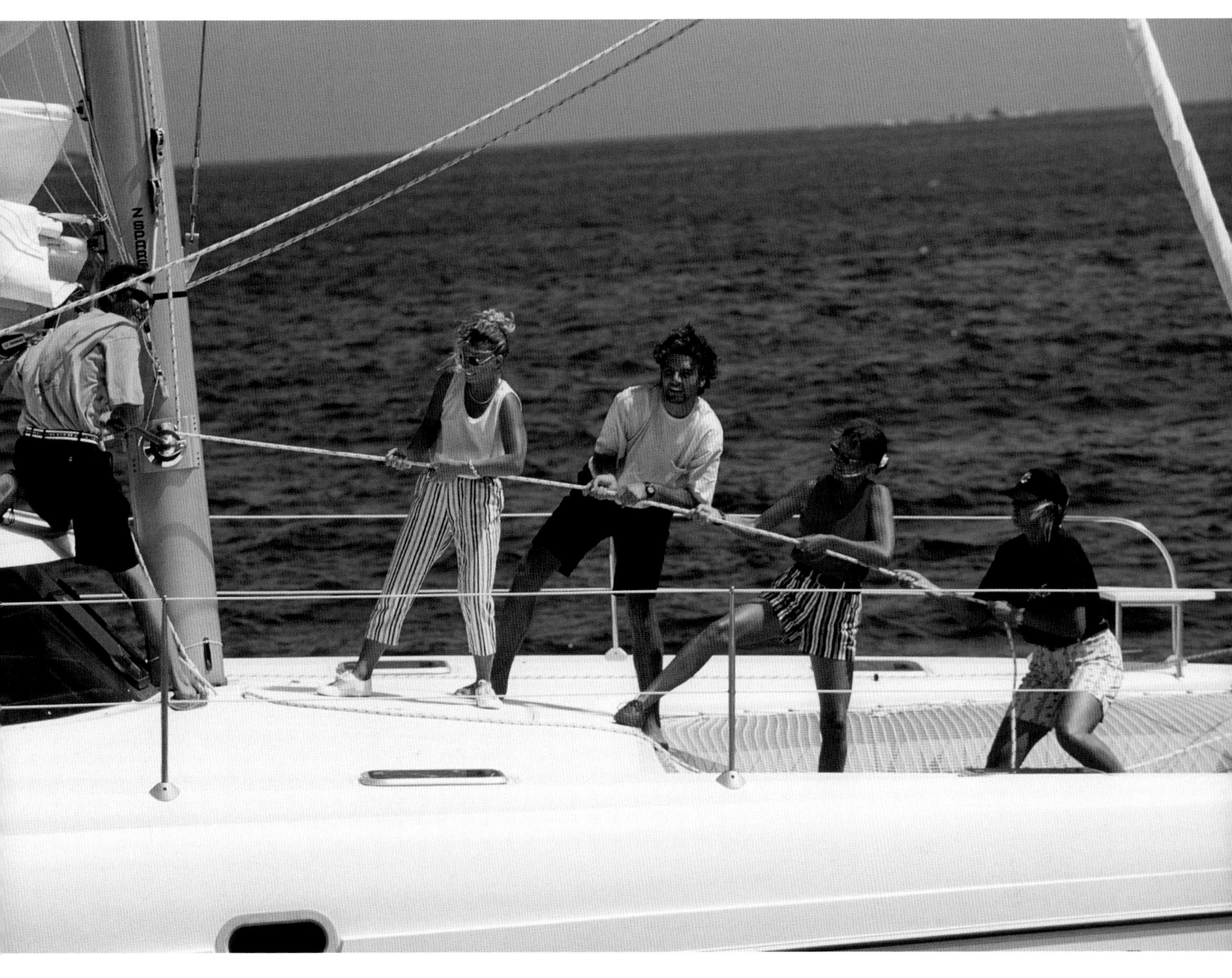

CATAMARANS was conceived and is published to precisely answer all the questions a newcomer to multihulls can possibly ask. That Gregor Tarjan is a naval architect specializing in multihulls, and thus familiar with the design concepts, is only one of the major ingredients in writing a comprehensive book. The fact that he has sailed thousands of ocean miles in a variety of catamarans, encountering every possible weather condition short of a hurricane, adds to his practical knowledge – invaluable when assessing the safety of these craft. If that's not enough, he is also a yacht broker and exclusive distributor for a number of yards which, in my opinion, gives him an advantage of knowing what today's sailors are looking for in a modern catamaran. He is in the unique position of being able to gauge the market and its changing trends. No other author of the previously published multihull-related books has this triple qualification.

If you are contemplating spending hundreds of thousands of dollars on a cruising catamaran, the small price of this book is probably the best investment you could possibly start with.

Charles K. Chiodi

above On most cruising catamarans the main halyard is conveniently hoisted with a push of a button via the electric winch from the cockpit. Here the entire crew gets some exercise and manually raises the mainsail – an easy operation that could even be done by one person.

INTRODUCTION

Catamarans are here to stay. Over the past decades they have established themselves in the charter industry and proven themselves as capable liveaboard cruisers. They can now be found in every harbor – from beach cats to 140-foot monster multihulls. Today the fastest sailboats are catamarans, clocking more than 700 miles per day. From circumnavigating vessel, to luxury yacht or passenger ferry – the multihull concept works! The evolution within the boating industry has matured sailors and their perception of the machines they take out to sea. This book was written to keep pace with these developments.

My childhood heroes were navigators and explorers such as Sir Francis Drake, Joshua Slocum and Bernard Moitessier. The vessels they took to sea were as different from a multihull as you can get, yet their adventures seemed as intriguing as the ships they sailed. Ever since I was a boy growing up in downtown Vienna, I felt myself drawn to the sea. Who knows, maybe the attraction stemmed from the fact that Austria is a landlocked country and could not have been farther from the ocean? My brother and I would save money to take the tram from the city center to the winding estuaries of the Danube River to experience our first sailing lessons. From these early days on I became hooked on sailing and longed for the adventures of the open ocean. The fascination with catamarans seemed just a natural progression.

Today, nearly four decades and almost 80,000 sailed miles later, while my two sons are sailing on beach cats and I am still learning, I am sure of this: perhaps my background in art has supported my realization that sailing is an art form. Just as we discover new techniques of how to singlehand a 70' catamaran or get off the dock in a crosswind, the sailing industry continues to evolve. There just does not seem to be an end to the learning curve.

Excellent books have been written about multihulls yet most of them are already outdated. Progress in the technology sector is outpacing all but monthly publications. Similar to the fact that by the time you walk out of the computer store with your new laptop, you find that your new purchase is already obsolete. Books written about the subject of multihulls face a comparable fate. Advancements in boat design and new construction methods have reflected the global acceptance of multihulls, new forms of seamanship skills, and a revolution in the charter industry. We Baby Boomers, and our insatiable quest for adventure, possibly have fueled the most significant growth in the boating sector – that of multihulls. Today more ferries and water taxis are built with more than one hull than ever before. In the past, developments of the modern catamaran had been hindered by the conservatism of designers, builders and sailors. Presently we see more progress in the

far right Bow-seats are often the best vantage point to take in the expanse of the sails, the sea and the wide decks of a cat.

world of multihulls, and their applications are reaching far beyond the yachting industry. The US military is producing high-speed wave-piercing catamarans, able to transport thousands of troops, including tanks at 50 knots. Minesweepers, cable-laying ships, dredging vessels and patrol boats... most are now catamarans. Shipyards, yacht brokers and charter companies, specializing in these craft are emerging in numbers as never before.

And they are getting bigger. Today's mega cats can reach a length of 150 feet. At the time of this writing I am involved in several superyacht catamaran projects. One of them is a 145' luxury cat, which will be built in Connecticut. The other could become the genesis of the second "Calypso," a reef exploration catamaran, which at 150' will not only be the world's largest cat, but also the first multihull featuring a helicopter landing platform.

The trickle-down effect of yacht races in terms of technology and reporting has created a brand-new awareness of multihulls that is here to stay. The exciting spectacle of high-profile sporting events such as La Route du Rhum, the Transat, and even the Worrell 1000 have attracted sponsors and millions of viewers.

A lot has changed from the editorial angles as well. Challenged by the multihull vs. monohull discussion, former authors were defensive of their subject. Thanks to these publications, multihull craft have been accepted in all nautical circles. Catamarans have finally established themselves and have been taken to new heights.

A number of transformations have taken place during the past decades; not only has the average size of a sailboat increased but traditionalist monohull sailors have greatly

far right Large, sliding, "patio" doors bring the outside in, and let the cook communicate with crewmembers in the cockpit.

matured and kept in step with the ever-changing industry. Sailors who once owned a "classic plastic" might now be sailing a lightweight cruiser/racer monohull or even a folding trimaran. Children of die-hard monohullers are now flying the hulls of their own beach cats. I doubt that these kids will ever go back to slow sailing and heeling. Their next boat very well might be a catamaran or trimaran. They will possibly charter a boat in the Virgin Islands, and chances are that it will be a multihull.

CATAMARANS is all about cruising catamarans. It focuses on design and seamanship issues with a special chapter dedicated to a catalogue of noteworthy multihulls. It might answer a lot of questions such as: why are catamarans typically faster than their single-hulled counterparts? Part 1 of this publication illustrates the characteristics and desirable attributes of multihulls. Are they really more seaworthy? Not everything about a cat is all rosy. I will objectively compare a monohull to its two-hulled equivalent and reflect on advantages such as stability, shallow draft and accommodations.

Isn't sailing in general simply a global stage for aero- and hydrodynamics put into practice? Part 2 examines various design attributes particular to catamarans. Updated publications, such as this book, are necessary as modern materials and developments have altered our manner of command of the wind and waves. Although the forces of nature have never changed, technology and design have. This book will keep you in the loop.

It does not matter which type or size of mono or multihull you sail – this publication aims to provide valuable insight into the world of cruising catamarans. It will improve your seamanship skills and understanding of boats and the sea in general. Part 3 discusses multihull handling and how to operate your catamaran in various conditions. Sailing is not all black and white, yet certain fundamental guidelines apply, which are surveyed. Sailing and delivering both mono- and multihulls across oceans contributed considerably to my understanding of the differences in behavior of both types in various sea conditions. Few publications or books to date have dealt with this subject.

In Part 4 you will discover a listing and brief descriptions of notable catamarans. As founder of Aeroyacht Ltd., an international multihull dealership, my insights into today's market will show you what is available in terms of production multihulls.

Some of the subjects in various chapters are overlapping. I do not talk about racing boats, or peripheral systems such as engines or electrical installations but will focus on core issues of catamaran design and characteristics. There are a limited number of possibilities to describe a multihull in a single word. When I use phrases "multihull," "twin hulled vessels" or "cats," I mean cruising catamarans and not trimarans or racing boats.

Many factors urged the conception of this book – including the necessity to describe the ever-changing industry and environment, and also the personal goal and desire to share with you the knowledge about these exciting new craft. Perhaps it is a consequence of my constantly evolving interest for these types of boats and the sailors who take them to sea that I chose to dedicate a better part of my life to cruising catamarans.

CATAMARANS is my lifetime contribution to this fascinating world.

Gregor Tarjan

HISTORY ABBREVIATED

Polynesians and Micronesians as far back as the 1700s used double canoes, and these were the forerunners of today's catamarans. In 1778 Captain James Cook wrote in his logbook about the enormous sailing craft that 'could carry a hundred warriors.' Indeed, there were all kinds and sizes used in inter-island travel. Some were small dugouts with single or double outriggers; others were 15 meters (50 feet) long. Captain Cook recorded sighting a war canoe in Tahiti, estimated at about 110 feet long and carrying nearly 200 warriors.

It is not within the scope of this book to go back 300 years to search for the roots of multihulls. For those interested in detailed history, I highly recommend Haddon & Hornell's 894-page book "Canoes of Oceania" (Bishop Museum, Honolulu, HI).

Every once in a while charismatic leaders come along who can turn the destiny of history. They invent something new, improve something that already exists, or unite people in a strange way. Not all are good, some turned out evil, like Nobel, Napoleon or Hitler. Others have given humanity a new meaning, like Curie, Martin Luther King or Desmond Tutu. On a much smaller scale, there was a newspaperman, a real promoter, who united those sailors who wanted a multihull but had no idea how to get one. He lived in Mill Valley, California, and his name was Arthur Piver.

Piver started drawing trimaran plans for sale in May of 1960, after he had crossed the Atlantic in his self-designed, self-built trimaran, Nimble. Soon he expanded the range into the 24-foot Nugget, the 30-foot Nimble, the 35-foot Lodestar, the 45-foot Victress, and as large as a 64-foot floating palace. Even though Piver was not a naval architect, he drew up very detailed, easy to follow plans and hundreds of his trimarans were built, worldwide. Soon he had a number of followers, like Jim Brown, Norman Cross, and a few independent designers, like Dick Newick and Ed Horstman. In other parts of the world, Lock Crowther in Australia and Derek Kelsall in the U.K. made a name for themselves. When Arthur Piver disappeared at sea while testing a new design to qualify for the OSTAR (Observer Singlehanded TransAtlantic Race), the multihull world expected a diminishing interest, but that didn't happen. Instead, more and more trimarans were entered in the OSTAR until, eventually, every race was won by these triple-hulled craft. Today, only those races that BAN multihulls are won by monohulls. For decades, trimarans ruled the multihull scene, and only a handful of catamarans were designed or built. The reason was primarily the superior windward ability of trimarans vs. catamarans – which was a deciding factor in the all-windward work in the OSTAR – and partially, the easier connection of hulls before the advent of today's high-tech materials. Without going into details of this last statement, suffice it to say that the multihull world has changed by a total turnaround to catamarans, discovering it to be the more viable cruising boat. Speed freaks, however, still vie for trimarans. The only considerable mass-production trimarans are the Farrier-designed/ Corsair Marine-built line from 24'-31' – and the Dragonflies, designed and built by Børge and Jens Quorning in Denmark.

If Piver is said to be the "inventor" of modern double outriggers which he called trimarans, a word that didn't make it into

Webster's Dictionary until just recently, then who "invented" the modern catamarans? Most multihull aficionados say it was Hobie Alter, the surfer boy from California. He was, indeed, the man who promoted them the most, but much before him it was Woody Brown of Hawaii who, in 1947, built Manu Kai, the first modern, fast ocean catamaran.

Today's catamarans are nothing like the double canoes of Oceania. To the contrary: early attempts looked more like a wedding cake than a sailing craft – there were so many layers piled up on top of each other. Soon it became evident that the uncontrollable windage presented by the superstructure was very detrimental to the sailing efficiency of the boats, not to mention the lack of aesthetic appeal to those who were conditioned to see seascapes with slim, shapely, heeling sailboats. In other words, "modern catamarans" were ugly. Except for one design.

In 1954-55 Englishman James Wharram designed and built the first modern catamaran that still resembled the Pacific outriggers. He named the 23'6" catamaran Tangaroa and promptly sailed her across the Atlantic with his wife, a female friend, a dog and 200 books. The boat had some flaws, the flat bottom pounded too much. So, reaching Trinidad in the West Indies, Wharram built a better catamaran, Rongo, that was a bit larger (40 feet), and sailed her to New York, then back to England in 1959. He wrote a book: "Two Girls, Two Catamarans" that is still selling well 38 years later.

Wharram designed a line of catamarans after that, all based on the Polynesian principle with swept-up bows and canoe sterns. They range from the 14' Hitia to the 64' Tehini. All his designs are very easy to build and sail. Thousands of plans were sold, worldwide, over the years. His own boat is Spirit of Gaïa, a Pahi 63 that has recently nearly completed a circumnavigation.

To a lesser degree, another designer, Rudy Choy of Hawaii, followed the Polynesian design/building concept. He was part of the C/S/K design team (Choy/Seaman/Kumulae), and their most noted creation was the 48-foot Polynesian Concept. Actor Buddy Ebsen campaigned that design, raced it against the U.S. Naval Academy Sailing Team and, eventually, donated his own boat to the Academy.

To bolster the multihull image and acceptance, MULTIHULLS Magazine organized a number of World Multihull Symposiums, notably in 1976 in Toronto's Harbour Castle; in 1985 in Annapolis, MD; in 1988 in Newport, RI, and in 1996-97 in Miami, FL. Verbatim transcript of the Toronto event was published in The Symposium Book (now out of print); followed by The Symposium Book II (available from www.multihullsmag.com).

Taking a clue from the successful OSTAR and 'Round Ireland & Britain Race, both British-organized events, the French did not

below "Rogue Wave" – a historic multihull designed by Dick Newick, one of the most accomplished multihull designers of our time. He attained international fame for creating sleek and swift racers and cruisers.

above A Pahi 31, one of the many hundreds of James Wharram-designed catamarans sailing throughout the world.

want to be left behind. They invented their own ocean races, the best known being La Route du Rhum, Saint Malo to Guadeloupe. It is run every four years, alternating with the British races. Other major races are the Québec-to-Saint Malo race, and the La Boule-to-Dakar Race. These events attract hundreds of thousands of sailing fans at the starting and finish lines and millions of TV viewers. Sailors became national heroes and sport idols like baseball players in America and soccer-players everywhere else. The French boating industry stepped up to the plate and created its own multihull designs. Major boat builders such as Jeantot Marine (now Alliaura Marine), Jeanneau (now merged with Beneteau), Soubise, and others searched out the best of the naval architects and yacht designers. First individuals, such as Marc Lombard (Privilège), Gerard Danson (Outremer), Erik Lerouge (Brazapi, Soubise); then design teams such as Christophe Barreau & Marc Valdelievre (Catana), Michel Joubert & Bernard Nivelt, and J. Berett & Olivier Flahault (Fountaine Pajot), Marc Van Peteghem & Vincent Lauriot-Prevost (Lagoon) created a French superiority not just on the race courses, but on the cruising grounds of the world. There are more French-built catamarans on the water today than all other nations' productions combined. Perhaps the best-known design firm for ocean race winning boats is Gilles Ollier's Multiplast (*Commodore Explorer*, *Club Med*, *Innovation Explorer*, *Team Adventure*, *Orange II* et al).

The history of production multihulls, however, did not start in France. That distinction goes to the U.K. (we call it England). The British Marine Industry was proud of Prout Catamarans (now Broadblue Catamarans), the largest producer of cruising cats. They produced such age- and sea-proven designs as the Scamper and the Sirocco, both 26', Quest 31, Quest 33CS, Event 34, Snowgoose 35 & 37, Prout 38, Escale 39, Encore 43 & 45, and the Quasar 50. The Prout brothers, Roland and Francis, had a competitor in Reg White, an Olympic medal winner in Tornadoes, who managed Sailcraft (now defunct), builders of such classic catamarans as the Iroquois 30 and 30 Mk II, and the Cherokee 35. Another British catamaran builder, Tom Lack, was nearly as prolific with the Catalac 8m, 9m, 12m cruising boats. Smaller boats by smaller manufacturers were known as the Heavenly Twins 26 and the Hirondelle 23. Another entity was Sandwich Marine, which built a little folding trimaran, the Telstar 27, designed by Tony Smith. Two-hundred and fifty-five Telstars later, he packed up his young family and his business and moved to the United States in 1980 to seek greener pastures or bluer waters. That company became known as Performance Cruising, Inc. in Annapolis, Maryland. Tony switched to building catamarans and just launched (at this writing) Gemini Hull #955. The early success of his Telstar haunted him enough to revive and improve the design and he launched the first American-built tri in 2005. Forty-four have been sold as of this writing. Another great Great Britain-born designer is Derek Kelsall, whose earlier creations were built in England, Ireland, and even in France. Since then he has moved to New Zealand where he is designing new ways of building boats based on time and expense-saving principles.

From San Diego to Maine and from Alaska to Miami there are very few multihull builders and even fewer designers. Prolific San Diego naval architect and trimaran designer Norman Cross passed away at age 75 in August of 1990; Dick Newick, originally from St. Croix, successful designer of day-charter boats, first moved to Martha's Vineyard in Massachusetts where he designed his most successful trimarans such as Rogue Wave and Moxie, among others; that was followed by a move to Maine where he dabbled into small catamarans and power cats; then he moved again, to Sebastopol, northern California and at age 80 is semi-retired. Maine designer and builder Dick Vermeulen first built the Maine Cat 22, a daysailer, but soon realized that there is not much call for that size boat and re-tooled for a 30-foot cruiser. That was so successful that he created a name for himself, and a reputation for quality and very friendly service, and soon attracted more serious sailors who were looking for a bigger boat. Although he can still produce the Maine Cat 30, his factory is turning out Maine Cat 41s at regular intervals. On the opposite coast in the

Northwest is Seattle-based Kurt Hughes whose sensible designs are popular because they fill the need between the Spartan Newick designs and the posh French cats.

I must mention the Land Down Under – Australia – where Lock Crowther, perhaps the most talented and versatile multhull designer, was turning out plans for homebuilders and for semi-production. The untimely and sudden death at sea due to a massive heart attack during his sailing vacation left his legacy in his young son Brett's hands, who then parlayed it into a mega design firm catering to the ferry-building industry. Other multihull designers, like Richard Ward and his Seawind Catamarans (SW 1000 & SW 1160), produce cruising yachts on an assembly line and sell the boats worldwide. Other notable designers in Australia are Tony Grainger, Jeff Schionning, Robin Chamberlin, Russ Turner (Jarcat), James Gard (Fusion), Perry Catamarans, Lightwave and Mike Waller Designs.

Neighboring New Zealand, a mere 1,000 miles away, produced Malcolm Tennant, the renowned multihull designer who created the well-known Great Barrier Express 27, Turissimo 9m, and Vorpal Blade 36 and others.

Not to be outdone by the "Other Continent South of the Equator," South Africa jumped onto the bandwagon when the Rand was at a low exchange rate (R5.30=$1) and the celebration continued when it fell nearly to 12:1. Builders could offer 35- to 50-foot catamarans at 2/3 the price of the French boats, and The Moorings, one of the world's largest charter companies, bought the entire production line of Robertson & Caine, the largest shop in Cape Town. They are now building exclusively the Moorings brand and the Leopard brand of catamarans, which are essentially the same with the exception that the Leopard is aimed at private owners and the Moorings' boats have charter layouts.

Other South African builders are Admiral Yachts, African Cats, Dean Catamarans, Fortuna Catamarans, Maxim Yachts, Sky Blue Yachts, St Francis Marine, and Voyage Yachts. Principal multihull designers are the Simonis

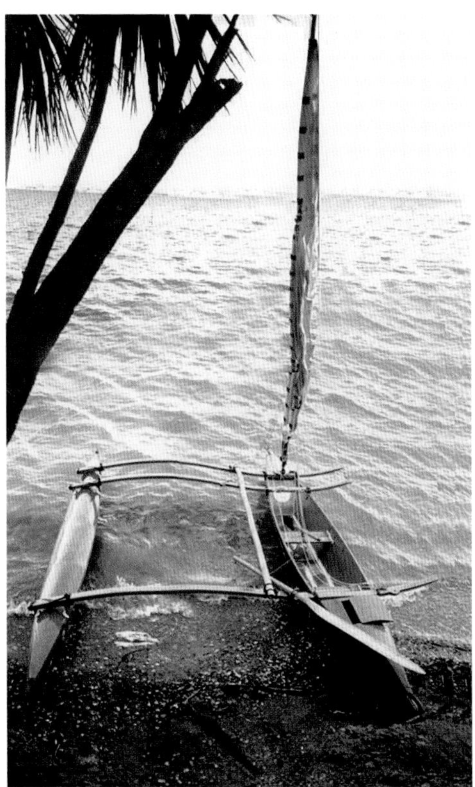

left Every modern multihull – catamaran or trimaran – finds its origin in the ingeniously simple outrigger style canoes of the Micronesian and Polynesian people. Workhorses for fishermen and traders, they safely carried natives across thousands of miles of ocean and were responsible for the migration of cultures throughout the Pacific basin.

Voogd Design partnership with offices in Cape Town and in Enkhuizen, The Netherlands.

The list of designers and builders could go on, but by the time this book is printed, there may be others coming out of the woodwork (no pun intended) or from the layup shed, because the multihull industry is growing in leaps and bounds. Even during the most recent years, when the global boatbuilding industry experienced a lull in sales, multihull production was up 18%. It is not just the number of catamarans that are growing, it is also their size. What was a reasonable 30-footer just a decade ago is now a "pocket cruiser;" the luxury catamarans of yesteryear are the run-of-the mill cruisers; and the luxury boats are now reaching mega-yacht status both in volume and in fit-out, such as the Yapluka and Blubay line, based in France. The Derektor Shipyard in New York State is in the production stage of Gemini, a 148-foot Marc Van Peteghem/Vincent Lauriot-Prevost-designed mega-cat.

Even on rainy days, the sun is shining on multihulls!

Charles K. Chiodi

PRESENT environment

Large day charter cats, as often found in the Caribbean, are the flag bearers of the modern cruising multihull. They have introduced flat and fast sailing to more people than any other sailing craft.

PRESENT ENVIRONMENT

The Big Picture

"So do they flip?" Long gone are the days when monohull sailors asked that question. At today's boat shows it is more an issue of "How many does she sleep?" The global charter industry, which is a multi-billion dollar enterprise, has embraced the multihull as a profitable platform. The notion of solo sailors pushing their giant catamarans or trimarans across the ocean has proven them not only as blindingly fast competitors, but also has demonstrated the multihulls' toughness in the worst sea conditions. In fact, they are so exciting that sponsors such as car manufacturers, fashion houses and producers of Hollywood movies have plastered colorful logos on their racers. On the other side of the spectrum is a new breed of environmentalists who explore the world's reefs and choose the sailing multihull for its low ecological impact, shallow draft, and stable, steady platform. The eco industry is booming and so is the awareness of the suitability of these new types of craft. Even marinas and boat yards all over the world now perceive the catamaran as mainstream and it is no more unusual to pull up to a dock in a multihull than it is with a jet ski. From Boat Shows' high-profile media events to environmental consciousness, perception and acceptance of multihulls has changed as much as the craft themselves.

Boat Shows are the presentation ground and testing venue of the current catamaran environment. They are an invaluable gauge of the growing public interest. When visiting today's boat shows, the abundance of cruising multihulls is mind-boggling. At an average Annapolis or Miami Boat Show, both belong to one of the most prolific multihull gatherings in the world, cruising catamarans typically take up more exhibition space than that dedicated to monohulls. Three dozen or more 40-plus-foot multihulls represent the present cross-section of models available on the market – from small 30' coastal cruisers, to folding trimarans all the way up to 60' or 70' luxury cats. Sailors have discovered the advantages of twin-hulled boats and manufacturers and designers have answered their needs.

The first thing I notice when visitors step aboard a multihull for the first time is the enthusiastic appreciation of the open and airy space provided. Usually they come from having inspected a mid-size monohull and are now exploring the catamaran section. Typically cockpit space, saloon and foredecks are double the size of those found on monohulls. Kids feel at home climbing into the various berths or jumping on the foredeck's trampoline while parents scrutinize navigation stations and locker space. This is quite different from years past when first-time visitors would be more concerned about the safety features and capsize issues.

It is actually quite interesting to compare the concerns and comments of sailors to those of 10 years ago. Usually boat shows are the best venue to study the first-time encounters

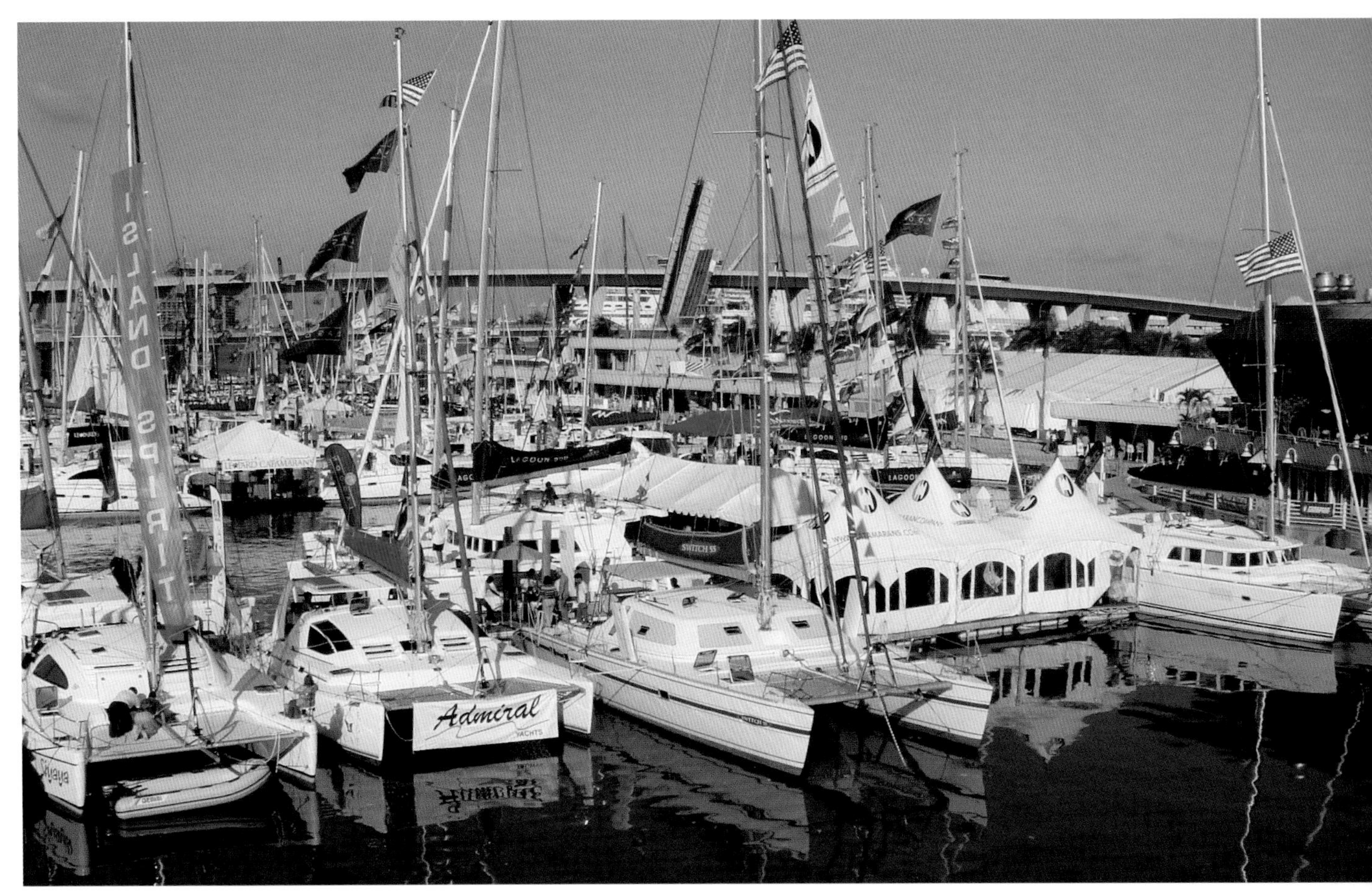

above At a typical Miami boat show, the catamarans on display usually take up more space than the monohulls.

of monohullers, who have either lost their way or have come intentionally to investigate the two-hulled boats. A woman's opinion is more often the decisive decision maker in the realization of liking or disliking a particular boat. Galley locker space, natural light and berth size is as much examined as engine access and fabric décor. It is a cliché to think that women only look at the galley. Today's female sailors are as skilled as men and it is often the spouse who takes the helm to bring a boat to a dock while the husband prepares lines and fenders.

And then there is thc myth of speed that still has not quite yet matured. "She must do 20 knots, right?" you hear people asking while stepping aboard a stately cruising multihull. More often a family boards a catamaran at a boat show or demo sail and the 15-year-old son gives the thumbs up and comments about his little beach cat and how cool it is to fly by his dad's old monohull. The media coverage of the 60' trimaran regatta circuit in Europe and the globe-circling monster cats have captured the fascination of millions. But, it has also created the false sense that all catamarans cruise routinely at double-digit speeds. Nevertheless, the breathtaking velocities of racing multihulls, usually attained in the roughest conditions, inspire sailors' constant quest to go faster. Multihulls seem to have become the ultimate platform for these ambitions.

With the larger size of multihulls also comes the ever-looming challenge of where to haul, berth and service them. Any catamaran over 35' could be considered large, which usually is a function of her beam. Compared to equivalent length monohulls, catamarans are almost twice as wide. Forget about finding a slip – a water berth surrounded by pylons – unless it is on an end dock. This realization was often the case a decade ago.

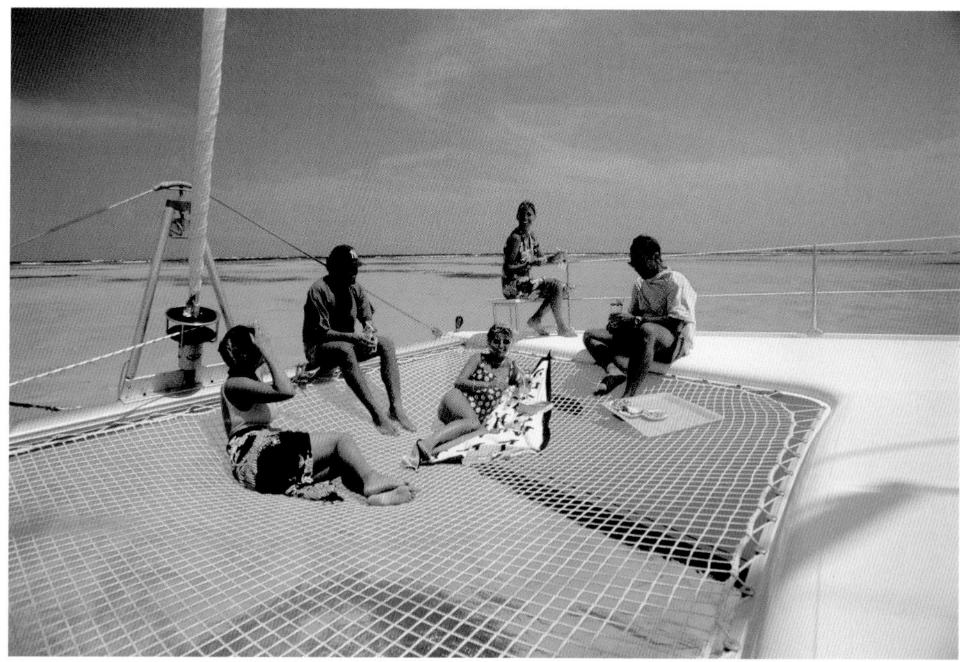

right The vast trampolines are playground and lounging space in one.

Today more and more marinas are catering to multihulls… and charging double the rent is a thing of the past. Yes, there still is a premium for dockage for a multi hulled vessel at crowded marinas but no one can turn their back on them anymore.

Current Perception of Multihulls

In general the pleasure boat industry, especially in the sailing segment, has experienced a definite upward trend in size. When studying the ARC, the Atlantic Rally for Cruisers, it becomes apparent that the average boat size has increased, and that there are now 20-30 multihulls participating every year. The ARC is usually an excellent indicator of the sailing industry's development and public sentiment towards certain craft. The many times I have participated in Transatlantic rallies – always on catamarans – it was interesting to see how often multihulls, which were often half the size of their single-hulled competitors, won over monohulls across the Atlantic. The barroom talk at the finish line of major races, where both mono and multihulls participate, has greatly changed the way cruising cats are perceived today.

I remember in the 2003 RAC (Rubicon Antigua Challenge), which is a sister event of the ARC, skippering a stock Outremer 45 catamaran with a delightful all-British crew. We were forced to start two days behind the fleet because we had to pick up an EPIRB (Emergency Position Indicating Radio Beacon) at a neighboring island. We were one of several multihulls in our race, but in the course of the 13-day Atlantic crossing we passed one monohull after the other – and they were getting bigger the closer we came to the finish line. At the end we beat 80' Swans and Oysters more than double our length. As we passed these larger monohulls, the communications between the yachts on VHF could be heard. The awareness and acceptance was apparent. There was no longer the question of 'are multihulls seaworthy for serious ocean crossing?' or cutting comments of past decades. But rather one could sense the monohullers' realization of having to compete against a faster and more comfortable adversary. Often the crew of the boats that finished behind us came and congratulated us with camaraderie and recognition of our accomplishment, and we felt immediately complimented by their urge to know more about our catamaran. There was a genuine interest to learn and understand how we were able to sail so much faster and how we coped with life aboard. Stories of the constant downwind rolling phenomenon that accompanies every monohull on a classic Trade Wind route were compared to our carefree spinnaker sailing. Tragic moments in the heeling monohull galley were evaluated to cooking gourmet meals on the level. Years ago most monohullers did not know what apparent wind was. Now they were listening intently when we told them of how we tacked downwind with a gennaker and were able to make better VMG than running at deeper wind angles with our spinnaker.

Our understanding of multihulls has increased but so has our exposure to them. It seems that cats have multiplied like rabbits. While writing these lines I am looking out over the waters of Long Island, New York. Eight years ago I would see two catamarans moored among hundreds of monohull power- and sailboats. Today I can count half a dozen. This might not be a quantum leap increase, but considering their scarcity, particularly in conservative New England, it is a significant number. Visiting marinas, and spotting them on the horizon when sailing, we are seeing more and more of these two-hulled craft. Even in the monohull stronghold of Newport, Rhode Island or Southwest Harbor, Maine, you will find cruising catamarans.

below A French 60' racing trimaran sailing at over 30 knots.

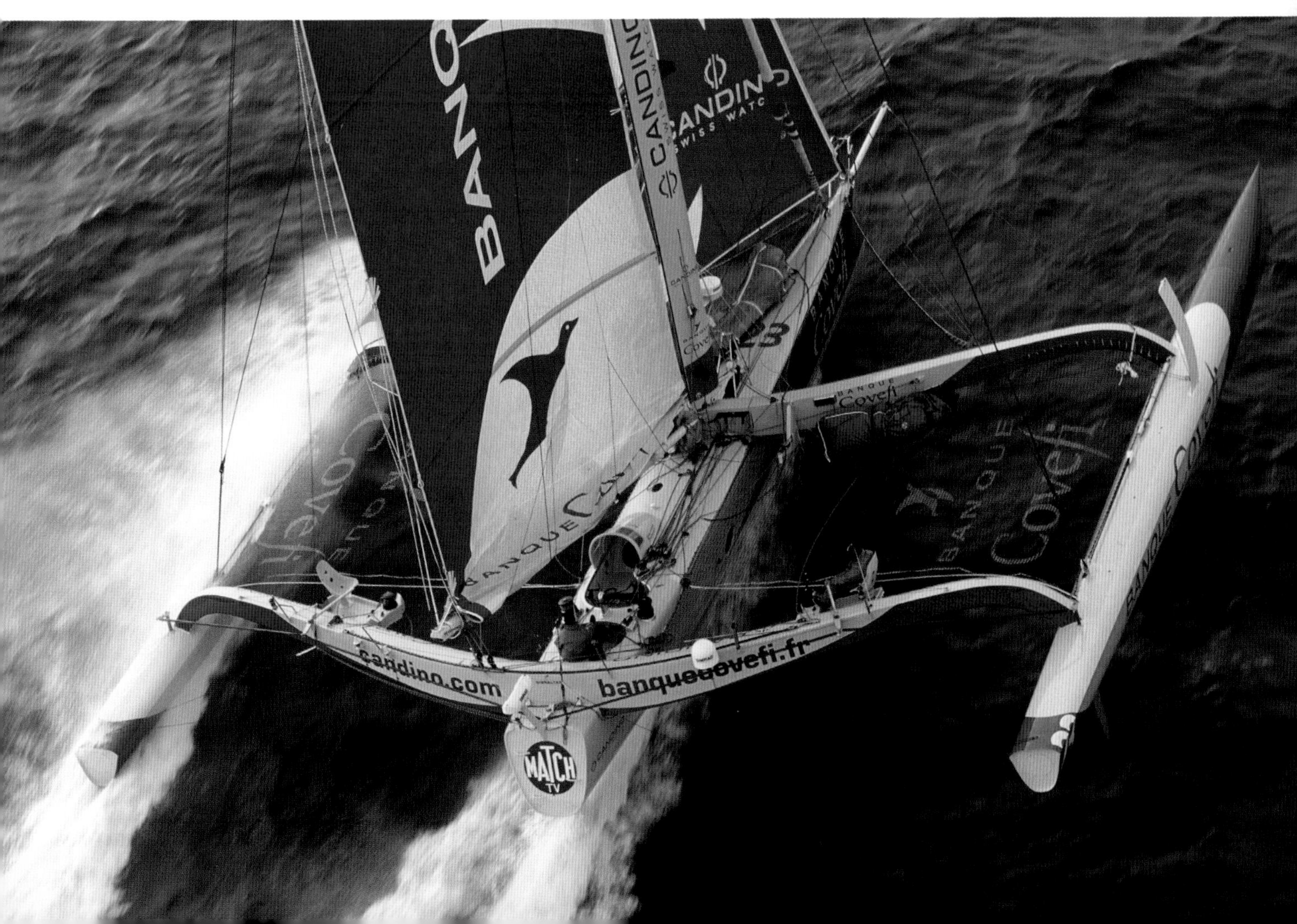

far right Aerial view shows the generous amount of deck space provided by even a mid-sized multihull.

below A quick-haul of this 45' cat assures fast turnaround times and minimum downtime for the yard as well as the owner.

Major sailing publications that were rather shy a decade ago regarding the issue of multihulls, are now appointing specialists to report on them. Moreover there are even dedicated issues in the general marine press, usually twice a year, to attract both readers and advertisers alike. Where we previously saw one magazine focusing on multihulls years ago we can now select from various international publications dealing with all aspects of two-hulled vessels.

Multihulls are now appreciated as the most comfortable sailboats available today. If you do not have the finances to purchase one, you can now time-share, lease or rent them everywhere. Shortly after the largest insurance companies deemed catamarans as safe, if not safer than monohulls, the charter industry exploded. Multihull rental companies have become one of the biggest promoters of these new types of vessels and they have provided an invaluable service towards making them mainstream today. It is hard to imagine a better vacation platform

than a multihull. With a catamaran's two separate hulls and large saloon, they offer unsurpassed privacy and socializing space. Viewing sailing magazines one will see most charter companies showing flashy ads of catamarans cruising in turquoise Caribbean waters. Thirty years ago, multihulls had the stigma to be unsafe and hard to handle. They are now "de rigueur" and everyone who can sail a monohull is able to operate them. The multihull bareboat industry is booming. After just a brief introduction and demonstration, vacationers are given the key to a 40' catamaran and they are off on their own. This would have been unheard of in the 1980s when the requirements to bareboat seemed much stricter.

Today there are sailing schools and courses catering specifically to this charter industry. Whereas years ago you would not be able to find institutions that would teach multihull sailing, you can now choose from a variety of nationally accredited organizations which gladly show you the ins and outs of catamaran handling. Upon passing a 3-day or one-week course, you walk away proudly with documents that pronounce competence in skippering a two-hulled monster that you never would have dreamed you could single hand.

Many people who considered multihulls as just another means of getting out onto the water are now living aboard their vessels. A majority has matured and progressed to their second or third multihull. Sailors who once represented the pioneering group, and were the first to purchase catamarans, have learned through their experience and are now applying their wisdom. Designers and builders alike are listening to these sailors and providing them with a better product. Today's multihulls are more attractive than the boxy hulks of 30 years ago, sail better than ever and most are built to last

Matira
HONDA

indefinitely. The trickle-down effect of the high-tech race boats and industry has produced a multitude of capable cruising cats that veteran sailors, as well as first-time buyers, can choose from.

World economy and globalization have had an impact on our small world of sailing, and multihulls in general. Real estate prices and waterfront property have greatly increased in value. Any dwelling near the shore is almost unobtainable and those who live by the ocean know this. Considering that the majority of the world's population can be found near coasts, and major cities are located on rivers, illustrate the fact that man likes to live by the water. For those of us who cannot afford those lifestyles, the large cruising catamaran makes more sense than ever. At almost half the price of a two-acre water-view home, you can now command your own island with the added benefit of relocation. You don't like your neighbors? Simply weigh anchor and sail to your next destination of choice. You could never do this on land unless you have a less romantic trailer dwelling or mobile home. More and more couples are packing it up than ever before. The power of the Internet and globalization has accelerated this free lifestyle more than any other phenomenon. Today you can be working in tranquility and comfort on the deck saloon of your catamaran, e-mailing your overseas partners, paying your bills, or surfing the Internet. We can now be as productive on our boat as we can from a tiny Manhattan office cubicle. The added benefit is that the view is nicer. Your cranky superior can be thousands of miles away, or you might have even "fired" your boss by starting your own enterprise. Multihulls, with their expansive and stable floor plan are becoming the number one boat choice for the entrepreneur or the new breed of part time consultants.

Political events such as the terrorist attacks of September 11th 2001 in New York City and Washington DC have also impacted the sailor's mind. For a brief time, shortly after that tragic date, more people packed their bags and left the New York City metropolitan area than ever before. It was "Destination Anywhere." The mass exodus reflected not only fear for life but also the disappointment in mankind and uncertainty of what the future might bring. This "Noah's Ark" phenomenon became evident in the multitude of cruising catamarans sold shortly after 9/11. The yacht broker community, as every commercial branch of the Western world, was worried, scratching their heads and spinning into a recession that lasted several years. Yet there was a small blip on the multihull sales radar. Disillusioned families moved onto a new boat, often a catamaran, and felt safer than ever before. Sitting pretty in an anchorage in the Florida Keys or Grenadines, they felt more secure than close to a metropolitan area. On their vessels, in sync with nature, probably made them feel united, safe and partaking in a fuller life than ever before.

Global prices for energy and oil continue to rise and play a great part in affecting a sailor's awareness. A decade ago few people thought about super-efficient propulsion systems for power and sailing vessels. Today we have numerous companies specializing in electric drives and hybrid power plants, and it was on a French production catamaran that this new type of propulsion system entered the pleasure-boat market.

It is no secret that a catamaran is more efficient in going from A to B than a monohull. She will require less energy, do it faster and be more comfortable. Passenger ferry companies around the world are realizing this by building multihull

below Haulout and service facilities throughout the world are catering to large cruising multihulls more and more. The largest travelift in North America is dwarfing this 55' catamaran.

above The expansive main saloon of an Outremer 64S can seat up to 12 guests in comfort.

vessels, which increase profitability. Initial investments for these types of craft might be higher than monohulls, but the quick amortization usually makes up for the difference. Passengers who board these catamaran ferries do not find them unique as they might have 10 years ago. Crossing a body of water at 30 knots on a high-speed catamaran ferry makes us think twice when scrutinizing them for our next boat form and we come to the realization that a multihull does make a lot of sense.

The warming of the earth's climate and the constant erosion of our planet's resources have spurred a new generation of marine scientists following the footsteps of greats such as Jaques Cousteau. The new "Calypso" type (Cousteau's boat of fame) used for purposes of marine research is often a large catamaran. A 100 plus-foot catamaran complements the demands of ecological awareness – sailing on free wind energy and gently slipping into the shallowest of the world's endangered reefs. At the time of this writing I am involved in the conception of several enterprises that look to build super catamarans as flag bearers of the eco cause. The boats will be floating laboratories, broadcasting centers and research facilities which will fly scientists and celebrities to the remotest locations with their onboard helicopter. Paralleling the fascination and adventure that Jacques Cousteau brought to our TV screens, these mega cats could inspire the young MTV-loving web-surfer generation. Soon we will be following dolphins with web-cams strapped to them, through exotic reefs via high-speed Internet.

Modern Pioneers

Sailors, adventurers and designers have shaped the multihull community as much as the ever-changing environment and technology. Multihull racers and sailors who have taken their boats on extreme voyages are constantly pushing the envelope of machine and human endurance. Their adventures have spurred the imagination and have provided valuable data and feedback to us all.

There are heroes like Pete Goss who first became famous by rescuing fellow competitor Raphael Dinelli in the grueling Vendee Globe race of 1997. His feat propelled him into the rock-star league and earned him a huge sponsorship package with Dutch electronics giant Philips. The boat "Team Philips" was a 125' monster cat designed for "The Race", a super tough, nonstop around the world event. This boat had me fooled, because I considered her a stunning breakthrough which might have worked. She was designed by one of the most experienced British multihull designers, Adrian Thompson. It can certainly be argued that the radical rig and hulls would or would never have worked. Apparently, the computer models and analyses of past experience said they would have, but, in the end, it was a disastrous failure which almost cost the crew their lives. The designer, although immensely qualified, never tackled anything of the nature or size of Team Philips. On the other hand, projects such as Team Philips are invaluable to the multihull community and in a larger sense humanity might still be sitting in caves, if there weren't heroes, adventurers and visionaries who would push the envelope.

below Sometimes the creativity of even the most experienced yacht transporters are challenged when hauling large catamarans through the busy streets of Paris.

My friend Yves Parlier, who is considered by most to be the best multihull racer in the world, is nicknamed "ET" for Extra Terrestrial. In one of the nonstop around the world races he lost his mast in the Southern Ocean. Possessed of superhuman willpower and strength, Yves fabricated a jury rig on "Aquitaine Innovations," his Open 60' and completed the race. He even started the engine on his crippled boat by tightly wrapping his mainsheet around the flywheel of the engine. By gybing the boat and spinning the flywheel he was able to fire up the diesel. The news he made shook the sailing world and since then, he has become one of the icons of solo sailing. But, Yves matured and was reaching for even more. In 2004 he launched "Hydraplaneur," a 60-foot-long 45-foot-wide, step-hulled, twin-rigged ocean racer. Tuning the boat and training with him was one of the most violent, yet rewarding sailing experiences in my life. The

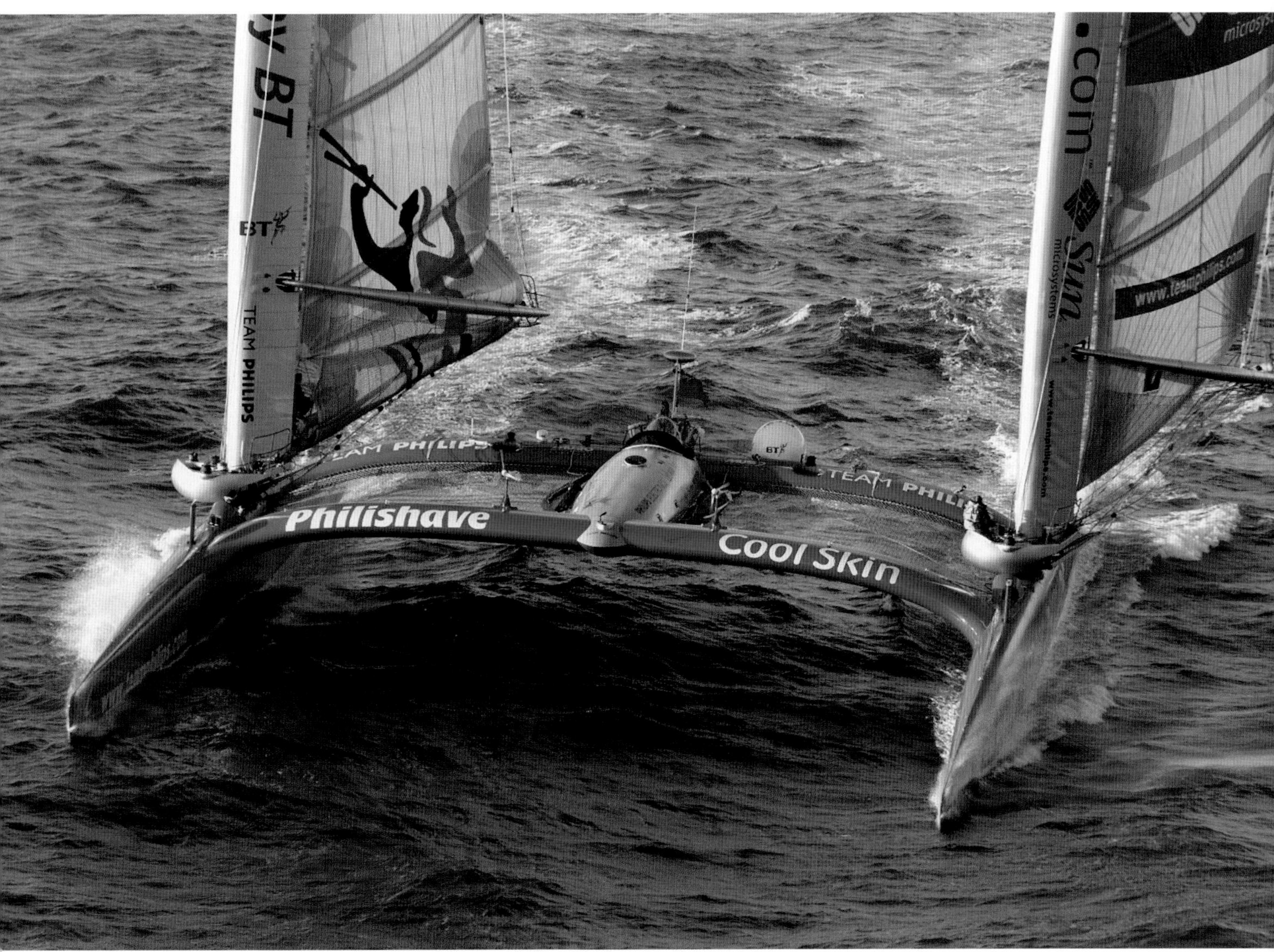

machine was built with only one objective: to go as fast as possible in any condition – without breaking. Yves has always pushed the envelope. In the summer of 2005, while delivering "Hydraplaneur" to our office in New York, his experimental monster cat encountered strong winds west of the Canary Islands. Yves tried to depower and reef the boat but had problems with the mainsheet. One moment of inattention and the boat capsized. Yves and the boat were rescued; he is now repairing "Hydraplaneur" back into shape to mount further ocean record attempts.

The natural love for ocean racing has enabled the French nautical industry to pull itself up to be ranked number one in the world in innovations and in the launching of competition events. Yves Parlier's project maintains this line of research to find new solutions for greater speed on the open ocean. In 1985 the first mandrel-spun Kevlar-shrouded carbon mast was introduced. In 1993, the first winch made of carbon fiber came onto the market. The year 1996 saw the first wing mast on a monohull and in 1998 the first transmission of video images shot on board ocean-racing boats were broadcast live on the web. You might have guessed it: most of these boats were catamarans. These important innovations have widely spread to other racers and have found important applications in the marine business and multihull community. It is no surprise

above The radical "Team Philips" on one of her maiden voyages effortlessly slicing through the water. Note the crew working in the mast pods at the base of the twin biplane rigs.

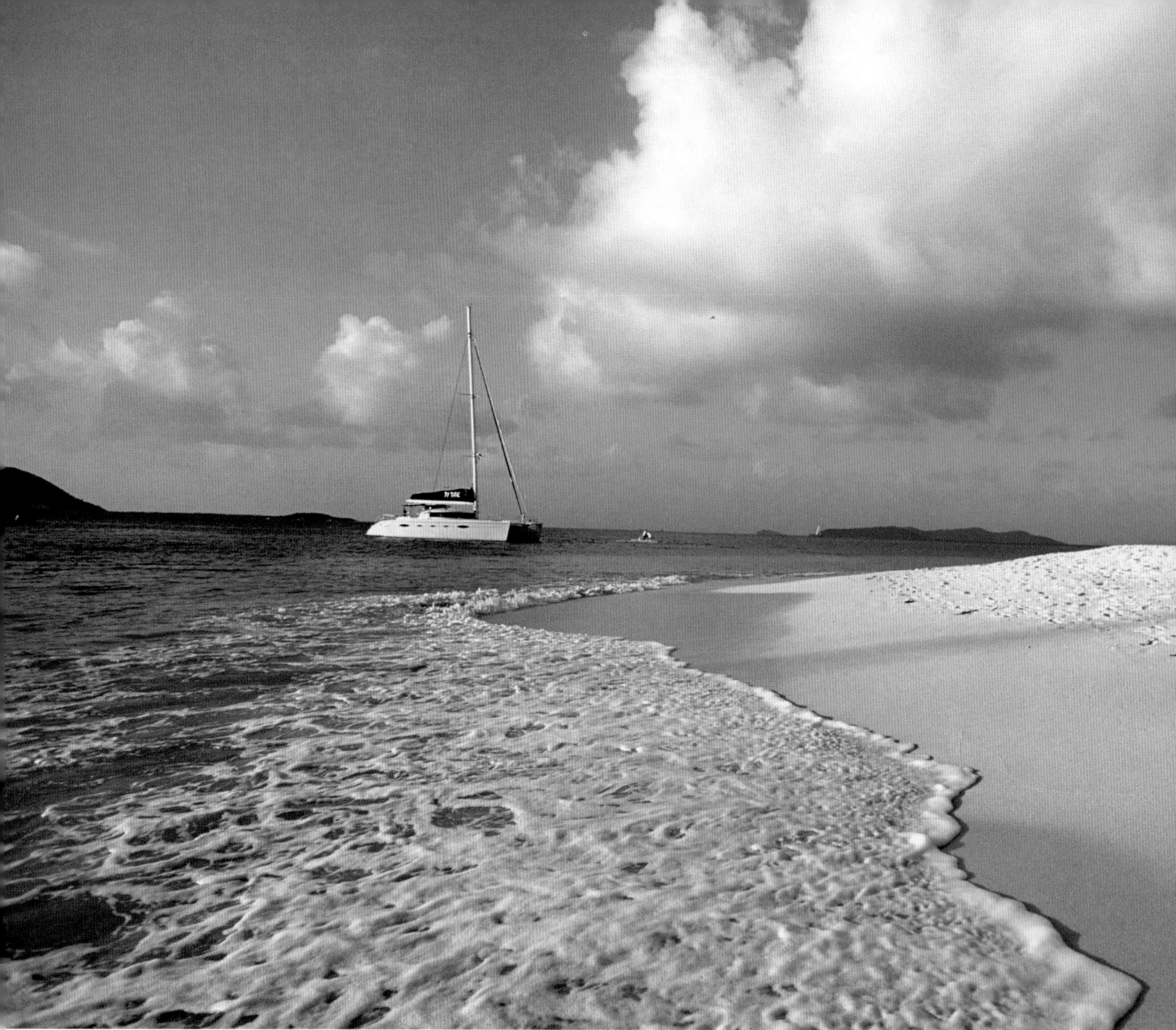

above The shallow draft of even a large 60' catamaran lets you avoid dropping anchor in crowded anchorages and allows the crew to wade to shore.

then that the most innovative cruising and racing catamarans come from France.

Countries around the world, such as South Africa, New Zealand, Australia, the Netherlands and the U.S., are contributing in great measures to the advancements of multihulls. But by sheer production volume of cruising catamarans and the popular fascination of the sport, France remains the leader.

General Manager of Fountaine Pajot, a French company, considered the largest builder of cruising catamarans in the world, is Eric Bruneel. Although he manages Fountaine Pajot full-time, he seems to be first a sailor and a "suit" second. Looking at his weathered face it is apparent that he spends most of his free time on the water, either testing Fountaine Pajots, or checking out boats of the competition.

In my professional dealings as a multihull distributor I met him at one of the major U.S. boat shows. Immediately, I had great respect for his approach to running his business and also for his sailing abilities. In 2004 he co-designed and built a 50-foot ocean racer "Trilogic" on which I had the pleasure to sail with him on several trips. The boat is extreme by measure of design, yet ultimately reliable and simple in terms

of systems and sail controls. On his first Solo Transatlantic Race, not only did he win, but he shattered the previously held record by more than two days. Months later he won the famous Fastnet race and now he is preparing his boat for La Route du Rhum. I have noticed the same amount of detail and careful approach in manufacture when examining the Fountaine Pajot cruising catamarans. Similar to Eric's approach to the design and construction of "Trilogic" all Fountaine Pajot catamarans are built for easy operation and dependability. I remember sailing with Eric out of Boston Harbor to my Long Island office, where he kept his boat over the summer of 2004. Sailing along at 12 knots, inattentive for just a second, we strayed off the narrow channel entrance and hit ground. I could feel Eric's pain as the shock reverberated through his boat. "Trilogic's" huge daggerboard received a good whack that split open the laminates and sheered a good 10 inches off the tip. Having the bonus of shallow draft we pressed on to Martha's Vineyard where we pulled the daggerboard and jury-rigged a repair. Eric's "can do" attitude and wholesome approach to sailing is felt in every one of his cruising multihull creations.

Objective & Mission Profile

My mentor and part-time lecturer Dick Newick, a personality whom I regard as one of the most prolific multihull designers of all time, summed it up: Space, Efficiency (low price) and Performance. You cannot have all three characteristics in a multihull. Two out of three, yes. For instance, you will soon find that a fast and spacious multihull will be expensive but, consequently, you can find a well-performing catamaran that will not break the bank but has little room. A multihull with a huge interior that is slow will not cost much either. This wisdom is the basis of all compromises. You will soon discover the enlightening truth that boats are not only the ultimate vehicle to adventure but also the definitive concession to our needs.

"The king is dead – long live the king." Although much has changed around us… the wind and seas haven't. Lately the North Atlantic Ocean experienced its most severe hurricane season, yet this statistic will become insignificant when looking at the big

below Eric Bruneel's reliable 50-foot "Trilogic" before winning the notorious Fastnet Race in 2005. In the previous year, he was victorious in the Single-handed Trans-Atlantic Race (STAR) and set a new course record.

above and right Yves 'ET' Parlier with his ingenious 60-foot racing catamaran "Hydraplaneur." This boat has the potential to challenge the dominance of the 60-foot trimarans and set new directions in the design of hulls and rigs for future generations of sailing craft.

picture. The forces of nature that man has tried to harness by inventing machines that fly, float, and drive have remained constant. It seems to be our continued quest to design stronger, better-looking, faster and more spacious catamarans.

And then there is man and his associated physical characteristics. The average man is 5'8" and has constant needs to keep his systems going. On an overnight cruiser you better have a bathroom, galley and berths, which have to have certain dimensions. Headroom will determine the height of the decks over the hulls and bridgedeck which, in turn, will characterize the exterior. This is why some of the smaller catamarans, say under 35', are at a considerable disadvantage. Much more so than a monohull, whose majority of accommodations are down below, literally under water level and out of sight. For a yacht designer it is so much easier to draw an attractive 33' monohull than a comparable same-sized multihull. Be aware of the too sleek-looking small catamarans whose bridgedeck clearance might be too low for safe offshore sailing. Bridgedeck clearance is another key consideration that is most vital to a seaworthy multihull. Both the height of the bridge deck and the room needed for a person in the saloon will determine the height of the coach house. Starting at 40 feet of length, catamarans begin to look very attractive and sleek, although there are some "toolboxes" around that force every cubic inch into a given length.

A lot of blame – now that we have praised them – goes to the charter industry, which commissions thousands of new cruising cats each year. In order to update their constantly abused fleets and with the goal to increase profitability, charter companies prefer multihulls with the most space/length/price ratio. This keeps acquisition costs at a minimum, yet maximizes revenues when renting to large parties. The only problem is that these types of charter cats often have mediocre performance and sometimes dangerous behavior in challenging sea conditions. Often hulls and bridge decks pound against waves and older catamarans purchased from charter fleets for a bargain can end up being a nightmare to own. This is not to say that there aren't good charter cats around that one can obtain at a good price and still enjoy. However, one should never forget the purpose of the boat and the forces the sea can throw at you.

If you are able to define the parameters of your next boat honestly, you will know what attributes it must possess to satisfy your needs. It is similar to mixing a fine tasting cocktail. Knowing what flavor you are trying to achieve will prevent you from mixing up a catastrophic mixture of spirits. You don't just throw in the ingredients hoping for a good result. Keeping priorities on the top of your list will make your mission to acquire the best boat a success. However, you will need to know what you want. Don't look for a heavy, luxurious boat if you will mostly day-sail. On the other hand, don't decide on a racy, narrow thoroughbred cat, even when the price is tempting, if your needs are for family cruising with substantial payload requirements. Retired racers often may be had for a bargain price and may present a great opportunity for some people who know what they are getting into. Yet, it can become an expensive and sometimes dangerous trap for the inexperienced. Budget and previous boat experience must also be considered and entered into the decision formula. A sailor operating multihulls with a greater amount of knowledge will have honed his approach to the subject of the compromise between performance and utility. He will better understand the limitations or advantages of certain hull types and their application to his needs. His decision-making process will be a faster and often a better one. Timing is also important especially if you have limited familiarity with large multihulls (at least for me "large" starts at around 35'). If your goal, let's say, is to go cruising with your family in about two years, start doing your homework soon. Knowing what type of sailor you are, or want to be, will eliminate most mistakes when trying to decide on a multihull. Having the discipline and honesty to compromise will make the search even more successful.

An evaluation method carried out in a systematic approach often works best. Making a hierarchical list of the most important parameters that one wishes for, with the most important starting from the top, usually helps, e.g.: Safety, Accommodations, Resale Value, Performance, Price, etc., all these will have an impact on each other and, of course, changing one criteria might alter the other.

See what size you can live with, need, and are able to sail by yourself. To my mind you should be able to singlehand any multihull in case your crew is incapacitated. Dreaming of a 60' catamaran makes no sense if you do not want to take crew and have doubts about your physical abilities. Ideally, not one single piece of equipment should extend beyond the strength limits of the weakest

below A sleek-looking Fountaine Pajot, Bahia 46, at Aeroyacht's Long Island dock.

above Some large catamarans are able to travel 300 miles per day, thereby providing the ultimate thrill ride for guests and crewmembers alike.

far right The airy trampolines of a large cat are the best place for relaxing and sunbathing.

crewmember. Don't consider a 32' multihull if you have a family of 8 and are thinking of a circumnavigation. Your payload might exceed the safe limits the designer had in mind and by the time you are at your destination you will put your boat up for sale. Or are you the type who needs to win every race aboard your next multihull? Looking for a bargain ex-charter cat that has the profile of a gothic cathedral will not make you happy either, even if your partner loves the interior room and locker space. Being realistic is often difficult, but it saves time and is the only approach to identify the boat of your dreams.

We yacht designers work in a decision spiral when determining what is best for our clients. You should be thinking along similar terms. What is my budget? With whom and where do I want to cruise? What length multihull can I afford and what space and payload do I need? Can I really singlehand the boat? What is the cost of the yearly maintenance? How much depreciation am I willing to accept? The resulting catamaran might turn out to be a 48' boat with a 16-ton displacement and too expensive. Consequently, you will fine-tune the initial parameters and ask yourself: Can I live with something smaller and do I require all that room? Will my spouse be happy? Do I really need to travel 250 miles per day in a high-tech boat that I cannot afford?

Eventually you will discover the sweet spot… where expectations and possibilities meet. This will be the starting point for profiling your ultimate multihull. Newick's famous saying that you can only have two out of three features is beautifully simple and makes ultimate sense, just like his graceful (efficient and fast, but small interior) trimarans. Perhaps the idea that all boats are compromises is a cliché but sums it up. Which features you are willing to give up in order to make other characteristics possible will become one of the biggest challenges when shopping for a cruising catamaran.

Decision Parameters

When deciding between purchasing one or the other catamaran it helps to evaluate objectively and score each parameter. Since Safety is the most important characteristic its rank should be multiplied by a factor of two.

In this example the X-cat might be a new, well-built production catamaran, which is compared to a Z-cat, a pre-owned less expensive alternative. Y-cat might be a new semi-custom high-tech boat, whose score lies somewhere between the two other vessels.

Decision Parameters	X-cat	Y-cat	Z-cat
* Safety (Design, Construction) Factor x 2	198	182	100
Value for Money (Boat for Dollar)	98	85	99
Live-Aboard Quality	95	99	68
Performance	92	99	99
Resale Value	91	75	65
Company Reputation & Experience	98	85	75
Construction Quality	95	88	75
Finish Quality	95	88	65
Warranty	98	88	50
After Sales Service	98	75	50
Reliability (vs. Complexity Systems)	92	75	65
Esthetics	93	93	93
Customization	85	99	65
Problem History (Relative to Numbers Built)	98	88	75
Sail Control and Handling	95	95	82
Total Score	**1521**	**1414**	**1126**
90-100: Excellent			
80-90: Very Good			
70-80: Good			
60-70: Acceptable			
60 and Below: Not Acceptable or Non-Existent			
* NOTE: Because of its Importance, the Safety Score Should be Multiplied by the Factor of Two			

"Those who fall in love with practice without science
are like a sailor who steers his ship without a compass,
and who never can be certain whither he is going."

~ Leonardo da Vinci

MULTIHULL characteristics

Flat decks without obstructions provide easy dinghy handling. A catamaran's swim ladder and transom steps are a safe and convenient way to get back on board.

MULTIHULL ADVANTAGES

Catamaran vs. Monohull

In order for us to appreciate the advantages of a catamaran it is important to be aware of their different attributes as compared to their ballasted counterparts. Although both types of vessels rely on watertight hulls to safely separate seawater from precious cargo on the inside, their stability is achieved via totally different means. Data of a typical 45' monohull will be compared to a 45' cruising catamaran, illustrating the diverse characteristics of both types of boats. Why are multihulls generally faster and do people really get less seasick sailing them? In this chapter we objectively investigate advantages of catamarans such as their stable and spacious environment, low draft and the fact that beginner sailors feel more confident.
But be aware, not everything is all roses. Although the well-designed and -built cruising multihull provides many rewards in terms of safety and handling, we will also investigate some of their drawbacks.

below An Outremer 50S tuning before the start of the famous La Route du Rhum.

Speed

Higher maximum and average speeds are what multihulls are all about and this is maybe the most important characteristic which lures monohull sailors to catamarans. L. Francis Herreshoff, a legendary American designer once said: "The fun of sailing is proportional to the speed of sailing." Let's be honest. Isn't it true that every single time we sail and see another boat heeling in the breeze, we want to catch it? Mostly we do it quite inconspicuously so that no one realizes that we are actually trying to overtake a competitor, but in the back of our minds we are always racing. Speed is more than just fun. There are times when we are actually participating in a race and by having a fast boat our chances to win are obviously higher. And what a joy it is to win!

In an incident at the Annapolis Demo Days 3 years ago, I sailed on an Outremer 45 on the Chesapeake Bay with 10 clients aboard, in about 12 knots of breeze. We were heavily loaded, had cruising sails and were certainly not in racing trim. My guests on board were in absolute awe, as we sailed faster, pointed higher and at

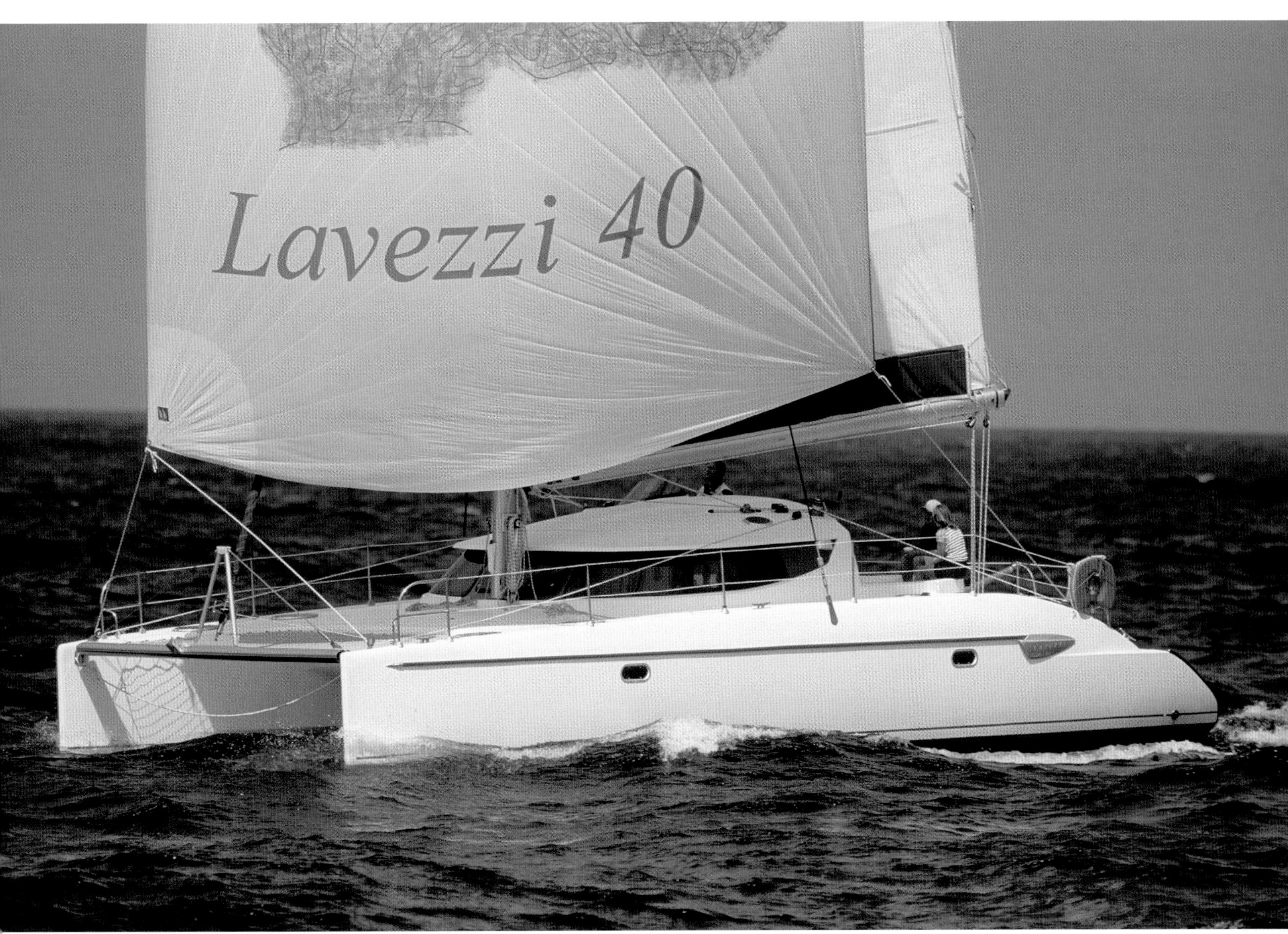

the end overtook a J-40 monohull with Kevlar sails, a boat that is considered by most to be one of the ultimate monohull cruiser/racers. The definitive speed comparison between monohulls and multihulls is most apparent at the annual Around Long Island Race (ALIR), which takes a fleet of ca.150 monohulls and a dozen multihulls past New York City, in a 220-mile offshore race around Long Island. The multihulls usually start about one hour after the leaders and it is not uncommon for us to have overtaken the entire fleet within the first 40 miles of the course. I have participated in 5 ALIRs and every single year we have an upwind start into strong headwinds. Many proponents of monohulls will say that sailing upwind is not the strength of catamarans, yet it is always on that first leg sailing to weather, where we pass almost the entire fleet. It is interesting to see monohull crews in their full foul-weather gear acting as "rail meat" taking spray, while we blast by on the level with cocktails on the cockpit table discussing sail trim.

Speed has won wars, turned commercial fisherman into wealthy business entrepreneurs and has been also a contributor to safety. In battle, a fast warship could outmaneuver its adversary or even run away from a boat with more firepower. Higher performance meant that Gloucester schooners, 100 years ago, could race against each other back to port and offer the freshest catch at the highest price. Just as in history, speed of a sailing yacht is important and gives a faster yacht more options.

above The new, all infusion-built, Fountaine Pajot – Lavezzi 40, powering along under asymmetric spinnaker.

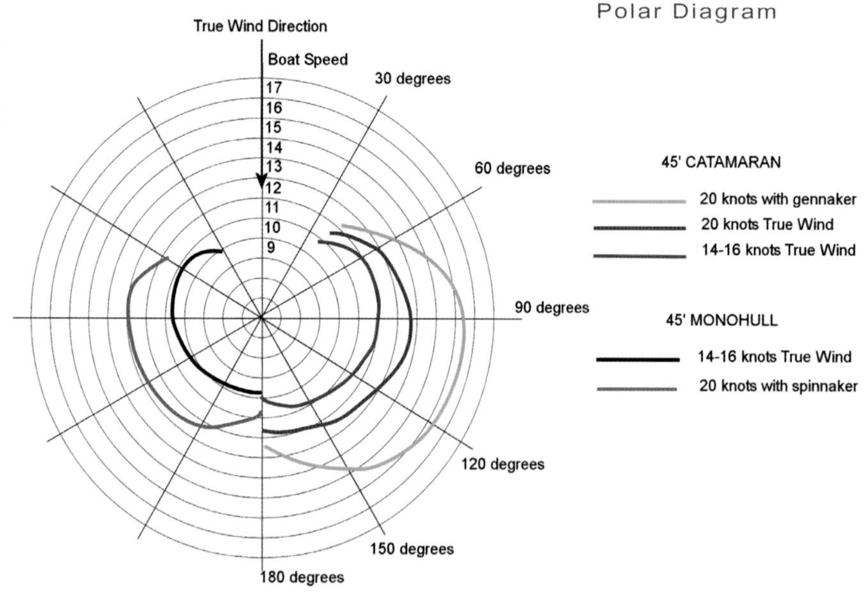

The polar diagram illustrates the varying speeds attained by a multihull, especially off the wind, where performance differences can be as high as 50% as compared to monohulls.

Personally, the most important benefit of speed of a multihull is the ability to outrun bad weather. Being able to average 11 knots on a catamaran, rather than 8 knots as on a monohull, will give you more options in your strategy of avoiding bad weather. Getting to your destination quicker and shaving off days on a transatlantic voyage will simply mean that you have mathematically less chance of getting the toilet clogged, running into a submerged container or falling overboard. Thanks to advances in radar, satellite and computer technology, a five-day forecast today is as accurate as a two-day forecast was in 1980. A multihull's higher speed will greatly contribute to easier and safer planning of ocean passages around weather windows, since exposure time will be less and meteorological prediction for shorter periods more accurate. Being able to sail faster will also introduce the concept of apparent wind to the strategy of efficient sailing.

Sailing upwind, the multihull will usually experience more apparent wind across the deck since she is sailing faster, hence the sails will feel more pressure, making the boat perform even better. The concept of apparent wind will greatly contribute to the joy of sailing, as it adds another dimension. When sailing towards a downwind destination, fast multihulls will be able to sail at smaller wind angles, often bringing the apparent wind forward of the beam, optimizing the angle of attack on the sails. Whereas multihulls will fly gennakers, Code-Zeros or asymmetric spinnakers, monohulls in contrast will set symmetric spinnakers off clumsy poles. Their boat speed will often cancel out the true wind, reducing the apparent wind and performance. The faster the multihull is the more she will be able to take advantage of the apparent wind and tack downwind towards her destination. Although she might be sailing twice the distance, she will arrive at the downwind mark quicker because her Velocity Made Good (VMG) will be faster.

Efficiency

The efficiency of a sailboat can be best expressed in how certain performance levels are achieved. We will compare the Displacement/Length Ratio, Sail Area/Displacement ratio and see how the all-important stability is achieved in both mono and multihulls.

The Power to Weight ratio (or Sail Area/Displacement Ratio) is one of the most important efficiency indicators in a sailboat. The higher the number the faster the boat will sail. The driving power of any sail-driven craft is the energy of the wind acting through the Center of Effort (CE) of the sail plan. The weight of the boat is the weight of the structure of the vessel, including its gear and equipment.

The formula for the Power to Weight Ratio or Sail Area to Displacement Ratio is:

$SA/D = SA / (Disp / 64)^{2/3}$

This ratio is an indicator of how much sail area a boat has relative to its displacement. A boat with a higher value will accelerate faster and get to hull speed with less wind. Again, all other boat parameters being the same, the vessel with the higher SA/D will be a faster boat. This is the basic power to weight measure.

Another important efficiency indicator is the Displacement to Length Ratio:

$D/L = (\text{Displacement in lbs}/2240)/(0.01 * LWL)^3$

The higher the resulting number the less performance a boat will have. This formula is especially indicative for monohulls, yet comparing a catamaran will show the relative difference. The displacement length ratio is a measure of a boat's speed potential. For displacement boats (most sailboats), speed potential is a function of waterline length (unless you are planing or surfing down a wave). Longer waterline boats can go faster. Lighter boats accelerate faster and reach hull speed with less wind. All else being equal, the boat with the lower D/L will be a better light-air performer. Lower displacement will also make a boat more sensitive to loading.

These two ratios together (D/L & SA/D) can give a good comparison of two boats' speed potential relative to one another. If our multihull has a SA/D of 27.7 and a DL of 117, and our monohull has a SA/D of 18.9 and a DL of 145, the multihull will clearly be a better performer. However, speed potential is not all there is to Efficiency.

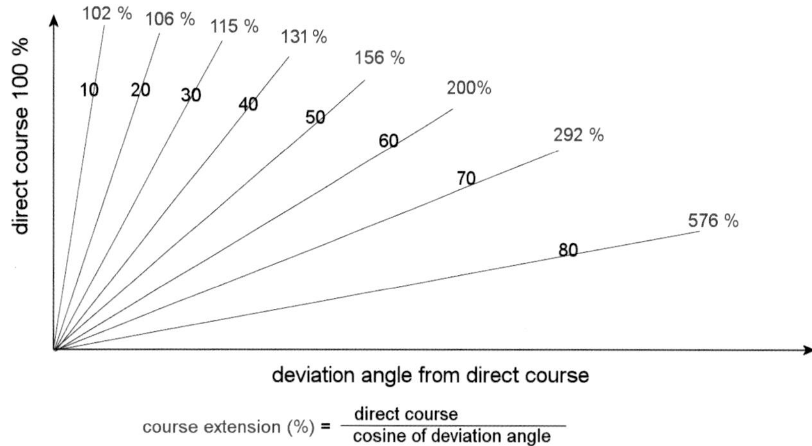

A simplified illustration showing the extension of the course as one digresses from the direct route. The calculation of VMG (Velocity Made Good) is based on this simple principle of the mathematical relationship between the cosine of the deviation angle and the Rhumb Line course. Diverting 20 degrees from the course adds only 6% to the distance, yet diverting 60 degrees doubles it.

Stability

In order to keep a monohull upright she will need ballast, which will resist the heeling force of the wind. Usually this ballast is in form of a weighted fin, often with a bulb attached to the bottom. The more a monohull heels, the more the Righting Moment (RM) and Righting Arm (RA) will increase counteracting the overturning moment. On a monohull it is the offset of the Center of Gravity (CG) of the keel from the Center of Buoyancy (CB) when heeled which will determine its stability. Depending on the type of monohull, often the weight of the ballast can constitute 30%-40% of the total displacement of the boat. This means that the only reason for the existence of tons of lead is the necessity to keep its carrier upright. The weight of the keel is just the beginning of a vicious cycle, because the structure supporting the keel has to be even stronger (and heavier) to prevent the keel from falling off. This means that the ballast of a monohull is just the starting point of a downward weight spiral and a keel actually increases the total displacement of

Specifications for a typical 45' cruising multihull and 45' monohull

	45' catamaran	45' monohull
Length (LOA)	45.0'	45.0'
Length (LWL)	43.2'	43.2'
Beam:	22.5'	14.2'
Draft:	24"up/7' down, 4' mini keels	5'-8.3'
Sail Area:	1,320 ft²	1,044 ft²
Ballast:	none	9,680 lbs
Displacement:	21,000 lbs	26,180 lbs
Displacement/Length Ratio (D/L)	117	145
Power to Weight Ratio (SA/D)	27.7	18.9

a monohull by more than just the weight of the ballast. Further, the attachment points on modern fin-keeled monohulls are comparatively small and inefficient in relation to the task of keeping an extremely heavy structure attached. This is not the end of the story. The heeling monohull will produce more water drag and also by necessity has a wider hull beam, which will suck the boat into a wave pattern, which will limit its speed, something that Archimedes already noticed 2200 years ago. The large bow wave that is produced by a fat hull shape will hinder the boat from surpassing its hull speed which is calculated as 1.34 x square root of its waterline length (1.34 x $\sqrt{WL}$). In the case of a catamaran, which has no keel to weigh the boat down, slimmer and more hydrodynamically optimized hulls, this theoretical hull speed rarely applies.

below Unlike an oceangoing cruising cat, the racey Corneel 26 can lift a hull if sailed hard.

Typically, cruising catamarans will have a beam-to-length ratio of roughly 50%, meaning a 45' long cat will be about 22' wide. This will not only result in a tremendous amount of space but also in a formidably stiff boat. A multihull will resist the overturning moment of the sails by its beam alone, without having fat hulls for form stability or a lead ballast. This results in a lighter boat, length for length, and a vessel with a higher speed potential, since the power-to-weight ratio will be higher.

Unlike Hobie cats or very light displacement catamarans, a cruising catamaran will never lift a hull. I have never lifted a hull on a cruising multihull and am often startled by novices questioning me: "Does she fly a hull?" On a well designed cat, theoretically, the shrouds will act as safety valves and break before the main hull could lift. Usually the breaking strength of the stays will be engineered to be less than the righting arm of the multihull providing a great theoretical safety valve. Honestly, I have never been in a situation where a mast shroud parted because of an excessive heeling force. The only time I flew a hull on larger multihulls was on racers, such as Formula 40 cats, 60' tris or 120' racing cats such as "Club Med." Their power-to-weight ratio is far beyond the normal scope of a cruising multihull and they are a subject of a different book.

When the extra weight of a ballasted monohull and its inefficient hull shape are taken into account, one can easily see that a catamaran is far more efficient and is simply

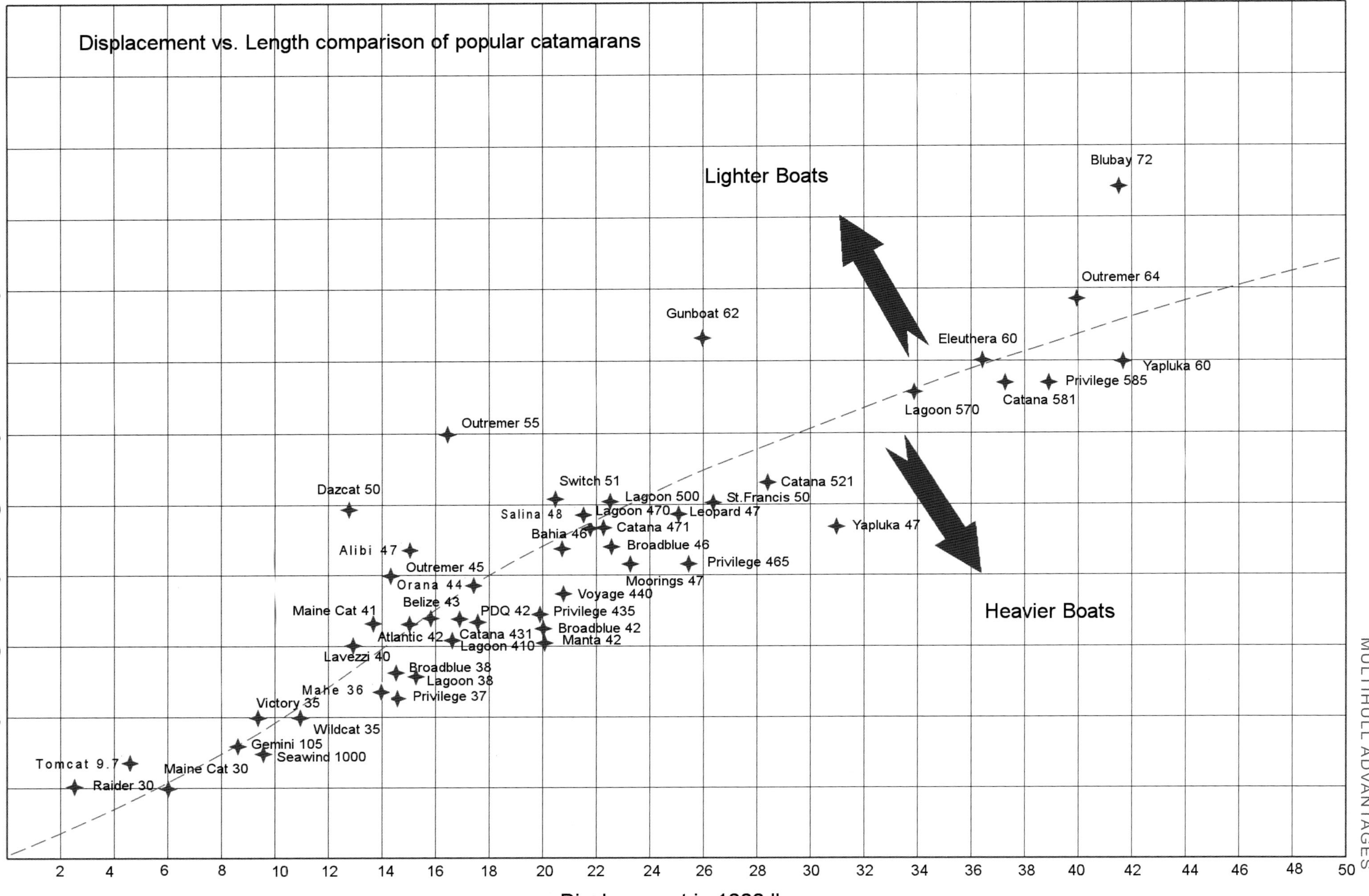
Displacement vs. Length comparison of popular catamarans
Lighter Boats
Heavier Boats
Blubay 72
Outremer 64
Gunboat 62
Eleuthera 60
Yapluka 60
Privilege 585
Catana 581
Lagoon 570
Outremer 55
Catana 521
Switch 51
Lagoon 500
St.Francis 50
Dazcat 50
Salina 48
Lagoon 470
Leopard 47
Yapluka 47
Bahia 46
Catana 471
Broadblue 46
Alibi 47
Privilege 465
Outremer 45
Orana 44
Moorings 47
Voyage 440
Belize 43
Maine Cat 41
PDQ 42
Privilege 435
Broadblue 42
Atlantic 42
Catana 431
Lagoon 410
Manta 42
Lavezzi 40
Broadblue 38
Lagoon 38
Maine 36
Privilege 37
Victory 35
Wildcat 35
Gemini 105
Seawind 1000
Tomcat 9.7
Maine Cat 30
Raider 30
30
35
40
45
50
55
60
65
70
75
80
2
4
6
8
10
12
14
16
18
20
22
24
26
28
30
32
34
36
38
40
42
44
46
48
50
Displacement in 1000 lbs.

a more hydrodynamically proficient structure. This fact usually translates into higher speeds, more miles sailed in a day, faster passage times and gallons of fuel saved. In eco-conscious times such as the decade we live in now, isn't this what sailing is all about? Traveling as efficiently as possible across the seas?

Safety

The fact that well-designed and constructed cruising catamarans are unsinkable makes them – at least in my mind – the safest platforms to cross oceans in. Usually their higher average speeds, shallower draft will also provide you with an active safety margin and their stable – non-heeling – platforms create a more secure operating environment. All these vital safety characteristics, essential to ocean cruising are lacking in a monohull.

Unsinkability is probably the number one safety issue regarding any boat venturing to sea. When we speak about an unsinkable vessel, I mean a boat not sinking to the bottom of the ocean if holed. Unlike the Titanic, which was claimed to be invincible because of her watertight compartments (actually many of them were only partial bulkheads, as they did not extend all the way through the boat), a multihull is usually unsinkable because of the way she is built. Most modern catamarans are constructed by utilizing composites whereby a core material, usually foam, is sandwiched between two skins of resin-impregnated cloth. This yields a very strong, rot-free structure, which is not only stiff and torsion resistant, but also makes the entire configuration float. The volume of the foam used in the core of the sandwich alone is usually more buoyant than the entire weight of the boat, including machinery, crew and cruising gear. The addition of watertight compartments, usually many more than on a monohull (if she has any) will contribute to any buoyancy in case of a collision. One should not be fooled by multihull manufacturers' claims. The term "unsinkable" might mean completely flooded and in the very worst circumstance, resulting in a capsize. However the fact remains, that one will be much better off on an inverted cat, presenting a great target to search teams, than bobbing in a tiny rubber raft and one's monohull miles below the surface. In my mind this fact alone should be one of the most important considerations for anyone traveling even two miles out to sea.

below The author's 43' catamaran, beached at low tide to rid the bottom of the hulls from barnacles and marine growth.

Some sailors who are interested in making the switch from their monohull to a catamaran do not seem interested in speed, relying on the argument that they are not racers. However after they realize that higher performance will allow them an active safety margin and more routing strategies around bad weather, more speed suddenly makes sense. We have often been caught thousands of miles from shore with a low pressure system looming to intercept our intended track. With the help of today's sophisticated routing software and weather prediction, multihull sailors can often evade the worst of storms. Sometimes the difference of 20% more average speed will result in avoiding gale-force winds and thus provide a safer passage.

Draft

Many of the planet's most beautiful anchorages and harbors lie in the remotest regions and most can only be accessed by vessels with a 4' or less draft. This is one of the reasons monohull designers have gone through great efforts to shave inches off 7' plus keels. On one hand they try to preserve the necessary stability yet need to balance it with the need of a shallower draft. The multihull does not need a deep ballasted fin to remain upright and can get away with twin low-aspect-ratio keels or completely retractable daggerboards or centerboards. It is not uncommon for catamarans up to 60 feet to have a draft less than 5'. Now imagine a monohull, with the equivalent volume of a 60' catamaran. That ballasted monster would be close to 85' and probably would have a draft of at least 12'! The fact that multihulls have less underwater appendages sticking out of the bottom also makes them safer, as there is less chance of grounding or hitting submerged reefs. Of course the chances still exist, since catamaran sailors would sneak into low water harbors, yet the consequences of touching the bottom will usually not be as catastrophic as on a monohull. Shallower draft will also give you more options in terms of which harbors you can find shelter in if you are out at sea and suddenly find yourself in trouble. Imagine having a sick crew member on board who needs to get to a hospital fast. Being able to quickly get him to land will be of essence and having more ports to choose from might save his life.

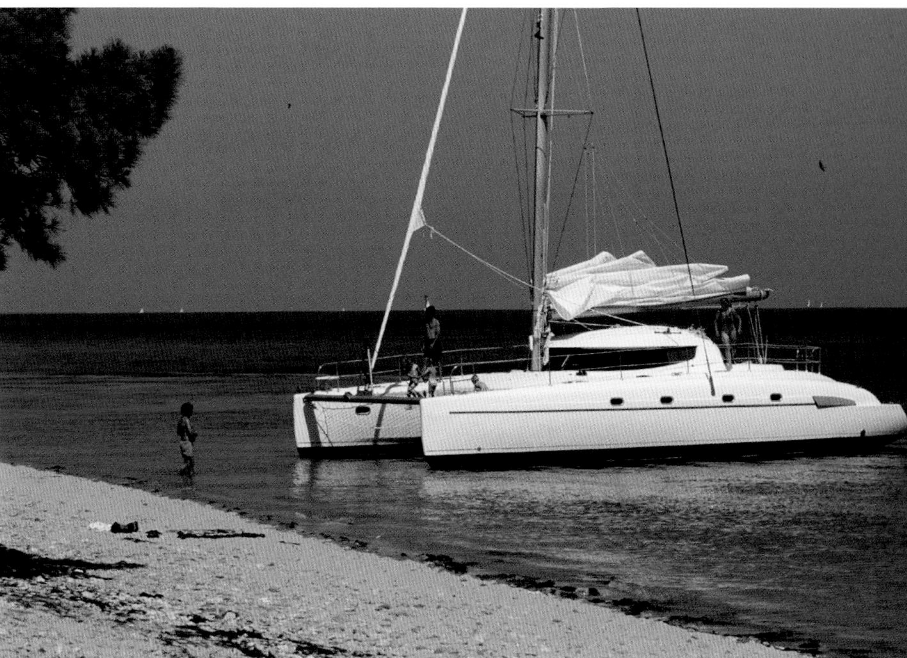

above As sandy beaches beckon, a catamaran's ability to come close to shore allows one to avoid neighboring boats and provides ultimate privacy.

No-Heel Environment

Cruising catamarans are also safer because they provide better shelter and a no-heel environment for their crew. This will result in less exposure, fewer seamanship errors caused by fatigue and a more refreshed crew at the end of a long trip.

I remember sailing into the middle of the Miami Boat Show in 2001 with "Alizé," a magnificent 64' catamaran after crossing the North Atlantic. The boat show with thousands of visitors was our first landfall after 6,000 miles of nonstop sailing. Although the vessel was big and comfortable, the crossing was challenging as we experienced very rough weather after leaving the Canary Islands. Trying to sneak out of the Mediterranean Sea in the middle of winter with inches of snow on deck and fierce headwinds was not easy either. Yet, at the end of the voyage my three crewmembers were in top form and the boat looked as if she had just come out of the factory. The most amazing fact is that nothing major failed on this maiden voyage of "Alizé," and she barely had 100 miles on her log before leaving the South of France. Maybe things would have been different on a monohull, which could not protect her crew from the elements as well. In the three days of the Canary storm the boat was sailing under autopilot at speeds of 20 knots and we once even hit 28 knots without touching the helm. Even in these rough conditions we found ourselves sitting around the stable saloon table eating three-course meals and enjoying fine French wine. (The bilges of the boat contained hundreds of bottles). Sitting at dinner, riding down huge waves, the feeling and atmosphere on the bridge deck was alert but definitely less stressed than it would have been on a monohull. I have been on 65' monohulls in less severe conditions and it certainly felt worse. Imagine sailing on a heeling boat in a storm and having to hand-steer unprotected at the outside helm. Chances are high that in those conditions and speeds the autopilot of a monohull could not hold the boat as easily, since the single rudder and keel would constantly yaw and change the angle of attack. The resulting cavitations and pressure could disengage the

below Here, a single reef in the main does not slow the multihull, but rather increases control and eases the stresses on the boat, an Outremer 64S.

Roll Angle vs. Human Effectiveness

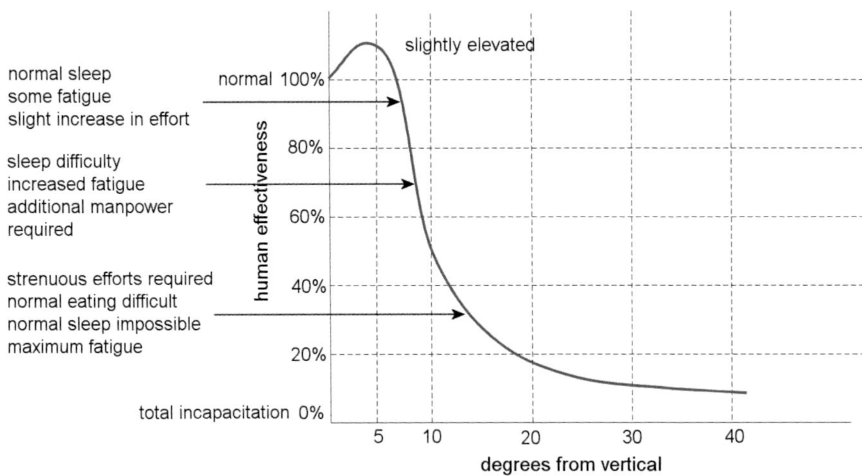

effect of roll angle from the vertical for prolonged periods

Roll Angle vs. Human Effectiveness

Studies by Warhurst and Cerasini of the Naval Ship R&D Center discovered that at a slight roll and heel angle, a human actually becomes more alert and his performance increases. However, as the roll intensifies, effectiveness and fatigue deteriorate until total incapacitation is approached beyond 45 degrees.

pilot at the most inopportune moment and result in a broach or even worse. Exposure to the helmsman, who would be forced to hand-steer for hours, would be unbearable and rotation of crew would be necessary. Fatigue would take its toll and making tactical decisions when one is tired is the number one cause of seamanship errors.

On "Alizé," we were mostly in the cockpit behind the protection of the coach roof, letting the autopilot do its work. We only took one single breaker into the cockpit when the boat accelerated overtaking seas. She buried a good part of her twin bows into the next wave face and the resulting impact created a deluge that drenched us 50' back in the cockpit, but that was it. The twin rudders, usually protected either by skegs or mini keels, always remained vertical, greatly assisting the function of the autopilot.
The long slender hulls also contributed to directional stability of our catamaran, which would have been in total contrast to the constant change of attitude of a monohull.

While on the subject of underwater appendages, on the transatlantic passage with "Alizé," we collided with a whale in the storm and did not even notice it because of the tumultuous circumstances. It was quite apparent when I stood at the dock in Miami admiring the boat with her owner when we realized that one of the 4' deep hull skegs was completely sheared off. It did what it was intended to do and sacrificed itself to save the spade rudder located just aft of it. Imagine a missing single rudder on a monohull in the middle of a storm. It would be a major incident. It is the same underlying redundancy that twin engines represent on a multihull. If one fails, you still have another to get you home. I think it is quite apparent that a well-designed, unsinkable, fast multihull with redundant systems, providing better shelter and a non-heeling environment will simply be a safer boat than a monohull.

The lack of heeling on a multihull goes beyond the discussion of safety as it is easy to understand that performing every-day tasks on the level become increasingly difficult when heeling. Most importantly, falling overboard and perishing at sea is the single most common cause of fatalities at sea and has happened even to the most experienced sailors (e.g. the tragic disappearance of Eric Tabarly off his own monohull in 1998). Slipping off the stable deck of a wide cat

Roll behavior of monohulls is quite different than that of catamarans. As waves are traveling from left to right, the multihull strictly conforms to the slopes, whereas the ballasted monohull will start a self-excited roll cycle, heeling the vessel far beyond the angle of the wave face.

Roll Behavior (Profiling) & Pendulum Effect

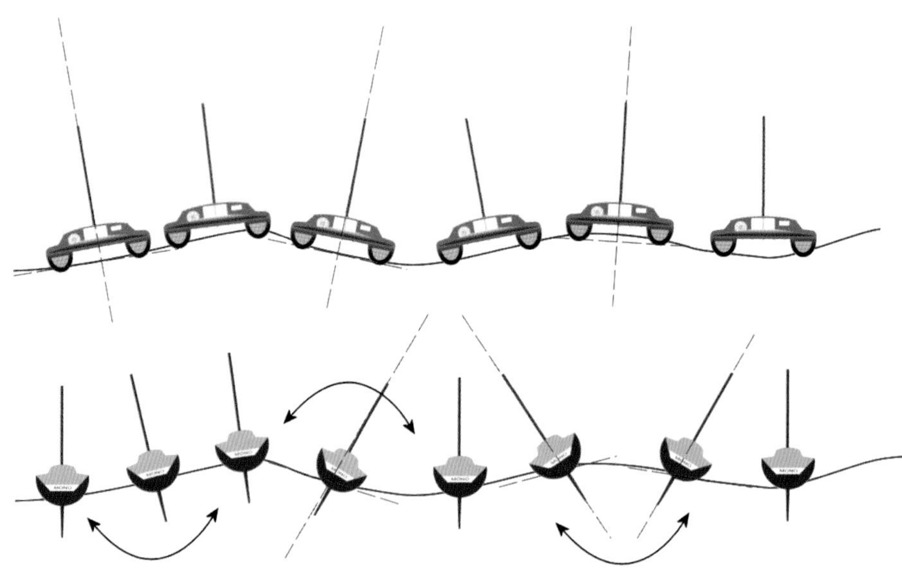

below Spinnaker sailing on a catamaran is not associated with cumbersome poles and endless rolling as can be often experienced on a monohull. Sail controls are simple, while traveling swift and flat.

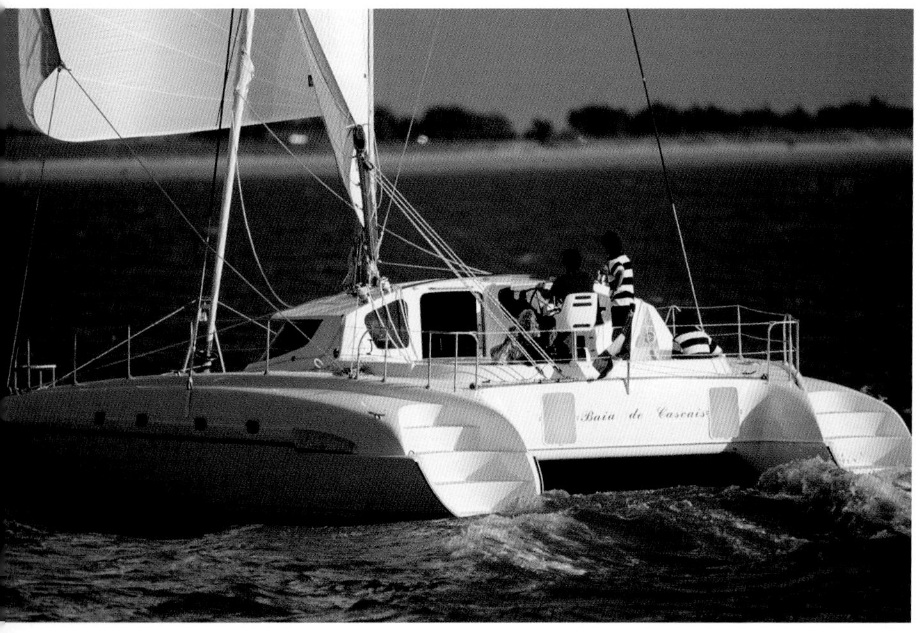

is much harder. Even retrieving a man overboard victim is difficult on a monohull and famous ocean racer Rob James, who slipped off his trimaran "Colt Cars," died of exposure before he could be retrieved. Interestingly, most drowned sailors are found with the fly of their trousers open, which says it all. The fact is apparent that it is much less likely for a sailor to fall overboard from a stable catamaran than a heeling monohull.

The Navy published an interesting study years ago, where test subjects were exposed to different responsibilities at varying angles of roll and heel. Interestingly, the effectiveness and degree of alertness of sailors increased up to 3 degrees of heel but radically diminished as time, roll angle, and heel angle increased.

Did you ever try going to the bathroom even in moderate conditions on a monohull? It is often an act of great contortions and almost comical in nature. One is balancing, trying to anticipate the ship's motion and not to mess up the environment too much. In storm conditions visiting the head on a monohull becomes dangerous. The confined space brings one's head in close proximity to the handles and edges and I have often been thinking of investing in a crash helmet before going to the bathroom. It is not to say that on a catamaran it is less violent, but at least one does not have to deal with the additional gymnastics needed to compensate for the heel factor. I have seen many burns on chest and underarms and heard countless horror stories of boiling pots of water flying

Stability at Varying Angles of Heel

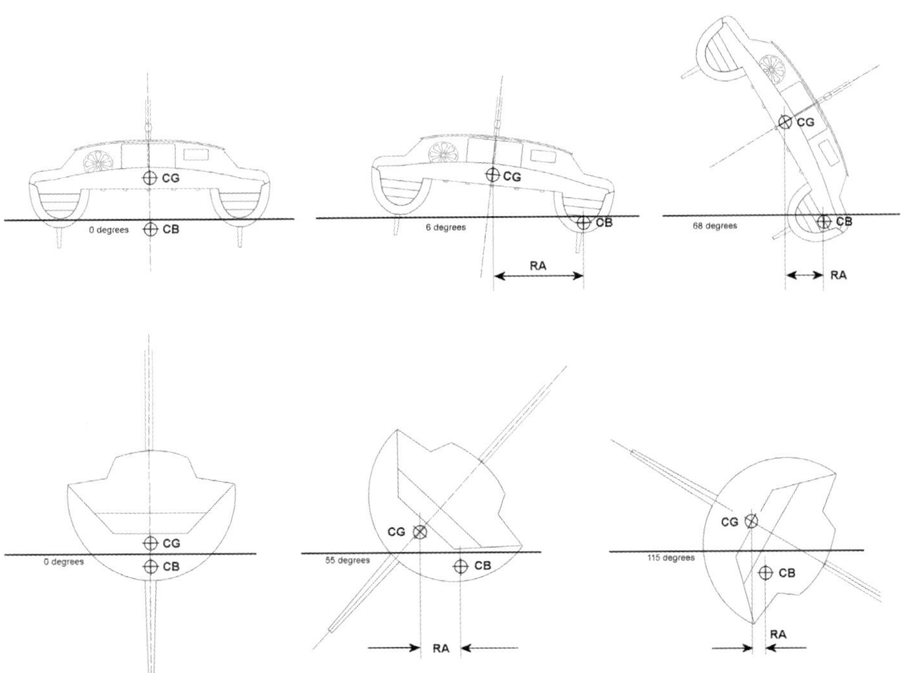

As the angle of heel increases, the relative position of the Center of Gravity (CG) and Center of Buoyancy (CB) change. Compare the Righting Arm (RA) and resulting stability of the catamaran at 6 degrees. It is almost twice as large as the monohull's at 55 degrees of heel. On the other hand, the ballasted keelboat retains enough RA at 115 degrees, whereas the catamaran is approaching its stability limit at 70 degrees.

through monohull cabins. On a single-hulled vessel there are even sadistic straps for the cook to tie him to the stove, leaving him little movement to escape from danger. It is very rare that cooking gear needs to be clamped to a stove on a multihull. Catamaran galleys are definitely safer places to handle scalding dishes and, in the worst conditions, bottles remain upright if placed into the sink. There is a reason that I have never seen a gimbaled stove or a cantilevered saloon table on a catamaran. Fiddles and door-locking mechanisms are often necessary on monohulls to prevent items becoming airborne. On a stable catamaran, wine glasses will remain on tables up to Force 8 conditions!

Seasickness, after the expense of sailing as a sport, is probably the single biggest deterrent, which keeps people on land. This condition is most uncomfortable and often the afflicted crew utter confused death-wishes to end their situation. Seasickness is caused by a number of factors such as anxiety, fatigue, thirst, hunger and cold, which all add to a sense of disorientation, yet the first and foremost cause of this malady is motion. In foul weather the heeling and yawing environment of a monohull is conducive to a sense of helplessness, where one must hide in the bowels of the boat, with diesel fumes and no air or open sea view. It is a fact that more people get seasick on monohulls than catamarans. The best remedy for a nauseous crewmember is to get him out into the open and keep him busy. Usually driving the boat and looking at a distant object on the horizon will help.

The catamaran provides a gentler motion and, in general, a more pleasurable sailing environment. The motion of the boat might be quicker, especially if sailing upwind, but it is usually perceived as more predictable. The high initial stiffness and moment of inertia of a cruising catamaran greatly help the human body to anticipate the next move of the boat. This is in significant contrast to the slower roll behavior of a ballasted monohull.

Having twin engines separated from the living accommodations, as is mostly the

below On some larger multihulls, even the head compartments are fitted with the finest wood-joiner work and rival those of a luxury estate.

case on modern multihulls, also keeps the sickening diesel vapors and noise away from the crew. In comparison, most monohulls have their engine buried under the cockpit with only the folding companionway ladder separating the smelly beast from the passengers. Novice sailors will also appreciate the better ventilation a cat can offer. Breathing fresh air and being able to see the horizon from a sheltered saloon will greatly reduce the anxiety associated with seasickness.

As we can see, safety has many faces and seasickness is possibly the ugliest of them all. More seamanship errors are committed by fatigued and queasy sailors than healthy ones. Creating a more habitable environment will thus contribute to the safety of crew and ship.

Space

Usually the very first comments boat show visitors make when stepping aboard a large cruising catamaran is related to the vast amount of room as compared to an equivalent length monohull. Close to ideal cockpit shelters, large amounts of storage, and 360-degree saloon views are just some of the space and layout advantages of multihulls.

Thanks to the wide beam of a multihull its volume is much more than meets the eye. We all know that for every additional foot in length, the interior of a monohull rapidly increases. This phenomenon is taken to the extreme on a catamaran where even several inches additional boat length will provide more of everything than ever dreamed of. This is most noticeable when experiencing the vast space of a catamaran's main deck.

The saloon and cockpit account for the major portion of a catamaran's bridge deck and usually span from the aft end of the cockpit to the central, mast-bearing crossbeam. Not only is this area the most comfortable part of the boat, since it is close to the center of gravity (CG), but it is also where most of the action takes place. In fact, more hours are spent in the cockpit or the saloon of a catamaran than in bed. In contrast to the typical monohull, where the cockpit is separated by a steep companionway ladder leading down into the cavity of the boat, a cruising catamaran provides a close to ideal surrounding.

Froude's Pendulum

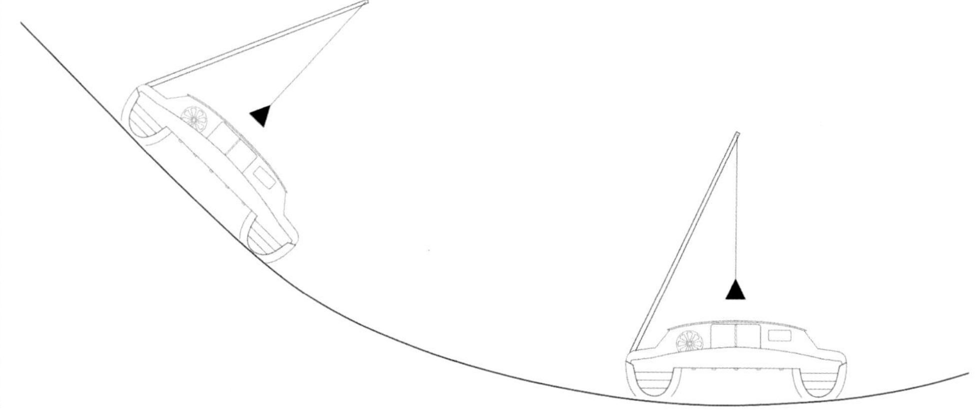

Froude's pendulum experiment proved that no matter how inclined the wave-face angle, the pendulum remained perpendicular to the sea due to the effects of momentum.

The cockpit, even on a 45' catamaran, has enough space to separate the helmsman from lounging crewmembers. Often the sheltered corner just aft and to one side of the saloon bulkhead is utilized for a fixed cockpit table. We often have 10 people on our boat without feeling cramped. There is sufficient elbow room for winches to be operated and usually the mainsheet traveler is either on the bimini arch or aft of the cockpit settee, well separated from passengers. On a monohull one sits "within" the cockpit, as one would in a bathtub. The helmsman will often have to squeeze by the huge wheel, and the sitting and lounging area is less than one third of that of a cruising catamaran. The bitter ends of halyards and lines quickly clutter the largest cockpit and make them look messy. On a monohull it is often unavoidable to be sitting or standing on a rope, which is not necessarily comfortable nor safe. The greater deck space of the catamaran also allows designers to route sail controls in such a way that they are not only strategically placed for efficient operation, but also out of harm's way of the passengers. This is one luxury that monohulls do not have either.

The bimini is an essential item on a cruising boat and in my mind is often underrated in its design. Few boats – monohulls and multihulls included – have smartly integrated or good looking biminis. Often one sees a beautiful looking yacht with sleek hull lines only to discover a ridiculous looking contraption of

above For half the price of a top waterfront condo, you could visit the most beautiful harbors and anchorages aboard your private island. Here the cockpit feels like an extension of the saloon; even the sliding moon-roof permits unobstructed view of the stars.

steel and canvas perched over its cockpit. Usually biminis on monohulls are more of an eyesore, as they are completely freestanding and do not benefit from the protective structure of the coach house as found on a catamaran. The only solution for the monohull is a small dodger, which protects the open companionway from spray and barely provides shade. In contrast, bimini structures on cruising catamarans are not only esthetically more pleasing as they can be tied into the deckhouse, but they actually do what they are designed to do.

The giant sliding saloon doors of a multihull invite the crew to enter the bright saloon from the cockpit, which is often on the same level. There are no steep ladders or steps to crawl over. Similar to an expansive patio, the living area created by the bridgedeck saloon and cockpit rival those of small penthouses. They truly are one of the best parts of a catamaran. One can entertain, cook, navigate or simply lounge with enough room not to be in the way of another crewmember. On long ocean passages, this is refreshing indeed. Some catamarans have the galley facing aft against the saloon bulkhead and feature a configuration resembling a bar. This permits the chef to easily pass drinks or food to guests in the cockpit. Try balancing beverages and plates up the steep companionway of a heeling monohull.

The 360-degree view from the saloon allows unobstructed sight forward and aft. In most cases the settee is placed against the forward side of the bridgedeck in order to create a transverse passageway for the hulls. The seating arrangement is usually slightly elevated to provide an outside view without having to strain neck muscles. In inclement

below Yapluka 70 saloon complete with wet bar and lounge area. Classic elegance and top workmanship at its best.

weather, seeing outside from the protection of the saloon is especially reassuring to novice sailors. On a typical 45' catamaran the dinette can seat 6-8 people for elaborate dinners without hindering the access and circulation in the saloon.

The galley is usually not far from the dinette. On most cruising cats the chef is where the guests are and is part of the social action. The cook is happy on a multihull, with plenty of storage space, ventilation and natural light. The front opening refrigerator does not necessitate acrobatics to get to the bottom of it and communication with the crew in the cockpit does not require shouting or hand signals. In short, even the galley on a small multihull is any chef's delight.

above One of the most overlooked features of good cruising boats is the forward-looking chart table, which lets you navigate and even steer the boat via push button controls in inclement weather.

Visibility Ergonomics

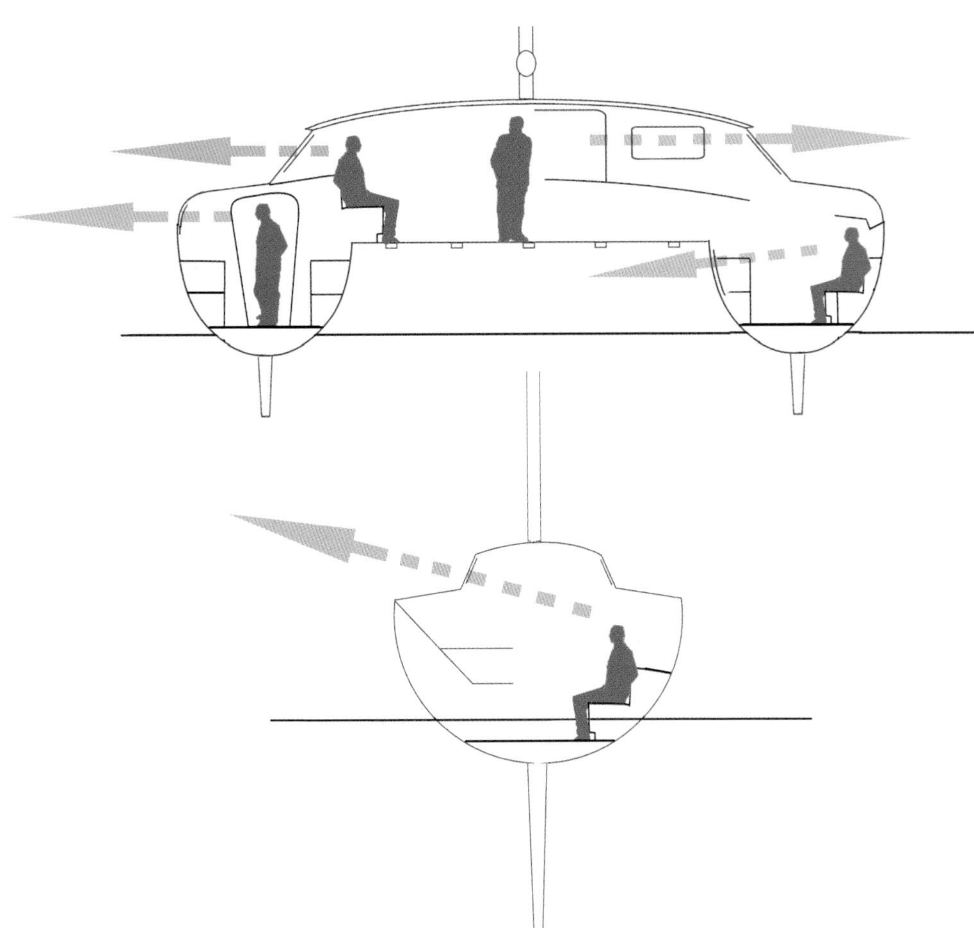

Whereas on a monohull, passengers live within the confines of the interior and often need to strain to catch a glimpse of the horizon, catamaran sailors reside above the waterline and enjoy unsurpassed 360 degree views, whether standing or sitting.

far right Wide, unobstructed teak decks are not only elegant, but also safe to walk on; however, they will require some maintenance to keep them looking good.

Storage space is usually (too) abundant on a catamaran. Where "deep-storage" items disappear into a monohull's bilges, the same goods are kept in house-hold type shelves and lockers. It is often frightening how many closets are found on a multihull. Sadly, sailors tend to stuff them full of items which are never needed. Everyone falls into this trap. I have often discovered items on our own boat, which rotted in the bottom of a dark bin, that I never even knew existed. It should be noted that one of the drawbacks of light multihulls is the erosion in performance when loaded. Therefore care should be taken to keep the payload within the designer's parameters.

Have you ever tried hand-steering a monohull from the inside navigation station? One is literally blind as there is no way to see forward. Usually inside helm stations are an afterthought on a monohull and it is rare that one finds a pilothouse boat with a proper forward facing navigation station. The majority of today's cruising catamarans have inside helm stations, which feature duplicate instrumentation and joystick helm controls. The operator has 360-degree view, can navigate, make course corrections and even tack (with a self tacking jib) while sipping a drink and comfortably seated. Abundant space and the unique layout of the multihull's bridge deck permit this invaluable feature. Anyone who has hand-steered a boat in torrential rain can appreciate the importance of an inside steering station.

The charter industry realized the practical nature of spacious money-making catamarans, which can often accommodate 4 paying parties or more. Well separated in the four corners of the boat, 2 couples sleep in each hull and guests sometimes do not even realize that they are not alone. The privacy provided by the hulls is unique and one could sleep undisturbed while another couple is watching a movie in the main saloon on the bridge deck.

Owner's layout multihulls feature an entire hull dedicated to the proprietor. Even on a typical 40' catamaran, a double berth aft is separated from a desk and lounge by closet space, while forward one can find en suite heads with separate walk-in showers. A cruising catamaran's abundant space and accommodation plan will provide a higher standard of living. Because of this the crew will find itself in a safer surrounding and a more ergonomically optimized environment than on any other vessel.

below A gourmet's delight and a chef's playground; the finely fitted galley. Although most galleys are found on a catamaran's main deck, they can also be placed in the hulls.

Boat Handling

Generous room, more possibilities for a smart layout and the non-heel environment of a cat will allow sailors to perform boat handling tasks much easier than on a monohull. Beginners will gain confidence

quicker, and a catamaran's redundant engine and steering systems will permit not only better maneuverability but also more efficient motor-sailing and the ability to beach the boat. Let's look at these characteristics in detail.

Many novice sailors are always astonished by the fact that I know people whose first boat is an 18-ton, oceangoing sail-catamaran. This should not mean that everyone can take a multihull around the world without experience, yet basic maneuvers are easier learned on a stable and more user-friendly catamaran. This greatly boosts operator confidence and because of that the learning curve is often steeper. The twin engines and high helm position of a cruising catamaran greatly facilitate docking and tight harbor maneuvers. A monohull's single screw will make a novice guess which direction the prop will "walk" and often bowthrusters are the only answer to back a big monohull into a tight slip. In contrast it will only take several times for beginners to understand the simple principles of the turning power of widely spaced twin diesels and soon maneuvers that seemed impossible are mastered with confidence.

below This is not the cockpit, but the flybridge of a large cat! A second helm station forward allows unrivaled views of the horizon and a sun pad provides lounging space for sunbathers; a stairway leads to the main deck below.

It is not uncommon to see women driving a multihull into a tight berth, while the husband prepares lines and fenders. The galley is certainly not the only place where our female companions feel at home and their reign has extended to the helm and beyond. It is a refreshing fact that I notice more women at the helm of a catamaran than on a monohull.

Have you ever seen a novice sailor clutching to the rail of a heeling monohull in a fresh breeze, eyes bulging, mouth dry and with an expression of apprehension? These will be involuntary reactions to a heeling and pitching environment, which is completely alien to dry land. Imagine the entire crew in foul-weather gear, huddled together and sitting in a cramped cockpit with water rushing by only inches away. Even worse, the novice is promoted to act as "rail meat" and is ordered to do something as useless as sitting on the windward deck. Now the wind increases and the captain orders the mainsail to be reefed. The boat turns into the wind, the mainsail flaps violently and the skipper shouts commands over the howling wind. The novice sailor starts wishing he were somewhere else as the monohull labors head into the seas, and waves crash against the bows causing spray to fly back into the cockpit. As crewmembers stagger forward to the mast and finally reef the mainsail, the boat is lurching to each wave, the boom is whipping dangerously from side to side and the noise and chaos is frightening. Our apprentice is ready to go back home, thinking that only experienced and tough seamen are made to sail the ocean. He feels that he is definitely not one of them. Of course, this example might be a bit exaggerated, but is often not far from the truth.

Reefing a boat, even on a multihull, can be a drama-filled event, where usually pulses quicken and crewmembers' alertness increases.

On a catamaran the novice would not feel that he is half submerged by sitting in a cockpit. Psychologically he would feel safer too, being high and dry on deck, many feet away from the water. Or the newcomer could be sheltered in the coachouse saloon and still be part of the action by observing the events from the safety of the settee. Even in the large cockpit he would be out of the way and not feel like a useless burden.

The beauty of a well-designed cruising catamaran is that one does not have to round up against the wind to reef the mainsail. This will reduce the excitement of the action and avoid the boat having to stomp into head seas, greatly eliminating the anxiety factor. Today's fully-battened mainsails and lazy jack systems allow a multihull to be reefed, even when sailing downwind. Apparent wind is reduced and the reefing maneuver is less taxing on boat and crew.

From running new sheets for the gennaker to performing a simple repair, actions are usually easier on a multihull with its wide and stable platform. For instance there is no need to tiptoe to a pointy bow to set and check the anchor. A multihull usually has the anchor resting on the front or central crossbeam with enough room to spare to attend to it. Making emergency repairs on a wide forward trampoline in the middle of the ocean (I have done my part) is so much easier than on a rolling stage as on a monohull. Even searching for an important item stored on

above Your private owner's suite, nearly 35' long; complete with dresser, lounge and a walk around – queen-size double berth, as found on the very successful Bahia 46 cruiser.

next page Pulling into a new harbor, the wide side decks are the best vantage point to take in the new surroundings and scout out anchorage locations.

Multihull Advantages and Drawbacks

Multihull Advantages	Multihull Drawbacks
Unsinkable – foam construction and more bulkheads	Usually more expensive, length for length
Non-heeling environment	Will stay inverted when flipped
Higher average speeds	Bridge decks can slam if not high enough
More interior space, 360-degree view, optimized layout	Not as easy to find dock space
Shallow draft – safer and more access to harbors	Performance decreases more rapidly when overloaded
Twin-engine and twin-rudder redundancy	Windage can be high
Safer sail-handling and reefing procedure	Quicker motion, especially sailing upwind
Better interior steering station – often forward facing	Not fleet-friendly racers
Better protection in cockpit against sun and rain	More maintenance
Better autopilot function	
Ability to beach and access for repairs	
Better maneuverability in harbor	
More deck space and user-friendly trampoline	
Better ventilation possibilities via emergency hatches	
More confidence-inspiring for beginners / less seasickness	
Longer range and more efficient under power	
Galley-up location	
Separation and privacy of twin hulls	
Lower environmental impact – more efficient	
Dries out upright	
Easier access from water via transom steps	
Better dinghy storage on davits between hulls	

far right One of the world's most magnificent, all-carbon luxury catamarans: the 102' "Allures" built by Blubay Yachts in France. She is able to travel at over 38 knots on wind energy, while wine glasses remain upright in the saloon.

your boat is certainly simpler with additional elbow room and better light, not to mention a more stable ground under your feet.

The shallow draft of a multihull will also facilitate emergency repairs as I have once experienced on our own 43' catamaran. In our shallow harbor where tides can be 8', "Flo" settled onto the shank of her mooring, which punctured one of the hulls. Being a composite built multihull with multiple watertight compartments, she only took on as much water until the buoyancy of the boat stopped the incoming water. Although I was up to my waist in freezing seawater, I could start one of the engines (good that I had two as one was drowned) and motor her right onto our beach in front of our house. It was a matter of hours until the tide left us high and dry, then we quickly performed repairs and patched the 2-inch hole. As the tide floated the boat in the evening, I realized that what was just a scare and a major inconvenience for me could have been a catastrophe on a monohull. The repairs cost me about a hundred dollars in materials and only some of our bedding needed to be replaced. Although I was later told that this was a freak accident and rather unusual for moorings to puncture boats at low tide, it happened to me. Had I owned a monohull the boat would have been a total write-off.

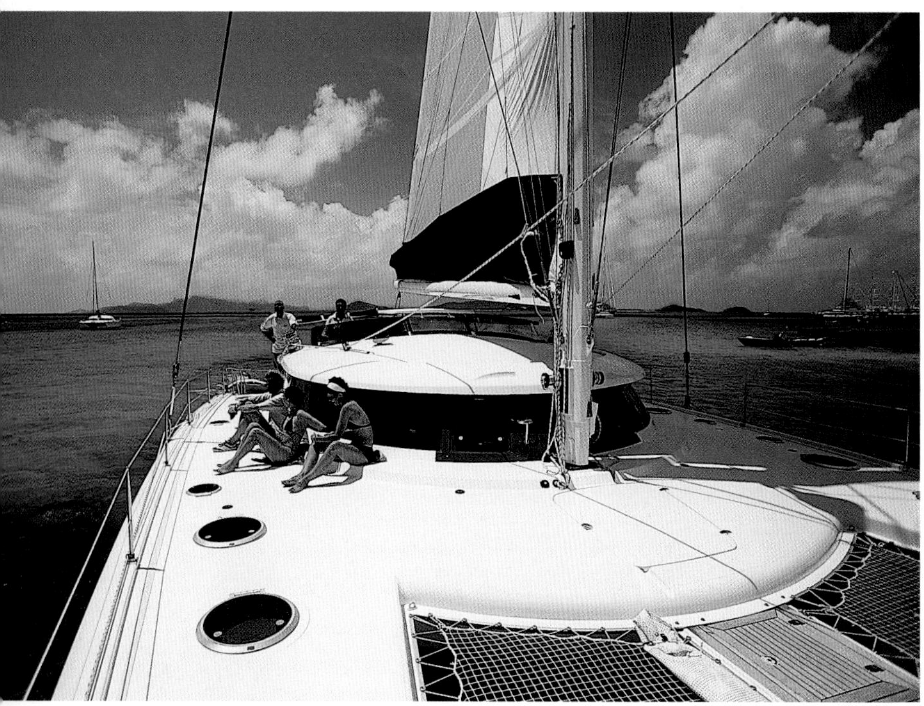

DESIRABLE attributes

The relaxing lighting in the saloon of this 40' cruising catamaran transforms the boat into a romantic retreat as twilight descends over port.

DESIRABLE ATTRIBUTES

Seaworthiness

Safety and seaworthiness, as Czeslaw A. Marchaj describes in his great book "Seaworthiness – the Forgotten Factor," should be one of the most important considerations when shopping for a boat. There will be many parameters to consider when buying a particular cruising multihull, ranging from price, looks, to how many she sleeps, but none should be weighed as heavily as seaworthiness.

below Gennaker sailing at its best! This large headsail can be quickly furled and provides instant horsepower when needed. Gennakers, also known as screachers, can even be flown in fresh conditions when running downwind.

Generally speaking, a seaworthy boat is one that has not only been expertly designed and constructed but also one that can show an impeccable safety record.

Even though most of us might be coastal sailors, the concept of seaworthiness is as important for someone who is about to start a family circumnavigation as for those who stay along coasts or in "protected" bodies of water. But don't be fooled – even the Great Lakes, Long Island Sound or the Chesapeake Bay can get very nasty indeed. Coastal sailors attempting a "hop" to the Caribbean or to Bermuda better be ready to face the worst the ocean can produce. One of the highest waves on our planet was measured in the Gulf Stream, less than 300 miles from shore. We all know that where the Continental Shelf begins and the waters get shallow near the coast waves become unstable and tend to break earlier. Consequently, it is not a surprise that experienced sailors tend to feel much safer offshore than close to land. Most of us are coastal cruisers; nevertheless the consideration of a tested, proven and seaworthy boat should be as important as for someone who ventures offshore.

Seaworthiness means different things to different people, but most will agree on following definition: The way the hulls at varying payloads move through the water, the ability to handle waves comfortably and safely at varying points of sail and, lastly, weathering storms and bringing ship and crew back to land unharmed. Well-designed and -built multihulls are one of the safest vessels afloat and in most cases it is human error that poses danger to crew and boat. By "human" I also mean the builder, which also necessitates a close analysis of the boat yard and construction parameters. As can be imagined, a well-designed

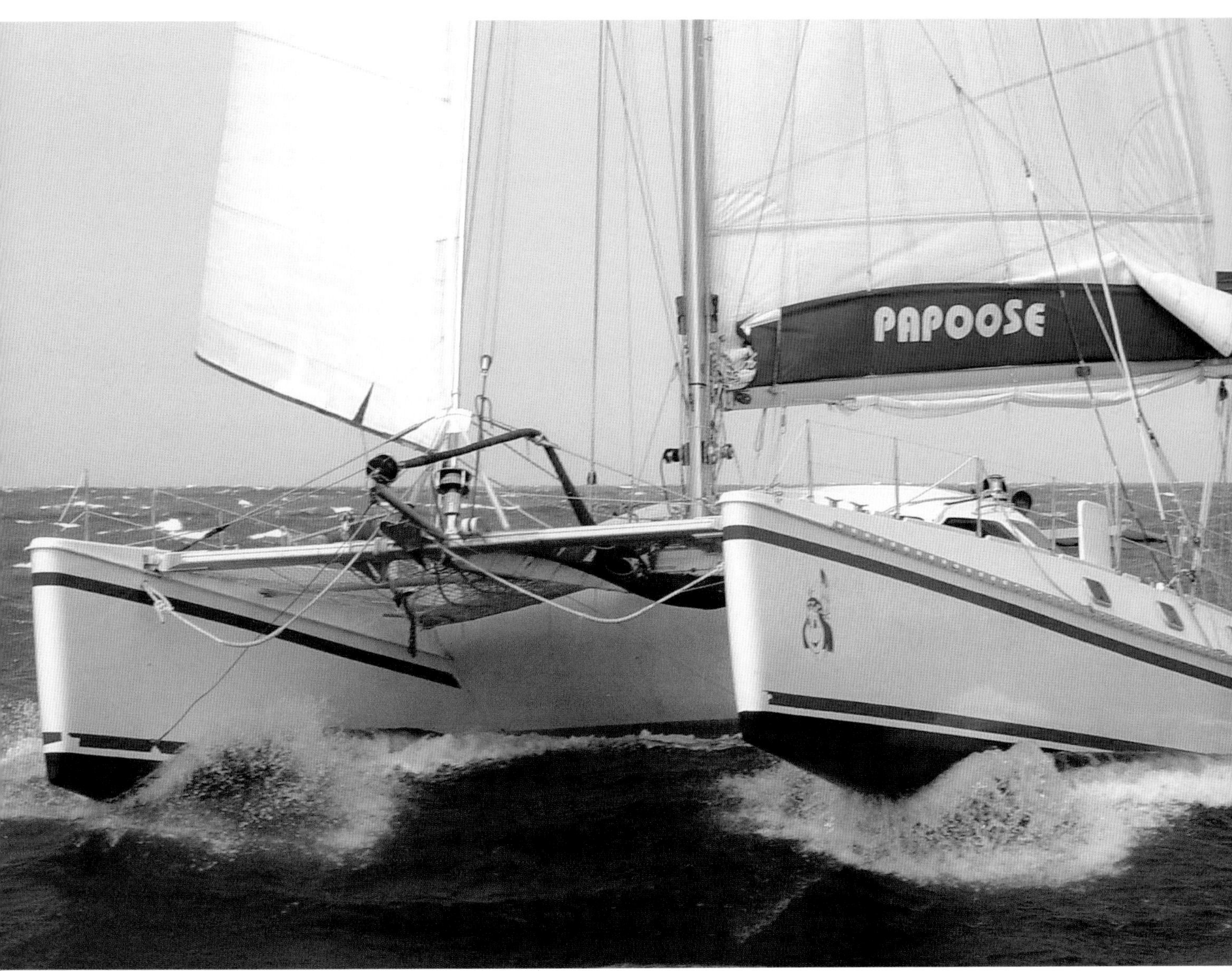

above A well traveled Outremer cat safely surfing before a building gale with a single reef in the main and the jib set on the opposite side.

vessel in experienced hands can still be a suicide machine if it has been slapped together quickly, or as in some cases of high-tech construction failures, has been built by inexperienced, cheap labor under mismanaged conditions. If one has a lemon, one is lucky if only ports will leak, or one might experience areas of delamination. In the worst cases, the boat might break apart in the most horrendous of circumstances. As we all know, catastrophes don't happen when it's blowing 15 knots under clear blue skies. Therefore, when shopping for a boat, the question of construction should be on the very top of the list.

Construction

Let's briefly look at the past, at the era before multihull mass production. The acceptance of multihulls in the '60s and '70s suffered tremendously due to the home-built boats of that time. Plywood and fiberglass, still excellent materials today, were the norm then. Even though these had an even greater forgiveness to building inconsistencies than today's high-tech composites, enough ill-constructed multihulls were built to give them a bad image. Many beautiful Pivers

above Split hull plugs of a Blubay 72 are filled and faired; a time-consuming and tedious process, but necessary for exacting results.

and Searunners, which were excellent designs, still exist. Nevertheless, I would guess an equal number of them, which were irresponsibly manufactured, simply rotted away at their mooring or fell apart, giving the early US multihull movement a bad start. In some extreme cases people even lost their lives due to shabbily constructed multihulls. One of the early production catamarans, maybe even the first ones that came from molds, were the great Telstar trimarans and the Iroquois catamarans of the '70s. These British-built vessels were mass produced in great numbers under controlled conditions and many are still sailing today. My friend purchased one recently and I had the opportunity to measure the heavy scantlings of the hull. If one can live with the narrow overall beam, the overbuilt and simple Iroquois is a great bargain. On the other hand, the legendary Wharram cats must also be mentioned. They were mostly homebuilt by amateurs, and represent the simple Polynesian concept of a safe, seaworthy boat. Thousands are sailing today and can be found in every part of the world. I even spotted one in Nepal!

A recent upwind sail on a new 47' production catamaran reminded me of the importance of construction and builder experience. The boat was built by a production builder, who built narrow, heavy cruising cats. The rig on this boat was recently tuned and all shrouds and mast stays were properly tensioned. We found ourselves sailing in brisk conditions, waves were about 4-6', the wind was getting stronger and it was blowing a steady 25 knots. The leeward shroud, which was tight when the boat was at rest, suddenly was extremely slack and was whipping through an arc of almost 2'! Not only did this represent a serious injury risk for the crew, compromise mast fittings and create an inefficient upwind rig but, more importantly, it showed the excessive flexibility of the entire structure. The boat would cycle through this athwartship contraction every 2 seconds and over the years might eventually do serious damage to the vessel and its entire sandwich structure.

Today's composite materials allow multihulls to excel as lightweight and strong structures in an often hostile environment, the ocean. But that also comes with a price. High-tech sandwich layup and construction must be performed in an absolutely controlled environment. Factors such as resin layup ratios, temperature, humidity and pressure are crucial to the strength of the final product. They leave absolutely no room for error or any deviations in working conditions. Therefore: *A seaworthy boat is only as good as its construction. Yard reputation is as important as its product.*

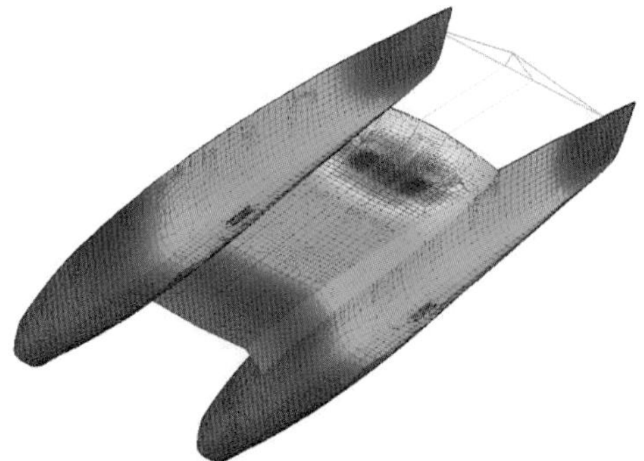

Blubay is one of the first catamaran manufacturers to apply Finite Element Analysis (FEA) to the engineering of their superyachts. On the recently launched Blubay 102, 150 Tons of mast compression have been calculated with the help of shroud-based strain gauges. By engineering safety factors, of between 3-5, FEA helps them determine safe working loads and properly sized support structures, without building them too light or unnecessarily heavy. It is interesting to note the high stress areas (in yellow) just ahead of the leeward daggerboard.

Design

above World headquarters for today's super cats: Yacht Industries' expanded state-of-the-art design and building facilities in Normandy, France.

The design of a boat is a beautiful science. Theoretical, practical and intuitive factors are fed into a complex design spiral and weighed against the compromises that need to be implemented. This process is repeated, results updated and fine-tuned until designer and client decide to stop and declare the result: "The Final Compromise or The Boat." Good sea boats evolve not only from tank testing, but also by constantly improving and changing the actual vessel. Often the rig, underwater appendages or even parts of the hull are modified to achieve this. Usually, if you see at least a dozen catamarans of the same design you could assume that they are good boats. But if you know that hundreds, even thousands, of them were built over decades, heard or read about them in numerous international magazines, it is almost a guarantee of a good product. The final confirmation of seaworthiness might be when one discovers that a particular multihull won numerous offshore races and awards, as well as having been consistently built in great numbers and whose owners have safely taken them to the most remote locations of the world.

The definition and discussion of seaworthiness and good design are complex and mean different things to different people. Even different sizes of boats will have to be analyzed by using dissimilar parameters. A 22' Tremolino, designed by Dick Newick, is a beautiful little trimaran and will be a safe boat to use in a protected bay or even for a daysail along the coast. More experienced sailors will think it even safe to venture offshore with her. Taken to the extreme, we all know that the French will not stop at taking anything across the Atlantic, but I think this is a different story, possibly of Latin heroism. That is why designers will usually start with parameters such as overall length, payload, operating environment, and the principal purpose of the boat. A 32' cat with the same design parameters as a 50' cat probably will have a lesser degree of safety factors, simply because of her shorter length and narrower beam. Although the smaller vessel might come through rough conditions in experienced hands as safely as the 50' cat, it will not be as comfortable nor "feel" as safe as the larger vessel. Which brings me to the following universal truth of sailing, performance and safety: At sea, given equal design and operating parameters, size counts more than anything else, and I mean waterline length. This is why a longer multihull with narrow hulls will usually be a faster, safer and more seaworthy boat than a shorter one with the same weight.

Length is an important consideration regarding seaworthiness, but so is stability and beam. There is an ongoing misconception about the relationship of the overall beam of a multihull (distance between outside of port hull to outside of starboard hull) and its

above "Neptune's Car" – a 50' Tektron/Shuttleworth design, tuning in New York harbor before the start of the classic Around Long Island Race.

far right Sometimes the best vantage point is from the masthead, where one can appreciate the vast expanses of deck area as found on this Eleuthera 60 catamaran.

below A friend's Outremer 55S, "Willow," docked at the historic maritime museum of Mystic Seaport, Connecticut.

dynamic stability. By building narrow hulls one actually increases the relative axis width (distance between port hull centerline and starboard hull centerline), which is the only interesting width in a catamaran. Having the same overall beam, a multihull with fatter hulls actually has a comparatively smaller axis between her hulls than a narrower one. This fact signifies the diagonal distance of a catamaran as an important design criteria. The longer the hulls and the narrower they are, the longer the diagonal axis will be and the more stable the multihull becomes.

Experience is invaluable in the world of boat design. Catamarans are as different from trimarans as monohulls are from multihulls. Different boats – different principles. When I worked with Dave Pedrick in 1984 on Dennis Conner's legendary America's Cup 12 meter "Stars & Stripes," he always reminded me: "If it does not break, it's too heavy!" In the same year I participated in the Olympic Star Class North American Championship, in which Dennis Conner's margin of beating me and the entire fleet was not only a result of the smallest detail improvements and modifications to his boat, but also a product of his immense experience. Again we see: it is the familiarity, skill and know-how in a particular field that produces winners.

If you are in the market for a cruising multihull, take the aspects of seaworthiness, construction and design very seriously. The brutality of the sea is often forgotten at boat shows, or when studying the glossy brochures. In the age of technology, gadgets and globalization, boating is perceived as being safer than ever. Nevertheless, the issue of seaworthiness, especially of multihulls with their higher speeds and loads, should be a top consideration even for a coastal cruiser. Designer experience and a reputable yard are as important as an impeccable safety record of a particular boat. Do your homework. Read all the books you can find on multihulls, talk to surveyors, authors, delivery skippers and designers. Chances are they will confuse you with their differing opinions. The bottom line is: Sail as many dissimilar boats as possible in as heavy conditions as you dare. Common sense will do the rest.

EXPLORER
WB
OUTREMER 55' Light

An Outremer 5
gennaker and f
confidently pov
Caribbean cho

CRITICAL ISSUES

Catamarans are vessels noted for their safety. This is part of the definition one would discover if one looked up the word "Catamaran" in a version of Webster's unabridged dictionary. Although the capsize scare of the pioneering multihull days has almost been eliminated, the capsize myth still exists. It is perhaps the most controversial issue and the one that always dominates arguments between proponents of the different camps. Ask monohull sailors what they think of multihulls and you will probably hear them argue the subject. Ultimately, one cannot answer people with uninformed prejudice if they don't want to listen. Capsize has been a particularly divisive topic and has accompanied the multihull throughout its development. The fact remains, however, that it is the least likely hazard the average multihull sailor will encounter.

We have to be very careful when discussing multihulls and capsize. This book is about habitable voyaging catamarans; therefore, the subject of capsize is discussed within that scope.

"The price of speed is accidents," as Dick Newick says. Lightweight racers, such 60' trimarans or the new Volvo Extreme 40 class will behave completely different in storm conditions than your average cruising catamaran. Even trimarans handle unlike cats. Racers take calculated risks to push speeds to unbelievable levels. While these boats do end up upside down from time to time, rarely is anyone hurt. Of course, the journalists and photographers who are present at most races make every effort to publicize pictures of the spectacular mishaps or breakups, crashes and back flips whenever they happen. And no wonder, in view of the sensational nature of the capsize, reports attract the occasional tragic news headline. The news media is perverse; to them "Bad News is Good News." Interestingly, these accident reports seem to fuel the multihull sport and attract even more followers and extreme racing designs to the circuit. Nevertheless, we have to be grateful to these pilots and their machines, who push the envelope of safety and technology. The trickle-down effect from the race circuit to the cruising community has benefited both monohullers and multihullers.

Cruising catamarans have a nearly flawless safety record. It is reality that in the four decades that production cruising catamarans have roamed the seas, only about two dozen capsizes of smaller vessels have been reported. Naturally these have occurred in the most extreme conditions and were all due to seamanship errors. That is a remarkable record especially if one considers the millions of miles that 6,000 or more production multihulls have traveled. That figure also includes the 1,500 bareboat charter cats. These vessels are often sailed recklessly by guests who have little or no experience on these types of craft, making the catamarans' safety record even more remarkable. I think it is obvious, especially in our court-happy legal society, that charter companies would do anything

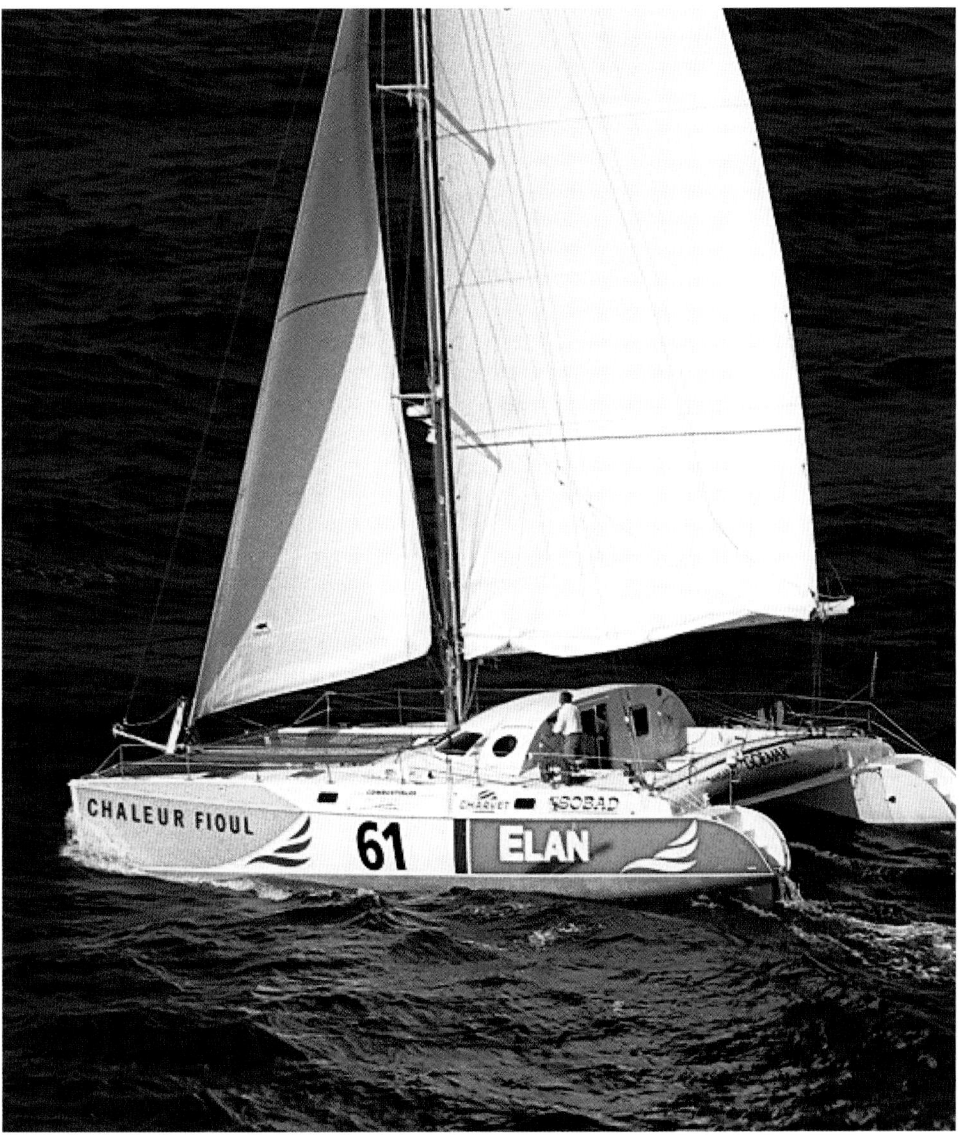

left European offshore regulations require racers to paint underwater appendages, such as rudders and daggerboards, high-visibility orange.

to avoid letting people sail dangerous boats. Capsizing in your cruising multihull is much less likely than overturning in your SUV.

As we have illustrated in the preceding chapter, a well-built and properly designed multihull is safer than its ballasted sibling because of its stability, speed and crew friendly environment. Most cruising catamarans are unsinkable, and the foam-core in the composite structure generally has enough flotation to keep the boat afloat many times over.

While monohulls often roll back upright after a knockdown, their lead keels will sink them like a stone as the vessel fills with water. Chances are so much higher that a monohull will vanish from the sea's surface because of a collision or faulty seacock, than a catamaran will capsize. Even then, your chances of survival are 100-to-1 in favor of a multihull. In the worst case scenario, an upside-down multihull provides shelter until help arrives. Escape hatches let crews access the cabin of a capsized boat. There have been some gripping sea stories of life aboard a capsized multihull, such as the Rose-Noëlle that drifted around the South Pacific upside-down for 119 days, helping her crew survive.

Monohulls need their ballast to come back up. And it is not always that keels stay

Stability Diagram showing a typical 45' cruising catamaran compared to a monohull. The Righting moments illustrate the static resistance to heeling. It can be seen that at a heel angle of about 30 degrees the cat has twice the resistance to capsize than the monohull. But, while the cat's stability is higher it is also diminishing quicker. At about 90 degrees she will capsize, while the ballasted boat still retains plenty of positive stability up to about 140 degrees. This graph is purely theoretical, as it is nearly impossible to heel a cruising cat or to even lift one of the hulls out of the water; 99% of catamaran sailing is in the 0-to-8 degree zone and this is where the multihull is infinitely more stable than the monohull.

Stability – Catamaran vs. Monohull

at about 8 degrees a catamaran has reached max. stability and starts lifting windward hull

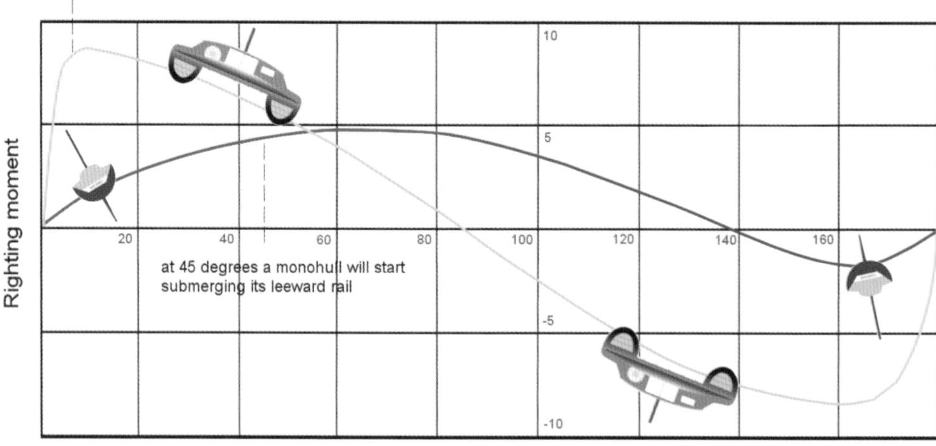

Angle of heel

attached as the following episode, reported by famous multihull sailor Tony Bullimore, illustrates. He sailed a 60' racing monohull in heavy weather: "I was just sitting on my favorite seat by the galley, and it was really nice for a couple hours, and I thought, 'well, everything is OK, I'm going to just ride through it.' Then, all of a sudden, there was a crack, literally like, CRACK. It happened, quickly and instantly. Within two seconds, the boat was upside down. I was saying 'please turn back, come on, come on, and get upright.' Then when she wouldn't come up, I realized the keel had gone."

Bullimore is still not sure exactly why the keel on his 60' monohull racer failed. He says it was as though all the forces just combined to be right at that split second, like a perfect karate chop, which is what it sounded like. The keel was not bolted to the bottom of the boat in the usual way, but was fitted through a slot in the hull and fixed to a false floor. The keel consisted of a carbon-fiber foil with a lead bulb on the bottom, which broke around the entry slot at the hull.

Mishaps can happen to all craft traveling the ocean. Any boat can be trashed by some combination of wind and wave, and you even may be able to tip the odds with help of knowledge and preparation. I have heard about a sailor who made four Atlantic crossings in 26' open cats, yet capsized a Beneteau 38 monohull in the Bay of Biscay and tragically lost a crew member.

Obviously, sometimes it's better to not be there in the first place. To that end, we have seen that multihulls have the advantage since they can escape a weather pattern more quickly and reduce their exposure time in bad conditions. However, nasty storms can materialize with frightening speed and it would be arrogant to suppose that there's always a way out. Successfully surviving a

below Smart life raft storage – easily accessible from any position. As most well-built cruising cats are made to be unsinkable, the life raft will serve as an escape from a burning vessel.

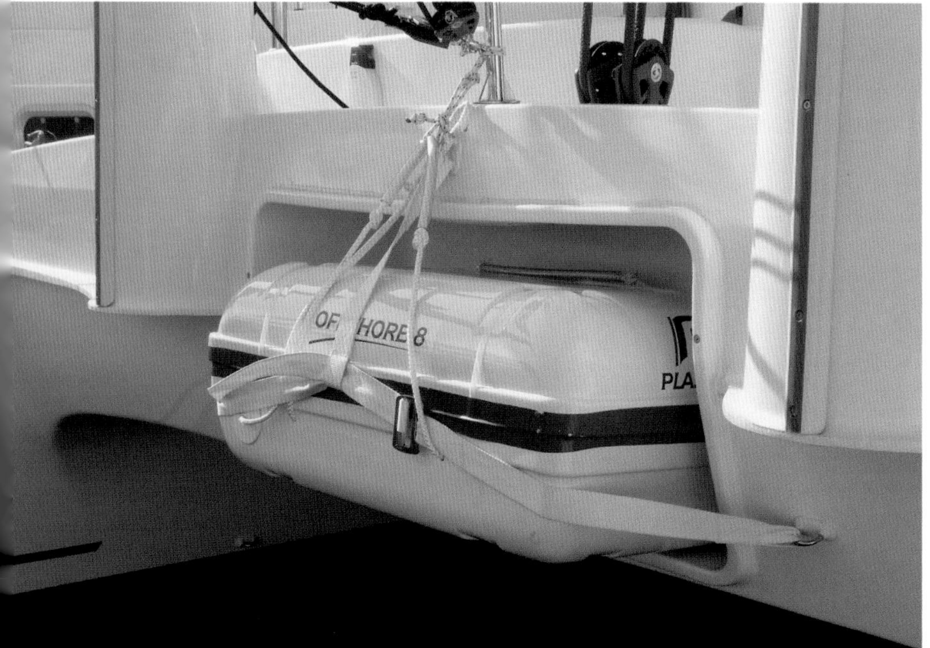

storm is a function of not only the boat, but seamanship, equipment and some luck. The reality is that multihulls have two exceptionally stable states: right-side up and inverted. Being in the latter attitude is neither recommended nor much fun. It is immensely difficult, even if one would try really hard to get from one position to the other. This is also the reason why it is impossible to technically re-right an inverted cruising catamaran without a crane, helicopter or a tugboat-assisted "tow over." On a tiny boat like a Hobie Cat, which possesses a huge power-to-weight ratio, re-righting without outside help is easy, but that seems to be logical, as these beach cats are as easy to turn as they are to bring back upright.

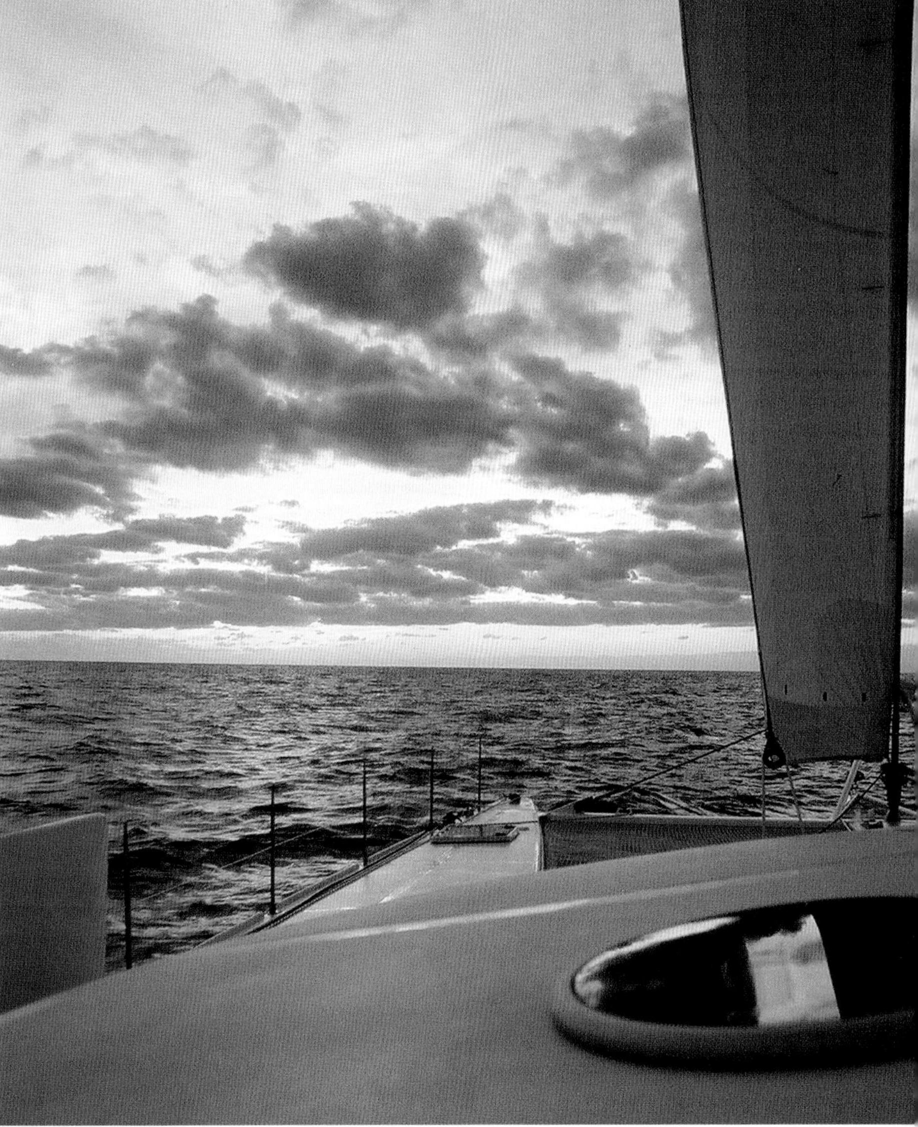

above Long transatlantic passages are rewarded by crystal-clear, starry nights and spectacular sunsets, neither of which can be found on terra firma.

Now brace yourself for this revelation: monohulls also have two stable states – floating on the surface of the sea upright or lying on the bottom of the ocean. Unlike multihulls it only takes a small unobtrusive hole to sink a ballasted boat and the consequences are much more serious. There are dozens of books about sailors trapped in small rubber rafts, fighting for survival. Most notably is Callahan's own account *Adrift*, which illustrates his epic endurance in a life raft after a collision at sea. His trusty sloop was hit by a whale and sank within minutes, dragged down by thousands of pounds of lead. Given the choice, wouldn't we rather wait for assistance on a large floating catamaran that still contains most of our food and equipment, than suddenly come to the realization of ending up as shark bait?

In past decades, there have been dozens of multihull capsizes, and only very few resulted in loss of life. OSTAR winner Phil Weld on "Gulfstreamer" and designer Walter Greene on "Gonzo" are famous examples. Both of these skippers cut holes in the bottom of the hulls of their capsized vessels and waited for help. It should be noted that both boats were racing trimarans.
Most, if not all, cruising catamarans have mandatory escape hatches. Unlike the name implies, their primary purpose is not necessarily to assist in exiting the boat (although they come handy for that too), but more importantly, to get back in, in case of a capsize. In an inverted position they would be just above the waterline and crew members could get in and out of the vessel without having to cut holes into the hulls. Capsizes happen when too much sail is carried for the sea state and wind conditions. It could be caused by: just the sea state, from wave action in combination with the boat's

own momentum (forward speed, pitch or yaw), or a combination of all three together. Interestingly, multihulls, when they capsize, do not flip sideways, but rather pitch-pole or tumble stern-over-bow. The stability of a multihull is primarily a function of its beam, length and weight as compared to its sail plan. The capsizing moment is the result of the effects of the wind, waves and momentum of the sails and structure of the boat. Because of multihulls' high speed, they could overtake a wave and stuff one or both bows into a wave face. The boat runs into a liquid wall and comes to a sudden halt, yet the mast tip keeps on going forward, slamming the boat on its back. Often this is a combination of too much pace and lacking reserve buoyancy (fine bows). Capsizes have also been known to happen when beating into steep waves with too little forward moment (not enough sails up), which throws the boat backwards, tripping it over its stern.

Capsizes can also be caused by extreme rogue waves or steep seas that catch a vessel beam-on. It is easy to imagine a towering breaking crest picking up a multihull, flipping it over in the process. In reality it is quite different as the catamaran, even one with properly designed shallow keels, will slide sideways. At the same time the breaking wave would lift the windward hull and as the wave rapidly passes under the catamaran the leeward hull would be picked up before an extreme heel angle is reached. Tank testing experiments have shown us that. Of course, it all depends on the steepness and speed of the wave and, in the end, no two situations are the same.

Of course, multihulls can capsize when one entire hull becomes flooded because of a severe collision destabilizing the entire platform. That is even less likely to happen, as modern catamarans have plenty of flotation in their structures and multiple watertight compartments. I can imagine that in storm conditions, and in the rare case of a steering failure with sudden, total loss of directional control, a multihull could capsize.

Of the very few capsizes that occur, most can be attributed to underestimating the circumstances, inexperience, or overconfidence. The primary reason (except collision-related or structural issues) is having too much sail up for a given sea state. It is a misconception that the number one reason is by the wind overpowering the catamaran and making her flip. On a monohull caught with too much sail, one is laid flat by a sudden gust. The very rare capsizes involving multihulls are caused by errors in seamanship in relation to the sea state. In extreme conditions, with too much sail up, rough and confused seas can turn a cat over before the sheets can be released or the sails taken in. On a monohull, most of the time one can get away by underestimating conditions. This is not so on a multihull as the immense initial stability lulls inexperienced sailors into a false sense of security. There is very little feedback to alert the crew of forces building beyond the safe limits of the boat.

far left Easy to maintain woodwork is practical and provides a feeling of warmth and a sense of quality. Note the escape hatch, which can be easily accessed and gives unrivaled views under sail.

below Escape hatches are mandatory by EU (European Union) regulations and can be found on all well-built cruising cats. They make great fishing ports when it rains and the boat is lying at anchor.

Average payload and pounds-per-inch immersion data for cruising catamarans.

Payload Data of an Average Cruising Catamaran

Overall Length	Pounds Per Inch Immersion (ppi)	Average Payload
30' LOA	730 lbs/inch	2,600 lbs
38' LOA	905 lbs/inch	3,700 lbs
45' LOA	1230 lbs/inch	4,800 lbs
55' LOA	1950 lbs/inch	7,500 lbs

It is therefore imperative to reef much earlier than on a monohull. On a ballasted boat one would reef primarily to the wind speed; on a cruising catamaran one should keep an eye on the sea state. An experienced skipper will know when to de-power the boat and reduce speed.

A fast boat, such as a multihull, can be deliberately slowed down in extreme conditions. A catamaran sailed with reserve (heavily reefed) can still keep pace with a hard-driven monohull, but will be safer and more comfortable than a ballasted keelboat pushed to its limits. In storm conditions multihulls will routinely surf at double-digit velocity, far beyond their theoretical hull speed, at which monohulls would strain. In strong winds, with the sails producing maximum power and the boat at full pace, close-reaching is the point of sail where there is the highest risk of capsize. However, you are unlikely to reach the stability limit or stuff a bow into a wave face, provided you are suitably reefed and in full control of your boat.

What actually happens if you do capsize? You will be scared out of your wits, yet your multihull will float with the bridge deck just above the waterline. Inside your catamaran it will be very unpleasant as anything loose will wash out of the boat. I know of multihull designers trying to engineer survival compartments, yet the boat will be uninhabitable in anything but a flat calm. The life raft could be inflated and secured between the upturned hulls and the dinghy would be used as a secondary shelter. In such an unlikely event one should always think about the worst case scenario. Check how easy or difficult it is to access the life raft, which ideally should be reached from both sides. Survival suits and the best foul-weather gear will provide better protection on the bridge deck than in the hulls where waves would wash about inside the accommodations.

Ultimately, the entire issue of capsize has been a controversial one for many years, yet the multihull has come out on top and the topic has all but disappeared from today's market. Modern awareness and the proof of their safety record has finally put it to rest.

Load Carrying

If catamarans were able to carry loads as well as single-hulled vessels, the majority of all boats would be multihulls. Ballasted keelboats can be weighed down with cruising gear and payload without great loss of performance, provided that the distribution of the weight does not negatively influence the trim of the boat. This is quite different on a lighter weight multihull, which can suffer if overloaded. This does not mean that a cruising catamaran cannot carry significant payloads too. Multihull sailors need to be pragmatic with their assessment of what they need to bring along, and often realistic means "not a lot of weight."

Cruising catamarans lure sailors into finding locker space for every imaginable item which they think they will need. In contrast to a monohull, storage space can be almost twice the size on a multihull, yet utilizing all of it could be detrimental to the performance and ultimately the safety of your boat.

Take our 45' mono and multihull as an example. Crew, their gear and provisions will weigh the same in boats of all configurations. Adding a payload of say 5000 pounds would represent an addition of more than 24% in weight for the catamaran, yet only 19% extra load for the monohull. It does not sound like a big difference, but if one takes the different underwater cross sections of the hulls of both types into account, the influence on performance is considerable.

A monohull has a wider waterline beam and therefore the load needed to depress the boat can be higher. That is measured as *pounds per inch immersion* of a vessel and depends on the prismatic coefficient of the underwater shape, size of the boat, and other factors regarding hull configuration. The slender hull shapes of a multihull are poor load carriers and without consideration for that it is easy to transform a light and agile catamaran into a slug. Narrow hulls are especially susceptible to overloading and, as seen in the table opposite, it is apparent how easy it is to burden a smaller catamaran with excessive payload.

Added weight will affect bridgedeck clearance and for every pound added, the critical distance between the underside of

above Transom platforms are ideal spots to disembark from and for taking showers after a refreshing swim. Many Caribbean day charter cats are profitable moneymakers and can often be seen sailing between islands with a full complement of 60 or more guests aboard.

above The Scape 39 cat, seen here sailing under Table Mountain, is an innovative multihull from South Africa, and can be shipped to any part of the world via a 40-foot container.

the bridge deck and water will decrease. Overloading a multihull is not necessarily dangerous as it will depend on the structure, the amount of weight added and, ultimately, on the reserve buoyancy of the hulls.

The pounds per inch (ppi) number will illustrate how many inches a vessel will sink below its waterline as weight would be added. The larger the water plane, or imprint area of the hull, the more load it will take to immerse. The pounds per inch number will provide a good sense of how sensitive a boat is to overloading.

Typically a full bodied catamaran with well-rounded hull sections will have better ability to carry weight than a slimmer, higher-aspect-ratio hull. A conservative payload of about 2,800 lbs is realistic for most cruising couples and, as we can see, this is easily attainable even for a smaller multihull. Often the hulls of fully loaded catamarans can be safely depressed 2-5 inches depending on their size and underwater shape. Payload carrying ability has a direct relationship to the boat's displacement and often sailors confuse the term weight and displacement. Displacement of a boat is actually the weight of the water which is displaced by the floating vessel. When designers talk about the designed displacement of a boat, they mean the weight of the water displaced, floating at the drawn waterline. At the end only one fact interests us: Where will our catamaran float if we add a certain amount of payload? Will this exceed the designer's estimate? Therefore, a multihull with a relatively high designed displacement is not necessarily a heavy or sluggish catamaran. It could mean that the boat has a large prismatic coefficient and its hull sections have been drawn with payload-carrying ability in mind.

Often designers and builders try to accomplish too much. Our market demands fast boats which can carry the contents of your average household. Remember Dick Newick's famous saying: "You can only have two out of three: Performance, low price and space." Obviously buyers want all three and often force builders into making compromises that affect the final characteristics of the boat. A designer will usually arrive at a payload figure by making an estimated calculation of stores, weight of the boat, and position of the waterline. Consequently, he will arrive at a displacement, which he computes from the underwater volumes. If he thinks that it is adequate he will fine-tune the list and analyze the exact weight of the boat, worked out by the number of square feet of hull and deck skins, the weight of the structural members, furniture, rig, systems, etc. If at the end the boat's total weight leaves inadequate amount of payload, he will go back to the drawing board (computer) and reshape the hull sections or allow for a lighter high-tech construction to permit the required payload.

Cruisers will inevitably add tons of indispensable (often unnecessary) items. Fuel, water, safety equipment and food will add thousands of pounds to a long voyage. Most manufacturers who try to market their boats as performance vessels (and most do) frequently design overly narrow hulls or succumb to the client's wishes by installing a multitude of subsystems, such as air-conditioners, generators, or huge refrigeration equipment. What started out as a performance hull has turned into a slow boat. The final weight of a boat will largely depend on the construction methods and materials utilized to build it. A low-tech, but price-efficient construction will not yield a light boat, and that directly affects payload.

Good design requires the closest attention to weight, therefore if sailors need to add their "unlimited general stuff" and still want to go fast they will have to go to a next larger size catamaran. I have seen two general mistakes being made over and over: buying a boat that is too large for the budget and buying a vessel that is too small for the payload required. If you are concerned about the payload issue then you should be using a guide to calculate what amount of gear you would need. For longer voyages, start off with the number of crewmembers and number of estimated weeks that you will spend at sea. About 70 lbs of clothes and personal items per crew is a good average. Carry enough stores, especially if you expect to make slower passages through light-wind zones. Fuel and water will be the heaviest items and will weigh about 8 lbs/gal or 1 kg/liter. Safety factors have to be added and the longer the passage is, the bigger the safety margin should be. Allowing an extra week for a transatlantic crossing is considered minimum. Drinking water should be calculated at about half a gallon

below The outside helm station of a 60' catamaran is the envy of even the finest monohull as everything is within reach and usually protected by a windscreen and an overhead bimini top. Main and jib sheet are close at hand, as well as engine controls, boat speed and wind indicators, chart plotter, radar and communication electronics.

per person per day, which does not include any water for washing. About 5 pounds of food is the average intake of crew, as well as drinking about 4 lbs of water. Dinghy, extra sails, ground tackle, everything must be considered when calculating payload. The result of all the above will be the extra weight needed for your cruise.

Payload capacity is vital to cruising. It can be improved best by choosing a strong, lightweight vessel which is long enough to provide adequate space. Keeping the above in mind, a liveaboard sailor, unless of minimalist mentality, should have as large a multihull as possible. As long as he understands the limitations and compromises a catamaran presents, he will be ready to cruise on the safest and swiftest vessels afloat.

below Simple pleasures of catamaran sailing are comfortably sitting at the wheel as you swiftly steer your 15-ton catamaran through crystal-clear waters.

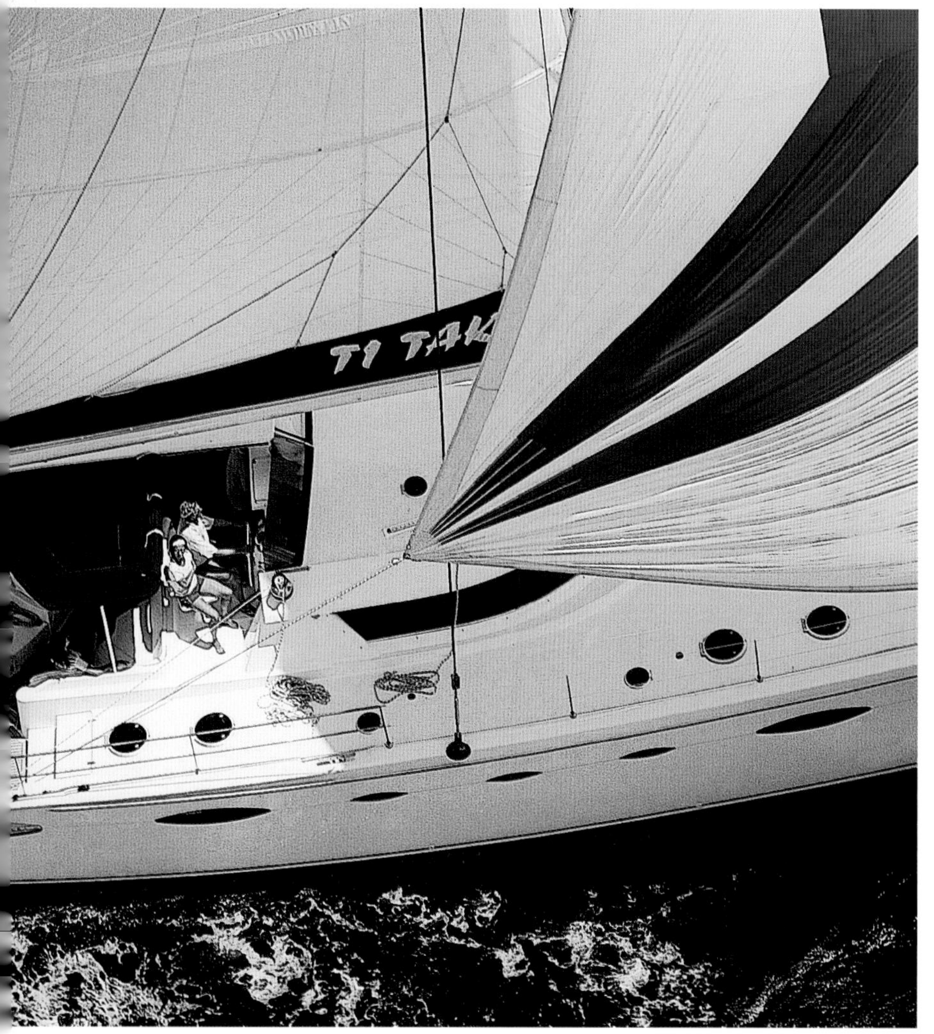

Cost

To budget for a cruising catamaran one must understand exactly what one is buying when initially purchasing the boat and how one will fund the running costs as the years go by. What scares some new sailors initially is the fact that multihulls are, length for length, typically 20% more expensive than their single-hulled cousins. But when one investigates further, it is not as bad as it looks. Length alone can be very deceiving. When the extra accommodations and volume are taken into consideration, most catamarans represent a better value.

"Two for the price of one." A cruising catamaran has two identical monohull floats and its total surface area is significantly higher than that of a single-hulled boat. On this count alone, they should be more expensive. Even when boats are offered in the marketplace, they are not differentiated by volume, weight or surface area, but by length. This is the first thing that buyers look at and usually the most important consideration. Boats are three dimensional objects and their sizes vary with the cube of their length. One has to see it to believe it, but a 48' multihull is twice the size of a 38-footer and a 65' catamaran is nearly double the size of a 45-footer. Unfortunately, cost also varies with the cubed length. The cost of a boat could easily exceed 20 times that of the same volume habitat on land, yet people still buy boats as an icon of freedom and adventure.

Parameters such as maintenance, insurance, depreciation and resale value must be considered as well, which can be significantly different than owning a monohull. For instance, depreciation of multihulls is significantly lower than monohulls. Most catamarans will hold their value better and in relative terms, one will lose less money when the time comes to sell. Typical examples are the fast and well-constructed Corsair trimarans. More than 1,400 of these folding marvels have been built and a 5-year-old one is as expensive as a new one. Just as any other commodity, a well-designed production boat will depreciate less over time and will remain popular.

Running costs and yearly maintenance can be higher than for a monohull, as there is more boat to dock, clean and service. Insurance, which was higher in the past, is about the same for both types, unless one is purchasing a very old or custom-made – one-off multihull. Haul-out expenses are always a concern for boaters and multihullers are no exception. Often it is not easy to find ramps or travel lifts close by which can handle 25'-beam catamarans. Yet, with the growing demand for multihulls and the huge charter industry to support it, more and more marinas and yards can accommodate catamarans for service and storage. These maintenance-related expenses are slightly higher than for narrower monohulls, yet can be offset by the fact that shallower catamarans can choose to use a beach for bottom cleaning, which a deep keel monohull cannot.

Molded fiberglass is a wonderful discovery and has allowed us to shape complex parts with the shiniest surfaces quickly, one after the other. Tooling (production of perfectly finished female molds) is essential for any boat sold today. Customers expect the gleaming surfaces and immaculate gelcoat finishes. It is not unusual for tooling of an average-size monohull to cost a quarter of a million dollars, and still no boat has been built, or sold. The volume of the sales and marketing efforts need to support the huge startup expenses, and that has cost many builders their enterprises. The extra surface area of a multihull requires proportionally more tooling and often these higher initial expenses are amortized into the building of the boats. Of course, the lighter and more high-tech a vessel is, the more it will cost. For every pound of construction weight saved by choosing to build with aramid or other exotic materials, it will cost you extra dollars on a monohull. It might be considerably more for a multihull, having more surface area.

Buying a new boat versus pre-owned will depend on the individual and the boat. Initially, the lower price of a used boat will seem like an obvious advantage, yet one must balance the pros and cons; is a pre-owned boat a money-saving bargain or is it destined to cost you more than it's worth? You can buy a 20-year-old 35' cruising monohull for less than $10,000. The market is flooded with old Bristols or Pearson monohull sloops, which feature

above Complex 3-D modeling of the next generation Blubay 138'. Today's sophisticated software allows designers and clients to shape and rework custom projects before they are started, facilitating the pre-design stage and making cost estimates more accurate than ever before.

far right A Bahia 46 catamaran in a deep, secluded anchorage. Note the long stern line tied to a rock ashore to keep the boat from swinging.

below A large catamaran's cockpit serves as an elegant outdoor dining facility; it rivals the atmosphere and experience found in the world's finest restaurants.

solid fiberglass hulls and are built to last. Try finding a medium-sized cruising catamaran for this price and you will be looking for a long time to discover abandoned plywood derelicts in the back of scraggy boatyards. Buying a used multihull should be attempted with much more caution, as sailing loads and structural forces are not only more crucial but also significantly higher than on a single-hulled boat. Hidden ghosts of past mishaps might be buried in the bilges and they will haunt you at the most inopportune time. To know the history of a used boat is very important… of a pre-owned multihull it is imperative. Good multihulls hold their value very well. The amount one usually saves when buying used must be carefully offset against much higher running costs, lack of full factory warranties and a compromise in systems, accommodations and general enjoyment of a brand-new boat. Usually, the extra dollars spent can be amortized in only several years when one buys new; in the meantime one is enjoying a safer and more up-to-date craft. In the end, the decision is personal. One should be aware of the advantages as well as the drawbacks when considering new vs. used.

Whether new or pre-owned, production or custom boat, a good cruising catamaran will cost money – a lot of money. It might very well be one of the most expensive items that you will ever purchase. But in relative terms it does not cost more to own a multihull than to own any type of vessel, as the expenses are related to size and the complexity of the vessel.

parameters

A typical view of a Carib
sunset from a stately Pr
495 catamaran, made b
builder Alliaura Marine.

DESIGN & DYNAMICS

Configuration & Basic Types

A multihull, just as any other type of boat, presents a series of compromises, and this applies to overall hull, deck and configuration as well. Concessions often have to be made because of space, performance or construction costs. In addition, the intended usage will be a significant factor in determining the shape and size of the vessel. Successful cruising designs will balance all parameters and only you, as a sailor, will know which type of catamaran will be suitable for your needs.

A monohull's characteristics, largely determined by the beam-to-length ratio of the hull and its displacement, will vary very little from another ballasted boat, as there is only so much volume you can fit into a single hull. This will establish the amount of accommodations, which will not greatly differ from one monohull to another, setting a stark contrast to a catamaran, where intended parameters vary so much more.

Basically, we can break down the major design considerations into: overall configuration, hull shape, underwater appendages, rig type and construction. Let's look at each of them in detail and see how they affect the dynamics and design of a multihull.

Class 1 – Open Bridgedeck Catamaran

If one thinks of an open bridgedeck-type of catamaran, images of Hobie Cats on one end of the spectrum, and giant-open ocean racing multihulls on the extreme end, come to mind. They have no fixed coachhouse roof and some of them, especially the small beach cats, only have nets strung between the hulls. Larger examples have partial composite platforms, which stiffen the structure and allow for cockpit seats and helm stations. Since without a solid coachhouse there is less boat to build, these multihulls will be generally lighter and have better aerodynamic properties than full bridgedeck-type cats.

Although few manufacturers and designers have attempted to build open bridgedeck catamarans for cruising, only the most die-hard campers will find them useful for liveaboard applications. Typical examples are the older MacGregor 36, Stiletto 27 and 30, the French KL27 and Corneel designs, which could be sailed hard by lifting a hull (something that you try to avoid when cruising with a fully decked-out boat). Some of these vessels even featured a tiny removable doghouse which provided some shelter for the crew. On smaller open bridgedeck multihulls the only living quarters are found in the confines of the hulls. Even on larger types, they are cramped and not conducive to long-term cruising. The advantages of these sporty vessels,

Basic Catamaran Configurations

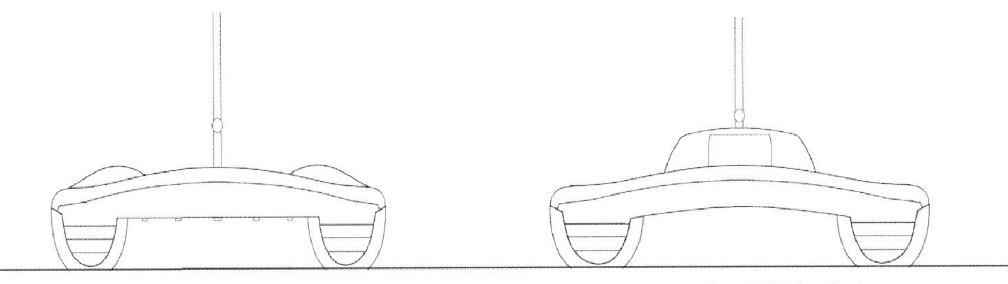

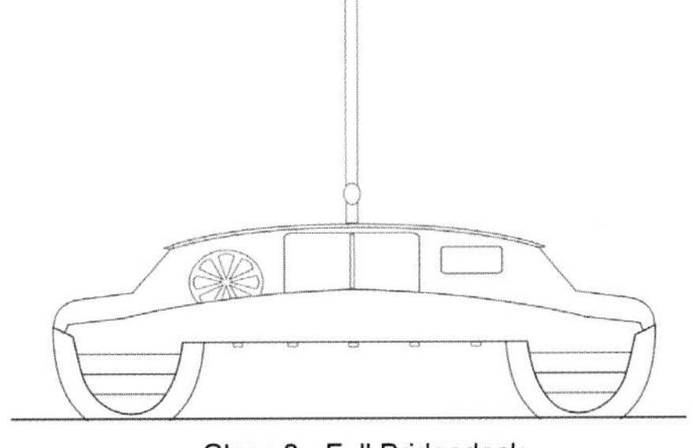

especially in sizes below 30 feet, is their lower cost, trailerability and lively performance. However, attention has to be paid that they not be overloaded or else one could easily turn a cat into a dog.

A large exception to the class 1 type of configuration is found in sizes above 30 feet, which could be considered as class 2. Manufacturers such as Maine Cat and a few other custom multihulls such as the Shuttleworth successfully combine an open-deck plan with a certain degree of cruising comfort. In order to provide some shelter for the crew, large semi-rigid biminis are erected. Not only are these afterthoughts unsightly and do no justice to the beauty of these boats, but they also add a considerable amount of drag, contradicting the nature of these athletic multihulls.

Large charter boats or "Day Boats," as they are called, also utilize the open bridgedeck layout to maximize cockpit space. These machines can entertain up to 80 passengers and are found in holiday resorts around the world. Correctly managed and marketed, they are big moneymakers and are considered the workhorses of the sea.

Class 2 – Partial Bridgedeck Catamaran

These are often referred to as cruising/racing types and, unfortunately, very few existing manufacturers still make them. Designs such as the older Edel and Outremer catamarans had a rigid deck and a small coachhouse, which was completely separate from the hulls. My own Outremer 43 "Flo" was of that category. She was a great sailboat and provided ample room for our family cruises along the U.S. East Coast. Similar to the class 1 vessels, the bridge decks of these types of catamarans are also shorter fore and aft, and the accommodations are simple.

Partial bridgedeck catamarans usually place simple sitting arrangements and nav-stations on the main deck. The balance of the layout,

below The Broadblue range of cruising catamarans are examples of full-length bridgedeck multihulls, providing plenty of volume for cruisers.

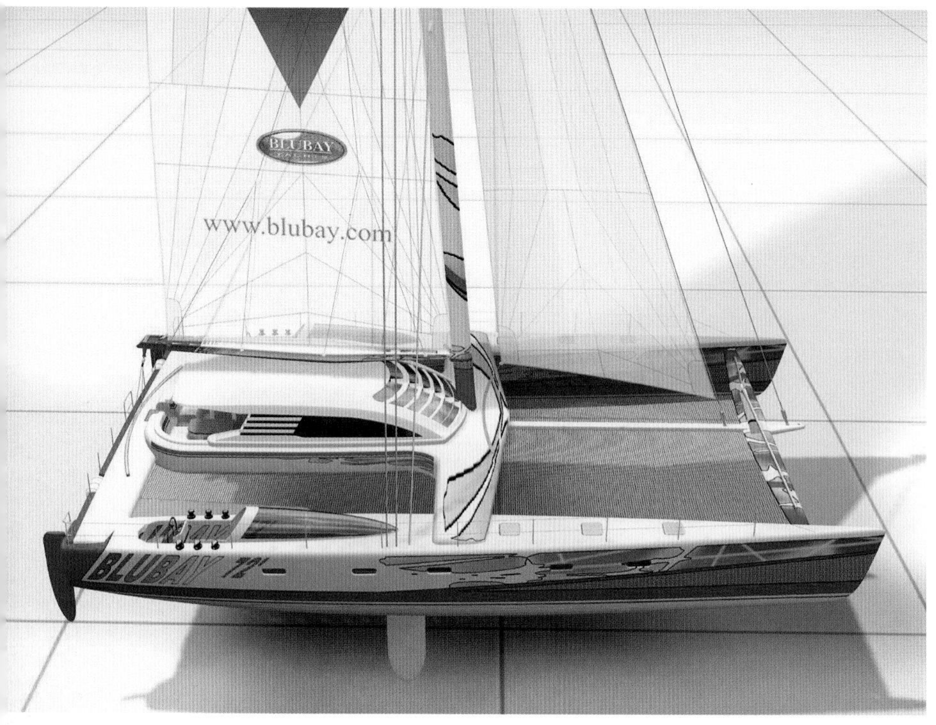

Advantages are good looks and light weight overall structure, but the fact that one can only access the hull compartments via the cockpit poses limitations for serious cruising or live-aboard applications.

Some years ago when Outremer was looking for a substitute for its 40 footer, I was asked to design an open bridgedeck type and came up with a compact 38' racer/cruiser with low profile and tiller steering. Unfortunately, lack of demand prevented the project from being realized and the Outremer 42 was born. However, I feel that a properly designed class 2 multihull is a fantastic compromise for the average weekend sailor. It is unfortunate that presently no manufacturer builds one.

above The Blubay 72 is a state-of-the-art, maxi-sized racer-cruiser featuring a separate saloon pod. She will cruise at close to 28 knots.

below The Gemini 105Mc, seen here in the Patagonian channels, is a popular full bridgedeck catamaran which, in capable hands, can be taken to the world's most remote areas.

such as the galley, heads and berths are often situated in the hulls. Most of the time, these multihulls only have sitting or crouching headroom in the saloon, unless the cabin sole is dropped significantly, compromising the underwing clearance. The Edel 35 was particularly notorious for her low bridge deck, although hundreds of them were built.

Class 3 – Bridgedeck Catamaran

Probably the majority of production and custom cruising catamarans belong to this category, which is the focus of this book. A bridgedeck multihull maximizes the use of space and features a solid deck with a coachhouse that spans the entire width of the cockpit. There is one main entrance into the boat via large sliding doors, and access into both hulls is through companionways leading down from either side of the large saloon. Bridgedeck catamarans are ideal for cruisers or liveaboard sailors. These vessels feature ample payload-carrying capacity and provide good protection for the crew. Helm locations are usually behind the coach roof bulkhead or in some rare cases on the aft end of the hulls behind the cockpit.

These class 3 multihulls contain all the comforts of home and feature a spacious

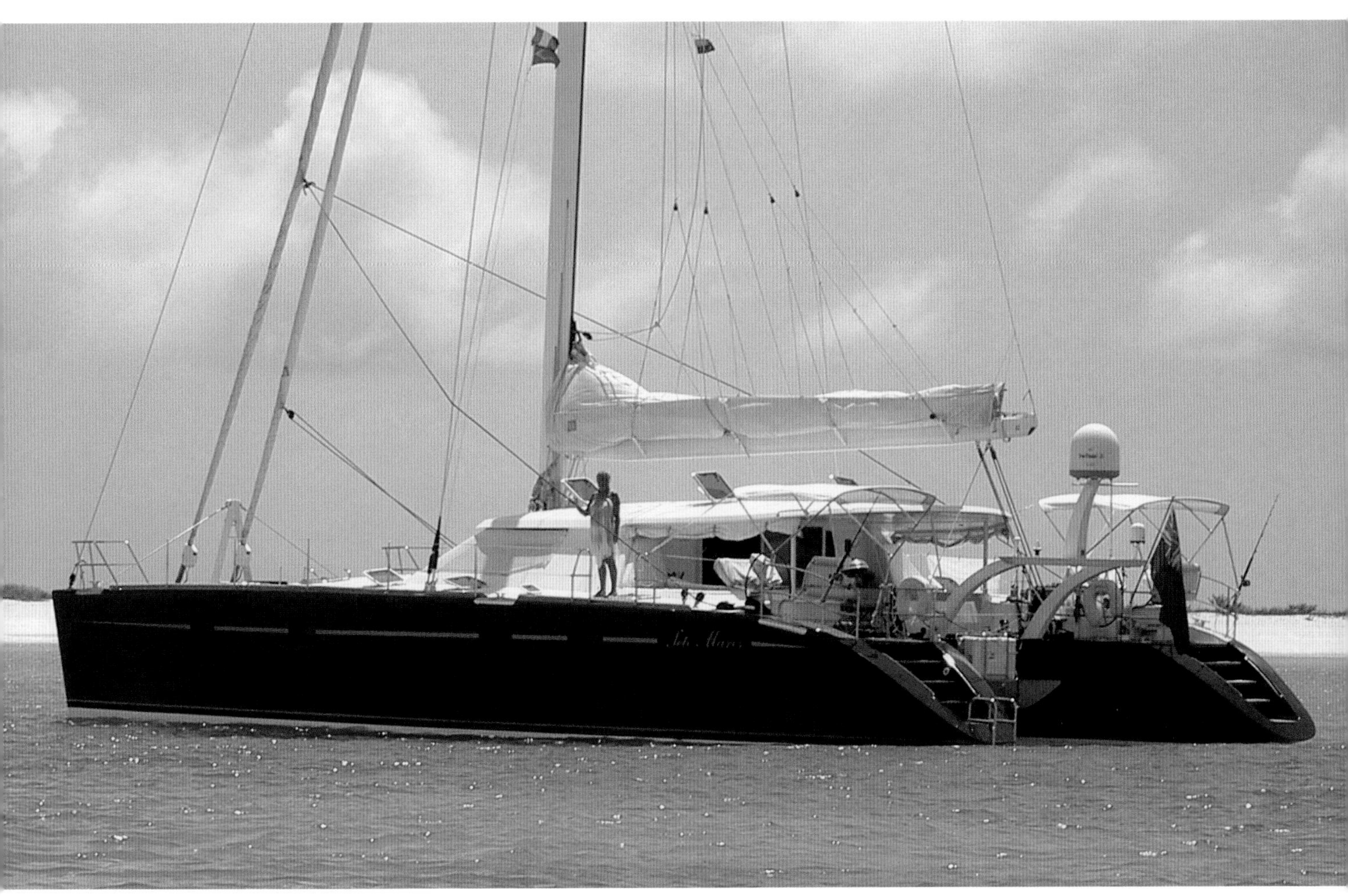

saloon, galley, and navigation station on the main deck. The coachhouse acts as a centralized core, spanning both hulls, which are usually reserved for heads, sleeping cabins and storage. Unlike any other type of boat, monohull and multihull combined, the class 3 cruising catamaran has an unrivalled "homey" feel to it. The wide cockpits are protected by biminis which integrate seamlessly into the coachroof. This not only looks good but creates an inside-outside space that is both practical and unique.

Large bridgedeck cats have the capacity and volume to carry most of the items you would find in your home. From dishwashers to the generators that power them, you can actually have it all. However, the desire to load up too much sometimes overburdens the vessel, compromising its performance.

On vessels larger than 40 feet, headroom is sufficient, although individuals 6 feet and taller might have to make compromises in the forward part of the saloon or in the extremities of the hulls. Designers try to balance the need for ample bridgedeck clearance and place the cabin sole high enough to avoid underwing pounding created by waves. Low, good-looking silhouettes can be found on larger catamarans, although some manufacturers have the "no holds barred" approach and make their boats look like a toolbox. Although this maximizes space, the chunky appearance is detrimental to the performance of the boat as it increases air drag. Finally, square coachhouses make catamarans look rather unattractive.

Some builders elect to pull the solid bridge deck all the way from bow to stern.

above This recently launched Yapluka 72' catamaran is seen here in full cruising trim and serves her owner-couple as a liveaboard world voyager and mobile office.

Bridgedeck pounding caused by waves is one of the drawbacks of low underwing catamarans. Moderate displacement, full-volume bow and stern sections, and a high and long bridgedeck will minimize, if not eliminate, annoying wave slap under the saloon sole. Although bridgedeck height is a very important parameter, it is a misconception that it is the only design feature to look for. One has to consider weight as well as its distribution and support by the hulls, especially in the extremities. Heavy, low bridgedeck multihulls might make great liveaboard vessels, but they should only be taken to sea by masochists.

Parameters Contributing to Bridgedeck Pounding

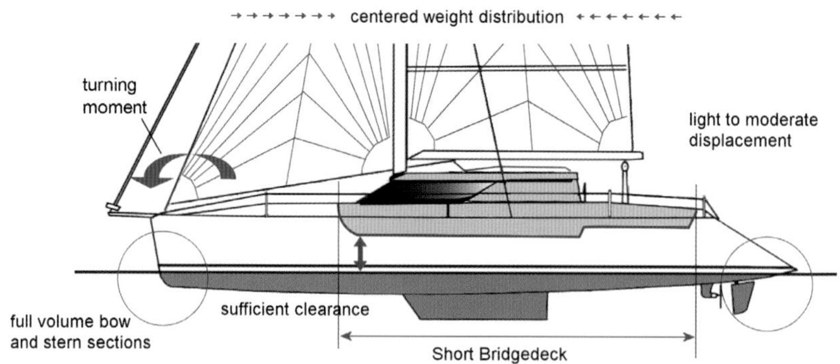

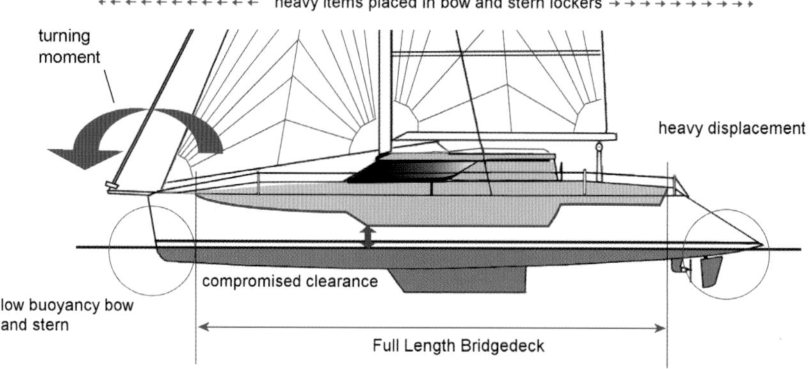

This is beneficial for stiffening the structure and making the most out of the available deck space. The Gemini catamaran is a very successful design which employs this layout. Yet designers who try to put too much weight into the ends must be careful. These types frequently suffer from excessive pitching in a seaway and display mediocre performance under sail.

below A partial bridgedeck cat, such as the older Outremer 43, was a swift boat but had the disadvantage of separate saloon and hull access.

Class 4 – Superyacht Catamaran

This book would not be complete without the mention of the new breed of luxury yacht: the Multihull Supercat. These magnificent vessels usually measure in excess of 100' and can sail on free wind energy at more than 30 knots without any heel. They feature living rooms the size as found on monohull superyachts twice their size, and require neither a dozen crew to run them nor large diesel engines. Very few builders in the world specialize in these types of vessels, yet their ideal application as large eco-expedition vessels, corporate entertainment platforms, or ultimate private yachts is unquestionable. Blubay Yachts of France seems to be on the forefront of this group as they have gained invaluable experience by being the only builder that has built a succession of composite superyacht multihulls upwards of 100'.

The world market for extravagant pleasure boats has been steadily growing, yet the catamaran platform for luxury sailing vessels has only recently been recognized.

Modern composite materials and high-level engineering utilizing Finite Element Analysis now permit the construction of large structures such as multihulls, which was not possible 10 or 20 years ago. The aeronautical and automobile racing industry have contributed considerably to the design and engineering of complex composite structures from which super-catamarans have greatly benefited. The use of aluminum has been the classic hull and superstructure material for large vessels around 60' and it is still a strong and economical build alternative. With the advance of composite technology experienced builders (usually French yards) are developing lighter, stronger and increasingly sophisticated super-yachts, providing clients alternatives that were unheard of just years ago.

Large catamarans, with their wide and stable platforms are becoming recognized as ideal structures for lavish, as well as exciting, pleasure boats. Their vast living accommodations and privacy layout make them ideal for people looking for an alternative to deep draft and heavy monohulls. In addition, their low-profile underbodies permit access to shallow harbors. The new generation of research vessels and oceanographic laboratory ships are frequently large catamarans. They project the image of eco-friendliness and efficiency as they are propelled by clean wind energy. Their shallow draft allows access to reefs and remote anchorages. Their wide aft platforms provide superior storage facilities for large dive tenders and even ideal helicopter landing pads. The demand for these types of superyacht catamarans worldwide is steadily growing.

below Large luxury yachts, such as this 100' catamaran, can easily accommodate several dozens of guests in ultimate comfort while, at the same time, they can sail at double-digit speeds. With world oil prices steadily rising, they very well might become the new breed of mega-yacht.

EVALUATION & coefficients

Spectacular sunsets in the Pacific turn the horizon into a brilliant spectrum of gold and orange colors.

EVALUATION & COEFFICIENTS

Various multihull characteristics and design features can be expressed in mathematical formulas. Their results are crucial and will give prospective owners a basis of comparison between different types of catamarans. These numbers are important, as they eliminate ambiguity and clearly display various advantages or concessions of a design, which would be hard to quantify any other way. Mathematical coefficients not only will provide insight into a boat's performance in varying conditions, they also reflect concerns about loads to be carried safely, speed and stability.

We have already mentioned the Displacement/Length and Sail Area/Displacement ratio in our chapter on Multihull Advantages, illustrating the point of a multihull's efficiency. Let's look at some other coefficients that give us an indication of a boat's performance.

What is performance and how do we really measure it? Most people who buy a cruising catamaran are not really interested in racing performance, yet desire high daily averages and passage times, which should be as short as possible. When choosing a large multihull, sailors look, above all else, for safety and comfort, long before the consideration for flat-out speed comes into the discussion. Nevertheless, performance is a highly important design consideration. No catamaran sailor wants to sail slower than a same length ballasted keelboat. Below are some useful coefficients, which will help compare monohulls and multihulls objectively.

below "Indigo," a magnificent Wormwood 70, sailing in sparkling Caribbean waters.

Bruce Number (BN)

The Bruce Number is very similar to the Sail Area to Displacement ratio although the formula is slightly different. It is the square root of the sail area in feet, divided by the cube root of the boat's displacement in pounds:

$\sqrt{SA} / \sqrt[3]{Displ}$ = Bruce Number (BN)

SA = upwind sail area (mainsail and 100% jib)
Displ = weight of the boat in pounds

Similar to the Sail Area to Displacement ratio, the higher the coefficient the faster the boat and better is its performance in light air. Typically a BN of 1.1 will be the threshold between fast and more sluggish multihulls. A heavy displacement monohull might have a BN of .7, whereas a modern cruising catamaran shows a BN of 1.3. Offshore multihull racers can have BNs of 2.0 and higher. The BN will also tell us about a catamaran's ability to withstand stronger winds before reefing. A boat with a higher BN is usually overcanvassed in strong conditions and will have to be reefed earlier than one with a lower coefficient.

On the other hand, they will be able to produce more "power" than their counterparts in lighter winds and perform better.

Sail Area to Wetted Surface (SAWS)

SA/WS = Sail Area Wetted Surface Coefficient

SA = upwind sail area
WS = total underwater surface area (hull and appendages)

This formula simply divides the upwind sail area of the boat (mainsail and 100% jib) by the wetted surface. This coefficient will give us a statistical indication of the multihull's light-air performance since in low wind conditions skin friction becomes an important factor. Monohulls can have coefficients of at least 7% more than multihulls.

above While sailing under spinnaker and experiencing virtually no roll at all, guests will always find a comfortable spot to relax on the foredeck, an impossibility on a monohull.

Hull Fineness Ratio (HFR)

The Hull Fineness Ratio, known as the hull's beam-to-length ratio, is an interesting number. It is derived by simply dividing the waterline length of the hull by the waterline beam of the hull.

Max. WL/Max. Beam WL = Hull Fineness Ratio
Max. WL = length of the hull at waterline in ft.
Max. Beam WL = beam of the hull at the waterline in feet.

Monohulls, when compared to multihulls, have low hull/fineness ratios. In Part 1 of this book, discussing "Efficiency," we saw that ballasted keelboats are limited to Archimedes' principle of hull speed (1.34 x $\sqrt{WL}$). Multihulls do not have these theoretical barriers, because their hulls are narrower.

The thinner the hull the faster it will be able to travel through the water. But, attention! It will also carry less unless you are on a mega cat. Typically, a 40' cruising catamaran's HFR will range from 8:1 to 10:1. Dennis Conner's

There are various methods of calculating the transverse stability of a catamaran. One of the simplest and most utilized techniques is establishing a relationship between the height of the Center of Effort (CE), displacement, beam and sail area. Multihull designer, James Wharram added safety factors of 20% to compensate for gusts and the dynamic environment of the ocean. Another method is described in the text below.

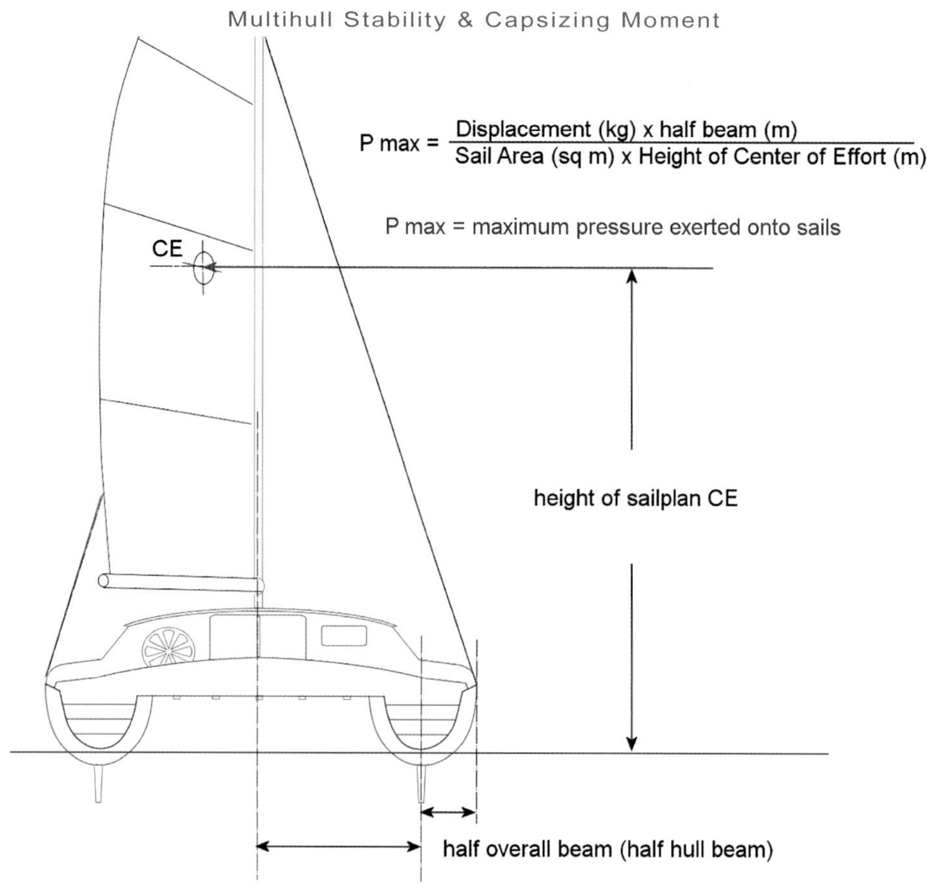

racing cat "Stars and Stripes" had a 16:1 HFR. Of course, the larger the boat, the narrower the hulls will become in comparison to its length. For example, the HFR of a 100' luxury catamaran may be 12:1, providing it with a high speed potential. However, monohulls can show HFRs of 3:1, though the comparison is complicated as their angle of heel affects the measurement.

One has to be very careful when analyzing the Hull Fineness Ratio of a cruising catamaran, because other factors such as the actual shape of the hull cross sections (Prismatic Coefficient, PC) can throw the analysis off balance. Go-fast sailors like to think that fine hulls are always fast. That is not necessarily true because a slim hull could have a large underwater volume, thus slowing it down. Consequently, a wide waterline-beam hull could have less drag than a narrower one. It could have a shallow underbody (low PC), which would be beneficial to load carrying (Pounds Per Inch Immersion Number, PPI) and early surfing characteristics at speed.

Stability Coefficient (SC)

This mathematical formula has been devised by the distinguished catamaran designer and sailor James Wharram and his team. This coefficient analyzes a multihull's ability (in a static environment) to resist capsizing due to wind.

$$\left(\frac{0.682\sqrt{W \times (.5\ Boa)}}{.00178 \times SA \times h} \right) \times .555 = CW$$

W = Wind speed, apparent, in mph
CW = Critical Wind Speed to capsize in mph
SA = upwind sail area in sq ft.
h = height of Center of Effort (CE) of total sail area
Boa = Beam overall

This formula will tell us how much wind it will take to overturn our multihull. By instinct we will know that a catamaran with a wide stance and a conservative sail plan will be very stable offshore. The SC formula will inevitably illustrate that a wider beamed catamaran with a tall sail plan will be as resistant to wind induced capsize as a short-rigged, narrower boat. This is not so if one considers the chaotic environment of waves and the real world of heavy weather sailing. It is interesting to note that a wide beamed boat (regardless of the SC) is more resistant to capsize in seas due to the effects of a higher moment of inertia. In an open-ocean environment, which is everything but static, the SC formula has little meaning. Nevertheless, it serves as a good basis to evaluate stability as a factor of wind force.

below When the wind suddenly comes up, all that is needed is a couple of turns on the jib furler to quickly reduce the headsail size. The catamaran will hardly sail any slower, but feel more comfortable.

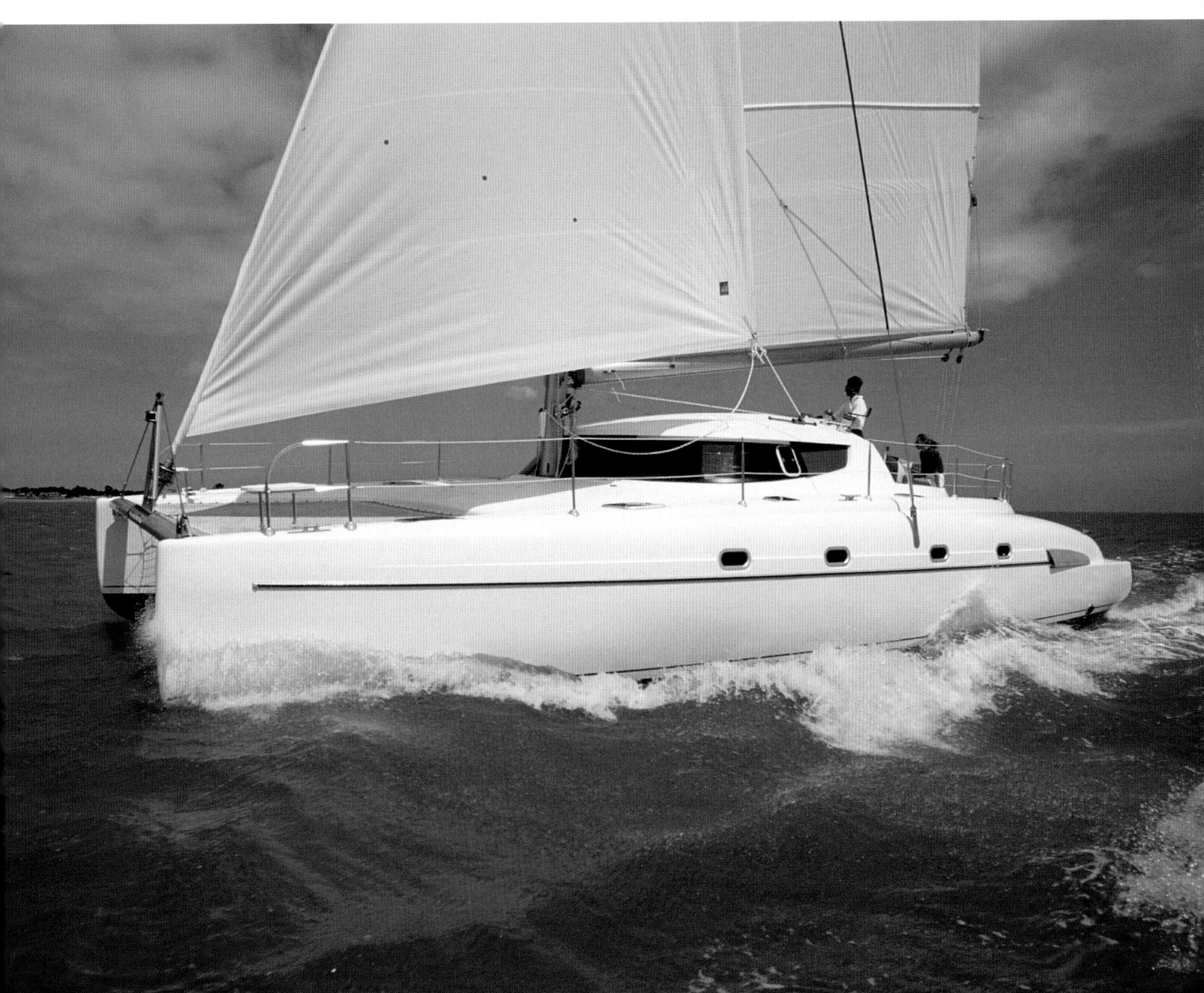

Wide hulls and a large overall beam will increase the overall righting moment of a catamaran. A word of caution: Excessive beam will reduce the fore and aft stability. Designers strive to compromise hull fineness ratios, place heavy weights towards the CG (Center of Gravity), and engineer hull and overall beam to achieve a seaworthy balance, which is safe, yet provides ample liveaboard accommodations.

Catamaran Stability Considerations

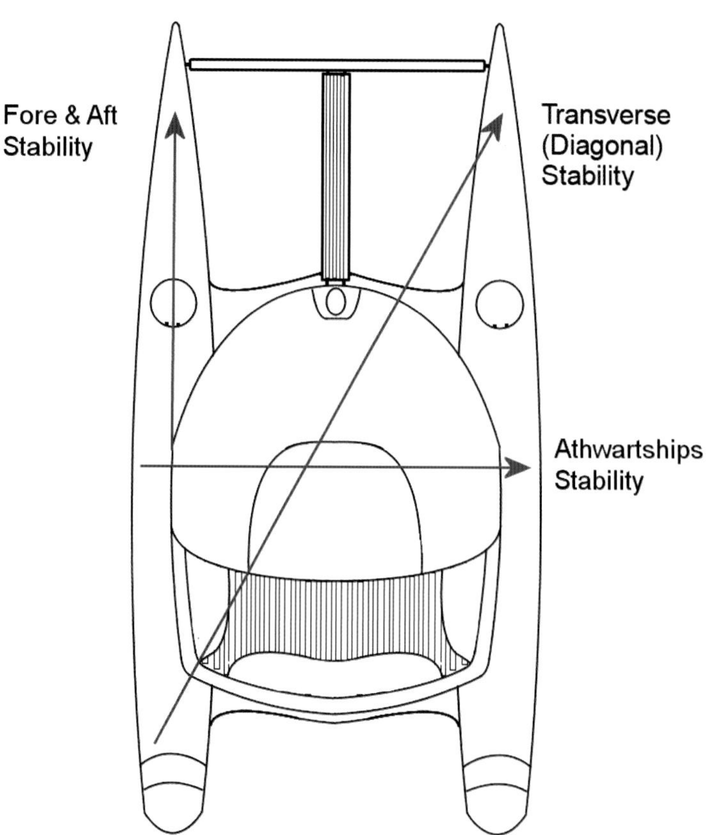

Diagonal Stability & Beam-to-Length Ratio (BLR)

Stability of a multihull, or the resistance to capsize, should be seen as three components. *Athwartship Stability* is one well-publicized type and the one often talked about. The other much more important types are *Fore and Aft* and *Diagonal Stability*. Fore and aft stability is established by the relationship between the boat's waterline length and the distance between the hull centerlines. It will reflect the catamaran's resistance to tripping. This relationship should be in the vicinity of 39% to 42%. For a seaworthy cruising multihull it is important maintain the proper ratio between length and beam, which, in turn, balances equal amounts of athwartship with diagonal stability. The goal should be to prevent the possibility of a sudden discrepancy of powers between fore and aft and sideways resistance. Most of today's multihulls keep these two component forces in equilibrium, making them extremely seakindly and safe.

Some early design multihulls were very narrow, partly due to the material limitations of that time. But things have changed. Contemporary composite construction allows designers to build wider boats without compromising stiffness. Production catamarans of today have a wide stance and have the benefit of greater safety margins in gusty wind conditions than their older cousins. Multihulls are sophisticated structures and true modern miracles. They provide a more comfortable ride and more interior room. Thanks to modern materials they weigh less and perform better than catamarans built only 10 years ago.

Some catamarans, especially production boats, which are very popular in the charter fleets, are growing wider by the year. The businesses who rent these beamy monsters adore them. Lots of room plus open decks are ideal for clients and the bigger (wider) the boat, the more paying guests can share the fees. But there certainly is a limit as to how wide is too wide. Extreme beam can be dangerous. It can lead to instability fore and aft and to excessive bridgedeck slamming, as the relative distance from the bridge deck to the water will decrease with an increase in width. A vessel with excessive beam might seem stable athwartships, but it will compromise overall stability.

We know that multihulls can, in extreme cases of seamanship error in wild storms, be thrown over from any side – front, back and beam-on. The best examples of this phenomenon are racing multihulls, especially Formula 1 trimarans, which have fine hulls for speed and huge sailplans to provide driving power. They are initially extremely stable athwartships (High Beam-to-Length Ratio), but have a tendency to become unstable fore and aft. They will surf down waves and reach a point where the power of the sails, and speed, will exceed the ability to keep the bows out of the water and the boat will pitchpole. This is the reason why catamaran designers usually draw their multihulls with a Beam-to-Length relationship of between 50% and 55%. The longer the vessel the lower that percentage becomes.

I am currently involved in the "*Gemini*" project, which presents an example. It very well might become the world's largest sailing catamaran. She will have an overall length of 145 feet, yet her beam will "only" be 54.4'.

above Asymmetric spinnakers on furlers are great inventions. They add instant sail area, yet can be doused in a matter of seconds when the wind picks up strength.

Please, don't worry. "Gemini" will not be tender and tip over in the slightest breeze. On the contrary, this monster will be one of the most stable craft afloat, although the beam-to-length relationship is only 37%. The relatively low beam-to-length ratio also involves the fact that the boat would be too heavy and building costs would be prohibitive if she were to have a standard 52% BL relationship. Most importantly, could you imagine turning a 75-foot-wide boat?

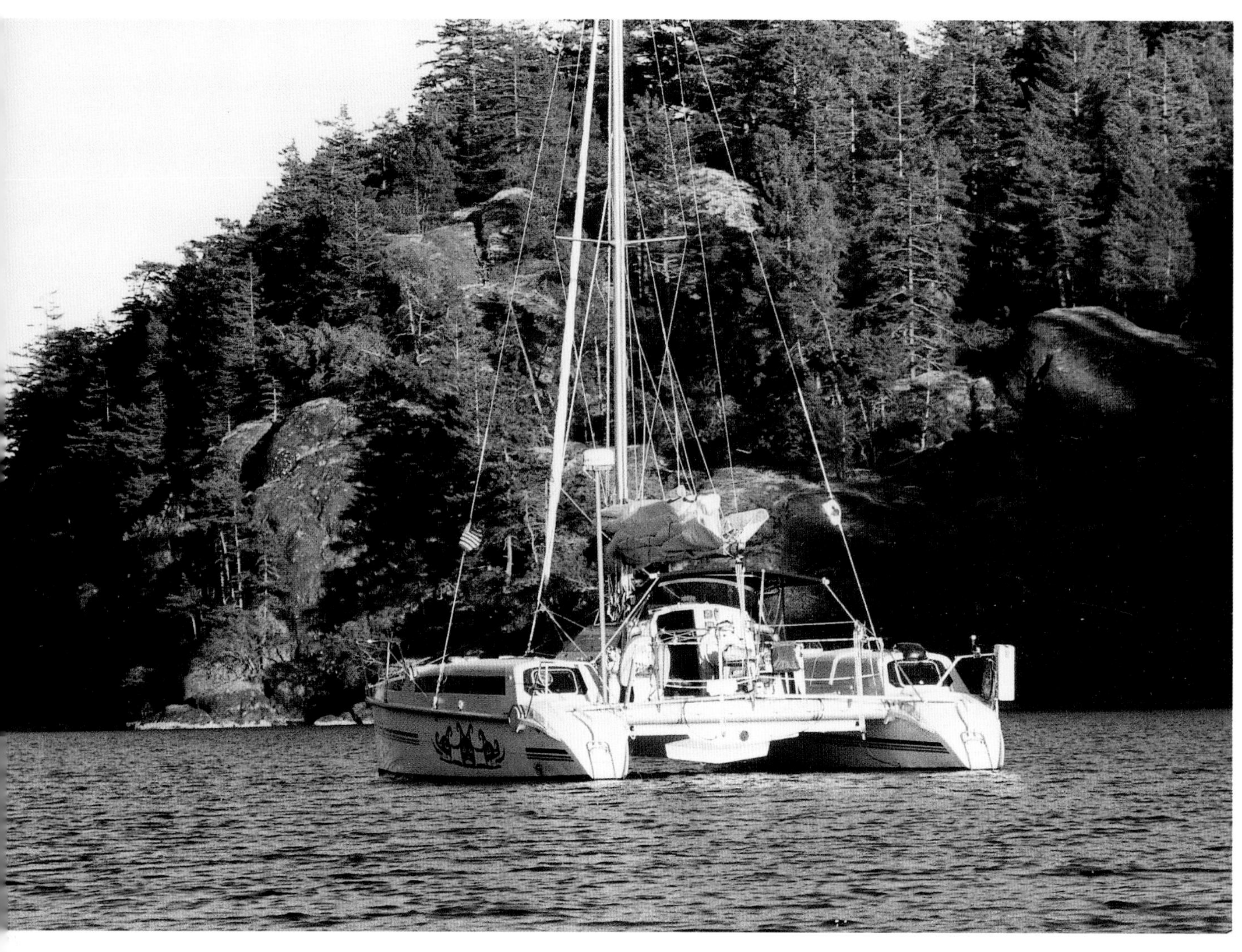

above Although this Edel 35 was a good-looking and popular catamaran, it suffered from excessive bridgedeck pounding, which was caused by only several inches of clearance between the saloon's underwing and the sea.

Obviously there is a sweet spot in the beam vs. stability question. Designing too beamy a boat will also necessitate more freeboard to preserve bridgedeck clearance which, in turn, will increase windage and complicate maneuvering. Unless sophisticated aramid construction methods are utilized, more beam will also add more weight and stress to the structure. Adding more mass will, to a certain point, help make the boat more stable, but where do we stop? Is it better to add weight or width to make a boat stiffer? Of course, both characteristics are interrelated as a beamier boat normally is also heavier. Just adding weight to a catamaran simply to make her more stable will not pay off. Consequently, making a boat too wide might increase living space yet it will also burden the structure, require a beefier manufacture, and yield an even heavier boat. Needless to say, a boat which is too wide will also create practical restrictions such as maneuvering, the ability to haul the vessel and much higher building costs.

Beam has a great effect on bridgedeck clearance, which is one of the most vital characteristics of a good cruising catamaran. As standard practice, the well-known rule of 1” of bridgedeck clearance for each foot of beam was a safe way to prevent excessive wave slap. The wider the beam the more the relationship changes and the necessary height of 1” per foot of beam needs to be increased to 1.3” or more. In the extreme case of overly square boats, that number will have to be closer to 1.8" per foot of beam. This will have a negative effect on any seaworthy multihull that has a bridgedeck saloon. The wide beam will necessitate a high cabin sole to remain a safe distance from the waterline. In order to provide standing headroom, the coachroof might be higher than practical, which could result in a boxy, high-windage multihull. Not only will this be unattractive, but also raise the Center of Gravity (CG) which really should be kept as low as possible.

More overall beam on the other hand (given that there is still sufficient bridgedeck height) has a less known benefit, as it reduces the possibility of hull-wave interference, which is particularly important for fast designs. The wave interaction between the hulls can lead to additional resistance, and especially in an agitated sea state, the formation of wave crests can pound the bridge deck. Most early narrow-beamed catamarans suffered from this phenomenon,

Ultimately, a boat's design has a major influence on its ability to stand against the forces of nature, and to keep occupants safe. Manufacturing excessively wide catamarans is like trying to market monohulls with super deep-draft keels. Both are totally impractical. We designers have to make sensible compromises and learn from past experiences of what has worked at sea by balancing the benefits of a wide boat with its disadvantages.

below This narrow-hulled Outremer 64 Light has completed her third circumnavigation with the same owners. Note the smooth underwing clearance, lacking any protrusions or steps.

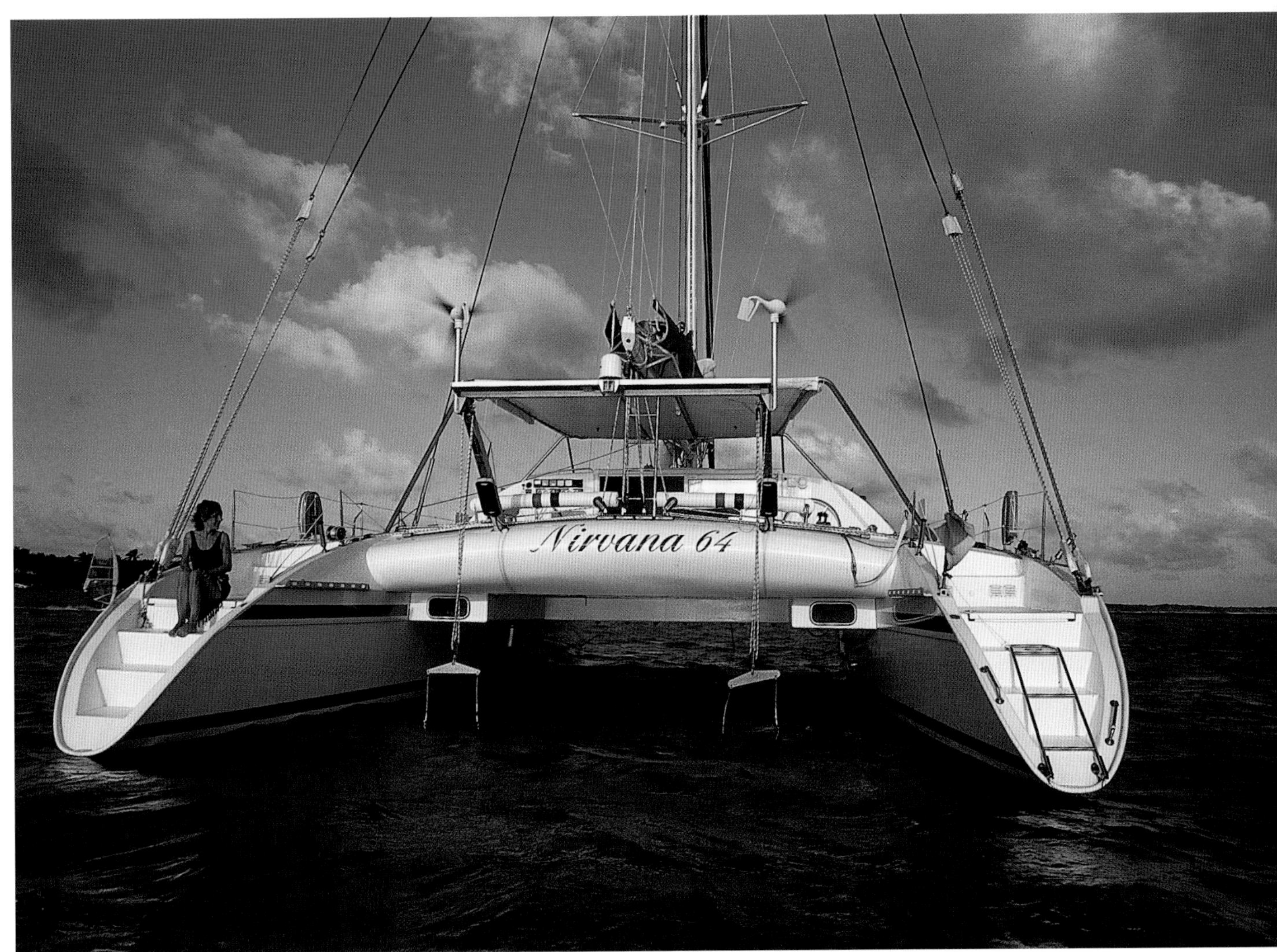

"A great cape, for us, can't be expressed in latitude and longitude alone.
A great cape has a soul, with very soft, very violent shadows and colors.
A soul as smooth as a child's, and as hard as a criminal's.
And that is why we go!"

~ Bernard Moitessier

TI TAK
TI TAK

HULL

Dinghies, windsurfers and every imaginable type of water toy can be stored conveniently on large catamarans and easily launched from the wide transom steps for shore-side pleasures. Note the twin life rafts located in special compartments on the massive aft crossbeam.

HULL

Shape & Resistance

A boat's hull shape and the distribution of volume are key factors in determining how it will behave in varying wind and load conditions. The underwater characteristics of a vessel are responsible for allowing a multihull and its cargo to travel through the water. The faster and more effortlessly the twin hulls can displace the surrounding fluid, the less resistance and more efficient a catamaran will be.

Typically modern catamaran designs have sharp bows to drive the vessel through the seas with as little wave making as possible. High freeboard assures a dry ride. Ample buoyancy helps keep the stems out of the water and spray to a minimum. Elliptical sections make up the first third of the hull, providing an easy entry in the water and some means to resist leeway. Towards the middle of the boat, gradually flattening out towards the stern, the sections become semicircular to help distribute buoyancy. These portions help carry payload and facilitate the hull lifting at speed. Basically, the majority of all cruising catamarans share these same underwater features.

Decades ago very seakindly, double-ended hull shapes were the norm as found in the thousands of Wharram catamarans. They were easy to construct, relatively slippery, and provided ample freeboard. Unfortunately they could not carry a lot of cruising gear, had cramped accommodations and were not the best windward performers. Their sharp V-sectioned hulls and rudders were their only means of resisting leeway as they had no leeway preventing devices. Similarly, the narrow asymmetrical type hull, such as found in the Hobie 16 beach catamaran, is hardly used in today's cruising multihull. The idea was to keep the underwater appendage to a minimum and eliminate any keels or daggerboards.

In contrast, the modern catamaran benefits from tank testing and computer-aided design. Composite molding technology allows for infinite shapes and each designer or manufacturer can now realize his idea of the perfect hull shape. Today's mini keels and daggerboards keep the cat hard on the wind and rival the weatherliness of monohull racers.

Drag on the hulls is the main deterrent to speed and has many components. We have to distinguish between water and air drag. Water-induced resistance can be further broken down into drag caused by wetted surface and wave making. Wetted surface, which is the frictional resistance the hulls experience when they are passing through the water, is the main cause of resistance at low speed. Wave making becomes more important as boat speed exceeds hull speed, or 1.34 x square root of the waterline length. Wave making resistance is not as easy to analyze and is more complex than drag caused by wetted surface; it is primarily a function of weight and, secondarily, of hull shape.

Pitch is another form of drag which can slow the boat down. This unwanted phenomenon is directly related to the buoyancy of the extremities and weight distribution. Wave-making resistance caused by the boat's constant plunging will slow a multihull, especially since it has less momentum to drive it through waves as compared to a single-hulled vessel. In addition the airflow over the sails will be disturbed by a constant change of attitude, further hindering efficient progress. Pitching can also be caused by placing items that are too heavy into the extreme ends of the multihull. In addition, various design- and construction-related issues can cause this problem, such as bridge decks extending too far forward of the mast and a high, heavy rig. Solid decking instead of trampoline nets, and/or large protrusions, which strangely some manufacturers claim break up waves, can also cause a hobby-horsing effect. Not only can this result in more wave-making drag than desired, but can seriously tire the crew. Any structure ahead of the mast can cause major slamming when having to face steep seas. Although many cruising catamarans, such as the Prouts, have been built with large bridgedeck structures extending forward to the bows, it is my opinion that an open trampoline, which poses no resistance to wind and seas, is imperative on a good cruising cat.

above High freeboard and angled-out hulls are trademark features of this capable Catana 521. Much thinking has gone into the hull shape of this catamaran, yet the pronounced step running along the inside of the vessel might create some wave slap in some conditions, a typical example of a compromise between space and performance.

Resistance & Performance

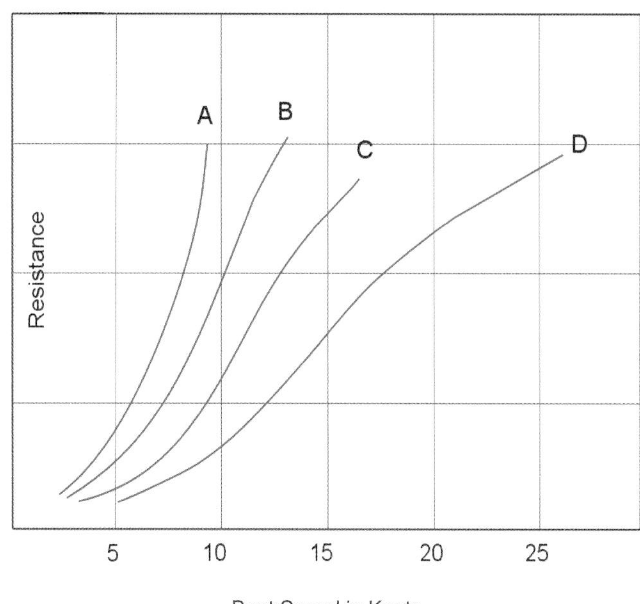

Resistance vs. Speed of four different vessel configurations

A. Traditional, heavy displacement monohull cruiser

B. ULD (Ultra Light Displacement) monohull

C. Typical performance catamaran cruiser

D. Racing multihull, with almost no wave making resistance

below A popular French catamaran, as photographed out of the water at the Paris Boat Show. Note that there are barely several inches of clearance between the bridgedeck and waterline. The pronounced forward knuckle of the nacelle is claimed to break up waves. In my mind however, there is very little that can resist the continued impact of seas, and any conflict between the wingdeck and waves should be avoided.

The cross-sectional profile of a hull will determine the wetted surface and drag. Its distribution throughout the length of the boat will affect payload carrying ability and buoyancy.

From the schematics at the top of page 117, one can easily see how the wetted surface of each type of hull section differs, yet retains the same cross-sectional area. At one extreme, the deep V-type hull partitions, as employed by the Wharram catamarans, have 25% more wetted area than the contemporary type oval and semicircular hulls. Although the V-type sections offer excellent resistance against pounding and travel efficiently through the water, they are poor load carriers and are rarely used in today's industry. At the other end of the spectrum, the semicircular and elliptical canoe-shaped hulls have the least wetted surface for a given displacement; therefore, it takes minimum amounts of materials to build them. They rely on lateral leeway resisting devices, such as mini keels, daggerboards or centerboards, to be able to sail to weather. Between the two extremes are an infinite amount of combinations and possible hull sections, all necessary to support the weight of tons of boat above them, yet facilitating progress through the water as efficiently as possible.

Narrow hulls will slice through the water with less disturbance and also have a lower moment of inertia. Yet they will also depress more and, in some extreme cases, also render less assistance in keeping the hulls from submerging. Designers are very careful not to take sharp entries to the extreme, as they can create a lot of waves that reach higher and farther aft, often compromising the bridgedeck clearance issue. Deeper hull sections will have a motion that is gentler and less jerky than a full-bodied, flat-bottomed hull. In contrast, flatter sections will resist the heeling forces of the wind and pitching motion far better. Since the water that is displaced by the hulls must end up somewhere, it is the responsibility of the designer to insure minimal wave impact as the boat speeds through. Sculpting the hulls, distributing the volume and determining the overall width and bridgedeck height, will all contribute to preventing the converging bow waves from hitting the passing boat. One can see there is a fine balance involving the entire design process, and the intricate shaping of a cruising catamaran's hulls must represent the culmination of all compromises.

Whereas the hull section cuts the hull vertically, the water plane area is a horizontal slice at the waterline. It is important in influencing the distribution of buoyancy of the catamaran and is a key factor in characterizing pitch, stability, and load carrying capacity. Many manufacturers employ very sharp bow sections with very little or no stem volume. In extreme conditions these forward sections work the hardest in keeping the stems out of the seas. Making them too fine can be dangerous. It should be noted that for a given length, the finer the hull beam ratio of a boat, and the fuller the stem section of the bows can be. The Outremer is an extreme example of this characteristic and features massive bows. Although they create more low speed resistance and wave making, big stems and a lot of buoyancy forward will permit the boat to ride with a nose up attitude when high-speed surfing in long seas.

The '80s experienced an interesting movement and the bulbous bow came into fashion. Many builders even retrofitted their stems and added underwater bustles of varying shapes. The late Australian designer Lock Crowther, who initiated this concept, realized the advantages of adding volume forward of the stem. The bulbous bow would act as a streamlining device to reduce drag. Interestingly, commercial ships around the world have been using this innovation to improve efficiency for years. However, it is questionable if smaller cruising catamarans traveling at varying speeds through relatively tumultuous surface water actually would benefit from the bulbs. On the other hand I can imagine the snagged lobster pots and driftwood that would get caught on a bow bustle which, in my mind, are significant disadvantages.

An interesting bow shape was developed by French naval architect Christophe Barrot, designer of the Catana range of cruising catamarans. I am sure that the influence of the boatyard's former designer, none other than Lock Crowther, also played a role in that innovation. The sections of Catana's stems look like a highly subdued bulb.

above Fine, elegant hulls are swift but will limit inside volume and payload. Note the emergency rudder-access deck-plate which can quickly be opened to fit a tiller directly to the top of the rudder post.

below Photographed from the emergency hatch, the radical hulls of "Hydraplaneur" show a pronounced chine and an underwater knuckle midships, similar to hydroplanes from the '30s. These features reduce resistance by lifting the boat out on an earlier plane than more conventional hulls. Disadvantages are a very wet ride and some pounding when sailing upwind.

above With one reef in the main and a couple of turns on the jib furler, this Outremer 45 powers through the finish line to win the ARC (Atlantic Rally for Cruisers).

They are tulip shaped and what starts as a voluminous entry at the waterline tapers upwards and then flares out towards the decks. The idea behind this is to increase the buoyancy of the bow section to reduce pitching, which further helps increase boat speed. Every single time the boat plunges, it creates not only more resistance but the airflow over the sails detaches and creates turbulence. The Catana's hulls are also canted outward, which help the boat's stability, but some people might find them awkward looking from some angles.

Another innovative hull shape is the one of British designer John Shuttleworth, as seen on the Tektron 50. He uses a flare almost along the entire length of the hull above the waterline to increase its volume, yet keeps the waterline beam to a minimum. It makes me wonder why we do not see more of these innovative hulls.

Freeboard is another important compromise between providing ample standing headroom for the crew on one hand, yet keeping weight and the vessel's Center of Gravity as low as possible. A disproportionate amount of freeboard, especially in lighter vessels, can create a host of disadvantages, such as difficulties in accessing low piers and unwanted windage, which can make slow-speed maneuvering difficult. Also, a massive freeboard looks unsightly and gives the boat a boxy look.

Just as freeboard can cause unwanted drag, the entire structure of a multihull could act

Percentage of Wetted Surface at the Same Displacement

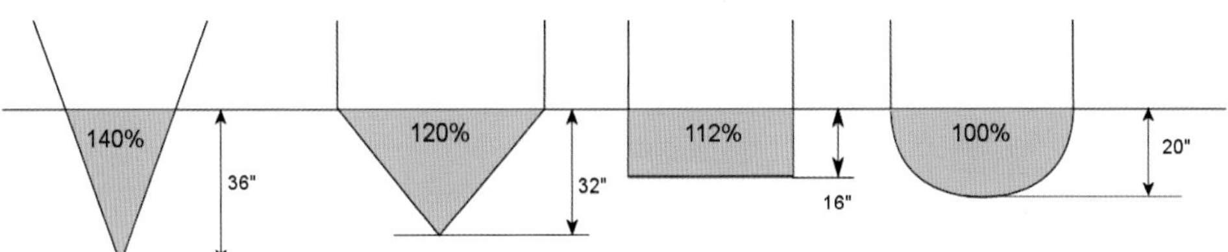

left Basic hull shapes illustrate different wetted surfaces at equal displacement. The semicircular cross-section has close to an ideal ratio of draft, wetted area and volume.

as an air brake if streamlining considerations are not taken into account. Designers therefore try to restrict freeboard to the minimum necessary. Windage can greatly affect a fast catamaran's performance and the wind pressure experienced by the vessel's hulls and superstructure can be considerable. One should not forget that the force is proportional to the square of the wind speed. This means that an increase in boat speed from 5 to 10 knots will result in an aerodynamic drag that is four times more. At 15 knots of boat speed the drag is nine times more than at 5 knots!

Aerodynamic drag is comprised of several components, all hinder forward progress. The most insignificant is the friction of the surface of the boat as the wind blows across it. Next in line is the drag of the sails as they bend the wind into forward motion. Finally, there is parasitic drag created by the boat's structure itself. It involves every part of the boat: hulls, coachhouse, mast and rigging. Therefore, the more optimized a catamaran's aerodynamic shape, the less drag and better speed. Keeping this in mind it is often surprising that there are still plenty of highly popular cruising catamarans on the market whose designers obviously disregard the requirements to streamline the superstructure. Although vertical windows create slightly more space in the saloon they make the vessel look like a tugboat. However subjective this criticism might be, the fact remains that bulky coachhouses have a decidedly negative effect on parasitic drag and significantly reduce a vessel's ability to sail to windward.

Resistance curves of equal weight vessels having different hull fineness-ratios show how the resistance wall at about 2.4 knots impedes wide bodied 3:1 b/l (beam/length) ratio hulls and actually prevents them from accelerating further. Slender hulls, such as 16:1 and even 12:1 b/l ratio vessels are hardly affected by this imaginary barrier.

Resistance Curves for Different Length/Beam Ratios at Equal Displacement

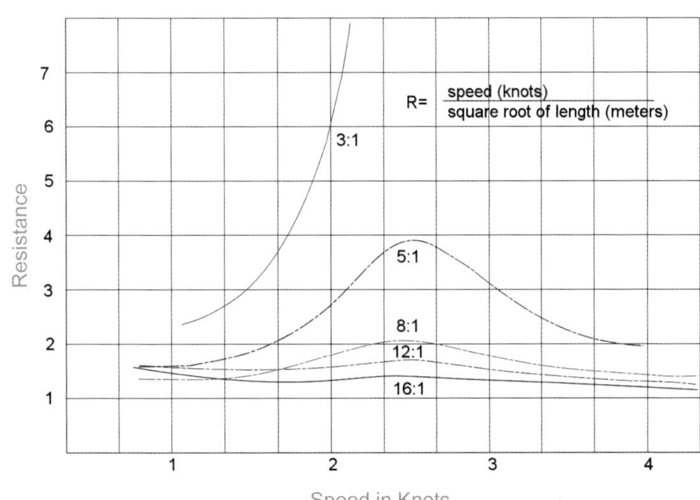

below The Catana's innovative bow section features flared topsides, a fine waterline and a bustle just below it – all contributing to optimizing its hydrodynamic properties.

APPENDAGES

Transatlantic passages can be week-long voyages; they are times for reflection, camaraderie and ultimate adventures, similar to high altitude mountaineering.

APPENDAGES

Keels vs. Daggerboards

Man has learned much from nature. Sailboats and their underwater appendages have been developed for their efficiency based upon centuries of observation, trial and error. As we all know, multihulls, as most things in life, demand compromises and we are often challenged to make concessions in one area in order to gain an advantage in another. This chapter will illustrate the basic virtues and some drawbacks of daggerboards and mini keels on catamarans, but will also focus upon their active and passive safety aspects.

Most multihulls in today's marketplace present two varieties. The majority by far of the production cruising catamarans are keelboats and have low aspect ratio, unballasted fins. Well-known French, Australian or South African boat manufacturers market their boats to individuals as well as to the charter industry and make a great product. Without sounding too general, these catamarans have very spacious interiors and are perfectly adaptable for liveaboard families or the charter trade. The multi-million-dollar charter industry has a pronounced influence on the requirements and design of their fleet, setting standards for cats intended for private ownership. Design parameters for these vessels are often centered around 2-week multiple family vacations in the steady Trade Winds and daysails between closely spaced islands of the Caribbean. Obviously, the features of these keel catamarans put less demand on pure sailing performance or extreme upwind sailing characteristics; instead they please by offering solid construction, liveaboard comfort and simple and reliable handling.

The other type of multihull is the catamaran with articulating foil-shaped daggerboards or centerboards. Centerboards and daggerboards both share the same basic concept, except that their deployment and stowage rely on different principles. The daggerboard is housed in a so-called scabbard, which is a heavily reinforced daggerboard trunk. It moves up and down while a pivoting centerboard is raised and lowered around a massive pin. High-aspect-ratio daggerboards are by far the most efficient foils. They have none of the problems associated with centerboards which, when fully lowered, are only braced by a small area on top. When beating in strong winds, loads on these trunks act as a giant lever, which constantly work to spread them apart. For this reason it is recommended to operate foils as pairs in heavier conditions in order to divide the loads. The large area of the remaining centerboard slot also creates a lot of unwanted turbulence, making them unpopular for performance-minded sailors. Lastly, the declining popularity of the centerboarders can also be attributed to the often large intrusion on the interior space these trunks create. Although the Gemini is a good example of a very popular and well-

Articulating Underwater Appendages

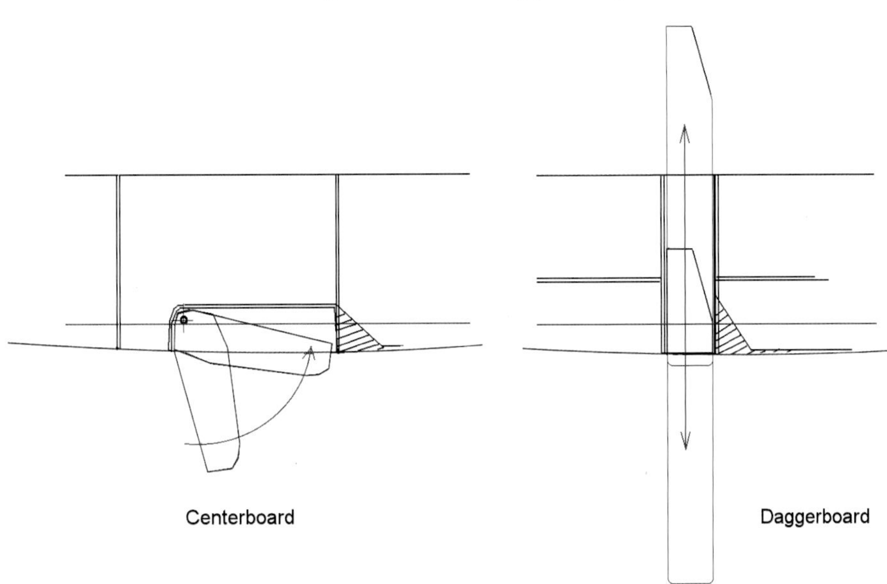

The centerboard provides excellent impact resistance as it can swing up into its case. However it is not as efficient as a deep daggerboard, which is better braced by its full-height trunk.

designed production centerboard catamaran, there are few other mass produced centerboarders around. It should be noted that one great advantage centerboards have vs. any other underbody configuration is they theoretically retract when colliding with an object. In spite of this, most offshore or performance-oriented sailors clearly favor daggerboards or low-aspect-ratio keels.

Daggerboard catamarans have several advantages over their keel counterparts, some are well known and others are more subtle and sometimes only recognized by people who have used them. Active safety aspects are advantages created by speed and the retractability of underwater appendages. I am a firm believer of faster rather than slower on oceangoing cruising catamarans. Many people might say that sailing fast is only for racers. But, let's think about this for a moment. The ability to reduce exposure time through speed is invaluable for cruisers. If, say, on a transatlantic passage you can shave off 5 days, then you have already increased your safety factor, in some cases by 25%. Not being a "sitting duck" is a nice thing, indeed. By having the choice, bad weather can be avoided, possibly eluding a spiral of negative incidences. In general, especially on long passages, a daggerboard cat will have a slight edge on speed over her keel counterpart. Although it must be said that the speed difference between a daggerboard and mini keel catamaran can often be minor and compensated for by good seamanship, a clean bottom and a light boat. Generally speaking, however, daggerboard catamarans will always be slightly faster than their keel equivalents, though the speed advantage of most daggerboard catamarans vs. keel catamarans is often exaggerated. On a typical day-sail a well-trimmed and tuned keel cat will hardly be slower than a daggerboard cat.
Cats lack the feeling of being in the "groove," that monohull sailors enjoy. Effortless high average speeds, acceleration and sustained high-velocity surfing are phenomena fast multihulls offer as compensation. It should be noted that anything (even a barn door) can surf in the right conditions. Even keel catamarans can get onto a plane at speeds of up to 30 knots down large seas. I know a veteran skipper who clocked his Bahia 46 at 28 knots on one of his North Atlantic deliveries and we often sail at over 20 knots in open ocean swells.

above Twin low-aspect-ratio keels are the only device supporting the entire weight of this 40' catamaran; it is perfectly balanced, simple and strong. The keels are completely foam filled and entirely sacrificial in case of a grounding; in case of a violent impact they would not compromise the watertight integrity of the boat.

Depending on sea state, daggerboard catamarans will out-point their keel relatives by several degrees. They will also experience 2-5 degrees less leeway, which one would think isn't much; however, in an uncomfortable 100-mile beat it adds up to being more than 17 miles closer to your destination.

Let's take a 45' catamaran: the lift (to windward) generated by a daggerboard is almost twice that of a low-aspect-ratio keel – and the drag, with the board retracted all the way, would be almost 20% less. The most recent generation of cats with large beams and stately bridgedeck houses benefit especially from high-lift foils, since the windage of their projected area can add up quickly. The same cats with keels usually suffer from excessive leeway and sideslip. Keel catamarans however, especially in a calm sea state, reduce this disadvantage as boat speed and flow over their keels increases. When running downwind in extremely strong conditions the fixed keels could act as brakes that one cannot disengage. Since they cannot be retracted, their volume and resistance slow the boats' progress and, in combination with the forward pressure of the sails, force the bows down. This is notably the case with catamarans that have excessively long bridge decks, heavy extremities and low-volume bows. The greater the friction in the water, the bigger the pressure on the mast, and the more the boat is burdened. On the other hand, the volume in the keels increases overall buoyancy and in some aluminum cats this cavity can be used as fuel or water tanks, effectively increasing stability.

On a daggerboard multihull a neat trick is lifting the daggerboards and tacking downwind. One can actually increase apparent wind by pointing up, inducing leeway and sailing faster to one's downwind destination.

Cruising catamarans are often presumed to tack slowly and react sluggishly to the movements of the helm. This is certainly true for some heavy keel catamarans but much less so for ones equipped with boards. In convoluted seas, some of the heavier keel cats' only option for a safe tack is back-winding the jib or gybing. Monohulls with only one fin will always tack quicker than multihulls, just as foil-equipped catamarans will be more responsive than keel multihulls. Modern hydraulic steering systems are easy to build. Most helm stations are located behind the main coachroof, often the only alternative for the builder. Mechanical steering will give the ultimate feedback and fun at the helm. However, most of the time the dependable autopilot does its work and could not care less about rudder feedback.

Another advantage of daggerboards is to afford better steerage under one engine. If you lose one engine and retract the board on the hull that has no power, but leave the powered hull's foil down, the boat will turn easier. Because of the retracted foil on the non-powered side, there will be much less drag-induced turning moment, the boat will be more balanced and the other side's lowered board will provide sufficient bite for "survival" steerage. Especially in high crosswind situations, a catamaran with both boards down can be easier to control than one with shallower keels. Usually harbor maneuvers under power are low-speed operations, and this is where twin boards excel yet again, and facilitate handling and precision docking. Daggerboard cats can also motor a bit faster, since by retracting the foils they have less resistance.

Keel and daggerboard cats usually have less draft than keel monohulls, which allows them to gauge the depth of shallow anchorages when entering unknown harbors. By lowering the boards, one actually creates a "safety depth." When they touch bottom, one still has the chance of raising them, performing a quick U-turn and getting into deeper water. With fixed non-retractable keels, especially with a monohull, groundings or unplanned bottom encounters could end tragically. At least a monohull can attempt to escape the grounding by quickly heeling the boat, reducing its draft and re-floating. Obviously this is not an option on a keel cat since if you get stuck in the mud you are forced to await the next high tide before you are off. Actually this isn't as bad as it sounds as you would be sitting upright on the hard and boaters around you might not even realize that you went aground. Crashing into a coral reef could be a different story altogether and only a haul-out will permit damage assessment and allow a repair. Depending on their design, boards could be rotated or flipped, and even repaired underway. In general, daggerboard cats with their boards fully retracted also have less draft than keel multihulls, allowing access to even more harbors and anchorages. They can be beached high up for repairs or inspections, increasing the window of exposure time between tides. On the other hand one should note that keel catamarans can be beached just as easily. They can be left sitting, high and dry, perched completely safe on their keels, without concerns about damaging the hulls or getting debris or sea life stuck into the vulnerable daggerboard trunks.
The following is an interesting account by Bruno Nicoletti, who is an old friend and one of the most low-key expert sailors I know. He has logged more than 130,000 miles (geriatric miles – as he calls them) on his 44' daggerboard catamaran. At a recent meeting with him in France we talked about his experiences of his record, double-handed,

Resistance to Pitchpoling

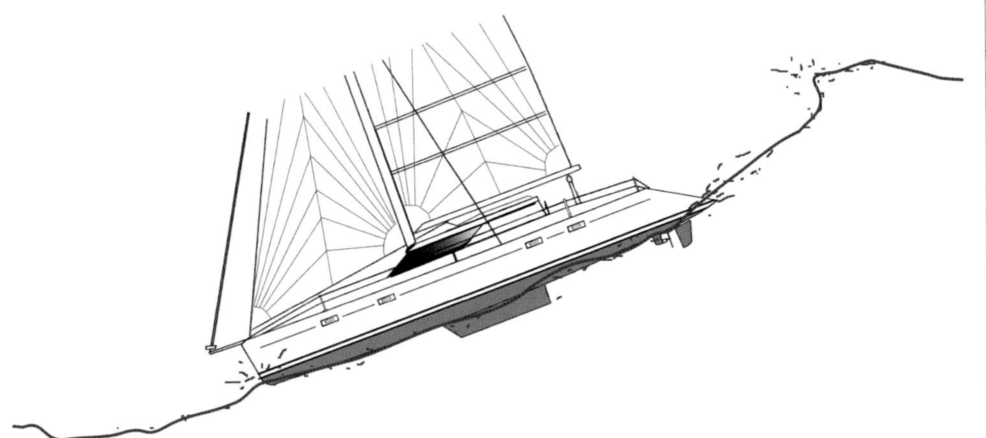

When surfing down long waves in strong conditions, resistance to pitchpoling is imperative. Full-buoyancy bow and stern hull sections, centered weights and a conservative sailplan will allow safe surfing speeds.

In some situations, raising the daggerboards will be of great advantage as it induces leeway, at the same time reducing resistance. In wind-against-tide situations, deliberate leeway will balance the boat against the opposite wind pressure. In light air, the catamaran will sail faster on a close reach than on a beam reach. Leeway towards the destination will turn the apparent course into a true course. In stronger winds, the same theory applies if the wind is aft of the beam.

Deliberate Raising of Daggerboards

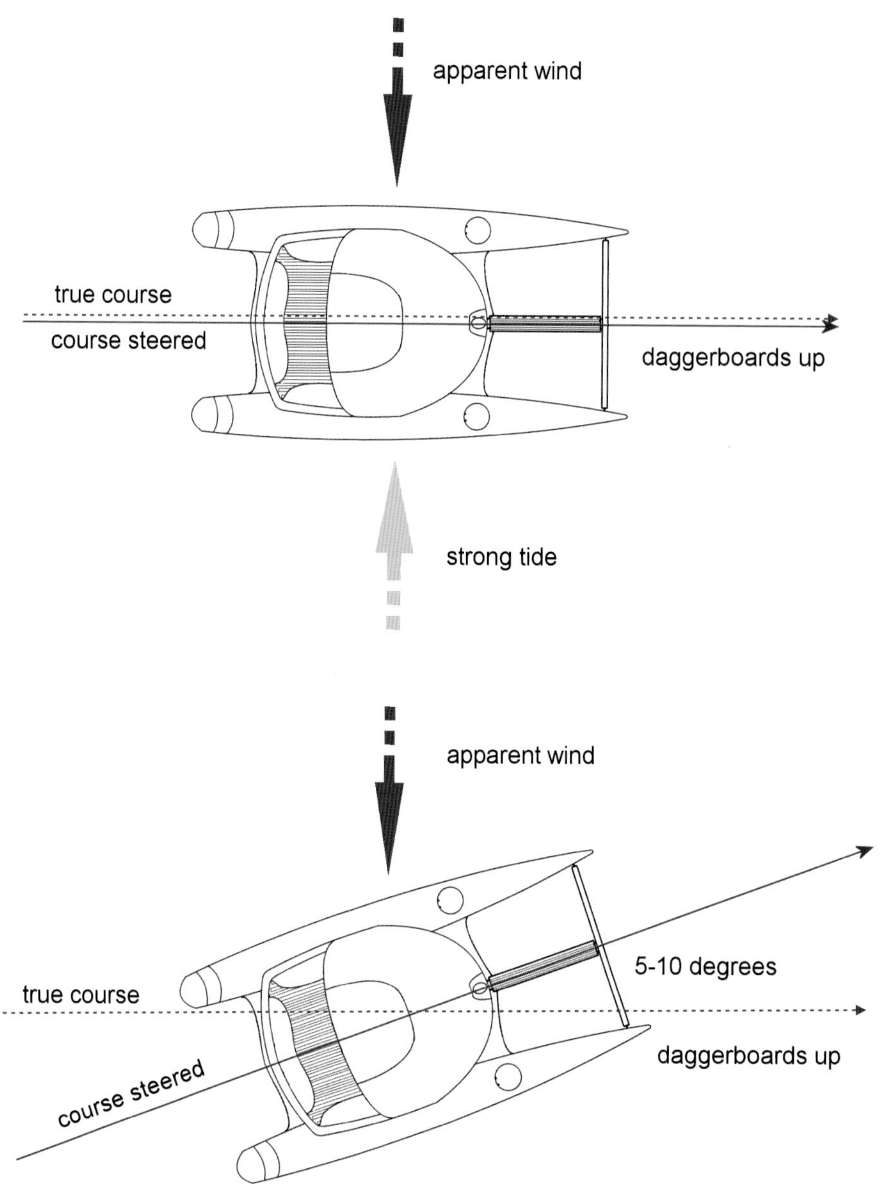

one-stop Southern Ocean circumnavigation at age 63. The French press compares Bruno to sailing legend Vito Dumas and has published his accounts in an article titled: "The Impossible Route." He explained that in the Southern Ocean, in the most convoluted conditions he would simply raise both boards, lock the helm to windward, and lie a-hull with no sails. "Brumas Patagonia" would safely slide down the steep faces of waves and drift minimally to leeward at about 1 nautical mile an hour, while he was either resting or reading. The turbulent water spoil of his sidewards drift would help keep the edge off cresting waves and often prevent them from breaking. While it was blowing 70 knots and higher, he felt very safe, and in fact, the world around him appeared to be "peaceful and quiet" as he mentioned.

It is not only in the Southern Ocean that one encounters steep, breaking waves. Major capes and the Gulf Stream are notorious for rough conditions where the ability to navigate safely becomes imperative. In those environments any proven and strongly built daggerboard cat would have a slight advantage if her boards were lifted, although a well-designed keel catamaran could get through unscathed. In extreme weather, and I am talking beyond Force 10, it is very important to enable a catamaran to sideslip rather than allowing the possibility of a trip, and maybe a flip. A catamaran's behavior in towering side waves creates vulnerability and the possibility to lift underwater appendages is essential, especially if one has lost the ability to steer.

The disadvantage of a keel catamaran in huge beam seas is more psychological than real, as these types of vessels, typically, also slip sideways. In survival conditions or emergencies, the use of parachute anchors, which force the boat into a certain attitude, are often thought to be the only solution for most boats. In my mind, this tactic should be used only if one has lost steering. Using a sea anchor places enormous strains onto the structure of the vessel and renders one helpless when the odd rogue wave smacks into the boat from a different direction. It is better to actively manage survival conditions by controlling and slowing the vessel with the use of drogues.

We have learned a great deal from the aerospace industry and the result is a technological trickle-down effect to monohull keels. Multihull designers and builders greatly profit from the advanced research that has been done in the field of NACA sections (National Advisory Committee for Aeronautics) and foil performance. Keels and daggerboards come in a variety of aspect ratios; most are based on low-speed foils, where drag/lift characteristics have been optimized. To increase lift even further some performance catamarans also utilize asymmetrical daggerboards, shaped flat on the outside (leeward) and cambered on the (windward) inside. As they can only be used one at a time, asymmetrical boards are somewhat limited in their adaptation for cruisers. Since multihulls do not heel, their underwater appendages are more effective in retaining positive flow than their monohull relatives. This is the reason autopilots burn out less often and can be used in heavier conditions on catamarans. As the monohull heels, not only is the upper part of the keel blanketed by the underbody of the vessel, but flow is also lost as the water slips past the angled keel to leeward. This was especially prevalent on the early IOR monos, which had extremely beamy, shallow bilges and high prismatic-coefficient center sections. To compensate for this loss of heel-induced flow, monohulls need deep-draft keels to make good progress to windward. The keel or daggerboard catamaran, on the other hand, can create lift more efficiently for the same keel surface area, not only because it has two keels vs. one, but also its minimal heel keeps its underwater appendages perpendicular in the water.

below A typical daggerboard will spend the majority of its time in the "up" position. It is lowered when beating upwind in order to reduce leeway or aid in the directional balance of the catamaran.

Safely Sliding Down Waves

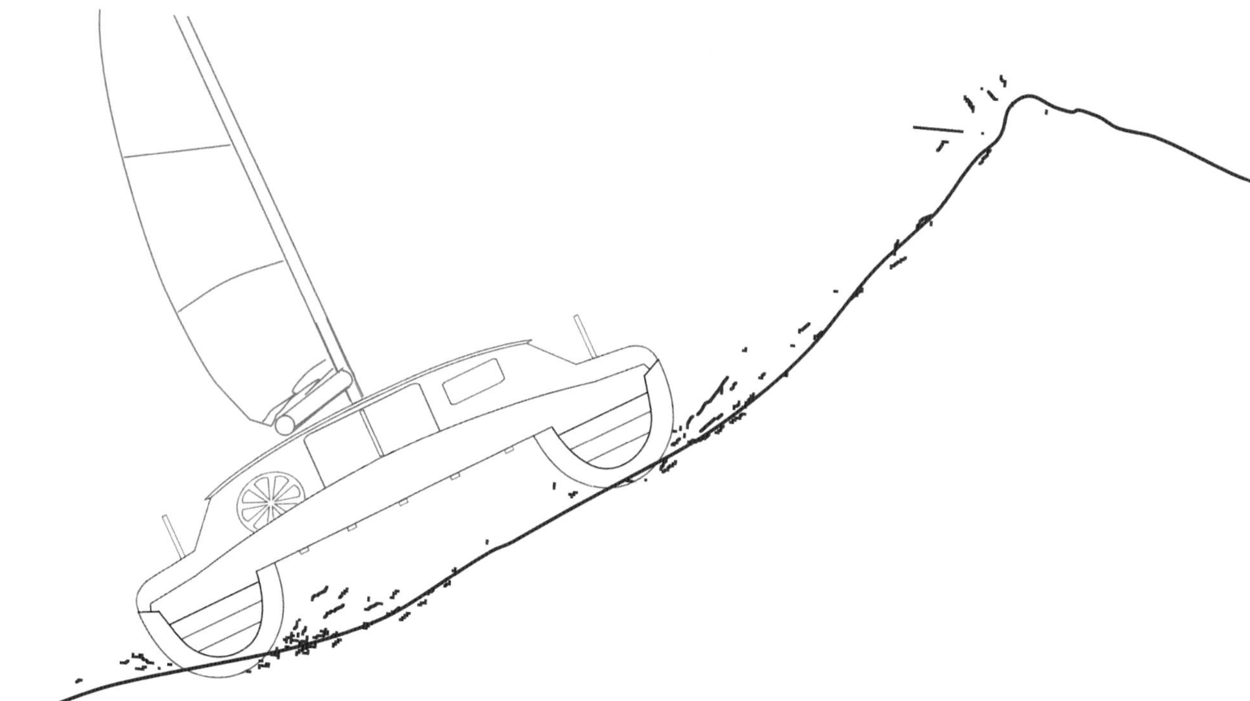

Well-designed cruising catamarans have the ability to slide down steep waves. Even multihulls equipped with mini-keels can safely resist tripping caused by too deep underwater appendages and/or low buoyancy hulls.

far right Long, high-aspect-ratio daggerboards have the advantage of being very efficient foils, yet in the up position can present considerable windage in a storm.

Usually daggerboard catamarans have a higher aspect ratio and are deeper than equivalent length monohulls since daggerboards are retractable and have no draft considerations. It is not surprising to see that in wind speeds starting at around 10 knots, a well-designed and sailed daggerboard cat will often outpoint and outpace a performance monohull. Even well-sailed keel catamarans often arrive earlier at an upwind destination compared to heavy monohulls. The few degrees they sacrifice of their ability to point to windward is often made up for by their higher speed and VMG (Velocity Made Good). This performance difference increases proportionally to the wind speed and is very noticeable in F4 conditions and beyond.

A well-known fact and possibly the single biggest disadvantage of daggerboard cats is the vulnerability of the boards and trunk in collisions. This is most detrimental in the case of poorly built and designed trunks, which cause flooding on impact. Obviously, this is not the case with keels, which would deflect a minor obstacle or, in case of hitting a container or whale, simply break off. The best protection against collision damage are sacrificial mini keels, which would simply sheer off, leaving the hull completely intact. Clearly, the most critical area in daggerboard design is the construction of the daggerboard trunk. It is usually heavily reinforced with massive gussets, especially at its aft bottom end, and extends from the bilge to the overhead. Typical forces on the trunk easily exceed the pressure of the wind on the sails. Dynamic forces of wave action and the shock loads of slamming into seas or solid objects require this area to be one of the strongest and best engineered of the entire vessel. Unfortunately, a lot of low production daggerboard catamarans suffer greatly in this crucial zone. Usually the foils are located just aft of the main mast-bearing crossbeam and are somehow tied into this unit to profit from its stiffness. The more "left over" daggerboard remains in the scabbard in the fully down position, the better it is braced, so it is not surprising to see foils that are 18' long for a 60' boat.

CATANA 52
CATANA

It is easy to see why a daggerboard catamaran is able to provide maximum lift via its twin vertical foils. Multihulls, which are equipped with shallow mini-keels will be slightly less efficient. The heeling mono will suffer the greatest loss of pressure.

Efficiency of Underwater Appendages

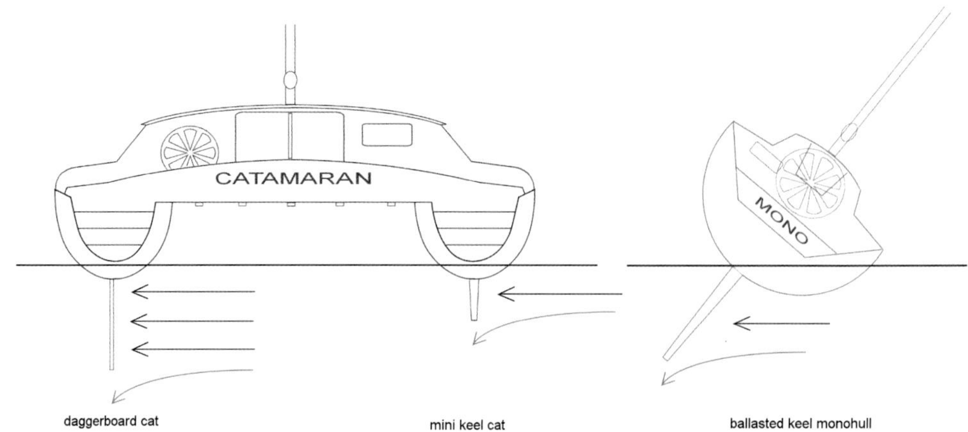

Builders who take their job seriously go to great lengths to make this crucial area as strong as possible. In a recent conversation with the manager of a reputable French production yard, he stressed that the daggerboard trunk is engineered and constructed seven times stronger than the composite board which it houses! In case of a violent impact, the foil, which has weak spots designed into it, will snap and leave the daggerboard trunk unscathed. It is a type of impact philosophy, or a safety fuse, just as it is employed on sacrificial fixed keels. Similarly, minikeels are a completely separate part of the hulls and will not allow water to enter them in case they break. The careful engineering and experience necessary in building reliable daggerboard or keel cats stresses the importance of a production yard which has built them consistently. This aspect should not be taken lightly if one ventures out into the open sea, even if it is only 20 miles offshore.

Builders of keel cats often add daggerboards to their designs, with the objective to market increased performance and safety. This usually results in a compromise when considering the hydrodynamic hull requirements of both types, which might differ substantially; proper integration, engineering, and construction become crucial factors.

Keels offer advantages – they do not need to be operated at all. They do their work silently, making one less thing to break. On the other hand, people who have never sailed with daggerboards think their operation is complicated. In fact, they are as easy to use as outhauls or travelers. In normal conditions with 2 people aboard – one pumping the daggerboard's uphaul line directly at the board, the other taking up the slack of the line – it literally takes 3 seconds to raise a 15' daggerboard. Single-handed, it is a 10-second affair, involving 2-3 wraps of the uphaul around a winch and 10 cranks. Most boards are heavier than the water they displace and often weigh 80 lbs. Lowering them takes one second by simply opening the uphaul sheet stopper and easing the foil down. Loads on the boards increase as the speed and pressure builds, so if one has the choice, these maneuvers are usually performed just before tacking. It is a misconception that the operation of daggerboards will only depend on the wind speed. Similar to reefing strategies, it is rather the boat speed – in regards to sea state, which, in turn, limits progress

– that dictates the proper positioning of the daggerboards.

Nothing is perfect, and this analysis would be worthless without mentioning the pros and cons of both the underwater appendages. Daggerboards, their surrounding structures and systems are more expensive to build, so builders prefer to stay away from them, if given the choice. On some catamarans, especially smaller ones, or those that have the trunk in the center of the hull, the interior passage in the hulls can be crammed. Again, it should be mentioned that an incorrectly designed and constructed daggerboard multihull can be more of a detriment than an advantage. In some cases it can be extremely dangerous. If the trunks are not massively reinforced, and if a violent collision occurs, one hull could flood and cause a capsize. One would be much better off with a well-designed and constructed keel multihull than a mediocre or untested one with daggerboards. Yet, daggerboards give you choices that keels don't. It is similar to the new generation of cars with Tiptronic gearboxes, which offer you an automatic transmission with a clutch-less manual override. By physically selecting the proper gear, torque can be adjusted to suit the conditions. The daggerboard-equipped multihull shares the same advantage. The boat can be fine-tuned to optimize the level of efficiency of the vessel's motion through the water. By adjusting the boards, one can achieve superior sailing characteristics, resulting in higher speeds and generally more fun on the water. Active safety aspects of reduced exposure time, better maneuverability and shallow draft provide significant benefits.

However, for safety reasons, today most catamaran builders opt for fixed keels and completely separate the keels from the hulls. This is a feature that preserves and protects the watertightness of the boat in the event of violent impact. Furthermore, if such a situation arises, it makes them easier to repair or replace. Fixed keels require no manipulation such as daggerboards do and always provide perfect protection for drive shafts, propellers, rudder blades and hull bottoms. Remember, daggerboards have to be in the down position to protect other appendages, while keels are always down. Lastly, the absence of a centerboard trunk means space savings in the interior of the vessel, which usually results in larger living area.

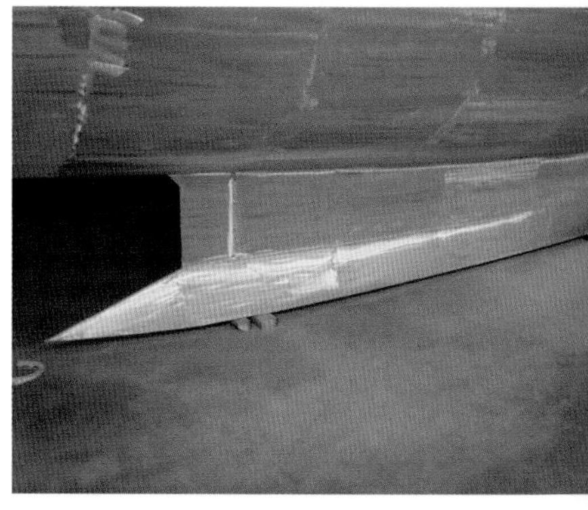

above Water tanks are conveniently housed within the aluminum keels, thereby creating a secondary watertight structure. The weight down low also contributes to a slight increase in transverse stability.

below Very low-aspect-ratio keels have the advantage of less than 4-foot draft as found on this 70 foot catamaran. Note how this cat is being transported. The entire weight of the boat is placed on the truck's trailer and supported by its very stiff bridgedeck alone.

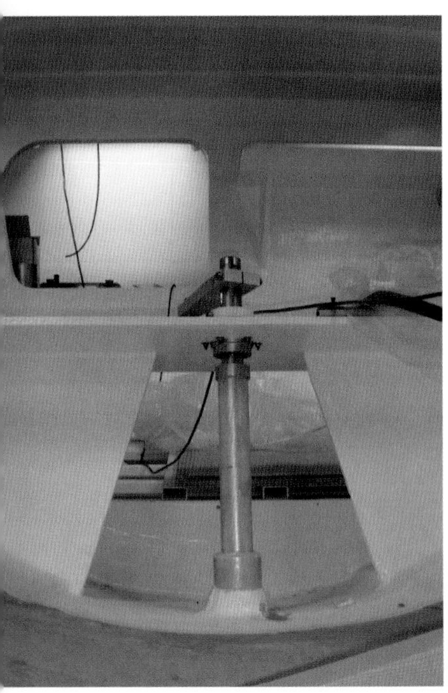

above Well braced on top and at the bearing end, this aluminum rudder post will provide years of service and even resist minor impacts with floating objects.

Today we continue to strive to find the perfect compromise in our vessels to satisfy our most important requirements. We should be deeply thankful for the thousands of keel multihulls that have revolutionized the charter industry and many good boats have evolved from this trend. Reputable daggerboard catamarans and well-designed keel multihulls will continue to be the choice of future generations of serious offshore voyagers. Both have their advantages and disadvantages and it is important to understand both in order to make the proper choice.

Rudders

While mini keels and daggerboards provide lateral resistance to leeway, rudders allow directional control and steerage. Catamarans always have twin rudders which contribute to their safety. Having reliable steerage on any cruising boat is essential and cannot be overestimated. Twin rudders provide positive redundancy, superior tracking, and reduce the loads on autopilots. Just as the majority of today's cruising catamarans are mini keelers, 90% of them are also equipped with fixed spade rudders. However, there are a number of variations that are perfectly suited for the various adaptations of a cruising multihull.

Usually multihull rudders are much smaller than their monohull counterparts. There are four reasons for that: First, there are two rudders, unlike the single one on a monohull, so the lateral area is combined. Second, a multihull will typically travel faster than a ballasted boat, therefore rudders do not have to be as large. The slower the boat the larger the rudder has to be in order to steer effectively. Have you ever seen the rudder of a tug boat? They are 3 times the size of your average door. Thirdly, rudders will always remain nearly vertical and so be more effective. Lastly, the narrow high-aspect-ratio hulls of a catamaran will help the boat track straight and not require a large rudder surface area as there is less directional correction necessary.

Designing a multihull's rudder is a challenge however. The performance window of a catamaran is much higher and a rudder that has to work at 3 knots must be prevented from cavitating at 25 knots when it surfs. Cavitation, or ventilation, as it is sometimes referred to, happens when, at very high speed, air is drawn down the low pressure side and detaches the flow of water around the rudder area.

There are also additional problems for multihull designers because the configuration of a catamaran, with its shallow hull, makes rudders much more vulnerable to impacts than on monohulls, which have a 7' keel protecting them. Normally the depth of the rudders are slightly less than the mini keels or skegs ahead of them, and their position should be roughly 20% aft of the lateral pivot point

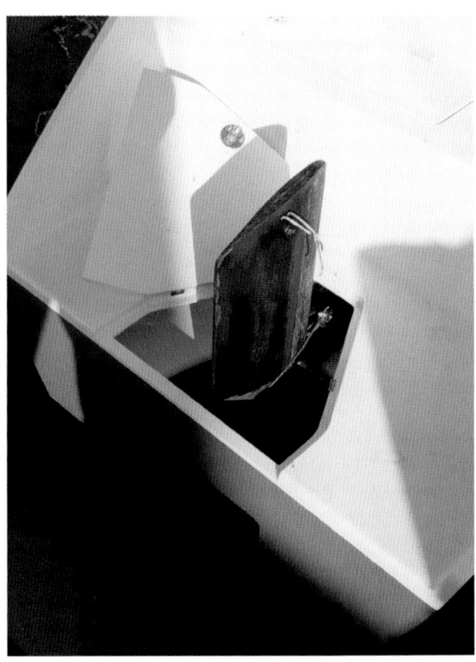

right A smart daggerboard lifting rudder mechanism as found on the Gunboat 49.

of the vessel. Generally, non-hydraulically operated rudders on multihulls are connected to one another by either a cross-bar tube or another type of mechanical linkage. This provides a straightforward and reliable system. If one side fails, one should have the ability to quickly isolate one rudder in order to regain proper steerage.

By far the most popular type are the spade rudders that are mounted on either stainless steel or aluminum (sometimes even aramid) stern-tube rudder stocks. In case of a failure emergency tillers can be quickly fitted to the top of the stocks. Fixed spade rudders are also referred to as "balanced," as the rudder stock enters the foil aft of the leading edge, leaving an area forward, which aids in turning the rudder. Spade rudders are usually located well aft for good lever action; they are also the most efficient type. Often the gap between the hull and the rudders' upper edge is less than one inch, making the hull act like an endplate. Spade-type rudders are straightforward to build and provide the most sensitive feedback to the helmsman. As many of today's multihulls are fitted with hydraulic steering systems, which are known for the absence of steering "feedback" to the helmsman, the spade-hung rudder nevertheless will be the best means to translate the forces back to the wheel. Freely suspended rudders are not without vices; they can snag lines and are vulnerable to damage, especially if they are not protected by skegs or mini-keels.

Another type is the skeg-hung rudder, which has the advantage of being mounted behind a solid appendage. It is not as easy to build and has less feedback than the balanced, free hung rudder. Both types should be designed to take the weight of the boat without damage when beaching.

Unlike the above fixed types, lifting rudders allow a reduction of draft. They can either be the daggerboard – vertically lifting type, hung on transoms – or built into hinging stern sections. Another variety is the centerboard kick-up type, usually hinged onto transoms. Presently only few production manufacturers equip their catamarans with lifting rudders. They are more expensive to construct, are complex in nature and lack the efficiency of the fixed rudder. Anything moving more than it must presents a potential weak spot, and the forces of Nature will usually find them at the most inopportune time. Having simple, reliable rudders is of the essence on a well-designed multihull.

below Beautifully finished in Aston Martin-blue, like the owner's car, this top-of-the-line catamaran is ready for launch. Note the anodes on both sides of the aluminum semi-balanced rudder.

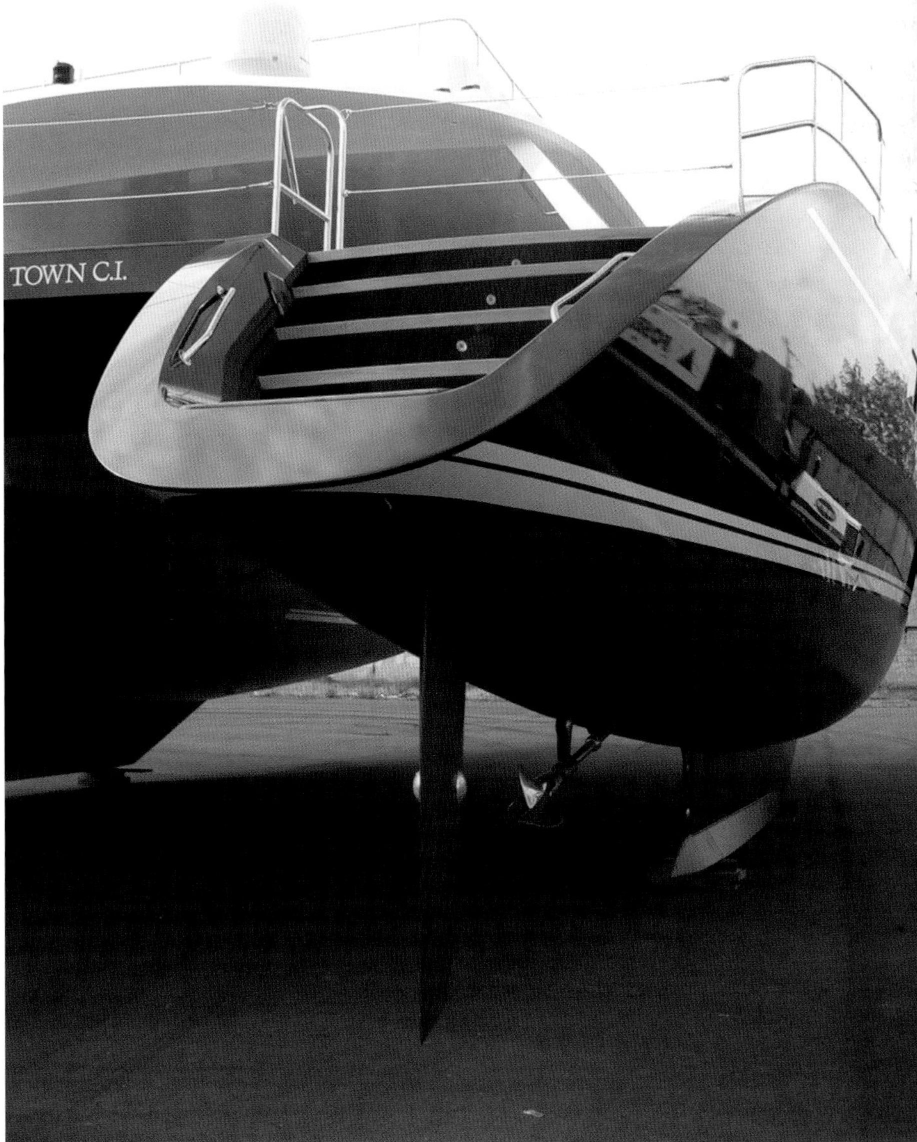

"The machine does not isolate man from the great problems of nature,
but plunges him more deeply into them."

~ *Antoine de Saint-Exupéry* – Wind, Sand and Stars

RIG

Halyard and reefing winches are firmly riveted to aluminum base plates and conveniently located at the foot of the mast, ready to hoist and douse sails.

RIG

Configuration & Types

Sailing in strong winds, deeply reefed, is one of the great pleasures of multihull sailing. With a properly reduced sail plan your boat might feel undercanvassed, yet will still show stellar performance. In contrast, a monohull might experience wild rolling and gusts will flatten her on her beam ends. A catamaran's easily driven hulls and highly stable platform have required designers to adapt the sail plan for a variety of operating conditions. Wide beam has great advantages of holding up the rig and keeping the compression forces to a minimum. Considering the many tasks demanded, a multihull's rig has to perform the same functions as any other sailing vessel's: be easy to handle, stay up and assist the sails in bending wind into forward motion.

The most common and practical rig type for multihulls is the 7/8 or fractional rig which will be our focus. Catamarans with a stiff structure and rigid bridge decks use this sail plan successfully. This trend is even noticeable in the monohull camp and today's performance keelboats are all utilizing fractional rigs. America's Cup yachts, mega sleds and Open 60 racers cannot do without them any longer. The advantages are obvious. A huge roach can be added to the mainsail area without it interfering with a permanent backstay as on a classic monohull masthead rig. French builders started putting 7/8 rigs on their production catamarans 25 years ago and someone has yet to come up with a better solution. They work, are reliable, and are here to stay.

The fractional rig is usually supported by only three stays – two shrouds and the forestay around which the jib is furled. Some people could argue that this is unsafe. But think about it for a second – any rig will fail if only one of its many stays parts under tension. The triangulation between shrouds and forestay is a nearly perfect geometry if boats were to sail only upwind. On a reach, however, the forward sheeting angle of the boom is limited by the aft staying position of the shrouds, and mainsails can chafe against them. Fortunately, fast multihulls, as we will discover later, will always bring the apparent wind much farther forward than their keelboat cousins, eliminating deeper sheeting angles altogether.

Forces exerted on rigs by wind pressure can be enormous, yet a catamaran's wide beam is ideal for keeping the shroud loads within manageable limits. Leading the shrouds outward to the deck's edge also reduces the compression on the mast, which is usually stepped on the central crossbeam. Whereas a monohull would heel in a gust, a stable cat will absorb the energy of the wind and translate it into forward momentum and simply accelerate the boat. It is a sensational feeling of rush when speeding up on a multihull – similar to being pushed back into a sports car's seat.

Modern fractional rigs employ roller-furling genoas and fully battened, large roach mainsails.

They are efficient upwind and are able to absorb huge loads. Catamarans, like any sailing yacht going to weather, will rely on a bar-tight forestay to preserve the shape of the jib and keep its draft forward. In this situation, one would tighten the forestay in a totally different way. A monohull must tension its backstay, boom vang or running backstays, which will not only have the desired effect of pulling up on the headstay, but will also try to drive the mast through the bottom of the boat. A multihull by contrast, which is lacking a backstay, will rely mainly on its mainsheet, and in some cases on runners, to tighten the forestay. Because of the fore-and-aft staying geometry, it is impossible to use the catamaran's shrouds to gain any effect on the forestay. By tensioning the mainsheet, the top of the mast is pulled aft and its midsection is pushed forward. This also results in flattening the main and removes the sail's fullness. Similar to a manual transmission in a car, one can thus depower the boat simply by the combined action of traveler and mainsheet. However, what one does not want is for the mast to bend aft in its center, resulting in exactly the opposite effect. The luff would move closer to the leach and create fullness, which would increase heel and weather helm. On some multihulls, runners, or running backstays, are fitted, which assist in tightening the forestay. More importantly, they support the mast when large headsails, such as gennakers or Code Zeros, are flown in heavier conditions.

Another advantage of the 7/8 rig is the fact that the forestay is shorter than on a classic masthead rig. A shorter forestay means less force to tighten it and less critical sag on the jib's luff. An added bonus is that the headsails are usually smaller, making handling easier. The smart aspect about the fractional rig is that it reduces structural loads wherever possible. A manageable-sized jib will not necessarily mean a smaller overall sail area, since the large roach of the main will compensate for the headsail size. The mainsail will also benefit from less back-winding from a smaller jib, rendering the important pressure zone more efficient between both sails.

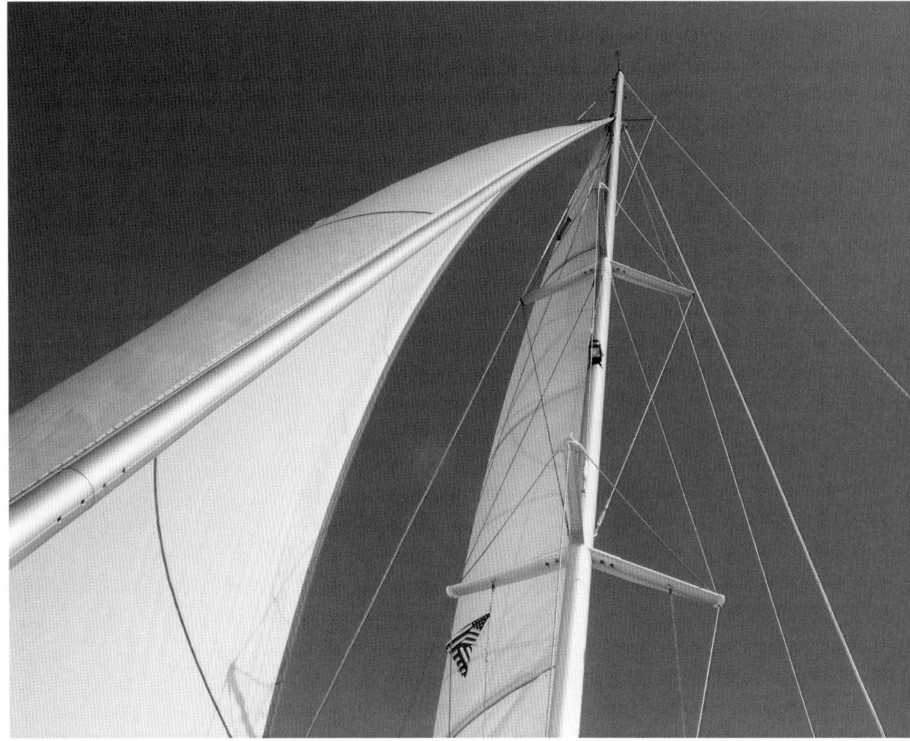

above The fractional, or 7/8 rig, is the most commonly used on modern cruising cats. It has the advantage of featuring a shorter forestay as compared to a masthead rig, which allows less luff sag and because it lacks a permanent backstay, also permits fully roached mainsails.

Shrouds on a monohull often have two functions – they keep the mast in column, and they prevent it from falling over. Fractional-rigged catamaran masts function differently. Single- or double-diamond stays hold the mast in column, while the shrouds serve only to hold the mast upright.

Masts on multihulls are always deck-stepped and are well supported via the heaviest component of the boat's structure, which is the central crossbeam. Although we have seen that the 7/8 rig will reduce the downward force of the mast, the compression at the mast step can be huge. This force has to be balanced by the tension of the forestay which, in turn, pulls up from the forward crossbeam. It is therefore key to have a stiff forward crossbeam, which still must be able to slightly articulate under a large strain in order to prevent it from breaking. Too often have I seen crossbeams that are laminated to the hulls. They will inevitably crack or be compromised as a result of the tremendous torsional forces in that critical zone. The best way to brace the crossbeam is in the form of a massive pin, flanked by large Delrin washers. Like a tree in a storm, they will allow a slight movement of the forward crossbeam, dissipating the twisting loads of the hulls.

below Nic Bailey's beautifully ingenious catamaran "Impossible Dream," especially designed and built for a handicapped sailor. She features a continuous, wraparound, one-level cockpit – foredeck, from which the skipper can, single-handedly, operate all sail controls.

One should briefly note an exception to the popular fractional rig, as used on the hundreds of Prout catamarans which were popular in the '70s and '80s. With a mast stepped more than halfway back, Prouts carried a tiny mainsail and because of that, a very large genoa. The advantage was the small main sail, which could be quickly reefed, as it was only an arm's length from the cockpit. The large genoa could simply be furled via a roller-furling drum. An added benefit was that the headstay angle was shallower, which exerted less compression on the mast. Some owners even claimed that because of that, the genoa created a component of vertical lift. I hope that this was true for their sake, as these vessels had very little bridgedeck clearance, were heavily constructed, and had full-length bridge decks all the way to the bows. Nevertheless, the sail plan seemed to work for that particular design, yet it appears outdated and inefficient by today's standards.

Stepping a mast on each of a catamaran's hulls has been done occasionally but never gained popularity for cruising. "Team Philips" and Yves Parlier's "Hydraplaneur" were prime examples of this rig, which is also referred to as the Biplane Rig. The advantage of this sail plan is that it divides the sail surface into two manageable sizes and lowers the Center of Effort, thereby reducing the heeling force. Effectively, more sail power for the same capsizing moment is achieved and speed is augmented. Biplane-rigged boats will also turn through the wind faster, since both mainsails are self-tacking and downwind they will not blanket each other. Winged out on either side, they will balance the boat and eliminate the need for cumbersome headsails. Disadvantages of this design are the tremendous forces on the two mast partners at the deck level in the case of freestanding masts and more drag up high in case the biplane rig is stayed with shrouds.

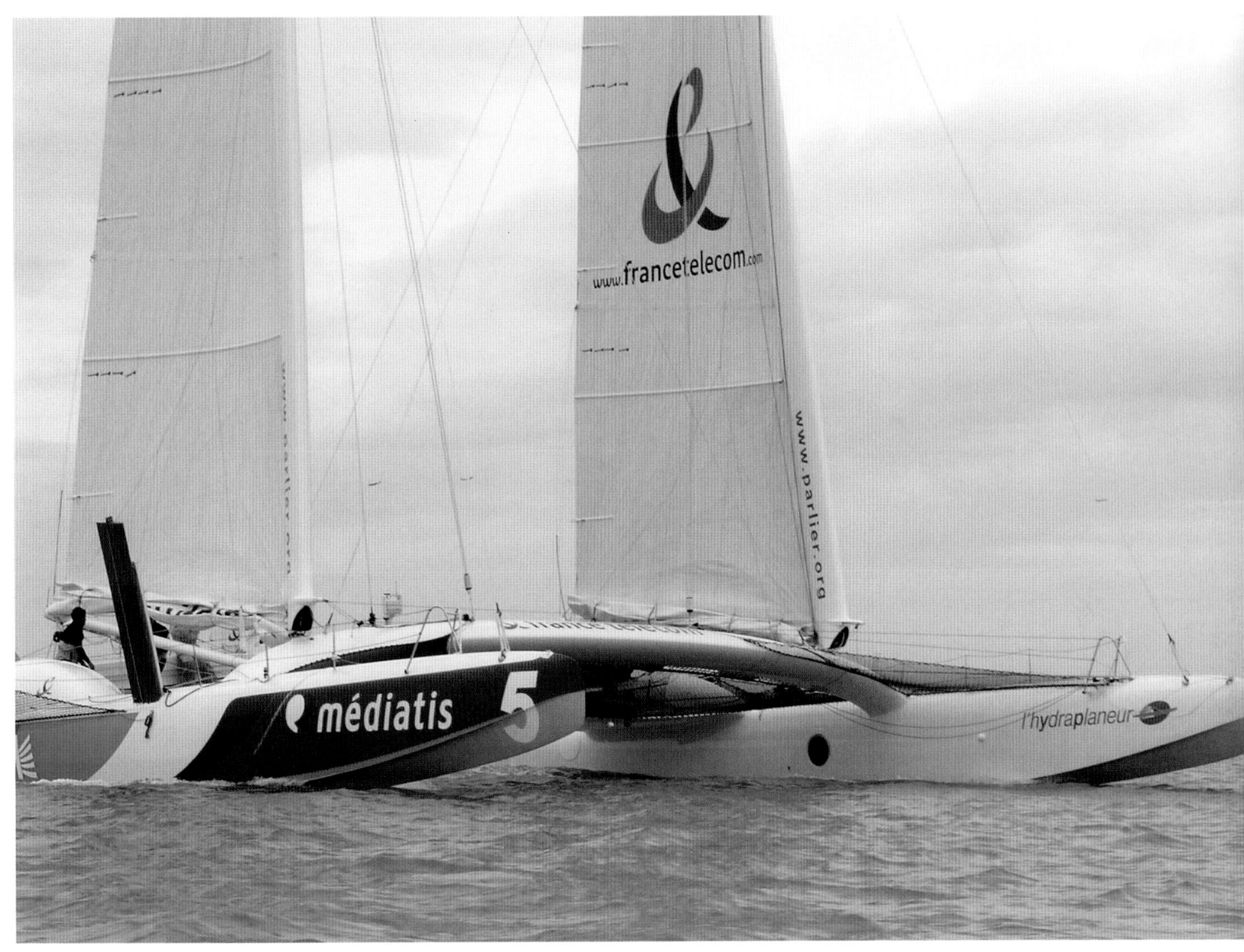

I was invited to test the 60' experimental ocean racer "Hydraplaneur" with legendary French superstar sailor Yves Parlier on a number of occasions. His biplane-rig masts were not stepped on deck but on the strongest part of the vessel's massive crossbeams. Compression of the rig was further eased by a mast brace, which acted as an articulating soft link high up by the hounds. Outboard shrouds were altogether lacking and smartly substituted by inner cross-stays. The mainsheet, in combination with the roach of the main and the forestay, always kept the independently rotating, twin wing masts stable in the fore-and-aft direction. The spreader link acted as a stabilizer while the inner shrouds assured athwartship stability.

Biplane rigs are an elegant way to rig a boat, keeping the loads low and allowing for a much lighter support structure. The added benefit of the twin rig is that in high apparent wind conditions – usually encountered on a fast boat – reefing the windward rig first also reduces some of the negative hydrodynamic pressure on the hulls. The faster the multihull, the more sense the biplane rig makes, especially for single-handing.

Mast

Most masts on production multihulls are fixed, non-articulating, aluminum extrusions and are therefore preferred for their reliability.

above Yves Parlier's radical "Hydraplaneur" showing her advanced stepped hulls and biplane rig. Note how the masts are stepped on the crossbeams and not on deck; this reduces compression loads and allows a lighter build.

Shroud, forestay and leach tensions are counteracted by the compression of the mast on the central crossbeam, necessitating this critical zone to be one of the strongest structures on a catamaran. Loads are measured in tons. In some recent mishaps, high-strung and under-built America's Cup racing monohulls broke in half because of these massive rig forces.

Rig Forces & Fore and Aft Bending

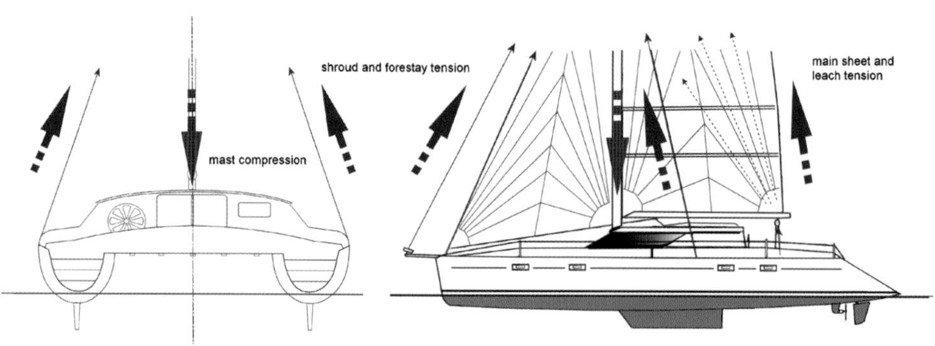

We should also look at rotating masts which, if properly designed, have advantageous applications even on a cruising catamaran.

As we have seen, multihull masts must cope with a large range of loads. Since momentary rig forces can be 50% higher than on monohulls, the entire rig and its support system must be stronger. This can either be achieved by beefing up the wall thickness of the mast section or by increasing its cross-sectional area. Both have their advantages and drawbacks, and it is again up to the designer to find the proper balance. Increasing the wall thickness of the mast will make it stiffer, but also heavier. On the other hand, enlarging its chord will increase windage and, if non-rotating, will spoil the important incidence of air onto the leading edge of the mainsail. Both solutions bear undesirable features, especially up high on a multihull. Another way to resist bending is to leave the mast section as it is and add more shrouds and stays, which again is not the best in terms of windage and air drag.

Halyards can exert a considerable amount of additional compression onto the mast; therefore, it is recommended that 2:1 halyards be utilized wherever practical. Long halyard tails might need more care in handling and stowing, yet the asset of having more purchase power to raise the mainsail, or haul someone up the mast, are additional benefits of a two-part halyard.

Often, increasing the mast's cross-section is the only way to accomplish column stiffness; yet being able to shape that larger section into an aerofoil, and streamlining it into the mainsail, seems to have additional benefits. That is where the rotating mast comes in. Similar to a fixed mast, it can be self-supporting and held upright by only three wires, yet because it needs to rotate the compression is less. Mast engineers' prime objective is to structure a column that resists bending under axial compression. But, unlike the fixed non-rotating mast type, there is less down force on the mast as it is allowed to pivot around a ball located at its base. Shroud tension is usually considerably less and the big advantage of being able to turn the mast's leading edge into the oncoming airflow will reduce windage. In fact, it will effectively "pre-bend" the wind onto the mainsail luff.

Usually the angle of attack of the mast can be changed with control lines and a purchase system, which is located under the gooseneck or close to the mast base. Being able to rotate the mast will clean up the turbulence on the all-important back side of the mainsail

below The absolute best way to attach shrouds to a multihull. Aramid lashings are very strong, extremely reliable and easy to visually inspect.

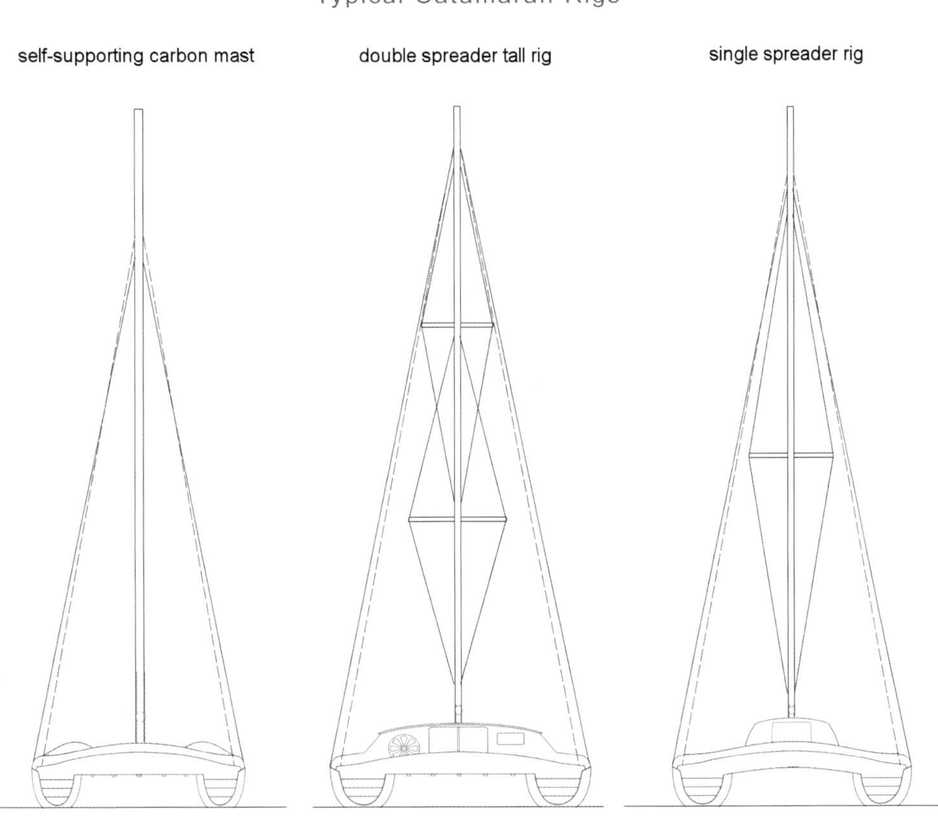

and will benefit both light-air and heavy-weather performance. The efficiency of the mainsail can be considerably improved by permitting mast rotation to the correct angle of attack in relation to the apparent wind. Most of the drive of a sail is developed on the low-pressure, leeward side, and reducing turbulence where it counts will be rewarded with higher speeds.

Rotating masts are not without drawbacks as we will discover. First, they can be considered a big moving part and we all know that whatever moves could shift more than we would want and break. Further, careful attention must be paid to the proper engineering of the hounds and the mast base. A lot of loads congregate in those zones, yet they must be designed to allow for safe operation and movement. Lastly, rotating masts present aligning problems for navigation lights and radar units. Often complicated electronic compensators need to be installed to allow for recalibrating rotation angles.

Wing masts are basically rotating masts taken one step further. Their cord is exaggerated and they can generate massive lift. Some advocates swear by them, some even say they are practical storm sails, yet in my mind they are too high to be used as heavy-weather sails and can easily overpower the boat. Since they cannot be reefed, they are impractical and cannot be recommended for cruisers.

Freestanding masts had a short blip on the monohull radar screen in the mid '80s, when Freedom Yachts built its mandrel spun carbon masts at TPI in New England. They made a lot of sense as they eliminated standing rigging. They were

below Forward crossbeams should always be attached to the hulls by a pin, by far the strongest way to deal with the massive loads experienced in these crucial areas. Small Delrin bushings allow minimal flex, thereby dissipating the slight torque movement of the beam. Some boats which have rigid attachments can develop fatigue cracks in that important zone.

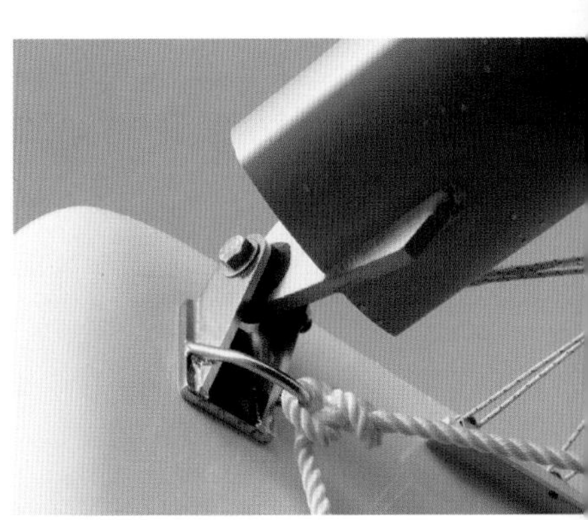

above With no one standing at the wheel, modern autopilots reliably steer the boat for days on end. Observe the poled out clew of the asymmetric spinnaker, braced to windward, to present more sail area to the wind.

all keel stepped and needed to be braced by massive structures at deck level. A monohull, which can dump wind pressure when heeling, can dissipate mast loads easier than a super stable multihull. Few biplane, free-standing rigs have been tried on catamarans, but the feasibility, especially in view of the deck loads, is questionable. The essence of a multihull is light weight and stiff construction. The need for heavy bracing would negate this philosophy. Most importantly, fast multihulls bring the wind forward and sail upwind all the time, which necessitates a decent headsail and tight forestay – both of these are omitted features on freestanding masts. Besides it would be nearly impossible to "keel" step a mast into a catamaran's hull.

Aside from the spruce and telephone pole rigs of the past, the most popular material for masts is aluminum and carbon. The subject of carbon fiber masts is a long one and best reserved for mechanical engineers. If one is looking for all-out performance, no matter what the price, carbon fiber makes a lot of sense. Any ounce saved up high in the rig is worth ten times its weight down low. Carbon fiber is a man-made miracle and its stiffness characteristics are among the best in the world. It is incredibly resilient in both tension and compression and shows great durability. And – it is very expensive! The truth is that one has to really weigh the benefit of a few pounds saved aloft versus the $80,000 it will cost to do so. However, carbon as a material has to be carefully scrutinized. In fact, it is produced in a variety of moduli and a top-quality aluminum mast could be better than a low modulus carbon type. Reliability is also an issue. Lately there have been a number of lightning strikes on carbon rigs, which could have something to do with their conductivity characteristics.
If I were to build a personal multihull racer, carbon would be my choice (if I could afford it). For an easily serviced world voyager, I'd take a good aluminum mast any day, and get a longer boat with the savings.

Sails

The main driving power of the working sail plan of a multihull is derived from its mainsail. Typically they are fully battened and loose-footed to permit maximum camber adjustment.
Due to the higher speeds of multihulls, sails are frequently cut much flatter and, generally, are also of heavier construction than those on a monohull.

Mainsails can have large roaches, which increase their area up high, where it counts. Winds aloft usually are stronger, and being able to capture them is of great advantage, especially in light air. Fully battened mainsails can have up to 60% more surface area than a conventional 18" roach as seen on the typical monohull main. The additional area can be applied either to making the boat go faster, or to reducing the rig height and the overall Center of Gravity (CG). But the efficiency of the sail plan increases with its aspect ratio, and the taller the luff is, relative to the length of the foot, the more power the rig will generate. However, care must be taken that the Center of Effort (CE) is not moved too high as that will affect stability, and might even induce pitching, which compromises airflow over the sails. Interestingly, the phenomenon of weather- and lee-helm on a catamaran can work in exact opposition to what is known to be true on a monohull. As the catamaran heels, it moves the CE athwartships and forward. As the hulls are depressed, the Center of Lateral Resistance (CLR) also edges towards the bows. Again, a delicate balance must be found to provide the most power with the least consequences in stability.

Designers have to dial in the correct sail area for each specific boat and application. A multihull should not be under-canvassed in light air nor easily overpowered in stronger conditions. Aside from mast height limitations and practical aspects of sail handling, the total sail area needs to allow for adequate performance and must be shared between mainsail and jib. Both sails, in turn, have to be in harmony with each other, since their combined Center of Effort (CE) is in direct relationship with the Center of Lateral Resistance of the underbody (CLR).

Multihull mainsails are fully battened, and what a fabulous invention battens are! Sailors can be grateful to the ancient Chinese seafarers for this superb feature found on every single catamaran. Reefing a

Lift & Pressure Distribution

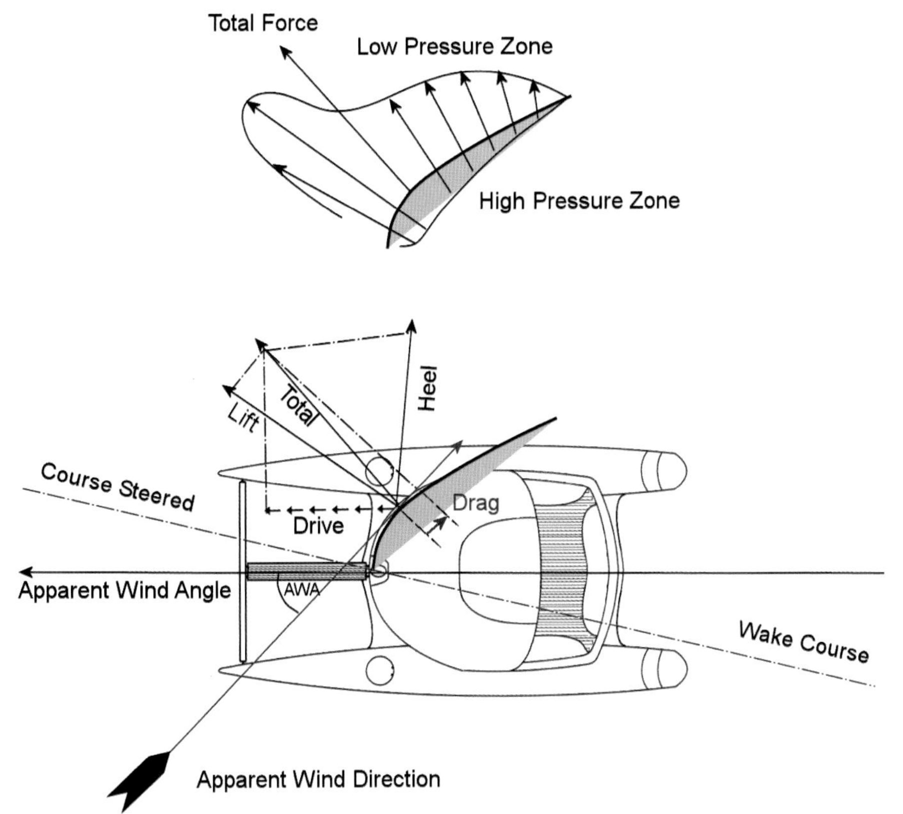

Most of the lift is developed at the leading edge of the sail where the low pressure zone is responsible for the forward drive of the vessel. Observe the varying strength of the forward force vectors and how they are distributed over the chord of the sail. The lowest pressure is generated in the first 20% of the width of the airfoil and the resultant total force acts through the Center of Effort at about one third aft of the mast.

above To eliminate cluttered decks some catamarans lead all sail controls via conduits underneath the bridgedeck to a centralized winch in the cockpit. Although this keeps lines neatly organized, any line knots or break could involve cumbersome rethreading, possibly under difficult circumstances.

catamaran's main will decrease material and human stress levels as there is no wild luffing, and the noise of the flogging sail will be completely eliminated by the stiffness of the battens. A catamaran's mainsail is silent and its shaped battens force the sail into an airfoil curve. That is especially helpful in light winds when there is not enough air pressure to stabilize a battenless sail and make it draw.

Battens support our mainsail's roach and they help us reef and stow the sail. Additionally, they prolong the life of a mainsail, since they spread the forces evenly across the cloth and prevent the material from moving and creeping. The best feature is their adjustability although only a few catamaran sailors take advantage of this. Screwjacks on either end of the batten pockets permit tensioning, consequently, one can change the curvature of the batten. That, in turn, will shape the chord of the mainsail. Of course nothing is perfect. Fully battened mainsails are not cheap, they can be heavy and, above all, airflow over them is difficult to read as they are so stable. Also, if one is not careful when gybing, one can also break them and single-handedly changing a batten on a 64 foot multihull at sea is not easy. Sailmakers have worked hard to make battens more reliable and nowadays they come in a variety of materials; solid or hollow fiberglass or carbon tubes are the most popular.

Usually mainsails are loose-footed along the boom. Their flatness is controlled primarily by the outhaul, mainsail traveler and sheet. Running backstays, if applicable, will assist too, while halyard tension and Cunningham controls move the draft forward.

Sails for multihulls have to be of bulletproof construction and reef points should be heavily reinforced, much more so than on a monohull. In the monohull world, boat weight dictates the thickness of material to be utilized to build a sail, leading to the deduction that a light multihull can get away with light sails. In fact, quite the opposite is true. The lighter the catamaran, the faster she will accelerate and the more pressure the sails will feel, necessitating extra heavy and flat sail construction. Luckily, advancements in sail materials, such as new Polyester composites, Carbon, Spectra and Kevlar are innovative fibers, which are both strong, light, and are ideally suited for multihulls. Considerations such as cost, durability, UV protection, chafe resistance and hygroscopic characteristics will be other factors that will dictate which sail construction to use.

Sail adjustments on multihulls, especially those that are fast, will have a greater effect on the vessel's response than sail trim on a slower monohull. The magic of apparent wind can radically change the angle of airflow, greatly influencing a catamaran's performance. Therefore, main and headsails have to be cut much flatter, unless the boat is heavy, which would require more powerful, deeper draft sails.

A key to safe catamaran sailing is the ability to lower the sails regardless of the apparent wind angle or sea conditions. You have to be able to reef instantly in any condition. Compression loads on battens can be huge and the bigger the mainsail, the higher the forward force against the mast track. Modern mainsail tracks and batt-car systems will assure that you can reef the mainsail even downwind. This is my preferred heavy-weather technique, especially when shorthanded in big beam seas.

The battens at the luff of the main are usually nesting in an end fitting, which has a freely articulating-but-strong attachment to the mast track car. The majority of these sliders rely on Delrin or other UHMWPE (Ultra High Molecular Weight Polyethylene) balls to reduce the compression load and friction of the mainsail. These ball-bearing type of cars must be carefully maintained since frequent heavy use eventually will result in failure. As an alternative one could opt for ball-less batten cars, which reduce friction via a Teflon-coated inner material. Although they might not be as efficient as roller-type fittings, they will need no maintenance other than an occasional hose down with fresh water.

Working headsails come in two varieties: the self-tacking jib and the overlapping genoa. Both have their merits and drawbacks.

below Some catamarans feature forward cockpits, which are located ahead of the saloon windows. The crew sits directly aft of the mast and all sail controls are close at hand.

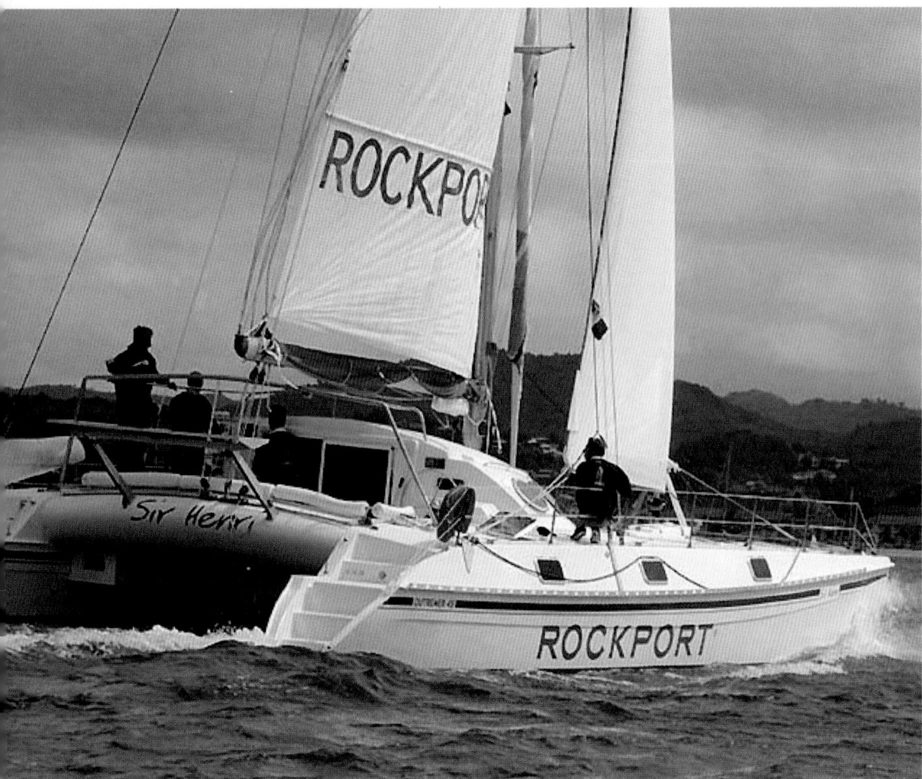

above "Rockport," an Outremer 45, winning yet another ARC Transatlantic Race. Although not as roomy as other cats in their class, the Outremer multihulls are known for their performance and strong, reliable construction.

far right Two common rig and sail handling features found on modern catamarans: the so-called "Seagull Striker," as seen here with a wire tensioner, and the reliable jib furler. Care should be taken to have enough wraps around the barrel and to lead the furling line fairly away from the drum in order to avoid reefing problems.

Whereas the self-tacking jib (the French call it "Solent") only has one sheet, it can swing through the wind without having to release the old and trim the new windward sheet, as on a genoa. The self-tacking jib, similar to the mainsail, has a huge wind window and a wide range of applications. It is a highly versatile sail and, if properly cut and reinforced, it can be reefed and used as a storm jib. Opponents might argue the added windage and inefficiency of a rolled up jib replacing a proper, hanked on storm jib. In my opinion, especially in extreme conditions, it is safer to stay in the cockpit and quickly roll the jib to a manageable size, rather than delaying the decision because of the risky trip forward to deploy the storm jib. We often have used the heavily reefed Solent successfully, even in F10 conditions and never felt the need for a storm jib. In case one is forced to sail to windward in heavy weather, a proper storm jib would certainly have the edge. However, if one has a choice when sailing in big winds and seas, it is always more comfortable to be sailing with the system. For that purpose a rolled up self-tacking jib is just perfect.

Roller-furling mechanisms are key devices for safe multihull sailing. They must allow smooth operation in any condition. The last 20 years have brought great advances in the engineering of sailboat hardware and long gone are the days when furlers would suddenly fail. There are a variety of manufacturers that make extremely reliable roller-furling hardware for any type of catamaran.

A self-tacking jib makes a lot of sense when single handing, or short tacking up a channel. Draft and twist can be adjusted with the sail's own jib track, which is usually just ahead of the mast step. To fine-tune it, barber haulers can be fitted to adjust the important slot between the mainsail and the jib. Especially if one is expecting to sail in strong wind conditions, the self-tacking jib (and autopilot) will become your best and most dependable friends.

In contrast to the self-tacking jib, the genoa is a headsail that is still seen on most monohulls. Since the clew of the genoa overlaps the mast, it requires a windward and leeward sheet to control it. One cannot tack without undoing one and trimming with the other sheet. The genoa, apparently invented by an Italian sailor, is a sail that will provide more power than the Solent. This is also the reason that it is utilized by most medium-displacement cruising catamaran manufacturers. Similar to the self-tacking jib, it can be rolled up and reefed to handle stronger conditions.

Gennakers, screachers or Code numbered sails are very large roller-furled headsails on a soft luff, typically flown from a bowsprit. They are sheeted to a block way aft on the outside rail and, depending on the wind speed and sea state, can be flown from a range of 45 to 170 degrees of apparent wind angles. Unlike the genoa and Solent, they cannot be reefed. Usually they employ a Spectra luff and need careful attention when it is time to take them in. Similar to reefing a multihull's mainsail in stormy conditions, and in exact contrast to our instincts, multihulls should have the wind aft of the beam when furling them. This will reduce the pressure and apparent wind, and make the operation manageable.

Sailing downwind on a catamaran is a pleasant experience and is not hindered by the distracting motion of monohull type rolling. Spinnakers come as two types, either symmetric or asymmetric, depending on their cut. Neither of these strictly downwind sails rely on cumbersome spinnaker poles and reaching struts, as found on monohulls.

The faster the multihull, the less a spinnaker will be necessary for downwind sailing, because the apparent wind will be brought forward. Gennakers will be used instead and the boat will be tacked downwind faster than running straight towards the destination. Besides, it is significantly more fun to have the wind in your hair and sailing on a reach than on a dead run. Spinnakers are usually hoisted to the same position as the gennaker, which is just above the hounds, or even to the masthead. A great innovation is the sock that the sail lives in. Like a giant snake, the entire contraption is hoisted before the sock is pulled up, exposing the sail to the wind. Similar to a monohull, sheets and forward guys stabilize the sail.

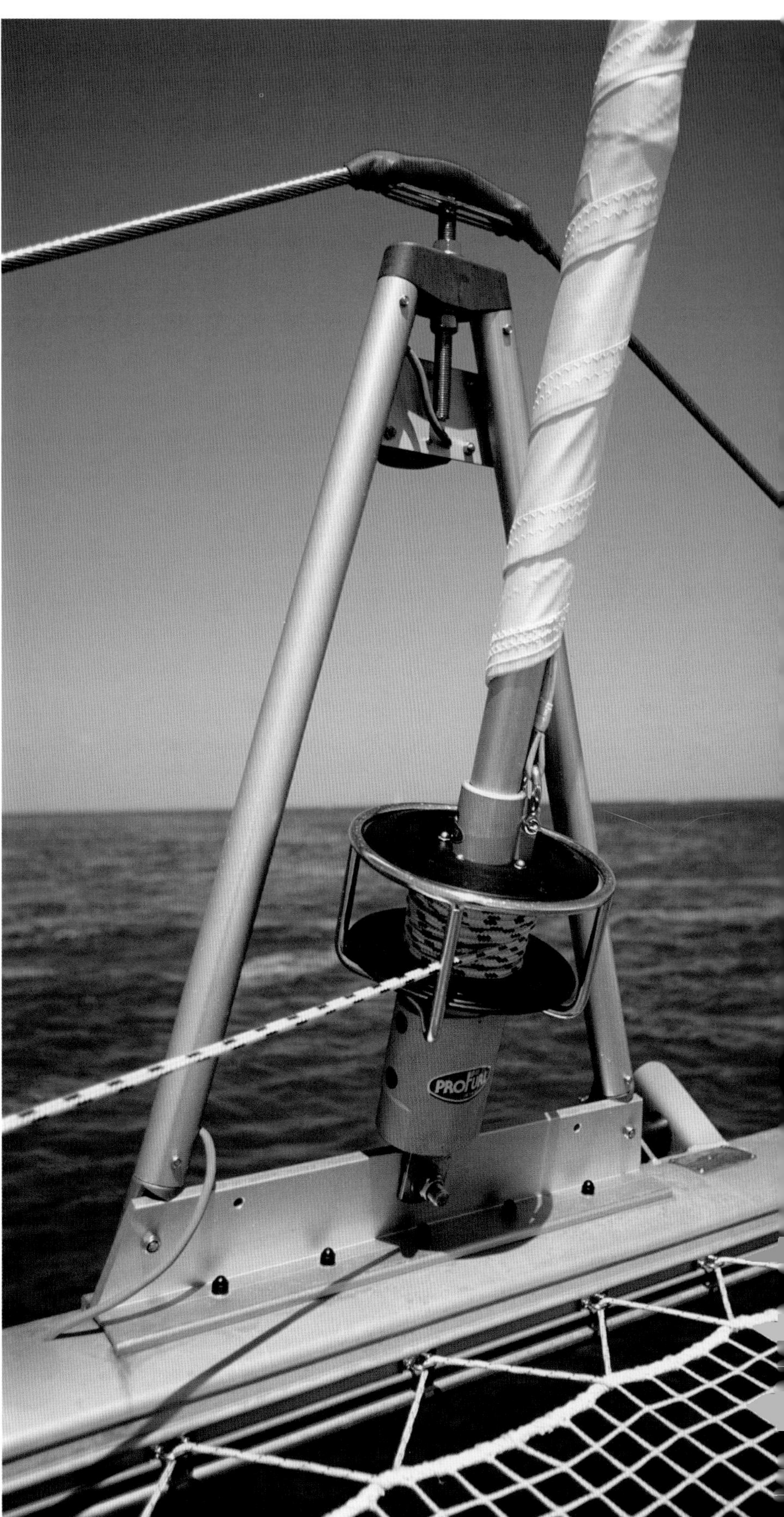

"The most beautiful thing one can experience is the mysterious.
It is the source of all true art and science.
He to whom this reaction is a stranger –
who no longer can pause to wonder and stand rapt in awe –
is as good as dead, his eyes are closed."

~ Albert Einstein

State of the art multihull
manufacturing assures a
consistent construction p
resulting in boats that wi
their value even after ye
hard service, eliminating
as often found in a totall
built, one-off, project.

CONSTRUCTION

Composite & Aluminum

I would rather take a boxy, heavy, but well-constructed boat to sea than a dubiously assembled fast racer. In fact, I would prefer to cross the bay in a well-built monohull before risking my life on an inadequately built catamaran. Most sailors will agree that careful construction, especially when it comes to multihulls, cannot be underestimated. Any boat venturing into the ocean must be built by exacting engineering principles and construction methods. Wide beamed catamarans will experience more complex and often higher loads than a monohull and, therefore, the greatest emphasis on bulletproof construction must be made. Since the main emphasis of this book is production cruising catamarans, we will focus on composite construction, which is the most popular building method.

The term "composite construction" implies a high-tech process, which actually it is not. From a tennis racquet to the book you are holding, everything manufactured could be construed as being made up of a series of parts. Even a hide and wood teepee built by Native Americans could be called "composite built." Similarly, the basic anatomy of a multihull is an assembly of a combination of suitable materials for the construction of a sailing machine that will have to face one of our planet's most hostile environments. It has to keep its crew safe, perform well and, on top of all that, keep a shiny finish.

In terms of production boat manufacturing, nothing can beat the advantages of sandwich construction. It yields a very stiff, mass producible and high-quality structure. In this process, the entire surface area of a boat, including hulls, decks, and often the interior components, are made up of FRP skins (Fiber Reinforced Plastic), which are separated by a core sandwich material.

The underlying idea of a sandwich laminate is to separate the two skins as far as possible to create a stiff panel. Similar to the classic I-beam, the farther apart the skins are, the stronger the structure. In fact, the stiffness of the entire configuration is directly proportional to the cube of the separation distance. The farther the load-bearing surface is from the center, the thicker the panel and the stronger the sandwich laminate will be. Of course, the lighter the core material, the better, as there is less to support. Although the I-beam example is a good one, it differs greatly from a composite skin of a boat since, typically, an all-steel I-beam is a homogenous structure, where each molecule has exactly the same properties. This just shows how intricate multihull engineering is, as different characteristics have to be taken into account before selecting the correct combination for a given application.

Plastic reinforcements come in different shapes, quality levels, and fibers, of which Kevlar, carbon, E and S-Glass are the most commonly used. Each of them has advantages over the other, yet all share the same function of adding strength and stiffness while adding minimal weight. Often, combinations of fibers, known as "hybrids," are utilized – depending on various load parameters in certain areas of the boat. Just like a Kelim (a flat woven, linen/cotton-blend carpet), Kevlar could be woven into carbon strands, or glass could be added to Kevlar to create just the right fabric. Every single fiber or core material stands out by having a unique characteristic, which is superior to the other, but there is not one overall winner. This is where composite construction excels. It takes the best features of each, and by assembling them it creates a stronger structure, which is far superior than the sum of its parts.

Polyester, Vinylester and Epoxy resins can be seen as the composite glues, for they bond the laminate structure. Each has its advantages. Epoxy resin has excellent secondary bonding qualities, superior resistance to water absorption and has the strongest tensile strength. Next down the scale is Vinylester, which is cheaper, easier to work with, and less sensitive to variations in the manufacturing environment, such as humidity, temperature and pressure. However, it is stronger and more water-resistant than Isophthalic polyester resin, which is the most economical yet has great latitude in the building process. Polyester resins can be handled in a wider environment and skill range, and can be repaired much easier. This is also why it is the number one choice of production builders who warranty their boats confidently for up to 5 years against structure and osmosis problems.

Similar to the skins, core materials must have unique characteristics as they have to separate the outer and inner laminates. Core materials must resist compression and shear forces, yet must also permanently stay attached and not delaminate from the two FRP skins. The most common core materials, such as Airex and Divinycell, are made of PVC. Sometimes balsa is also used as a core material as it is superior in its compressive strength and exposure to the sun. Balsa wood's drawback is its dry weight, which can become even heavier when exposed to moisture. That is also the reason why PVC is the most popular core as it has excellent hygroscopic properties and hardly absorbs any water.

Vacuum-bagging techniques assure that the sandwich structure stays together until it cures and hardens. In that process the wet composite is covered with an airtight barrier-film, and by creating a vacuum, physical pressure is applied as air is removed. This assures that all layers adhere to each other without creating any voids. Far superior techniques are the various infusion processes, which, basically, all work similarly. The idea is to inject a controlled amount of resin into the dry laminate, apply pressure and at the end, extract by suction the unused glue. This method ensures the

above In the world of molded catamaran construction, the product is only as good as the female mold it is pulled from. Here an infusion mold is undergoing final inspection and polishing, before the composite layup process commences. A well-built mold can produce over 150 boats before starting to warp.

Relative Impact Resistance & Cost of Fibers (scale of 0–10)

	Cost	Impact Resistance
E-Glass	2	8
S-Glass	3	10
Kevlar	6	9.5
Carbon	10	2.5

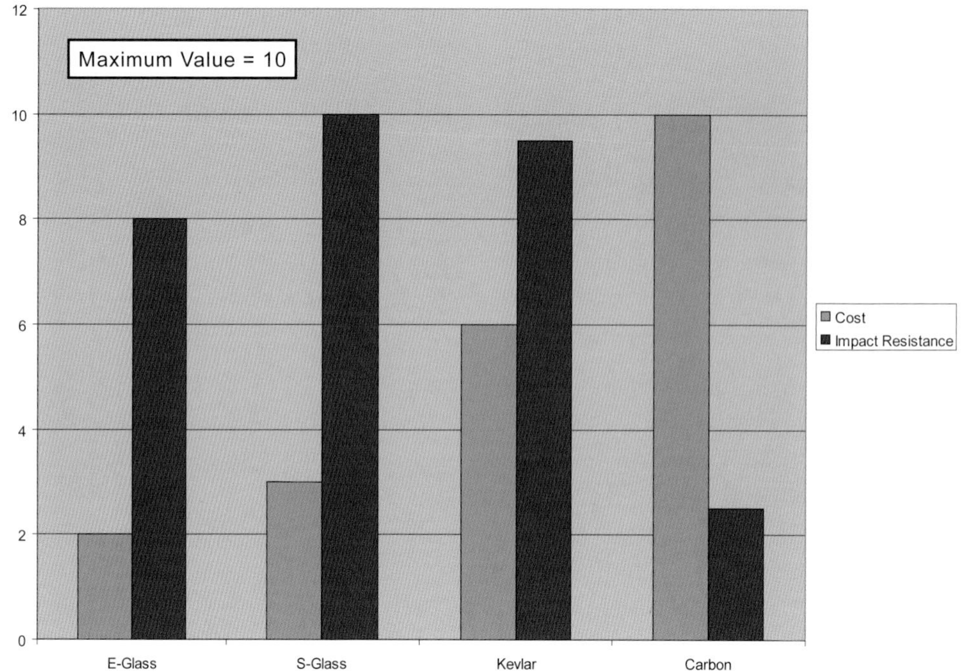

Relative Tensile Strength & Stiffness of Fibers (scale of 0–10)

	Tensile Strength	Stiffness
E-Glass	5	2
S-Glass	8	3
Kevlar	10	7
Carbon	8.7	10

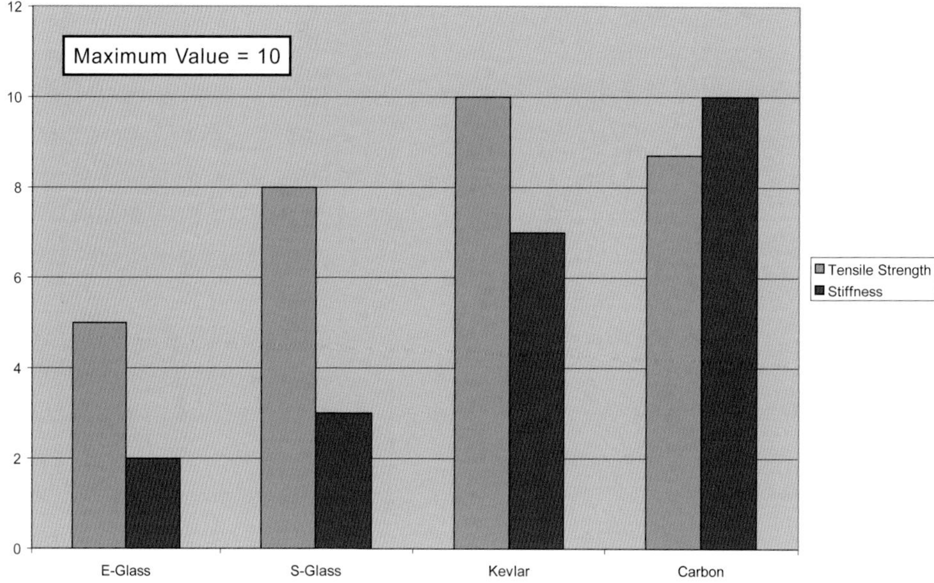

ideal resin-to-fiber ratio and prevents the accumulation of unreinforced resin into pools that might weaken the structure. Resin is only as strong as the structure it bonds, similar to household glue, which is only as solid as the surfaces it cements.

The entire lamination process is set up in gigantic female molds, which are mirror polished to perfection. It is not unusual for a 45' catamaran to have only 2 molds for its entire outside skin, including hulls and decks. In these molds the boat is built from the outside in, starting with the release agent (usually a wax), gelcoat and the sandwich laminate. There are no more hull-to-deck joints that can leak, as the two giant halves are laminated from both sides. It is like putting a lid on a steel box and then welding the seam. Gone are the days of infamous hull-to-deck leaks.

Normally the bilge areas of the hulls are left without core. This has the purpose of strengthening the lower part of the hull and to prevent compression due to the weight of the boat when beaching. Closely spaced bulkheads, usually composite, divide the hulls, while longitudinal stringers run along the side of the boat. This system divides the interior into a stiff grid system, which serves as a basis for the interior. Most manufacturers fit the majority of the accommodations and overhead before the deck is laminated to the hulls. To assure a perfect finish even these surfaces are composite panels, which are taken off female molds. From countertops to shower compartments – everything is molded to perfection.

In the end, composite construction is really a fancy word for saving weight without losing strength. Different areas of the vessel experience different active and static loads. Instead of building an entirely homogenous structure throughout the entire boat, greater strength is provided to locations that need it, whereas other areas that are stressed less are built lighter. It all comes down to the Finite Element Analysis of a given section, which defines its strength requirements. It can be achieved in many ways, either by heavier scantlings (more layup or denser, stiffer or thicker foam) or more exotic materials (carbon and Kevlar).

Typically it takes up to 6,000-8,000 hours to build the average-size multihull. They are very expensive structures; we are all reminded of that when visiting the boat shows and checking the sticker price. Yet, they are incredibly complex machines and have to work reliably for decades. Boats are exposed to forces beyond imagination – humidity, heat, freezing cold, impact with waves and salt water, one of the most corrosive substances in nature. Still, they have to sit pretty and look good from the inside and outside, provide all amenities of home, and they had all better perform and always function, even after long periods of sitting at a marina unused! Presently, there is no known shelf life for composite boats. The technique was started in the mid-1950s and boats built at that time can still be found floating in the back alleys of the Caribbean. Molded composite construction has made multihull production feasible, if large numbers of a certain model are built. Not only does that require sufficient market demand, but a large organization with dedicated engineers, craftsmen and sales people who stand behind their product. It also demands good design, for who would spend hundreds of thousands of dollars to develop tooling just to produce a series of mediocre vessels? But it has happened, and companies went down with their boats. Builders who construct less than a handful of multihulls per year and/or constantly have the urge to modify their design are better off using one-off construction techniques, such as strip plank on male molds or aluminum.

below A "plug" (male part, which forms a female mold) is being board-sanded and prepared for tooling. Great care is required at this stage as any imperfections at the shaping process will be transferred to the female mold.

Sandwich Panel Under Load

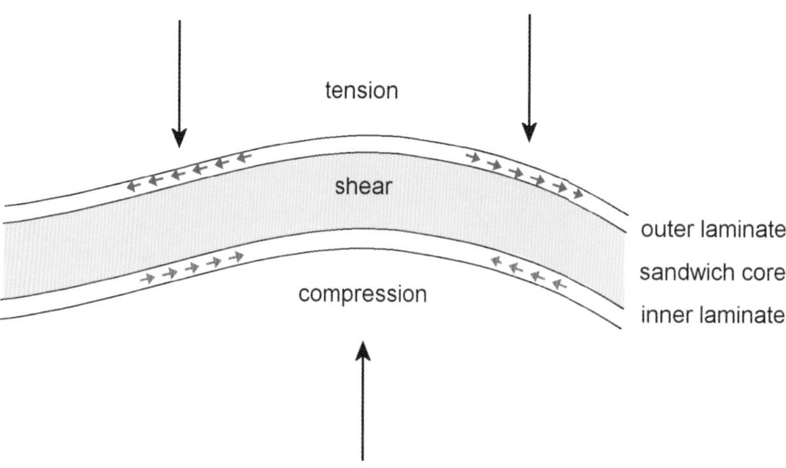

Aluminum is rarely used on multihulls of less than 50 feet unless performance is way down on the list. New materials such as AluStar and Silium metal multihulls will save up to 15% in the structure, but small metal boats are heavier than they have to be and there is no way around it as this example will illustrate; unlike on ballasted monohulls the smaller catamarans' superstructure surface becomes a significant part relative to its entire displacement. Imagine a cruise liner weighing many hundreds of tons. The weight of its heavy metal hull and deck represent only a small percentage of its entire mass of machinery, passengers and stores. In contrast a tiny 18 foot beach cat has nearly 100% of its entire weight in its structure. Building the "Titanic's" hull and deck out of lightweight composites would have made as much sense as building the small beach cat out of metal. Of course, this example is extreme, but illustrates the point.

Relative Tensile Strength & Stiffness of Resins (scale of 0–10)

	Stiffness	Tensile Strength
Polyester	6	8
Vinylester	6.8	9.7
Epoxy	10	10

Relative Tensile Strength & Stiffness of Resins

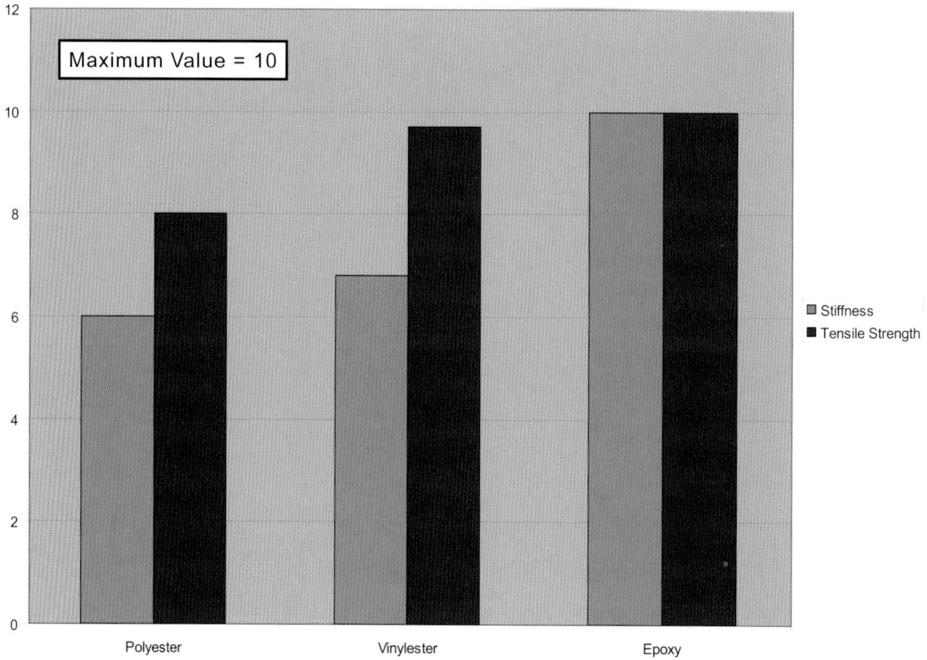

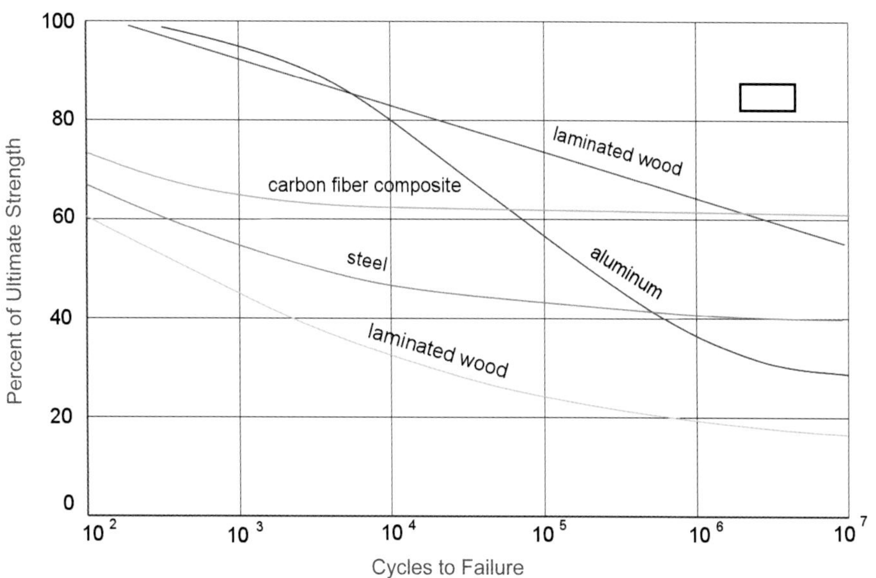

Tensile Strength

Various building materials possess different strength characteristics. It is interesting to note how their durability to cycling loads change as they weaken with use. Composites, such as carbon fiber or aramid layups, show the highest strength even after millions of cycles. Aluminum, which starts out as the strongest boat building material, loses two thirds of its strength after seven million test cycles, whereas carbon fiber is hardly affected.

Aluminum multihulls need to be welded with metal plates of a minimum practical wall thickness and this makes them heavy in sizes under 50'. Although most aluminum catamarans have thicker plating in the bilge area, becoming progressively thinner towards the topsides and deck, the structure is still heavy. Yet, builders cannot change the characteristics of the material and match it to the loads, thereby saving weight as in a composite construction. Typically a small aluminum multihull will be up to 15% heavier than its composite cousin. This is a lot of unnecessary weight. Not only the surface structure, but also the required, heavier engines, tankage, and hardware to drive the boat, will add to the load dilemma. Even history shows where aluminum multihulls had reached their limits. The handful of racers built in the '80s were a disaster, because they were either too heavy to win races or too light and broke apart.

In larger sizes, however, aluminum makes a lot of sense. Expensive plugs or molds do not have to be made and tooling as in composite construction is entirely eliminated. This is the reason that for non-production, one-off multihulls over 50', the usage of aluminum is hard to beat in terms of strength and cost. Tankage can be built into keel areas, fully utilizing the volume and also providing extra safety by creating a double bottom. Reputable shipyards radio-graph their welds and check them for accuracy before issuing a certificate of compliance to quality-classification societies such as Bureau Veritas, Lloyds or DNV. As long as galvanic corrosion is monitored, aluminum boats will never leak and are easily repaired in even the remotest cruising areas. This makes aluminum the most cost effective choice for large luxury vessels or open-ocean research catamarans.

For a production series, multihull composite construction is unbeatable, but in sizes between 50' and 200', customers for one-off catamarans have the choice of opting for aluminum. A composite custom catamaran might be slightly more expensive to build but will have the edge in performance and sailing sensation. For clients looking more for comfort rather than speed, aluminum is

next page bottom An advantage that building with aluminum has over composite construction techniques is the lack of expensive tooling. Often, just plywood jigs are erected on the shop floor, around which the boat is taking shape. In the foreground the flybridge coaming is being erected.

far right Finished aluminum hulls are only as smooth as the countless hours of sanding the filler makes them so it is imperative that, at the welding stage, the plates are fitted as accurately as possible. The best builders employ expert welders and allow less than 2 mm of weld tolerance.

Finite Element Analyses are highly complex computer studies of what is really happening to the structure of a 130' catamaran under maximum righting moment, sailing upwind. The entire surface area of the construction is divided into thousands of load cells, which provide feedback of the stresses involved. This allows engineers and builders to design sufficiently strong composites yet not overbuilding and burdening the vessel with unnecessary weight, which in turn needs to be supported, making the boat even heavier. Fascinating to see are the high stress zones (yellow and red) where the jib sheet leads are located on the coach house roof, the leading edge of the bridgedeck and the rudder stock on the leeward hull.

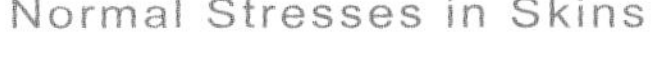

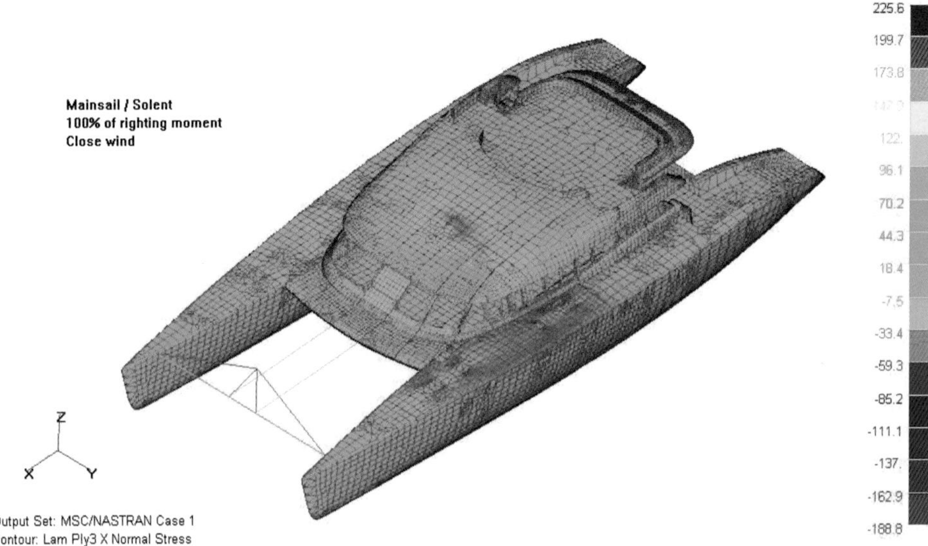

a sensible choice. Any owner who considers a fast yacht would choose a multihull. Opting to build a 35' catamaran in metal would be a contradiction to his mission. Nevertheless, aluminum has its virtues for larger yachts, one-off research vessels or work boats – the larger they are, and the less the focus is on record breaking performance, the more aluminum construction can be justified.

Finite Element Analyses and computer modeling are used to analyze complex engineering structures. This is a simulation technique whereby a mathematical model of a multihull is subjected to known loads and consequently properly engineered composites can be determined. Complex structures such as catamarans are suitable subjects for this clever method. Finite Element Analysis, which just recently made its way into the mainstream of pleasure boating, basically determines which areas of a multihull experience specific loads. Designers add safety factors to these results and can engineer laminates to deal with these forces, thus resulting in the optimum strength-to-weight ratio. Although one can apply Finite Element Analysis to metal vessels, one cannot fine-tune the structure as much as a composite boat. A given aluminum plate is simply what it is. It is the smallest denominator in the construction puzzle. As recently as a decade ago, engineers could not make composite construction viable for mega yachts; the explosion of the software industry and aramid fibers have changed all that.

"I made companionship with what was around me,
sometimes with the universe
and sometimes with my own insignificant self."

~ *Joshua Slocum* – Sailing Alone Around the World

MULTIHULL seamanship

The biggest factor for assuring the safety of the crew and boat is proper seamanship. It is an art form and can be practiced for years. Even after many ocean passages, prudent sailors will always discover something new to learn.

MULTIHULL SEAMANSHIP

Sailing is an Art and there are no defining right or wrong ways to perform maneuvers on a boat. Polynesian seafarers who plowed across the Pacific already knew this thousands of years ago. Their knowledge of navigation and seamanship was handed down by the leaders to their heirs and treated like a closely guarded mystic treasure of knowledge. Their expertise in navigation and sailing giant oceangoing multihulls was responsible for the successful colonization of distant islands. Polynesian mariners did not have the advantage of today's high-tech materials, electronics and sailhandling systems. All they could rely upon was their ability to handle their multihulls in any weather. So let's remember, however well designed, constructed and equipped your cat is, the one thing that will ensure its safety are experience, understanding and above all good seamanship.

It is my firm belief that every sailor should be able to singlehand his multihull unless the boat is set up as a fully crewed yacht. The importance of this cannot be emphasized enough. Most cruising catamarans are manned by a husband and wife team with occasional guests, who are usually novices. If one of the principal operators becomes incapacitated, it is up to the remaining crewmember to navigate and return to a safe harbor. If sailing is an art, single-handing is its highest manifestation.

I have sailed close to 80,000 miles on different types of vessels, monohulls and multihulls alike, and feel fortunate to have had the opportunity to share the adventure of the open ocean with people who have become my closest friends. If you are able to sail for a week with a stranger you will get to know him better than knowing anyone on land for a year. Getting along with your crew on ocean passages and weathering storms with them will bond you in a special way – unknown to people on terra firma.

In my many Atlantic crossings on different types of catamarans I have experienced days of calms but most of the time, moderate conditions, which did not test our skills. However, I remember very well, and so does my crew, the three days of a Force 10 storm that intercepted us in the middle of the Atlantic in winter. At the end we got through it because of our efforts as a team and by applying the art of seamanship.

Sailhandling – Monohull vs. Multihull

Sailing trim on a catamaran does not differ greatly from that on a monohull, yet to a large extent it will depend on your experience, the actual boat you sail, and your perspective. Since the basic sailing concepts

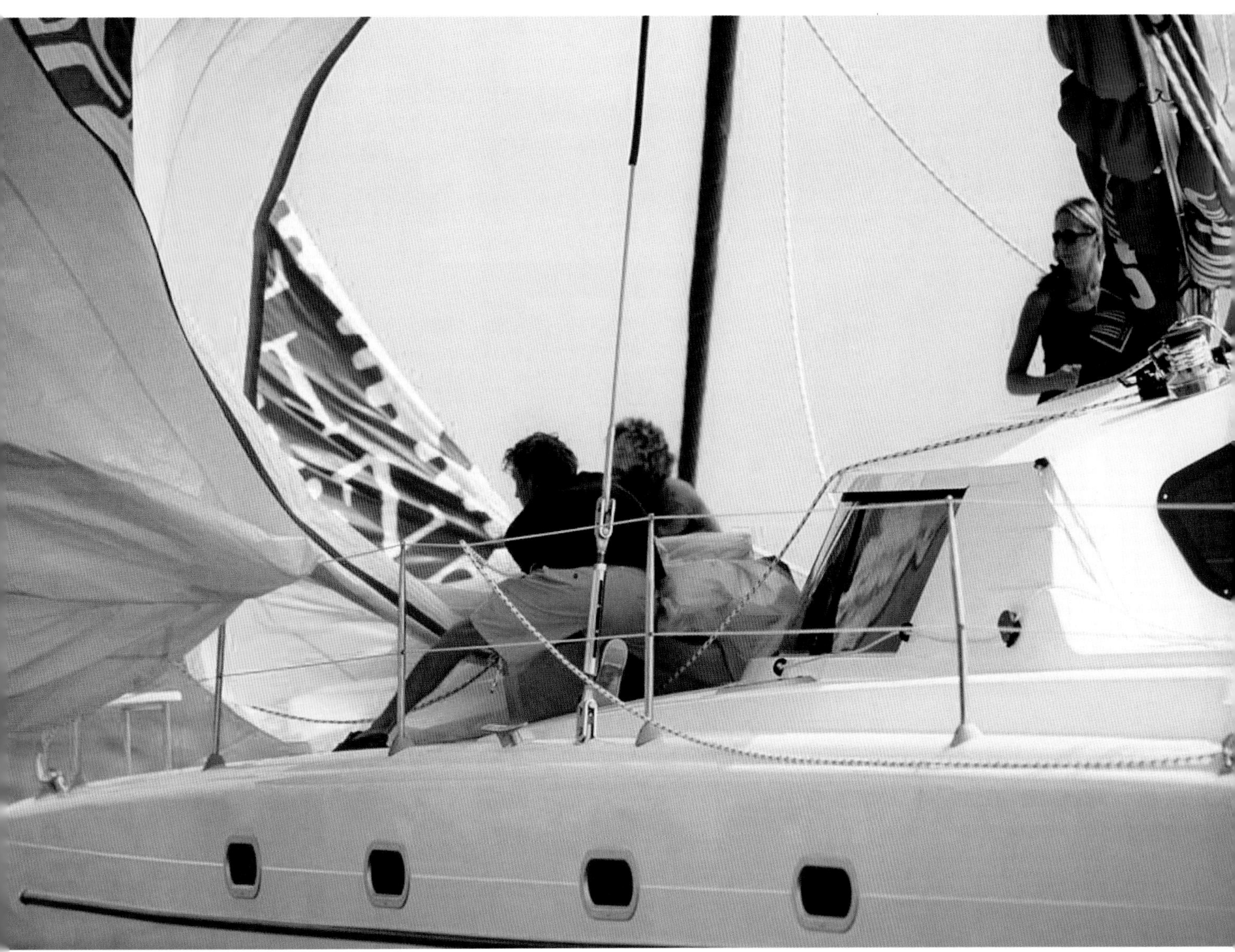

apply to multihulls as well, you'll find the experience similar to monohull sailing with subtle but important differences. Those new to the sport have few preconceptions about how a multihull should perform. They find multihulls relatively easy and forgiving boats to learn on as they aren't trying to subdue years of monohull sailing instincts. Becoming proficient at sailing in general, and at sailing a multihull in particular, become one and the same. While experienced monohull sailors have a firm foundation in basic techniques they need to get over the mindset of comparing multihull sailing to sailing one-hulled ballasted boats. Once they can do that the process is easy.

The boat you learn on tends to become your benchmark for what sailing is all about though handling varies remarkably between different designs. Despite the huge strides in market acceptance over the past few years there is still a tendency to lump all multihulls together. It is remarkable how cats differ more from each other than monohulls. Some sailors learn on a true cruising catamaran, quite a different experience from sailing a high-performance model.

Your viewpoint on what sailing is all about also influences your approach to multihulls. Some sailors aren't really sailing unless they are heeled over, cold, wet and tired. If you

above As the halyard is eased, gathering the spinnaker, even without the help of a spinnaker sock, is easy work for the crew on the spacious trampoline of this 43' catamaran.

above Barreling along with 12 people aboard, at over 14 knots under spinnaker, is both safe and fun on a stable multihull.

can relate to those sentiments you'll probably be disappointed with sailing a multihull. I personally have always taken great pleasure in the comfortable, protected sailing and quick passages a cruising catamaran provides.

There are also plenty of psychological adjustments monohull sailors might have to make when switching to a catamaran. We have seen that most midsized, cruising cats have either low profile fixed keels (draft typically ranges between 2' to 4') or daggerboards for which the depth can vary from less than 24" with boards up to over 8' with boards down. It's a major adjustment for monohull sailors to cruise on a shallow draft multihull. It's not unusual to see them hyper-ventilating the first time they sail fast in five- to six-foot-deep, crystal-clear Bahamian water.

Catamarans have no use for heavy ballast since their comfort and safety depend on their ability to remain perched on top of the waves. Good performance is linked to the designer's recommended payload, which is usually relatively light as compared to the boat's displacement. One reason many live-aboard and charter multihulls lack sparkling performance is because they've been loaded in excess of the designer's recommendations. You'll need to get used to the handling of a light displacement boat. Multihulls can accelerate rapidly; they may lose their way quickly upon heading into the wind, much to the annoyance of novice sailors as they attempt to anchor, approach docks or come about. In general you'll need to head up closer to your desired stopping point than you would in a ballasted boat (a little unnerving in the beginning) and maintain boat momentum to make good gains to windward.

While multihulls sail faster, the sensation of speed can be less than on a monohull due to one's higher seating position relative to the water and virtually no heel. Cats don't plunge and labor through the waves like a heavy displacement boat and simply sail faster with relative ease. They stay on the water's surface so their motion is lighter, quicker and less sustained in one direction. Some long-time monohull sailors miss the steadiness and responsiveness of a keelboat, but most have an easier time with the multihull motion. Others find it just as easy to be seasick on a catamaran.

One of the first things you notice is the lack of heeling on a cruising cat. There's no need for constantly bracing yourself or your gear at unnatural angles. Sailing is more comfortable and less tiring which translates into greater enjoyment and safer operating conditions. Searching for a downside to level sailing, I'd say there's a lack of feedback that heeling provides the helmsman. With no appreciable heel and a reduced tendency for weather or lee helm on a cat, it's more difficult to tell when it's time to reduce sail. One must rely on boat speed and boat motion relative to the seas. Multihulls have no real ability to spill a gust of wind by heeling; they typically translate excess wind energy into acceleration, which demands slight adaptation. Rapid acceleration is most noticeable on light displacement multihulls with high-performance rigs. I thought I knew what boat acceleration was until I sailed a Formula 40 cat on Long Island Sound with Olympic sailor Keith Notary. She went from 12 to 22 knots in the blink of an eye, quite normal, for high-performance cats.

Cruising multihulls not only accelerate quickly, but they maintain higher average speeds than monohulls. In moderate conditions, even slower cruising catamarans sail as fast as monohulls, and attain higher top speeds in fresher conditions. High-performance cruising cats, however, can surf at 20 knots or more. Sailing in high-speed mode is quite different, partly because everything happens much faster and partly because the Apparent Wind is brought far forward, to the point where a broad reach on a monohull becomes a close reach on a fast multihull, and a beam reach becomes close-hauled sailing. Most cruising multihulls on the market perform somewhere in between; as a rule you can expect to maintain smaller sheeting angles and flatter sails for a given True Wind Speed.

Catamarans have lots of room topsides for sail handling and crew maneuvers. They usually have full-width travelers for the mainsail, and those designs with bridgedeck cabins have the added advantage of a saloon area, almost on the same level with the cockpit, providing good visibility of the surrounding water. This allows crewmembers to stay in touch with those in the cockpit and the general sailing conditions around them. It's not unusual for one crewmember to help navigate while at the same time tending to some domestic chore in the main cabin.

Because of the lack of helm feedback, you may initially find it difficult to hand steer a straight course, especially sighting over the wide foredeck of a catamaran. The secret is to either sail by the jib's telltales or line up a point relative to the boat and use this mark as a reference. One will be surprised, however, how little one actually touches the helm on longer passages as 90% of the steering is performed by the autopilot.

It may sound, and in fact it is, a contradiction to say that in many aspects catamarans are easier to sail. They provide more shelter than a monohull of the same size, no heeling, and often simpler sailhandling. But because multihulls sail so much faster they present circumstances that monohull sailors hardly experience or even know exist.

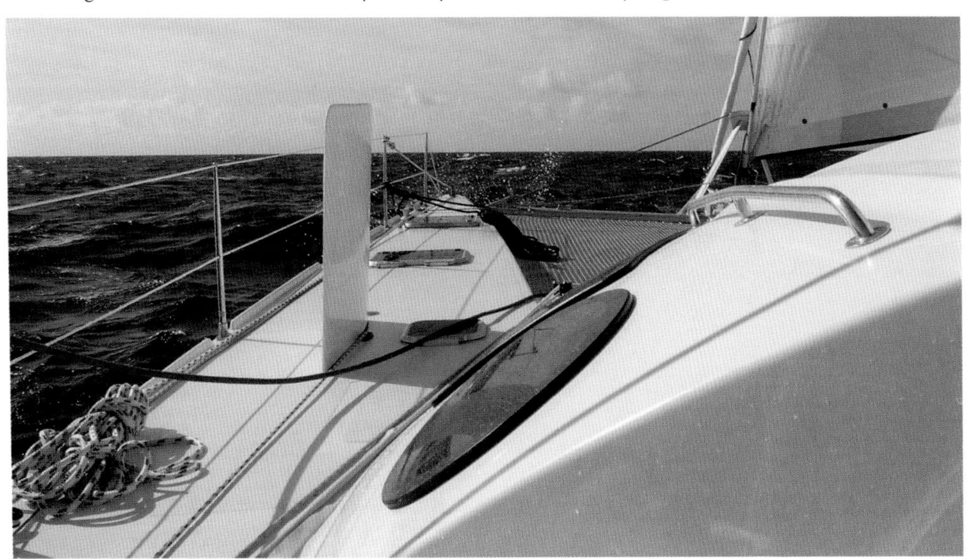

left Sailing under mainsail and jib, the gennaker is pre-rigged and at the ready, to instantly add sail power when the wind lightens.

far right It is often easier to learn sailing on a non-heeling boat, such as a large cruising catamaran. With its high steering position and flat decks, even children feel more comfortable taking over the helm.

On fast catamarans it is highly important for sailors to be savvy. Navigation and anticipation must be earlier and reactions to fast-changing conditions must be made quicker. Since multihulls are wider than single-hulled boats, more stable and sail faster, they have to be handled in a different way. Catamarans have been sailing in the Western world for approximately 50 years. We have learned much from previous sailors, some of whom were pioneers of their time. Recent developments in engineering and design have created a new environment and the best boats ever. Although their handling is based on some older principals, there has been a constant push to attempt maneuvers differently and to improve on seamanship. Let's look at them in detail.

The Magic of Apparent Wind

In order to fully understand key seamanship issues, the phenomenon of Apparent Wind should be recognized, since most of them relate to this fascinating principle. Probably the first thing monohull sailors will notice when sailing a high-speed catamaran is the fact that a large percentage of the time the wind is forward of the beam. The reason is that a multihull is faster and draws the Apparent Wind forward. Apparent Wind is comprised of several components: the speed and direction of travel of the boat and the True Wind. True Wind is the direction and force of wind we would feel when stationary. Say you are sailing at 7 knots and experience a True Wind from 90 degrees off the starboard beam. The resulting Apparent Wind would be 12.4 knots. This would mean that you (and the sails) would be feeling 12.4 knots of wind pressure. With the same True Wind Speed however, sailing directly downwind at 7 knots, the boat would only feel 3 knots of Apparent Wind, as a large portion of Apparent Wind is cancelled out by the forward speed of the boat.

In the table below, it is clear that at 45 degrees the catamaran will achieve its highest VMG at 8.5 knots. Every multihull has a different "sweet spot" at varying wind speeds. The boat's polar diagram and vessel heading will be decisive factors towards the choice of course to be taken.

In an extreme example, offshore racing trimarans which sail upwind at 20 knots would be constantly close hauled. The faster they sail, the higher the Apparent Wind is accelerating them further, consequently bringing the wind almost to dead ahead. Theoretically this can be construed as a self-limiting play of power, in which the sails of our fast multihull would start to luff. At this point the boat could not go faster or sail closer to the wind.

If you think this example is a wild thought reflect on following everyday play on the

Best Upwind Course VMG Table for a typical cruising catamaran:

Boat Speed (Knots)	3.00	4.00	5.00	6.00	7.00	8.00	9.00	10.00	11.00	12.00	13.00	14.00	15.00
Angle to True Wind													
(half tacking angle)													
35 degrees	2.60	3.30	4.10	4.90	5.70	6.50	7.40	8.20					
40 degrees	2.40	3.10	3.60	4.60	5.40	6.10	6.90	7.70	8.40				
45 degrees	2.10	2.80	3.50	4.20	4.90	5.70	6.40	7.10	7.80	8.50			
50 degrees	1.90	2.60	3.20	3.90	4.50	5.10	5.80	6.40	7.10	7.70	8.40		
55 degrees	1.70	2.30	2.90	3.40	4.00	4.60	5.20	5.70	6.30	6.90	7.50	8.00	
60 degrees	1.50	2.00	2.50	3.00	3.50	4.00	4.50	5.00	5.50	6.00	6.50	7.00	7.50

relativity theory. Let's say you are driving north at 55 mph, arm stretched out the window and the True Wind is blowing from the north at 55 mph. You guessed it. You would be struggling to keep your arm straight, as your hand would experience a storm-force wind of 110 mph. But at the next exit ramp you decide to get off and go back south where you came from. Driving south at the same speed your hand would experience no wind at all. Correct! Zero wind, although it is still blowing a good 55 mph outside. Bizarre, isn't it?

On a fast multihull, Apparent Wind can be very deceiving, especially in strong downwind sailing conditions. We often carry heavy-weight spinnakers or gennakers at up to 35 knots of True Wind. Tell this to a monohull sailor – he will think you are bragging or losing your sanity. Yet sailing downwind in strong conditions, fast catamarans will travel at double-digit speeds and cancel out part of the True Wind, making it feel like a breeze on deck (allowing us to carry the large headsails). But, this can be tricky as any increase in True Wind would not be felt; once it is time to reef quickly, it may be too late. Even worse, if there is a small snag, such as a sheet parting or a block exploding, one would have to slow the boat immediately. Doing that would radically increase the wind to gale force and one would be caught with too much sail up. Furthermore, at high surfing speeds, your boat could be overtaking seas and come to a halt by stuffing the bows into a wave face, abruptly coming to a stop. Wind speed would suddenly double and all hell break loose. It has happened to all of us and only experience has taught us to be especially alert under such circumstances.

We all know that the wind speed is higher on mountains and the principle is similar at sea.

above An Outremer 50S hard pressed and sailing upwind at close to 10 knots. In these conditions she would rival the speed of the best monohull racer/cruisers.

This is due mainly to surface friction of the earth and water. Depending on the height of the rig, the wind pressure at masthead level can be as much as 25% higher than at deck level. This also changes the Apparent Wind and its angle of incidence on the sails. Since the art of good sail trim is to adjust sails to a constant Apparent Wind angle along the entire height, keeping this variation in mind is important when trimming to adjust twist in main and headsails.

Adjusting the sails will generally have a much larger effect on a fast catamaran than on a slower one. This can go both ways. It can slow you down if you overtrim, yet can also bring higher gains. As a basic rule, the faster the boat, the more sensitive the trim.

While monohull traditionalists will miss the heeling, performance catamarans offer a different thrill – acceleration. In gusty conditions it is not unusual to go from 10 to 15 knots in under 5 seconds and a broad reach will instantaneously turn into a beat. Whereas the monohull will waste a lot of wind energy by heeling, the wide-beamed catamaran will transfer the increased forces into a rapid forward rush. The wind is drawn forward and this demands constant alertness from the crew, who will have to trim to get the most out of the boat. This change of wind does not mean that you have to be running back and forth constantly to adjust the sheets. You will find a groove and average window of sail settings where the boat will cruise along at a respectable pace. Yet in strong winds one must remain vigilant and always be aware where the wind is coming from and observe its strength. Your boat's acceleration changes the wind strength and direction. Both must be monitored.

My dear uncle Eddie still does not believe that I often sail faster than the wind. "Impossible," he insists. It is true, though. Under the right circumstance even a light and well-sailed cruising cat can sail at 10 knots in 8 knots of True Wind. Low drag hulls will accelerate the boat and a powerful gennaker will draw the wind forward, making the sails "feel" 14 knots, allowing the multihull to sail faster than the True Wind. The boat will literally "feed" on its own wind. One day, maybe, I shall put a bet on it and prove it to my uncle...

Maneuvers Under Sail

Upwind Sailing

The ability to sail upwind better than your opponent has won races, saved lives and won wars. Sailing high on the wind is the most challenging point of sail, as even the smallest sail adjustments will have a significant effect, not only on your course and speed, but also on the boat's motion. Wind and seas will batter the boat and changing your heading by only 3 degrees might let the boat move faster through short choppy waves, increasing Apparent Wind and thus allowing it to accelerate.

When discussing optimal sail trim in light air, it is up to the individual to determine to which degree the best adjustments can be achieved. I know sailors who cannot sit still and constantly fiddle to get the sails drawing just perfectly at the slightest change in conditions. Others will relax in the cockpit with a cocktail and simply be happy that the boat is moving at all. When singlehanding, our autopilots will become our best friends, as they give us the freedom to leave the helm to adjust sails and perform maneuvers. In light-to-moderate conditions to about 25 knots you may chose the level of effort towards accelerating the speed of your multihull. In winds above 30 knots – and depending on the accompanying sea state – you have no choice. You have to be on top of the game as issues of seamanship enter into play.

Years ago multihulls were considered to have poor windward ability but modern cruising catamarans have proven quite the opposite. Those boats with sleek topside profiles, efficient hull shapes, and daggerboards or centerboards will point the best. But even on a cat with bridgedeck accommodations and integral keels you can make better way to windward than equivalent-length monohulls, if you know what you're doing. One trick is to not pinch a multihull as close as you would a heavy-displacement monohull. By footing and falling off just a bit you will maintain momentum and higher average speeds, thereby avoiding making excessive leeway.

Retaining speed is especially important when getting ready to come about, since good momentum helps draw you through a tack smoothly. All tris and most high-performance cruising cats with daggerboards tack with little effort. The balance of the cruising multihulls now on the market come about less quickly (especially if they have excessive windage), but usually without problems. Vintage cruising cats tend to come about in a rather stately fashion. Light winds with choppy seas are always a bit of a challenge, since it's hard to gather the momentum needed to overcome the seas in those conditions. You might occasionally have to backwind the jib to avoid being caught in irons, but the technique should only be employed if necessary, since it tends to slow your progress.

When you're ready to come about on a catamaran, do it decisively, and make sure you are close to the wind but still maintain good speed. Trim the main hard before tacking. This allows the main to act like the aft section of a wind vane, helping swing the boat into the wind. Find a lull in the waves and bring the helm over smoothly, and keep

below The author's wife, Flo, and two friends sailing off Table Mountain, not far from the most southern of the world's promontories: Cape of Good Hope.

Airflow and Sail Turbulence

Downwind, when wind angle is the greatest, turbulent zones behind and on the perimeters of the sails are the greatest. With proper sail adjustment, airflow is smoothest on a reach, running nearly parallel with the boom angle. This is also the point of sail where forward momentum is maximized. Upwind the wind is compressed by the jib and mainsail resulting in smaller pressure vortexes to leeward. Except on a downwind course, telltales are the best indicators for proper trim.

Airflow & Sail Turbulence

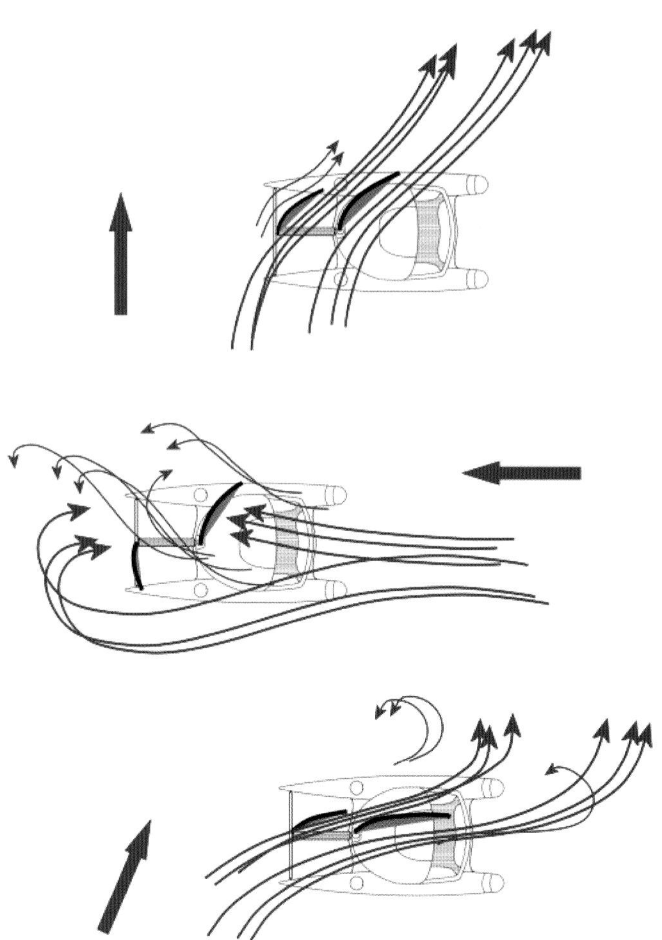

it there until you approach 45 degrees off the wind on the new tack. At that point slowly reverse the helm to bring the boat onto your new heading. As you pass through the wind, ease the main a bit to reduce the wind vane effect which is no longer needed. If you lose momentum during the tack and need to backwind the jib, delay the release of the headsail sheet until the back side of the jib has filled and is pushing the boat off the wind. As soon as you're well through the wind, but no farther than necessary, release the windward sheet and haul the leeward sheet in quickly to get the boat moving forward again. Always trim the jib first and then the main. Allow the boat to pick up speed before moving close to the wind again.

When close-hauled in a monohull in windy conditions, standard practice is to head up when hit with a gust. This prevents excessive heeling, which could result in a knockdown. On a high-performance cruising multihull luffing up is still the best course of action when you're temporarily overpowered while sailing very close to the wind, since falling off could make the boat accelerate rapidly. The traveler should be eased all the way to leeward, thus flattening the mainsail. Another way to cope with gusts is to use a square-top mainsail. The square top blows off in a gust, serving as an automatic first reef. What one should not do is release the mainsheet, which would create the opposite effect of what is desired, making the mainsail fuller.

The telltales on the jib will be the single most important gauge of how well you are doing. The slot effect between main and jib will be key to a proper pressure balance between both sides of the sail. This is even more true in light conditions. As a rule, the lighter the wind, the less you should trim. Over-sheeting the sails is the most common mistake when sailing in light-to-moderate winds. It will stall airflow and reduce speed.

Upwind, you pick your safe course and sheet the jib in first, until proper flow over both sides of the luff is achieved. The telltales will be the best indicator of your adjustments. Once that has been accomplished the main will be trimmed to match the jib's leach shape, accelerating the air through the slot. Back-winding the main will be hard to spot since the battens will hide any signs of the mainsail luff stalling. So, care should be taken not to over tighten the jib. Mainsheet, traveler, halyard, outhaul and Cunningham tension will control twist and draft. Depending on the sea state and weight of the boat, you will dial in power when the wind is light (more fullness and twist) and the opposite, in flat water and stronger winds.

Usually the boom should be midships, and when sighting up the mainsail, the leach should have a moderate luff. The chord of the sail should have a consistent airfoil section with its deepest draft one third aft of the luff. Walk forward and sight back between the slot. When all telltales are streaming straight back on both sides of the sail, there should be a harmonious, almost parallel, distance between the leach of the jib and the belly of the mainsail. All leach telltales on the main, especially the lower ones, should be streaming straight back.

In ghosting conditions care should be taken to move about delicately and make small gradual adjustments. Monitoring the knot meter will reflect on your trim's success. Keep the weight out of the ends of the boat and your catamaran will make its own wind.

On daggerboard cats, use the leeward board fully lowered to give you the most lift. As you gain speed or bear off the wind, the daggerboard can be gradually raised. Familiarity with your boat will tell you how much you can comfortably raise the board under various sea and wind conditions. You'll have to allow for additional leeway when going to windward in any shallow-draft boat. Daggerboards help reduce leeway by reaching down into deeper water. Recommendations from the builder or designer and your own experience will tell you how much to allow in various sea conditions. High speeds and strong winds can make it difficult to raise the board. You may find that you have to bear away and reduce speed temporarily to ease the pressure on the foil.

Cruising multihulls, with their associated steering system and modest helm feedback, will let you sense very little if the boat is experiencing weather or lee helm, unless something is really wrong. Generally, an over-sheeted main and less powerful jib will produce weather helm, whereby the

below Leather-covered steering wheels are minor details, but they make a difference when having to hand-steer on a cold, clammy night.

above Most sail controls on catamarans can be led back to the cockpit. Even halyards and reefing lines are routed aft via turning blocks. Although this increases friction and also means more mess in the cockpit, it is often worth the tradeoff of not having to clamber forward to the mast in inclement conditions.

multihull has the tendency to round up – or turn into the wind. Not only will this increase the force on the rudders, but will use more electricity for the autopilot's operation and produce more drag, slowing the boat unnecessarily. Remember that you have two rudders, therefore twice the drag of a monohull under the same circumstances. Adjusting sails for balance is therefore imperative.

Reaching

As in monohulls, reaching is the fastest point of sail on a cat and wind angles might change by 50 degrees in gusty conditions, even at relatively low speeds. Special alertness is required to extract maximum performance out of your multihull. A catamaran's agility and light weight will put more significance on the slot effect between main and jib, and both sails should be trimmed to an open position.

Sailing an acceleration curve is a maneuver that effectively can be performed on a cat to create Apparent Wind. Sailors who know how to perform it will fully exploit their multihull's efficiency. An acceleration curve is simply making the boat feed on its own wind and thereby speed up. One starts on a heading where the wind is blowing from well aft of the beam, say about 130 degrees apparent. At this angle main and jib should be given time to start drawing and working in unison. Similar to upwind sailing, trim the jib via the indication of its telltales and sheet the main so that its leach curve is parallel to the jib. Make sure that you are not back winding the main by either over-sheeting the jib or letting the boom too far out. The most common mistake at this point is to over-trim the sails and stall them. Be patient and let the boat accelerate. If the True Wind is at 10 knots you might be starting to sail at 4-6 knots. Now, as the boat accelerates and the wind is brought to about 90 degrees apparent, sheet in both sails to adjust for the new wind angle. Speed will continue to build. Keep powering up and "tease" the boat to go faster, hardening up on the sails, until the wind is forward of the beam. At this point you might see an Apparent Wind of 15 knots and be traveling at close to 10 knots.

A barber hauler should be rigged to provide a better headsail shape, especially on a reach or run. An additional line can be used which is led from the toe rail aft via a snatch block, or even the windward (lazy) sheet can be cleated off to the leeward toe rail to force the clew of the headsail outboard.

Barberhauler to Provide Better Headsail Shape

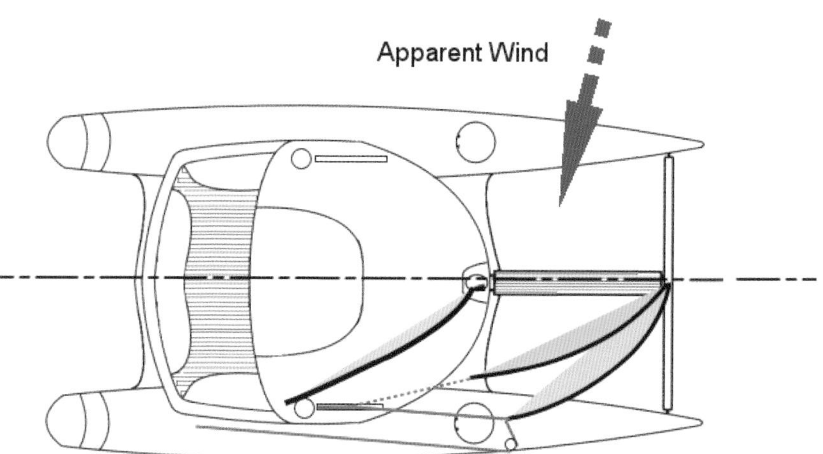

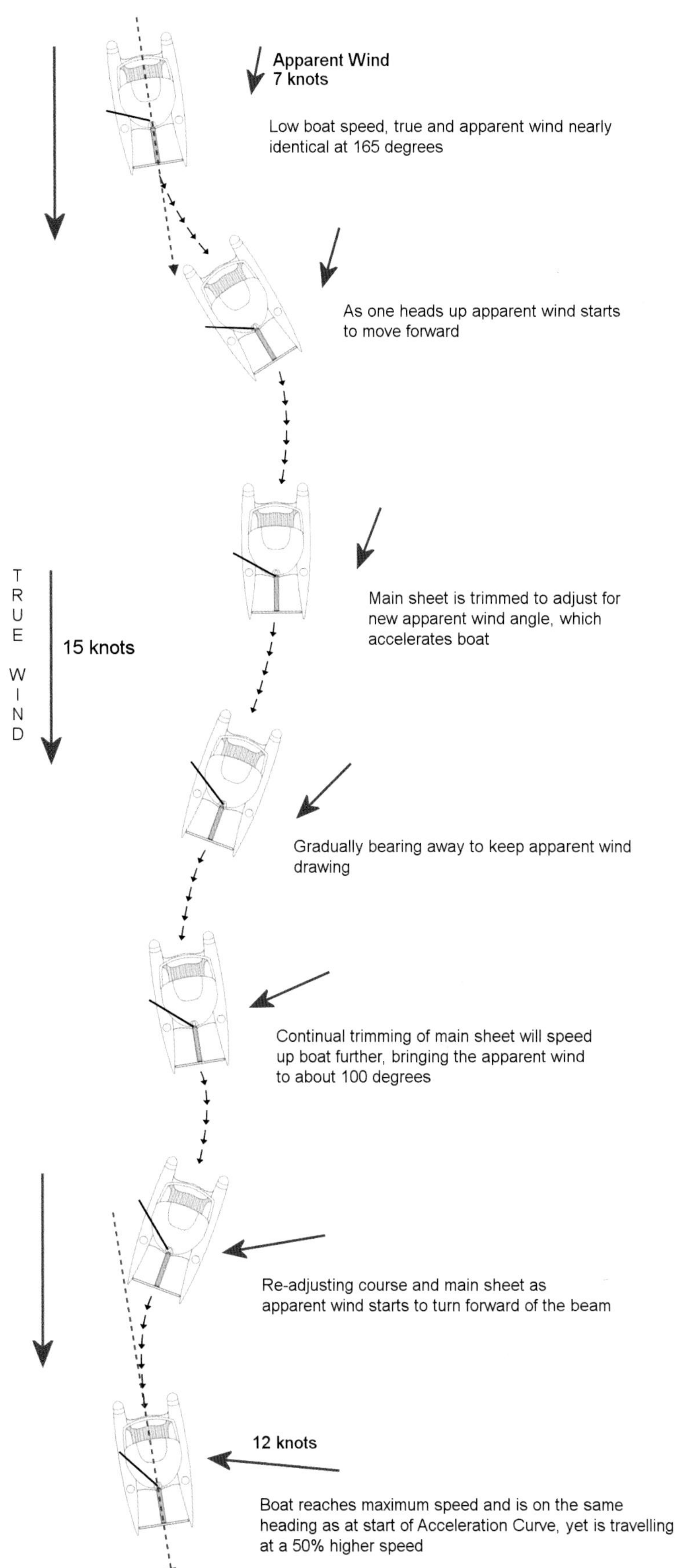
Apparent Wind & Acceleration Curves
Apparent Wind
7 knots
Low boat speed, true and apparent wind nearly identical at 165 degrees
As one heads up apparent wind starts to move forward
Main sheet is trimmed to adjust for new apparent wind angle, which accelerates boat
TRUE WIND
15 knots
Gradually bearing away to keep apparent wind drawing
Continual trimming of main sheet will speed up boat further, bringing the apparent wind to about 100 degrees
Re-adjusting course and main sheet as apparent wind starts to turn forward of the beam
12 knots
Boat reaches maximum speed and is on the same heading as at start of Acceleration Curve, yet is travelling at a 50% higher speed

On faster cruising multihulls it is possible to speed up the boat by sailing a series of acceleration and freeing curves, while at the same time trimming the sails to compensate for the more advantageous apparent wind which one creates. The higher the wind, the less prominent the weaving course needs to be.

Profitability of Downwind Tacking

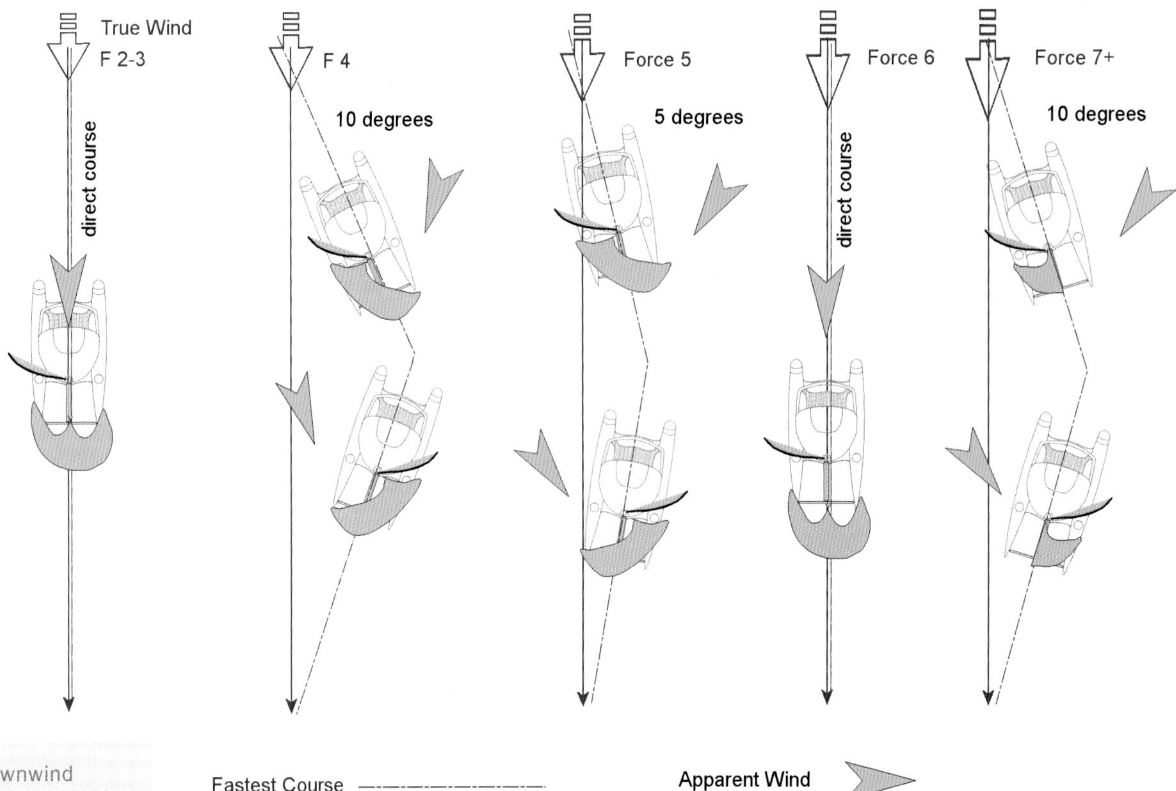

Profitability of downwind tacking depends on factors such as boat performance, wind strength and sail combinations. In an F2, dead downwind, it might pay to sail directly to one's destination by flying a symmetric spinnaker. A course deviation of 10 degrees in F4 conditions will be more advantageous and one would set an asymmetric kite. In an F5, it would be faster to sail more direct, but as the wind increases to F6, a symmetric spinnaker will result in the best VMG. In fresh F7 winds, a genoa could be flown, and tacking downwind at 10 degrees would get you to your destination fastest. Every multihull will be different and this example only illustrates a particular boat. With the help of today's sophisticated, on-board instruments, VMG can be instantaneously recalled via a push of a button. If it is safe, chose a course that optimizes your boat's VMG (Velocity Made Good).

Mainsail twist control is just as important as sheeting angle and it can be controlled via the traveler and mainsheet. A huge advantage that multihulls possess is their wide travelers, which span across the aft crossarm. This means that you have a 20-foot-long traveler on a 45' multihull. Make full use of it. A multihull's wide beam eliminates the classic boom vang and, in fact, I don't remember ever seeing one on a catamaran. Besides, vangs put major loads on fittings and mast, and I have discovered more broken booms on monohulls because of them than I care to remember.

Similarly the jib can be controlled by the sheet lead position. The farther forward it is, the fuller the sail is shaped. You can considerably improve the shape of the sail by rigging a barber hauler, which is basically a secondary leeward sheet, taken around a snatch block placed in a strategic position and led back to a winch. In fact, you can even use the lazy sheet and rig it to leeward as a barber hauler. Learn to use this device to control your jib. A barber hauler does not need to be a fancy multi-part tackle on a track; it can be made from most anything, including just a length of line led from the clew of your jib to an appropriate turning point and back to a winch. By playing the two sheets you can hook the clew of the jib towards the centerline of the boat for more power, or force it open for better airflow.

Key to fast reaching is the main/jib slot. Both sails must be in harmony and work together, accelerating the wind and creating a Venturi effect. Try standing in that slot. When you feel the wind almost twice the force than in the cockpit you know that you are doing something right. The sails are drawing perfectly and the boat is humming.

The farther aft of the beam the wind is, the less critical sail trim becomes. This does not mean that one should not try to sail as efficiently as upwind, yet the fact that the Apparent Wind will have somewhat smaller angles of variation will not necessitate constant adjustment of the sail controls. This is true for downwind sailing in light conditions and quite the opposite in 30 knots and upwards, where one should be fully alert to increases in True Wind.

Downwind

Generally, the spinnaker and gennaker are the two types of sails which are utilized for downwind or reaching conditions. Which sail to choose will depend on your intended course, wind speed and sea state. Both types can be very powerful so they should be treated with respect, especially when one is sailing short-handed. The ability to furl them at any time is imperative.

In speeds varying from 5 to 20 knots true, the gennaker (or screacher), depending on the cut, can be utilized to sail as close as 45 degrees or as deep as 170 degrees. As we will later see, it will be wiser to sail at a closer wind angle, increasing your VMG to leeward. Conversely, the stronger the wind and the more agitated the sea, the deeper you should sail. Gennakers are usually built for light-to-moderate conditions. Care should be taken that the Apparent Wind never exceeds the intended fabric limitation of the sail. I should remind myself, as I have blown out too many.

Sailing downwind in a multihull is a breeze, with reaching typically a preferred point of sail. When sailing from a close reach to a beam reach or from a beam reach to a broad reach in a multihull, trim the sails as you would for a monohull. Ease the sheets until the leeward telltales flow aft evenly. The main difference from monohull sailing is that fast catamarans bring the Apparent Wind farther forward, so that for a lot of downwind sailing the sails are set as though for a beam reach. Fast cruising multihulls are often seen flying asymmetrical spinnakers with the headsail up, which is an advantage for racing. Slower cruising multihulls differ less from monohulls when sailing downwind, although flatter sheeting angles are typically needed to maintain proper sail trim.

When the destination is dead downwind, fast cruising multihulls usually "tack" on a broad reach course and gybe 90 degrees through the wind. This technique produces the fastest speeds and the fastest passage between two points. Slower multihulls usually sail closer to dead downwind, but with little heeling; the typical rolling motion of a monohull is all but eliminated and the tendency to broach does not exist.

below Spinnaker drops can often involve the entire crew. Great care should be taken not to lose the halyard when unclipping, a mishap that has happened to all of us.

right Colorful spinnakers, such as this tri-radial kite, are often set by using a spinnaker sock to hoist and douse them. Note that the one pictured is on a furler, which makes handling a simple one-man operation.

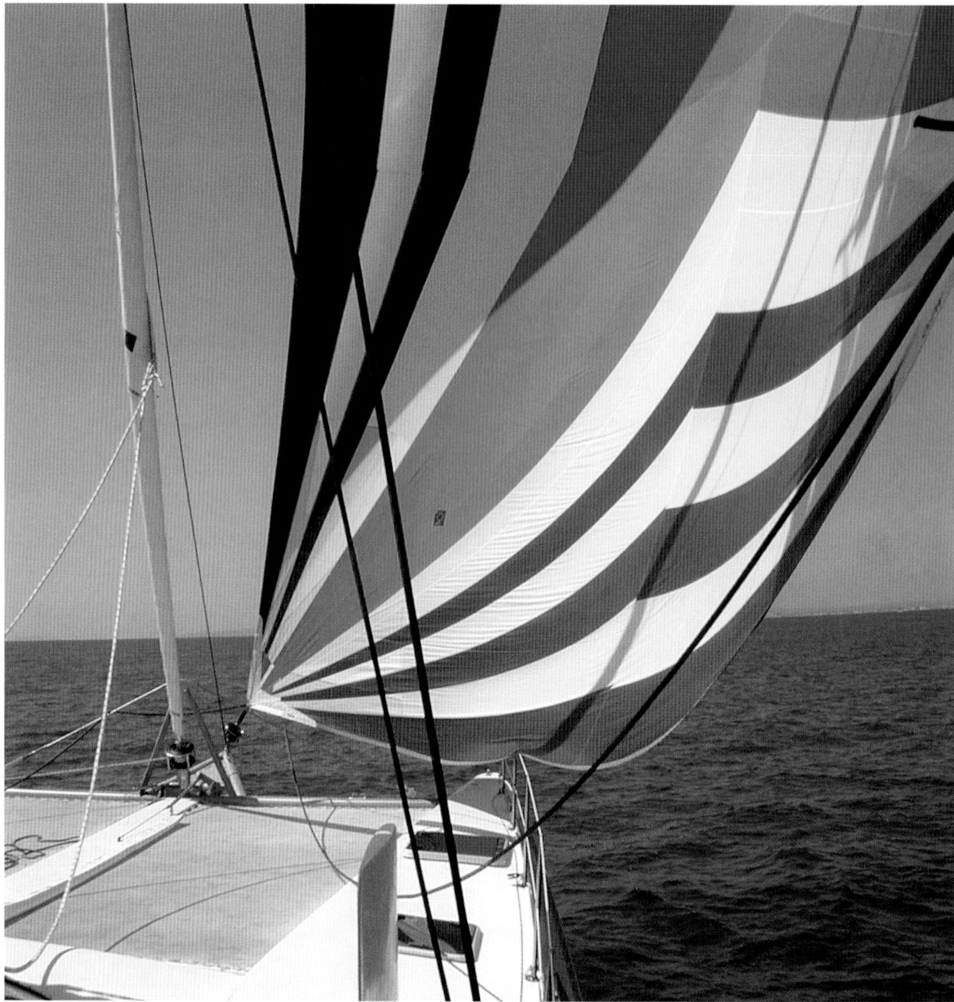

Spinnakers are made of nylon and can be cut either with equal leaches or different length sides, hence the distinction, symmetric and asymmetric spinnakers. The higher the Apparent Wind angles, the more an asymmetric spinnaker or gennaker should be used. However, the deeper one is sailing, meaning with the Apparent Wind close to dead astern, the more power a symmetric spinnaker will provide. Since on a fast cat the wind is brought forward of the beam, these boats only have an all-around gennaker or asymmetric spinnaker.

Cruising multihull sailors seem to favor asymmetrical spinnakers for downwind sailing in light winds. The tack of an asymmetrical spinnaker is supported by a line from each of the outward bows of a cat. These huge sails can be set without a pole due to the wide beam of a multihull, although a bowsprit permanently mounted on the forward beam of a cat allows the tack to be tightened using only one line. When flying a spinnaker on a multihull you need to be aware of the moment when the sail should be taken down. Higher boat speed downwind means lighter Apparent Winds, and it's easy to get caught in True Winds too strong for spinnakers. On a fast multihull, heading downwind temporarily depowers the sails just as luffing up does when going to windward.

When sailing downwind in light winds trim the spinnaker first by sheeting it in until the sail begins to stall, then ease the sheet until the leeward telltales flow aft evenly. If the headsail can be carried, trim that next in the same manner. Lastly, set the main traveler and trim the main.

If your boat has daggerboards, keep the boards down partially for a beam reach to minimize leeway, then raise the boards gradually as you sail farther off the wind. Experience will tell you exactly where to place the boards in various conditions. Sometimes it helps to keep a foot or so of daggerboard down when running to improve tracking.

The gennaker can be hoisted when the Apparent Wind is lower than 20 knots. It should be set with the wind between 80 and 110 degrees. This sail requires special precautions, in particular in the handling of the running backstays, if applicable. If the boat is set up with running backstays to counteract the forward pull of the gennaker, the runners should be on tight. If possible they should not be left in jammers but locked on a self-tailing winch. Many rigs that failed collapsed because of jammers pulling out of the deck, suddenly releasing the runners and snapping the mast. One should think about dousing gennakers when the Apparent Wind exceeds 20 knots. When this powerful sail is furled, it can be lashed to the trampoline and left attached to the bowsprit end, if conditions permit. Make sure it is safely tied and cannot blow over the side or fill with water. There should never be a permanent line from the bowsprit to the top of the seagull striker. Instead the bowsprit should be held up with the spinnaker – or spare halyard. This will prevent the risk of losing the forestay and rig in case the gennaker halyard fails and the sail goes overboard and fills with water.

Light-displacement catamarans occasionally surf down the backside of waves. They can sometimes surf at speeds approaching True Wind Speed, which brings the Apparent Wind to zero and causes the headsail or spinnaker to temporarily collapse. A spinnaker in that situation may wrap itself around the headstay. If it wraps tightly, you may need to gybe the mainsail to allow it to release itself. When freed, gybe back to your original course. You can help prevent spinnaker wrap by temporarily over-sheeting until the Apparent Wind picks up again. Repeated surfing and cavitation of rudders might indicate that you have too much sail up for the wind and sea conditions.

Velocity Made Good (VMG)

Often called downwind tacking, it really should be referred to as gybing, as one is going through the wind stern first as one would in a gybe. Often novices will think that pointing the ship's bows directly towards the destination is the fastest way to get there. Well, there is a surprise: The faster your multihull and the lighter the wind, the more you will sail away from your destination.

VMG vs. Boat Heading

Performance sailors use the acronym VMG (Velocity Made Good) to express boat speed relative to the direction of the wind. The concept holds that for any given sailing condition and desired course, there is a single combination of boat speed and true wind angle that equates to the optimum VMG. On any point of sail – upwind or down – the longer we can maintain the best VMG, the better our cumulative performance.

VMG = boat speed x cosine (angle sailed to the true wind). In this particular example, it can be seen that by bearing off to an angle of 57 degrees to the True Wind, one can optimize VMG to one's destination. Although one will sail a longer course, VMG will be higher and one will arrive at one's goal faster. VMG depends on the polar speed diagram of one's catamaran and the cosine of the angle sailed to the True Wind.

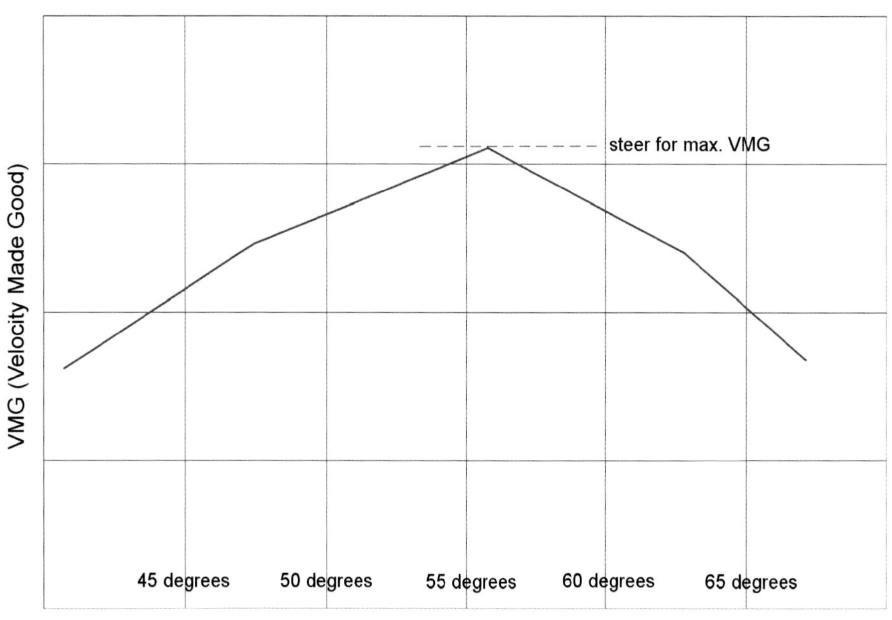

Asymmetric Spinnaker Controls

Similar to a symmetric spinnaker, which has two equal leaches, the asymmetric kite is flown without a cumbersome pole. Two sheets and a pair of fore guys are sufficient to stabilize and trim the spinnaker, which is usually hoisted and doused with the assistance of a sock. The guys can be replaced by a bowsprit, which would have the effect of better securing the sail's clew in a fixed position.

far right Battens assure a quick, non-snag, mainsail drop. Because of their weight and mast attachment via sliders or ball-bearing cars, friction is eliminated and therefore the main sail can slide down the instant the halyard jammer is opened. Be sure, however, to always keep a couple of wraps on the halyard winch before opening the jammer in order to ease the sail down with full control.

Apparent Wind vs. Course

Note how in the diagram the (blue) True Wind vector is always the same length as it represents equal strength on all points of sail. The Apparent Wind (red) however, changes dramatically in strength and direction, especially on an upwind course. This example illustrates why it is often more advantageous to tack downwind rather than sail on a dead run.

On a straight downwind course, the Apparent Wind will diminish as the (yellow) Boat Wind will cancel out part of the True Wind. On a reach and beat the Apparent and Boat Wind become greater than the True Wind.

Asymmetric Spinnaker Controls

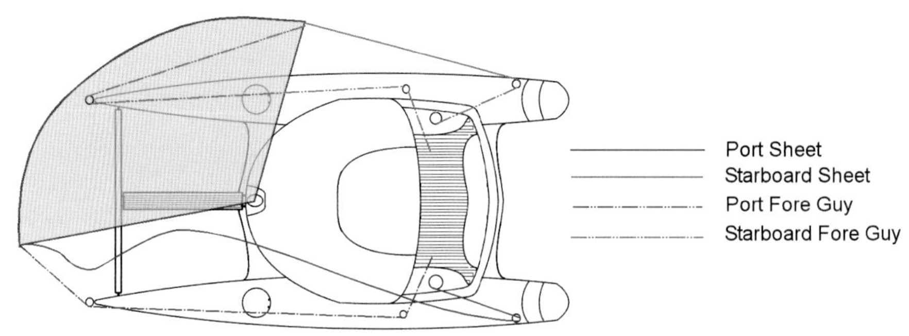

Apparent Wind vs. Course

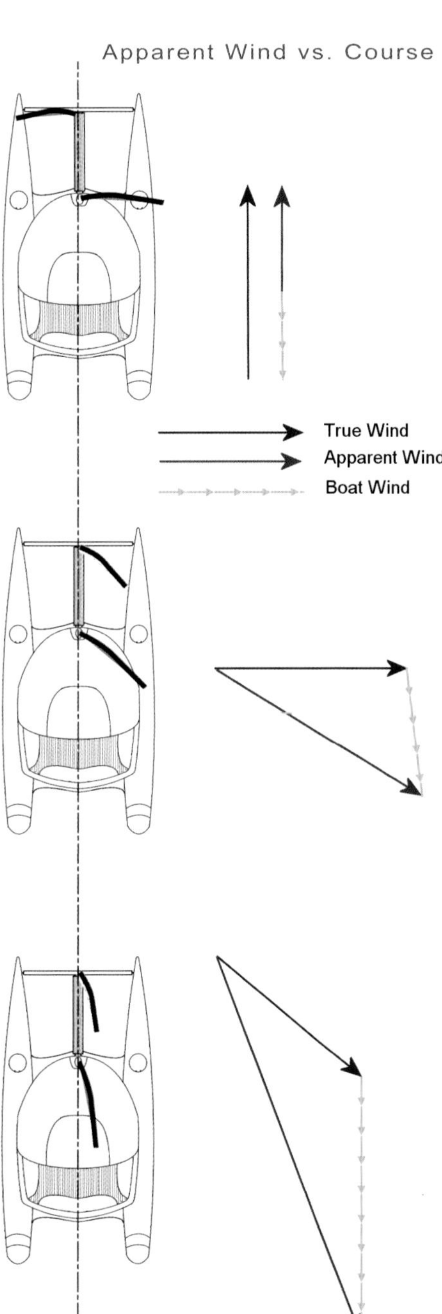

You will get to the yacht club bar earlier than if you would have taken the "Rhumb" (as in direct, not Rum as in drink) Line.

The farther downwind your destination is the more it pays to perform a series of gybes. This is especially true in winds under 15 knots true. VMG or speed made good towards your goal is an important concept to understand. It is inherently associated with Apparent Wind and your best boat speed as compared to sailing a certain course. The skipper's decision whether or not to diverge from the Rhumb Line will depend on the wind speed, the sea state and the multihull's polar diagram. Generally, in light air, multihulls will go appreciably faster if the Apparent Wind is brought forward. This means if you are sailing on a broad reach, it will pay to steer upwind and sheet in, especially if the wind is fluky and inconsistent. Heading changes do not have to be excessive. A course correction of only 10 degrees could make a substantial difference, resulting in an increase in Apparent Wind pressure and 2 knots more speed. Needless to say other parameters, such as un-navigable areas, vessel traffic and sea state, will also have to be accounted for.

Just as paying attention to the jib telltales when sailing upwind or on a reach, downwind sailing will have you scanning your boat's instruments. Your true/Apparent

Wind speed and direction indicator and your boat speed gauge will become your best allies. It will be key to keep the Apparent Wind angle constant, and by monitoring the wind gauge or masthead Windex, one simply steers, or lets the autopilot steer, a course relative to a constant wind angle. In fresher conditions, your multihull could be accelerating down a wave and start to surf momentarily, bringing the wind forward. One would bear away to keep the sails at the angle to which they have been originally trimmed. This will assure that all sails are drawing, even if the boat will slalom slightly. It sounds more complicated than it is, but in essence this is sailing a downwind acceleration curve and maximum speed will be attained.

Battens

Similar to the Chinese junk rig, a modern catamaran's mainsail is stabilized with battens, usually 4-8, depending on the size and aspect ratio of the sail plan. The advantages are easy reefing and their ability to extend the roach, thereby increasing the sail area. Battens also prevent wild flogging in the wind when reefing or hoisting the sail. This will greatly reduce the crew's stress level and increase the longevity of the main. Disadvantages of battens are their weight, and the fact that they are another part to fix and replace in case they break under shock loads such as accidental gybes in strong winds. Broken battens need to be replaced before they tear the sails. The pros of battens far outweigh their negative aspects however, and catamaran sailmakers have been using them as standard equipment for the last 15 years. Battens come in different shapes and sizes, but the most popular are solid fiberglass rods.

When partially rolling up the genoa while reefing, the headsail lead block should be moved forward to keep the sheeting angle constant to assure optimum sail shape.

Geona Lead Position

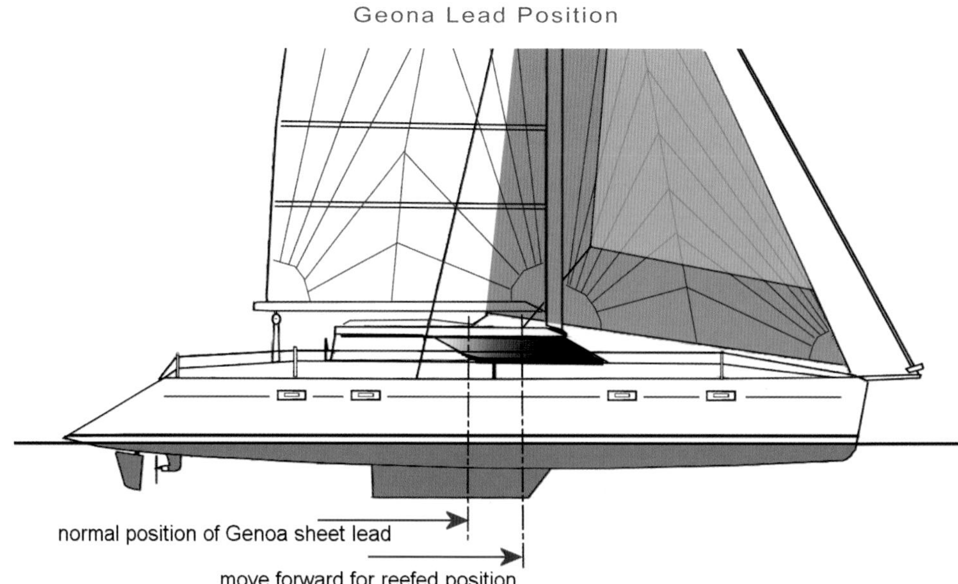

below This is what you want to see when looking up the rig – mainsail and jib drawing in harmony, without stalling the air in the all-important slot between both sails. Note the boom bars, which assist in handling reefs and help keep the lazy jacks spread in order to facilitate gathering the main once it is dropped.

More exotic materials such as Kevlar and carbon tubes are lightweight but expensive.

Special end fittings fix the battens to the mast track and most of the time adjustment screws are on the leach side. By being able to dial in the batten tension, the sail shape at different heights can be controlled. Depending on the weight and configuration of the catamaran you will not need to adjust batten tension often, once they are set. The lighter the boat, the more effect the alteration in tension will have on the sail shape.

Generally, you want a fuller sail in light conditions when sailing through choppy seas on a heavy boat. Wind speed, sea state and boat weight will be the most important parameters when looking to power up. Consequently, the opposite is true when sailing in flat water in stronger winds with a light boat. All three factors, or a combination thereof, should dictate the degree of fullness the main and jib should have. Of course, outhaul, halyard, Cunningham, traveler and sheets will have the greatest cumulative effect, yet batten tension will contribute its share. The more the battens are under compression, the more they will bow and the deeper the chord of the sail will become. Often you will see an S-curve in a batten when sighting up the main, which will be evidence of too little tension.

Reefing

The reliability of a simple reefing system is imperative. As much as they are a great help to monohulls, rarely do we see in-boom furlers or in-mast reefing systems on multihulls. Their higher loads and the fact that most multihulls have fully battened mainsails, which makes even in-boom furling complex, don't lend themselves to any other way of reducing sail except the slab or jiffy reefing system. This is by far the mostly reliable and best system to reduce the size of a catamaran's mainsail.

Even if one only considers oneself a coastal sailor, reefing lines should be ready and pre-fed through the respective leach cringles. Reef systems vary but having only one line for each reef (leach and luff) which, along with halyards, can be led back to the helm,

above Usually, catamarans hardly lose any speed when reefed, but gain more balance and control. With a single reef in the main and a reduced jib, the Bahia 46 is ready for an increase in wind strength.

will add to friction and greater mess in the cockpit. The advantage is that one does not have to climb forward to the mast to reduce sail. No matter what system one employs, it is a good idea to pre-feed at least 2 reefs out of the typical 3 reefs. This will prepare the boat for the worst conditions, without the need to rig lines when the wind suddenly increases. The leach of the mainsail is often equipped with reefing blocks, which are designed to ease loads, prevent chafe and make reefing easier. It is, however, my experience that a well reinforced, simple reef cringle is stronger and actually will be better in preventing chafe. In addition, it will be lighter, one less part to break and cannot foul.

Furling the jib is straightforward and beefy roller furling hardware has made the trip forward to handle jibs unnecessary. As you control the jib sheet, slowly ease it out until the sail starts to luff sufficiently for the reefing line to be hauled in. In stronger winds the line will wrap tightly around the furler, therefore it is important to have enough tail to completely furl the sail. When you partially furl the sail, the jib lead should be moved forward to retain proper clew-lead geometry and prevent a full sail. It is a good idea to check the furling line for chafe often and to double it up via a lashing when leaving the boat at a mooring for extended periods.

I often hear discussions concerning experiences in gale conditions and the necessity to reef at certain wind strengths. Very seldom, however, is the sea state mentioned. In my mind multihulls are much more affected by the sea state. Wave height and intervals are the primary consideration when making the decision of when to reef. Of course, wind and sea state go hand in hand, yet often the waves do not correspond with the wind, as they might be left over from an older low pressure system. To simplify it, there is one basic rule of thumb associated with reefing: on a monohull you typically reef to the strength of the gusts, while on a multihull you reef to the strength of the lulls. Most catamarans are just as happy with reduced sail and you will be surprised how little speed you really lose with less sail. Slow down to a more moderate speed. Think of it as similar to slowing down your car when you come to a rough road by shifting into a lower gear for more control.

At what point does one reef? This is the most common question concerning multihull safety. The answer is deceptively simple and an often heard principle: "It is time to reef when you first think about it." This is not meant to disparage the importance of knowing that time. As you acquire more experience with your boat, the more "feel" you will get for the process. From the subjective point of view, when you begin to feel uneasy, apprehensive or concerned, it is time to reef. When the boat no longer has its feather-light touch at the helm, it is time to reef. When the lee bow seems to want to plunge and bury, it is time to reef. When you are no longer strong enough to crank in the sails, it's time to reef.

Reefing, as referred to in this section, includes both headsail and mainsail. As a rule, for masthead rigged boats going upwind, start by partially reefing the jib first; downwind, reef the main first. It is hard to generalize about fractional rigs. Sailing under main alone is typically far more controllable if the boat remains balanced. The fully battened mainsail, which has the most sail controls, is held on two sides by spars, and can be given optimum size and shape. Generally, it is important to reef main and jib together in order to assure that the boat remains in balance. For instance, simply reducing the main to the third reef and keeping a full jib will result in lee helm. Although less of an issue, but still possible, is severe weather helm. This happens when you only furl the jib but leave a full main. The stronger the wind, the more you will feel imbalance, which puts unnecessary strain on the autopilot and increases drag as the rudders are over-compensating. Therefore, always reef main and headsails together.

To sum it up, reefing depends on the force of the wind, the sea state, point of sail and the capabilities of vessel and crew. Above all, remaining humble and respectful of the elements will make you a better sailor. Following wind speed benchmarks will assist in determining when to reef which sail.

Reefing Chart for mainsail and jib (not accounting for sea state)

Sustained Apparent Wind Speed	Mainsail with 4 Reef Points	Jib (on Roller Furling)
< 15 knots	Full Sail	100%
15 - 18 knots	Full Sail	100%
18 - 27 knots	1 Reef	100%
25 - 32 knots	2 Reefs	70%
30 - 37 knots	3 Reefs	50%
35 - 45 knots	3 Reefs	20%
40 - 50 knots	4 Reefs	20%
> 50 knots	4 Reefs	0%

In light-to-moderate conditions, the mainsail can be reefed in a conventional way by heading up, easing the main and luffing. Yet, if you are overpowered by a strong beam wind, especially in big seas, I prefer to reef the mainsail by running downwind. This might sound completely untraditional and unorthodox, but modern mainsail sliders and a proper procedure will assure success. Since wind and sea state will demand reefing, rounding the boat head into the wind will only increase Apparent Wind and can expose a catamaran at speed to dangerous centrifugal forces. Beam seas are the most dangerous for a multihull and should be avoided at any cost, even if only for seconds. Conversely, falling off avoids this critical sector of seas; Apparent Wind is reduced and the motion of the boat is easier. Easing off the halyard and pulling on the reef lines will force the sail down. "It is not pretty," I always tell my crew, because the battens contort into S-curve shapes before they drop into the sail bag. Here is a little trick: to prevent battens from jamming against the mast you can load up a luff reef, or downhaul, and release the halyard when momentarily bearing away. The Apparent Wind will be briefly reduced, compression on the battens eased, and the main will slide down. Your lazy jacks will catch the excess sail and prevent it from billowing out. Reefing downwind is far more controllable and safer than having to turn the nose of the boat into the teeth of a gale and taking the waves onto the beam.

When you take a reef in the mainsail it is important to relieve the strain on the jammers under the boom, whose clutches can quickly chafe through them. Lead reef lines to winches instead.

On longer open-ocean passages, where rough weather is expected, it is particularly important to double up the reef.

By dead-ending a strong line around the boom, passing the end through the leech reef cringle, and tying the bitter end tightly around the boom, one has a second way to secure the reef. By easing the reef line slightly, one can then divide the loads between the two lines. This will subdue squealing of the

below Gennaker and spinnaker sheet blocks are located as far aft as possible in order to accommodate the geometry of the large sails that they help to control. These blocks experience massive loads and must be secured with adequate backing plates beneath the deck.

leech blocks (if used) and prevent premature chafe, which could cause the reef lines to part. Acrobatics must be employed to perform boom work, therefore during this operation it is recommended to always wear a safety harness and have another crewmember spot you.

Daggerboards

The majority of today's cruising catamarans are equipped with mini keels for reliable and hassle-free operation. There are fewer than a handful of production daggerboard catamarans, which provide the sailor slightly more pointing ability and other advantages as illustrated in previous chapters. Their operation is generally straightforward via either a single uphaul line in case the board is heavier than water, or by an additional downhaul to keep the foil lowered, in case it is more buoyant.

Needless to say, when trying to point as high as possible, the leeward board should be fully deployed. The finer the hulls of the catamaran and deeper the foils are, the more they will contribute to getting the multihull to windward. In very rough conditions, when the boat will be thrown around by wind and waves, it is a good idea to divide the loads between both boards and only let them halfway down.

Marking the daggerboards at deck level will help indicate a "control" depth and assist in judging when they will be extending deeper than the rudders and thus aid in protecing them in case of a collision.

For a more detailed description of daggerboards and their use, please refer to the "Appendages" chapter.

Tacking

Just as many early skeptics of multihulls believed that catamarans could not sail upwind, they also alleged that they could not tack. It is true that because of a multihull's lighter weight, wider beam and more windage, turning through the wind will be slightly more hesitant than on a ballasted boat, which carries its momentum through the wind. Decisively performing the maneuver, however, is not less successful or complex than on a monohull.

In moderate conditions, tacking is straightforward. The traveler must be centered and the vessel must be sailing as close-hauled as possible. It is surprising how often one sees sailors trying to tack a multihull from a reach. This frequently fails, especially when the winds are light and the sea is choppy. In light air you should put the helm down smoothly and sail through the turn. The lower the wind speed, the more essential it is to be sailing upwind at full speed, just before turning through the wind. In very light conditions and/or in lumpy seas, it might be necessary to sail an acceleration curve starting with a reach, and sheeting in to close hauled as one is gaining speed. Depending on windage and sea state it might be helpful to briefly backwind the jib, before sheeting in on the new heading. This will assist the bows in turning through the wind. Key to a successful tack is the skill of quickly sheeting in the jib on the new heading. If the boat feels like it is going to stall, release the traveler and main sheet immediately, as they will try to force the bows into the wind. Helm action should be continuous and decisive, but not too fast as to create rudder cavitation. Using the wind and rudder angle indicators will often help in determining when the turn has been

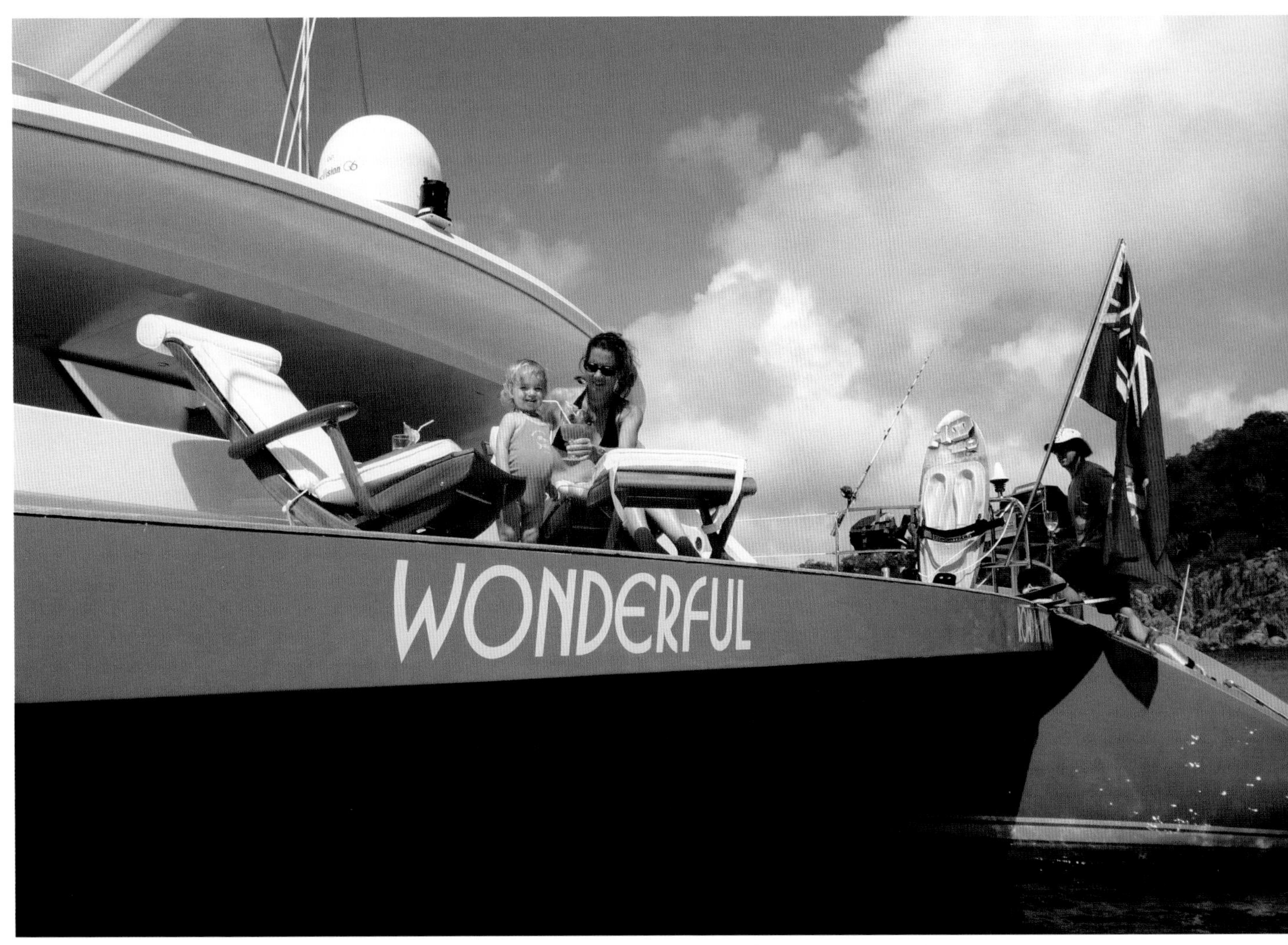

above The aft sun porch is a place for the entire family, and conveniently houses everything from surfboards to the yacht's fishing gear.

completed, after which the rudders should be straightened. Simply pushing the "auto-tack" function on the autopilot will turn the boat 90 to 110 degrees through the wind. As in upwind sailing, telltales will indicate proper jib position for the new heading. Once the boat has gone about, sheet the jib in first and only once it is drawing correctly, adjust the main. In light conditions, fall off to a reach until speed is gained, and then go on an upwind course, if so desired.

If the boat is equipped with daggerboards, the windward board should be lowered just before the tack, and while still sailing upwind on the old heading. Just as the vessel is going about, the old leeward board should be quickly lifted to avoid raising difficulties because of water pressure. Also keeping the new windward board down will help the boat pivot better. This fact is also the main reason why daggerboard cats tack quicker.

Stall Recovery

In the worst case scenario you can stall during a tack, when there is not enough momentum, or did not sheet in the jib quickly enough. This is not a disaster, as a catamaran can be sailed backwards smartly. All you have to do is release all sheets and, as the multihull is pointing into the breeze, the wind will push you back as if reversing a car. With the wheel turned to point the bows onto

Stalling a catamaran will happen to everyone. Knowing how to quickly recover will be key, especially in extreme conditions, when rudders and other gear could fail. First, release the main sheet and traveler, reverse the helm and backwind the jib towards same side as the rudder tips are pointing. After letting the boat drift back so that the wind is at least 30 degrees off the bow, turn the helm to leeward while quickly sheeting in the jib. Once the headsail is drawing, straighten the helm and trim in the main sail. Even when single-handing, recovering from a stall can be done in less than 30 seconds.

Catamaran Stall Recovery

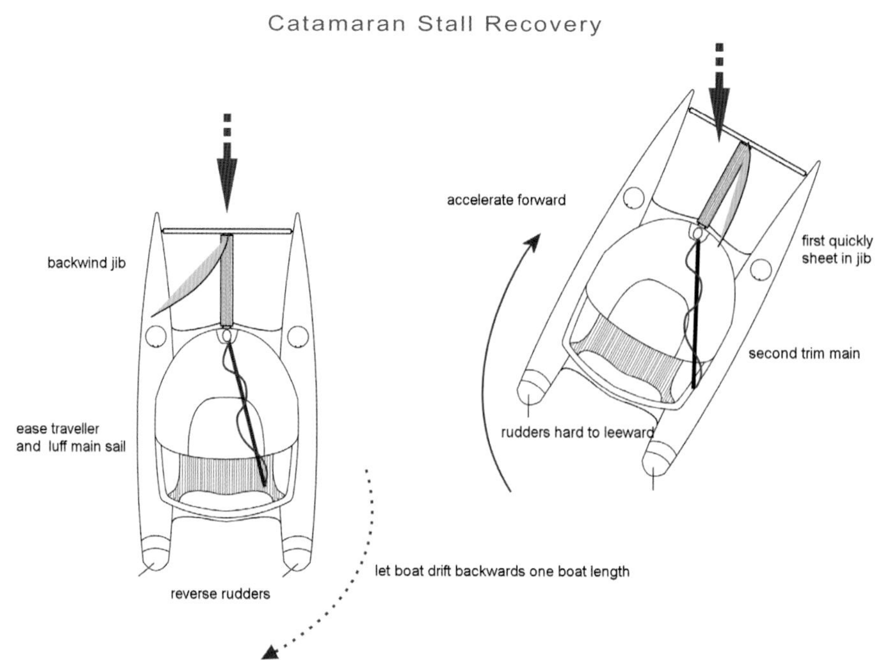
accelerate forward
first quickly sheet in jib
backwind jib
second trim main
ease traveller and luff main sail
rudders hard to leeward
let boat drift backwards one boat length
reverse rudders

the new heading you will be able to sheet in the jib and power away onto the new tack. In many instances the jib can be left backwinded to accelerate reversing. It is important to give yourself plenty of room astern until the boat is clearly pointed in the proper direction. You will quickly be able to adjust the sails (jib first) to sail off on the new tack. Of course, you can also cheat and switch on one of the engines to help you.

Gybing

In contrast to performing this death-defying maneuver on a monohull, gybing is child's play on a catamaran, thanks to its wide traveler. On a monohull gybing can be an act of terror as the boom cannot be braced as well. Often, as a monohull goes through the wind, the sudden heeling and momentum shift caused by the gyration around the keel whips the boat onto the other tack. In extreme conditions monohulls can even broach. Gybing on a monohull in strong winds must be done under absolutely choreographed conditions to avoid rigging damage to gear or personal injury. Boat speed is usually low as compared to the Apparent Wind, so the boom and mainsail can swing across with considerable force. By contrast, gybing on a catamaran is quite different because of the reduced Apparent Wind, wide mainsheet track and the excellent tracking abilities of a wide twin-hulled vessel.

To properly gybe a cruising catamaran, trim the main as you steer downwind and pull the traveler amidships. Bear away to gybe the mainsail. As the headsail becomes blanketed by the main, gybe the headsail. Ease the traveler and mainsail for your new heading. The key is to maintain as much boat speed as possible in order to reduce Apparent Wind. This principle applies to the strategy when gybing a very fast racing cat. You want to sail at maximum speed and start from a broad reach, and don't steer dead downwind before the gybe. This would only reduce boat speed and make the conditions similar to a monohull. It is more advantageous to bring the helm over steadily, while at the same time quickly centering the traveler and trimming the main. Gybe through about 90 degrees until you are sailing on the opposite broad reach course.

Gybing on a catamaran should always be controlled. I remember my days on our Olympic Class Star boat, which looked like a miniature version of an America's Cup Yacht – narrow beamed, with a deep keel and a massively long mast and a boom that swept the deck. Unfortunately the traveler was only a mere 23" wide! Gybing meant simultaneously trimming and easing numerous wires, sheets and stays, yet ducking just at the right instant as the boom whipped around to fulfill the process of decapitation. Single-handedly gybing a Star boat in fresh conditions was a challenge. Of course, the Star could not be reefed, transforming the procedure into a circus act.

Gybing a cat with an asymmetrical spinnaker or gennaker complicates the maneuver slightly, but is not difficult. When performing an "outside gybe," the boat passes through the wind, as one gradually releases the working sheet and allows the sail to be blown outboard. When the wind is on the opposite quarter, quickly haul in the new sheet. Of course gennakers or asymmetric spinnakers can also be gybed more conventionally by completely furling them and then adjusting the sheets to the new tack. This is called an "inside gybe."

Modern catamarans are easy to gybe; in some conditions it can be the preferred maneuver as compared to the tack. To summarize, when gybing a cruising cat one should be sailing as deep and fast as possible. This will reduce the Apparent Wind and keep the turning angle to a minimum. Just before going stern through the wind, the mainsail should be quickly sheeted in and the traveler centered. The jib should be also trimmed to midships. Similar to tacking, the steering should be decisive and continuous and then wind and rudder angle instruments should be referred to for assistance. Once on the new heading, head up slightly and trim the traveler, main and jib before committing to your new heading. Effectively you would be sailing a mini downwind acceleration curve to increase Apparent Wind.

Docking & Under Power

Maneuvering a multihull under sail in tight anchorages, or around docks, requires some practice, particularly with cruising cats that lack good crisp response to the helm. Give yourself some additional time and distance to turn, and be aware of how quickly a multihull can accelerate in a gust or come to a stop once headed into the wind. Play your main and jib just as you would with a monohull. However, it is best to approach a dock under power, with all sails dropped for maximum control.

below The practical center cockpit of a Chris White-designed, Atlantic 48. Although not nearly as spacious as more conventional aft cockpits, it has the advantage of placing the crew close to the most vital of the yacht's controls.

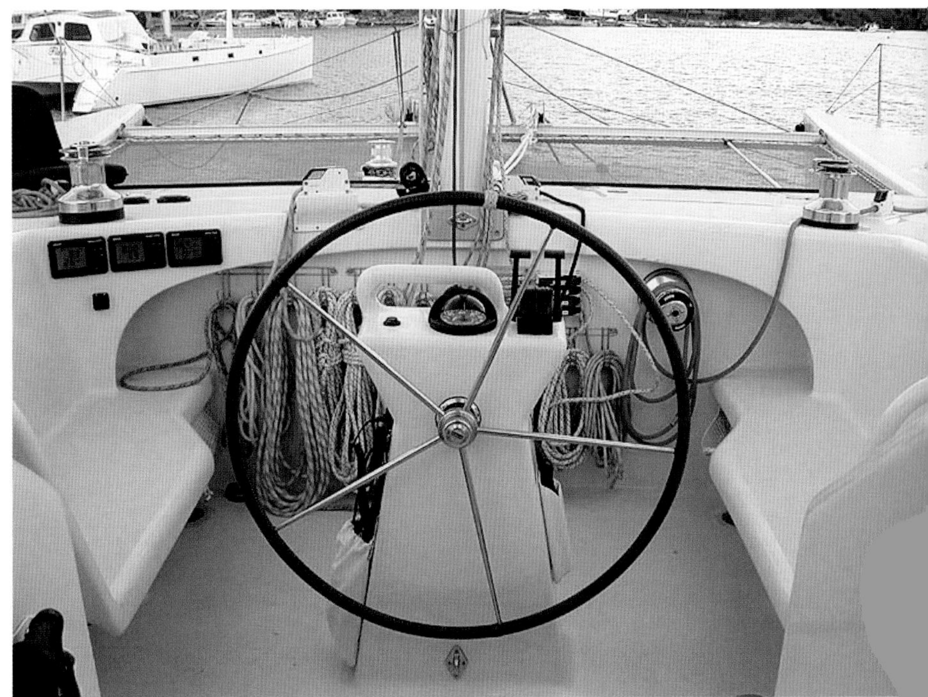

above "Willow" finally docked in St. Lucia after our longest transatlantic passage, which lasted more than 21 days; she was the second multihull to finish in the 2004 ARC.

Catamarans have twin engines, one in each hull, which not only contribute to their safety, but also to their maneuverability. There are no issues with "prop walk" and by simply putting one engine in forward and the other in reverse, any catamaran will turn on its own axis.

Modern diesels have become bulletproof and are the number one choice for cruisers. Whether straight shaft or sail drive power trains, both are reliable. Sail-drives will have a space advantage, often permitting the engine to be moved farther aft, gaining space in the interior. Their early corrosion problems have been totally eliminated and sail drives are seen on most production multihulls today. Propeller size and pitch must be properly engineered to avoid cavitation at any speed and they should, preferably, be of the two-blade folding or three-blade feathering type to reduce drag when sailing.

It is important to remember that rudders need water to flow over them in order to be effective, making them useless under 2 knots of boat speed. When maneuvering to a mooring, around obstacles or a dock, slow down sufficiently to control your approach. If your speed drops to under 2 knots, it is important to center the helm (check the rudder angle indicator) and only utilize the twin engines for steerage and yaw adjustment.

Daggerboard catamarans have the advantage of retracting both boards when motoring and thereby can reduce some drag. However, when approaching docks under power in high crosswind situations, they should be lowered in order to provide bite and help resist drift.

Motor-Sailing

Catamarans generally also have a much longer range under power than monohulls because their narrow hulls offer less resistance and their overall weight is less. Yet even when sailing in very light winds, one engine can be run at medium idle, doubling the Apparent Wind and substantially increasing boat speed. Heavy monohulls will not be able to do this. If you have the choice you should run the leeward engine, as it will give you a slight kick to weather when motor-sailing to an upwind destination.

It is amazing how well a multihull will track on one engine, and most of the time the autopilot needs to compensate by less than a couple of degrees. The lighter the boat the more pronounced this advantage becomes. When all sails are dropped in a calm, motoring on one engine will power you along nicely at almost 75% hull speed, yet you would be using only half the amount of diesel. This is a huge advantage when planning transocean passages, effectively doubling your catamaran's operational range.

Anchoring

above Twin windlasses keep the anchors at the ready for instant deployment when needed; they are placed well aft for convenient operation. Hundreds of feet of heavy chain and rode are located in the chain lockers, just ahead of the mast. Note the removable "passarelle" which serves as a gangplank when disembarking.

A shallow-draft multihull is a joy to anchor. Usually the ground tackle is ready to deploy, either located on the forward crossbeam, or even better, at the central mast bearing beam, closer to the center of the boat. A bridle can be pre-rigged and one simply has to attach it via a snap shackle to the anchor chain after the anchor has set. Bridles will absorb the loads and distribute them via triangulation to both bows. In tight anchorages care must be taken as catamarans might have different swinging characteristics in cross-tide and wind conditions than neighboring boats. Catamarans are more affected by wind as they present more windage than single-hulled boats. But due to their shallow draft, multihulls have more anchoring areas to choose from. Being able to locate a spot close to the beach, upwind of the mooring field, one has the advantage that the holding power for a given length of chain is greater, as the length of the scope will be relatively longer in shallower water. The added benefits of a shallow draft cat is that one is closer to the beach, usually in the lee of a headland and upwind of other anchored boats. This greatly reduces noise and smell pollution created by your cruising neighbors.

Everyone seems to have their favorite style anchor and sailors usually form their own preference when it comes to the selection of the ground tackle. The truth is that there is no single perfect anchor type for all bottoms. Sand, mud, and kelp sea bottoms will be different than rocks and coral conditions. Every anchor has different holding powers in different environments. Therefore, at least two different anchors should be carried on board. Large-but-lightweight anchors, which even can be dismantled, such as the FX type Danforth-style, are a great backup to always keep aboard.

Nylon rode and chain should be adequate for even the deepest anchorages and a scope of 7:1 must be respected, especially if one is expecting a blow. Properly sized nylon line is a great shock absorber and dissipates gust loads. A 30-foot chain leader will help hold the anchor shank down and prevent chafing on the sea bottom, especially if one is moored in coral beds.

It is a misconception that lighter multihulls will need lighter anchors or moorings than monohulls; due to their higher windage they will require at least the same ground tackle as single-hulled boats.

Multihull anchor and ground tackle size guide lines:

Length of Catamaran (ft.)	Min. Chain Leader Length	Main Anchor	Chain Size (high tensile)	Nylon Diameter
30' to 35'	30'	25 lbs.	3/8"	3/4"
35' to 40'	30'	35 lbs.	7/16"	7/8"
40' to 50'	36'	45 lbs	7/16"	1"
50' to 60'	42'	60 lbs.	1/2"	1 1/4"
over 60'	50' +	75 lbs. +	1/2" +	1 1/5" +
* It is recommended to carry a back up anchor of at least the size of the next lower category				

"We shall not cease from exploration,
and at the end of all our exploring we will arrive where we started
and know the place for the first time."

~ *T. S. Eliot* - Little Gidding

Cascais

HEAVY WEATHER tactics

As passing storm swells let the boat surf towards safe land, the crew is happy not to have broken anything. On this rough transatlantic passage we chafed through half a dozen boom preventer end-lashings; a still intact one can be seen attached to the cleat, next to the runner-block.

HEAVY WEATHER TACTICS

Scores of books have been written about heavy weather sailing, but few of them address the particulars of multihulls and their individual considerations. Monohulls have more commonalities as a group, therefore there are more general guidelines. Storm tactics for multihulls will depend more on the capabilities of crew and vessel than any other factors.

Barreling along at 18 knots in strong winds can be thrilling and is a highlight of multihull sailing. Making no seamanship errors will be as important as the simplest rules of keeping all lines neatly organized and kink free. Often tangled lines have gotten sailors into more trouble than anything else. Keeping a neat cockpit and thinking ahead are the cheapest insurances against mishaps.

In heavy weather the boat should be set up with appropriate safety lines and attaching yourself to them must be mandatory, even if one only ventures briefly into the cockpit. All crew should wear full gear and always have their life jackets at the ready. Each member should have a strobe, knife and whistle permanently attached and there always should be a big knife with a serrated edge mounted in the cockpit to quickly cut a jammed line, if necessary. Basic safety drills, location of life saving equipment, rafts and throw-able MOB devices must be known to each crewmember. Everyone on board must understand the crucial function of EPIRBs, VHFs, firefighting equipment, as well as engine operation and bilge-pump system. It is all really common sense.

If in the highly unlikely event that you capsize, stay with the boat at all costs. Rig one life raft or dinghy to the underside of the bridge deck, fly a kite and wait for help. Never, ever separate from the mother ship as your chances of being spotted will be close to zero in a raft. Staying warm, hydrated, and clear headed will be as important as keeping crew morale up. Salvage as much food and water as you can and secure them, as waves in the interior will wash them out any opening. It has been suggested to await help in the upturned vessel, but unless it is a perfect calm, it will be impossible. Wave surges in the cabins will be violent and there will be leaking battery acid, foul smells and floating objects that will force you onto the upturned platform of the bridge deck.

Storm strategies will depend on the sea state. The shorter and higher the wave faces, the more critical correct seamanship will be. It is my opinion that the use of sea anchors should be carefully weighed and avoided if one can actively deal with the conditions. In theory, they work well if conditions do not change. The crew can rest and the multihull will make nominal drift downwind, provided there is minimal searoom. But the sea is a chaotic environment and waves do not always remain in one and the same pattern, direction, and period. The forces and loads on the boat when tied to a parachute type device can be huge.

True and Apparent Wave Height

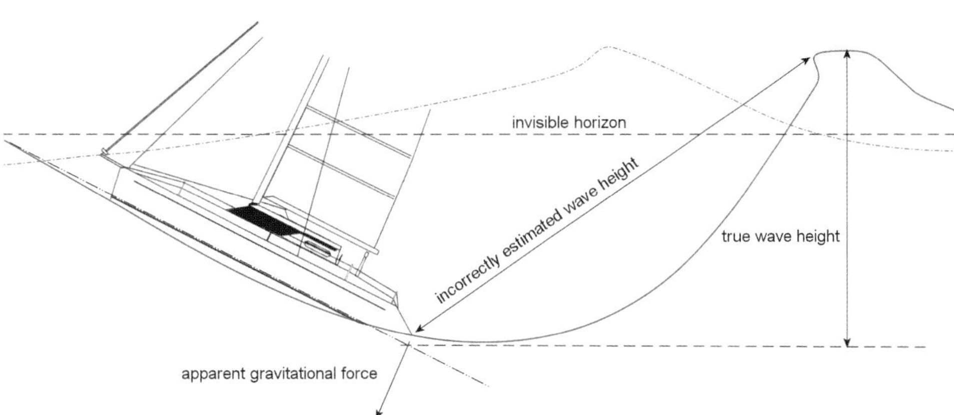

Wave heights make great subjects for sea tales, but the altitude of seas are often overestimated. Especially on smaller vessels, when the horizon is hidden, one feels that the seas are steeper than they actually are. The apparent gravitational pull makes one think that the boat is sailing parallel on the horizontal plane. Usually however, the boat is already ascending the next wave, leading to estimation errors as high as 50% in judging wave heights.

Imagine your boat hanging off a sea anchor and suddenly a wave from a different direction slams into the boat from the side. As the boat is not moving, actually drifting slightly backwards, it will not have any possibility to handle this odd rogue wave. The catamaran might be overwhelmed and rotate around its longitudinal axis and flip. Most cruising catamarans that have capsized were constricted by sea anchors. In one well-documented incident, the parachute's lines caught under the rudders and turned the boat.

A sea anchor might lull you into a false sense of security and your vigilance will be reduced. Being caught with your guard down is the most dangerous situation, and I feel it is better to actively deal with storm conditions, rather than letting the boat drift off a sea anchor. Besides, retrieval and deployment are risky, and if not done properly the first time, they can subject crew and boat to more risks.

This is not to say that a parachute anchor does not work. On the contrary, many multihulls have ridden out hurricanes with these devices. Personally, I would want to position the boat to sail with the seas if there is sea room. The vessel's speed should be adjusted to the wave period and therefore would reduce the relative impact of waves. If one's cat sails too fast, even without sails up, a drogue or warps could be dragged behind the boat. Streaming warps off a stern bridle will also be helpful if the boat has lost steerage. It will keep the bows pointing downwind. Ideally, seas should be taken off the rear quarter in order to present the longest diagonal axis to them. This will be the most stable attitude, and a good multihull will be able to handle the most severe conditions. A well-working autopilot, an alert crew, and a strong boat will get you through anything. Concentration will deteriorate as the conditions worsen and any mistake will be very difficult to rectify. Your margin for error will be minimal and advance thinking and anticipation will be key. Approaching a safe harbor during heavy weather can be nerve-wracking and should be carefully weighed with the risk of running aground and encountering much rougher than usual inlets. Often standing off will take discipline but be safer.

Again it should be mentioned that everyone manages differently with storm conditions and there is not necessarily only one right or wrong way to do it. Making the vessel's speed work for you and being able to

Safely slowing the multihull is accomplished by streaming warps or trailing a special drogue. A large bridle is either fastened to the windward hull or to the sterns.

Streaming Warps or a Drogue to Slow Down

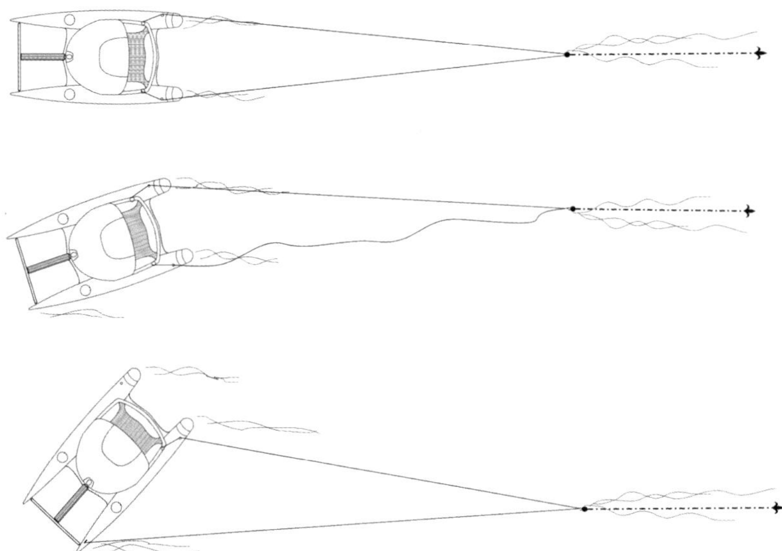

outrun a system will reduce your exposure time. Drifting slowly downwind tied to a sea anchor will expose you to bad weather longer. The advantage of a fast catamaran should be used to get you out of trouble, or even better, by using today's advanced meteorological forecasts, you might be able to avoid it entirely. Yet, once you are in storm conditions, slowing down the boat to retain full control will be challenging.

If there is no sea room, or one is forced to claw upwind, reducing speed to minimize wave impact is imperative to the comfort of the crew and safety of the boat. Finding the right groove between stalling and too much speed is important. You do not want to be caught by a wave slamming into you, bringing you to a halt. This could end up in a lack of steerage and, in the worst case, you could be flipped backwards. Always keep on sailing at a manageable speed and if your boat has daggerboards, both boards should be down one third only. Head closer to the wind towards the top of the wave, and fall off as the boat sails down the slope. This will aid in keeping the sails drawing and boat speed in check. Structural shocks upwind in very strong winds can be very tough, so find the right speed. Reducing your main to 3 or even 4 reefs and furling your headsail for balance will drive you to weather. We all know that this will not be comfortable, but if there is no choice other than to windward, one will manage until conditions have abated. Flatten sails as much as you can to depower the boat. If you need to tack, plan ahead, do it decisively, and with plenty of momentum. You do not want to be caught in irons while drifting backwards. Loads on the rudders with the boat going in reverse can damage the steering, leaving you crippled.

Running off at a controllable speed is the safest way to handle a storm. If you are deep reaching or sailing downwind with the storm, retract both boards if your boat has daggerboards. In the event that the catamaran is skittish and hard to steer, lower one foot of daggerboard on both sides. Long, well balanced, high-aspect-ratio hulls, especially ones equipped with skegs far aft, will track well, even without boards. A tiny amount of jib sheeted hard amidships might be all that is needed to point the boat downwind. Reduce the boat to a speed where you are just a fraction slower than the waves.

Keep in mind that the term "slow" is relative as this could still mean that you are traveling at well over 15 knots!

Sailing with the beam to the storm and seas should be avoided at any cost. If, because of say navigational issues, one has no choice, both daggerboards must be lifted to assure sideways slippage.

Heaving-to is a tactic which lets the boat sail controlled, almost stationary, and should be used only if one has no more alternatives. This could be caused by crew exhaustion or mechanical issues with the boat. When heaving-to, the helm is locked to windward, a tiny scrap of jib sheeted to weather, and/or a heavily reefed mainsail can be set. The traveler should be let off to leeward and, theoretically, the multihull will steadily work herself to windward. At 40 degrees, she will either be stationary or slightly fore-reach. This does not work on all multihulls and different mainsail and jib combinations should be tested. Also letting the main or jib luff slightly will take speed off the boat, if

far right Boarding via the transom platform, any guest will easily find his/her way to the spacious cockpit by walking down wide, teak-covered steps. Notice the lack of any sail controls or helm station – they are all located out of the way, on the flybridge above.

so desired. Catamarans with daggerboards should only have very little windward board down to avoid tripping.

Similar to "heaving-to" lying-a-hull differs from boat to boat. In this attitude the boat will carry no sails at all and fend for herself. In case of daggerboards, retract them. Most boats will take the seas on their beams (not my favorite) and let the waves pass under them by surfing sideways. Just as trying to avoid the use of sea anchors, this tactic should only be reverted to if one has exhausted every other possibility.

There are a few generalities that will help you learn about heavy weather sailing tactics. Fine-tuning the sails will help depower the boat. As the wind increases, move the mainsail sheeting point to leeward. This is one of the best features of multihull sailing. Multihulls have wide travelers and an extensive sheeting base which allows for more choices for sail trim than narrow boats. Ease off the traveler to move the main to leeward and use a strong outside rail attachment point, such as a cleat or toe rail track to move the jib to leeward. As the wind strengthens, reduce camber and flatten the sails. Double up preventers and reef lines to create backups and divide the loads. In the end, knowing when to reef and how to control your cat is the most important skill to develop to prepare for heavy weather sailing. Practicing maneuvers in strong conditions will raise your level of confidence and prepare you for the worst Mother Nature might have in store for us.

Heaving-to is an important "parking" technique that should be practiced by every catamaran owner. One tacks from a close-hauled position and either luffs the mainsail or furls it completely. Once on the other tack, the jib is left on the "wrong" side and the helm is turned hard to windward. Every multihull will behave differently, and one has to experiment how hard the headsail must be sheeted in or how far the rudders must be turned. Keel catamarans will behave slightly differently than daggerboard cats. The headsail will keep the bows turned away from the seas, while the rudders will prevent the boat from presenting her beams to the waves. In the heave-to attitude, the catamaran will fore-reach and slightly drift to leeward.

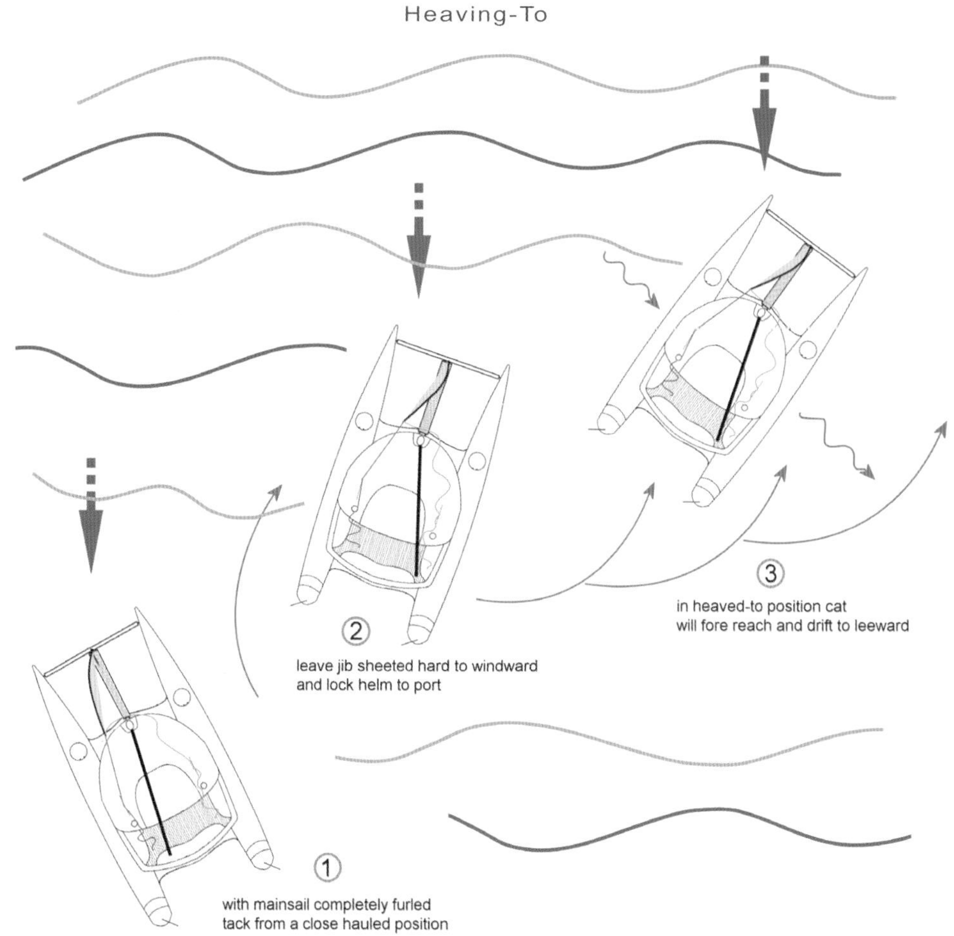
Heaving-To
2
leave jib sheeted hard to windward
and lock helm to port
3
in heaved-to position cat
will fore reach and drift to leeward
1
with mainsail completely furled
tack from a close hauled position

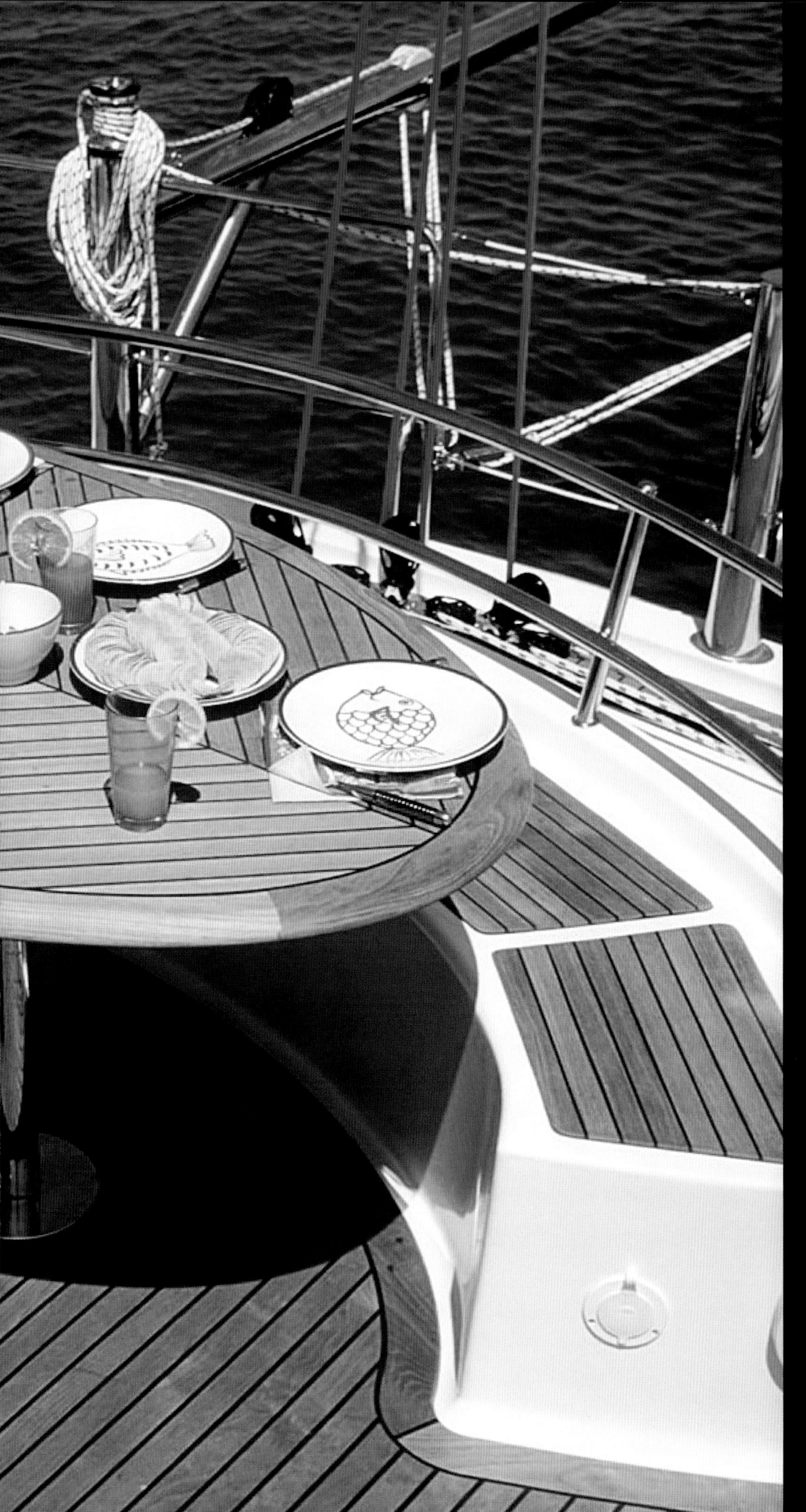

NOTEWORTHY **multihulls**

A teak-covered table and seati
surfaces are not only practical
but give the yacht a feel of lux
Six to eight guests can easily
around the cockpit table of this
60' cat.

NOTEWORTHY MULTIHULLS

In the following chapter I have attempted to objectively present and illustrate some of the popular cruising catamarans which are available today. Purposely omitting custom boat builders, the multihulls in this section represent about 90% of today's production cats.

My company, Aeroyacht Ltd., an international dealership specializing in multihulls ranging from 35'-200', has seen several new builders come and go over the past few decades; the following yards seem to have passed the test of time. Readers who are shopping for a catamaran have the possibility to consult our web site, www.Aeroyacht.com, which features tests, movies and pictures, and keeps track of the newest developments of popular cruising multihulls.

In my quest to include all manufacturers, we have contacted yards and dealers around the world. This catalogue of cruising cats will permit the reader to glance at features and characteristics and quickly compare one model to the other.

LOMAC
LOMAC

ATLANTIC 55

Specifications

Length .... 55.6'
Beam .... 28.4'
Displacement ..... 26,800 lbs
Draft .... 3.8' / 7.10'
Mast Height........ 75'
Fuel .... 200 gal
Water................. 160 gal

The Atlantic series of catamarans are the original center-cockpit, aft-pilothouse design multihulls. Designed by Chris White in 1984 they have gone through 22 years of continuous development and provide cruising sailors with a blend of comfort, safety and sailing performance. Construction is modern epoxy/glass/carbon composite and the boat is built in Cape Town, South Africa. The outstanding feature of the Atlantic 55 is her center cockpit, situated ahead of the saloon coachhouse. Although one is often exposed to spray when sailing upwind, one can conveniently take shelter in the spacious saloon, which houses an excellent inside helm with a wheel. The aft cockpit features generous lounge and storage areas. Unlike other cruising catamarans, Chris White has cleverly managed to keep the fineness ratio of the hulls to a minimum, yet he has designed sufficient payload-carrying ability for a couple with children and occasional guests.

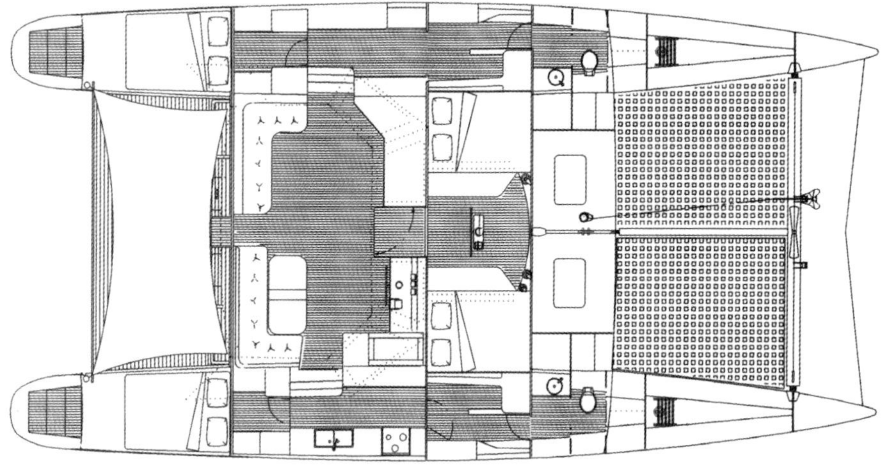

BLUBAY 100

Specifications

Length .... 100'
Beam .... 43'
Displacement ..... 44 tons
Draft .... 6.2' / 14.8'
Mast Height........ 123'
Fuel.................... 1,585 gal
Water................. 792 gal

With the recent introduction of "Allures" in Cannes, France, the first of the Blubay 100 series of super cats has been launched. This mega catamaran can only be described in superlatives, as no expense has been spared to create not only one of the most beautiful and comfortable, but also the fastest superyacht in the world. "Allures" will be able to travel in excess of 35 knots rivaling any vessel at sea. Daggerboards can reduce her draft, providing access to shallow harbors, which would normally be denied to mega yachts of her size. Her designer, Jean-Jacques Costes, brings with him 30 years of big-multihull experience and his company, Blubay Yachts, also works with Airbus industries on aeronautical engineering projects. The Blubay 100 is the largest, all-carbon structure ever built. Strain gauges constantly monitor loads, which can be observed at either the two flybridge helm stations, or the expansive interior navigation center. From her aramid rigging and carbon mast to her specially selected fine interior joiner work, this Blubay 100 will provide her owner with many seasons of cruising pleasure and will remain a landmark of catamaran engineering for many years to come.

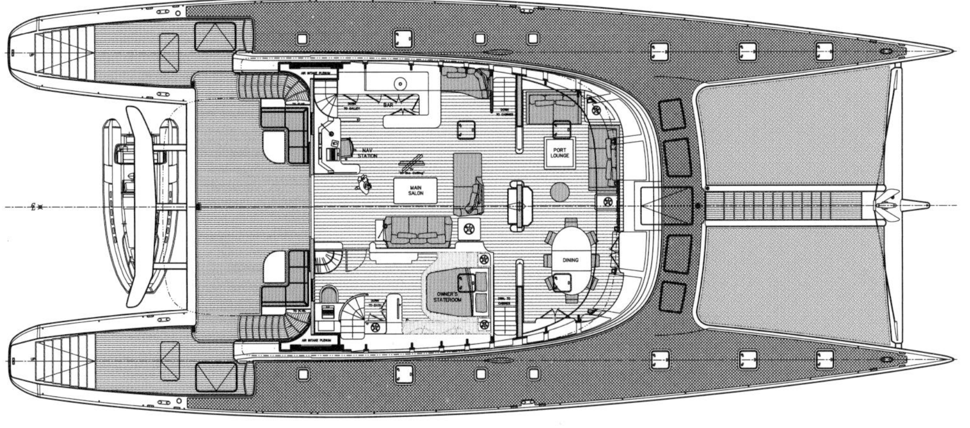

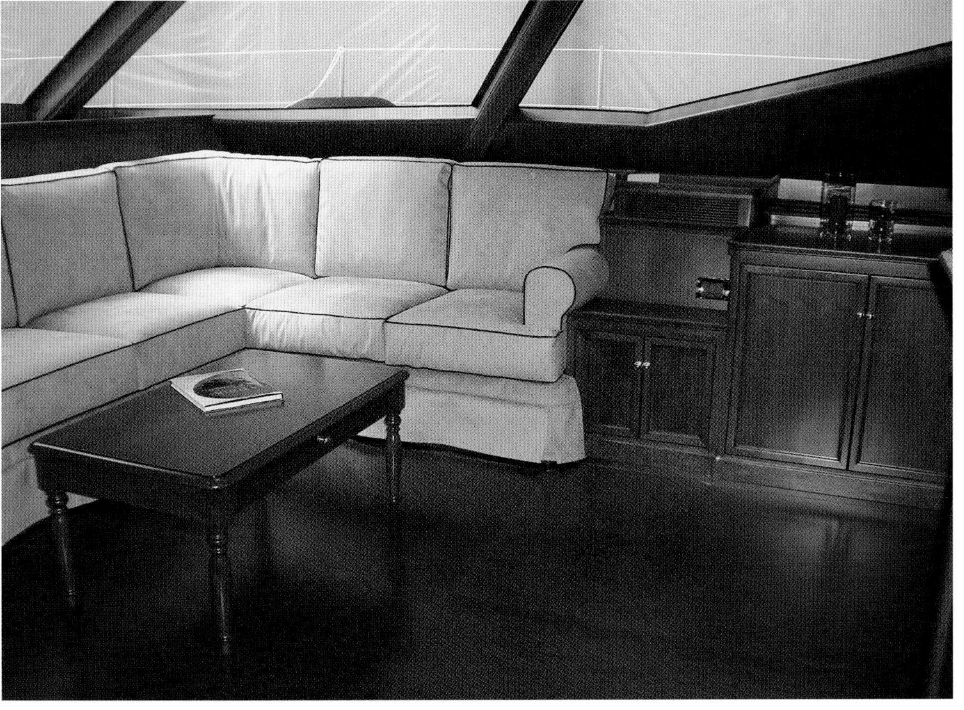

BROADBLUE 435

Specifications

Length .... 43.5'
Beam .... 22'
Displacement ..... 22,430 lbs
Draft .... 4'2"
Mast Height........ 62'
Fuel .... 117 gal
Water .... 125 gal

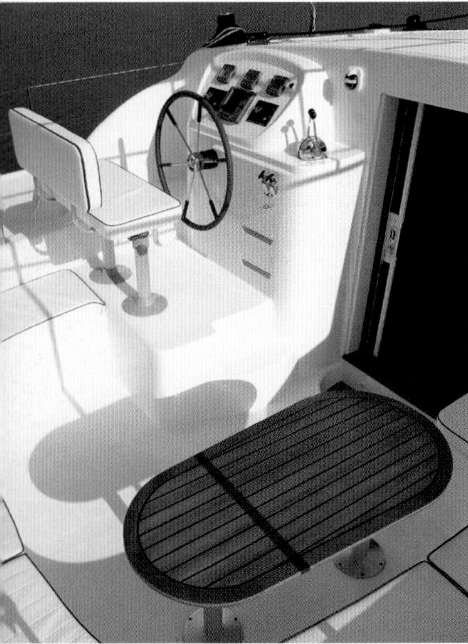

The Broadblue 435 is an updated version of the famous Prout line of catamarans, which made its mark in the '70s and '80s. In the tradition of British offshore cruisers, the interior is well finished and offers quality craftsmanship and elegant joinery. Available as an Owner's version (3 cabins, 2 baths), Charter version (4 cabins, 2 shared baths) or customized interior, the Broadblue 435 is a stately vessel which emphasizes liveaboard comfort and safety.

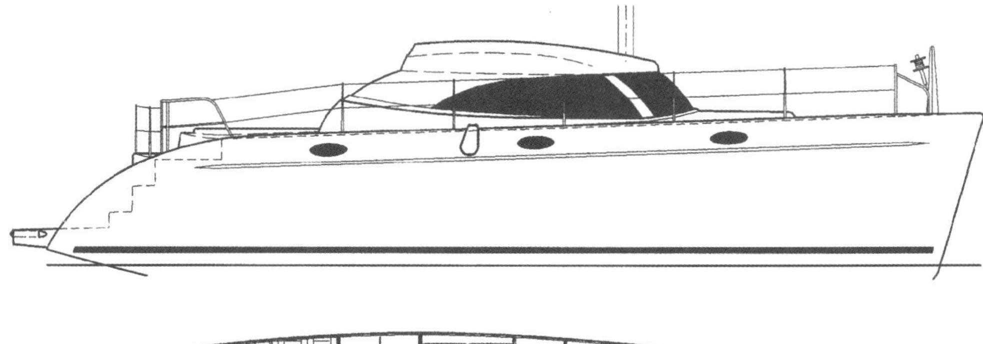

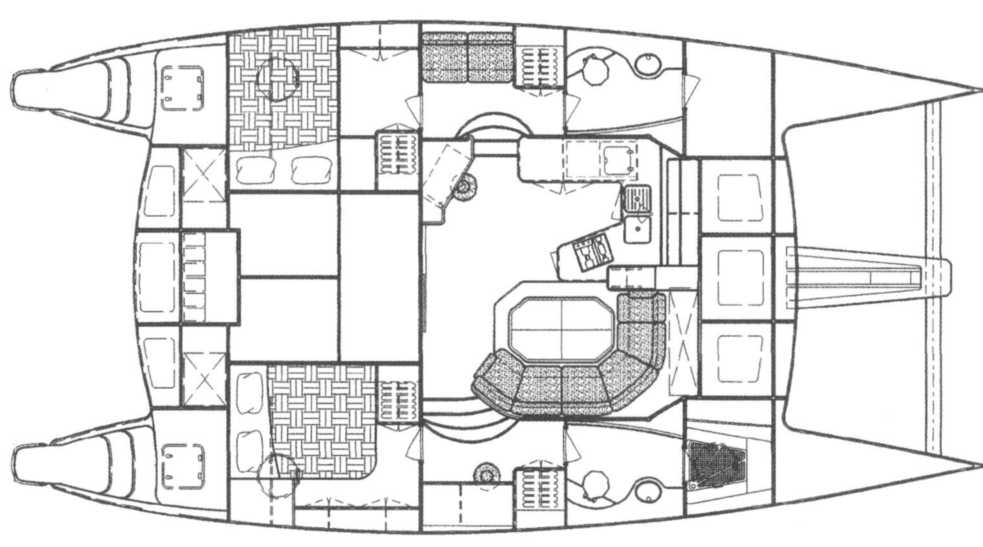

02

CATANA 52

Specifications

Length .... 52'
Beam .... 28.2'
Displacement ..... 44,000 lbs
Draft .... 4.5' / 8.6'
Mast Height........ 78.7''
Fuel .... 211 gal
Water .... 211 gal

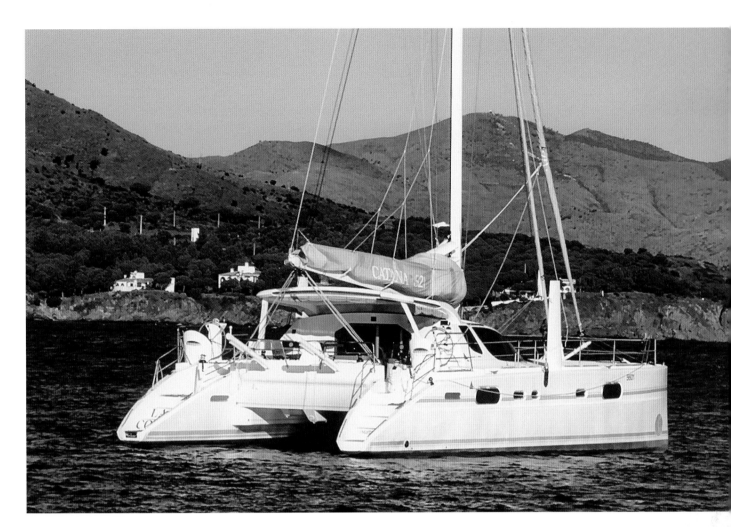

The Catana 52 represents a high-tech production catamaran, which is equipped with retractable daggerboards, a rarity on today's market. She is constructed using aramid fibers in her composite skin and her standard gear includes items such as a washer/dryer, watermaker and a carbon mast. A smart, passive ventilation system, flat decks, which facilitate getting about the boat, and centralized sail controls are just some of the innovative features of the Catana. Unique design details are her inclined hulls, which add to her stability, her tulip-shaped bows and very high freeboard. Although this increases interior volume, the windage can be substantial and the boat's visual appearance may suffer from some angles. Large hull windows, elegant fittings and a choice of two layouts make the Catana a swift and well-fitted catamaran.

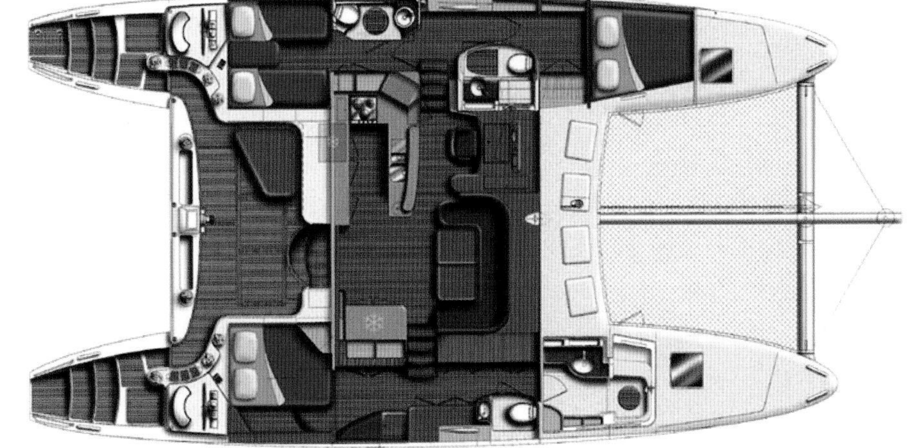

DOLPHIN 46

Specifications

Length .... 45.9'
Beam .... 24.2'
Displacement ..... 24,250 lbs
Draft .... 3.7' / 7.5'
Mast Height........ 65.6'
Fuel .... 118 gal
Water................. 118 gal

The Dolphin 46 is a cruising catamaran, built in Brazil. Her interior is richly finished with local hardwood trim, teak-type flooring, and finely fitted cabinetry. Her twin daggerboards help her point going to windward and reduce resistance when sailing off the wind. She sports a semicircular saloon table, providing space for 8, while the cook has an unobstructed view from his forward facing galley. Nearly vertical saloon windows help reduce heat radiation from the tropical sun and her built in hull portlights provide an airy and light hull interior. The Dolphin 46 is a catamaran that has broad appeal to sailors who care not only about well appointed amenities, but the feel of the yacht underway.

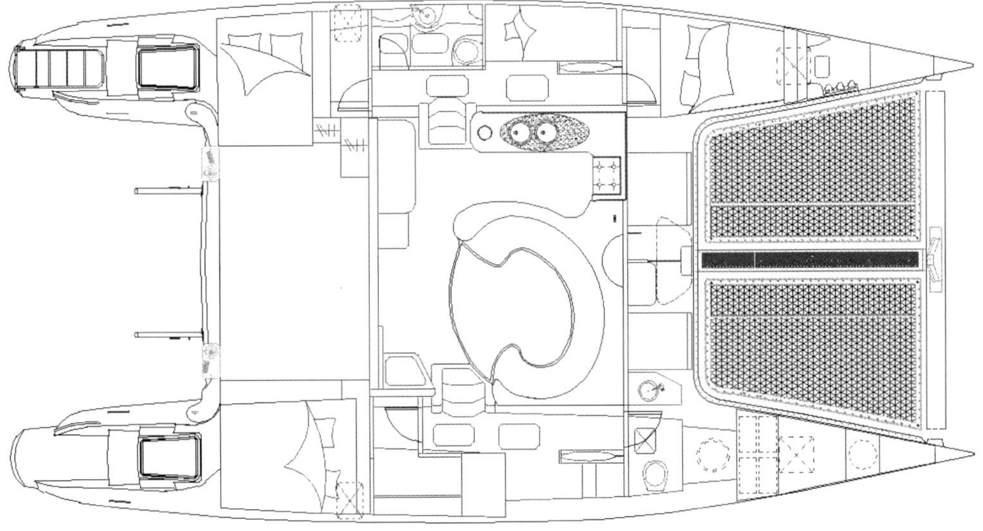

FOUNTAINE PAJOT – ELEUTHERA 60

Specifications

Length .... 60'
Beam .... 28'
Displacement ..... 38,500 lbs
Draft .... 4.7'
Mast Height........ 78.8'
Fuel .... 158 gal
Water .... 213 gal

Starting from her introduction in the Fall of 2004, the Eleuthera 60 became Fountaine Pajot's flagship and instant success. As one of the largest one-piece infusion composite structures in the world, this catamaran not only enjoys the 30-year experience from the world's oldest multihull builder, but also a bulletproof construction, which will assure longevity and good resale value. As with all Fountaine Pajot cruising catamarans, emphasis is placed on excellent sailing performance, reliability of the ship's systems and ease of handling by a couple. The Eleuthera 60's overhanging coach roof reduces sun glare and heat, contributing to her good looks and has become the trademark of the entire line of Fountaine Pajots from 35 to 75 feet. As one of the best values on the market the Eleuthera 60 is available in 4 interior versions, of which one is shown below.

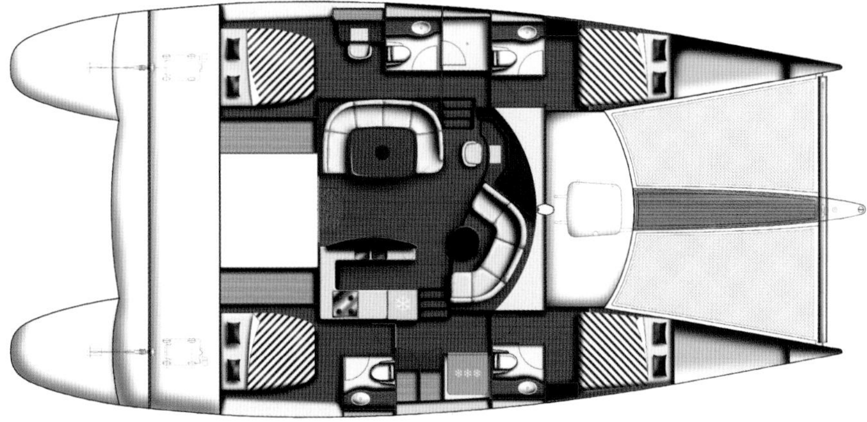

GEMINI 105Mc

Specifications

Length .... 33.6'
Beam .... 14'
Displacement ..... 9,600 lbs
Draft .... 18" / 5.5'
Mast Height........ 46'
Fuel .... 36 gal
Water................. 60 gal

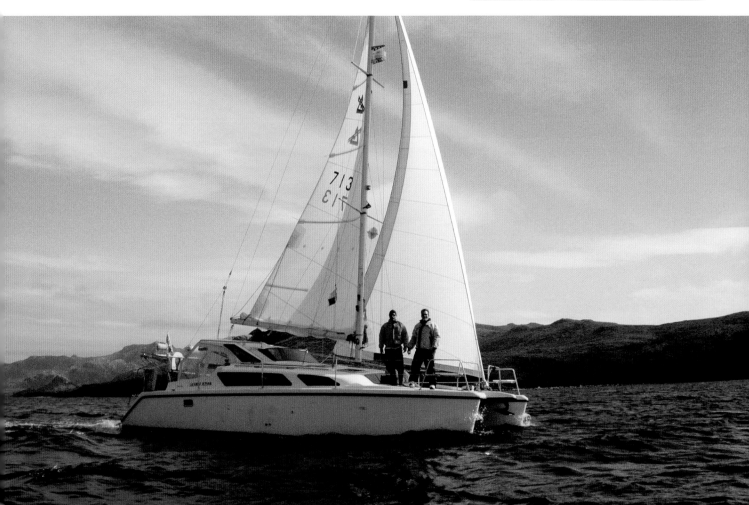

The Gemini 105Mc is a phenomenon. With close to 1,000 boats sold in the last decade, Tony Smith and his family have dedicated their lives to the production of one the most practical and cost-efficient catamarans. The Gemini 105, which is built near Annapolis, MD features centerboards which can absorb minor impacts by retracting. A masthead rig with a large genoa keeps the mainsail size manageable and also permits the mast to be placed farther aft for better balance. The Gemini's smart features, such as a hard dodger, integrated bowsprit and circular traveler for the gennaker tack and an innovative yet open layout plan, offer liveaboard couples a practical surrounding. Another outstanding feature of the Gemini is her true ability to ghost into the shallowest harbors. A unique propulsion system consisting of a single 27 HP diesel connected to a "Sillette Sonic Leg" can swing up, just like the liftable rudder, which greatly adds to the safety of this catamaran. If one keeps a conservative eye on payload and does not overload the boat, the Gemini 105 is possibly one of the best pocket-size cruisers available today.

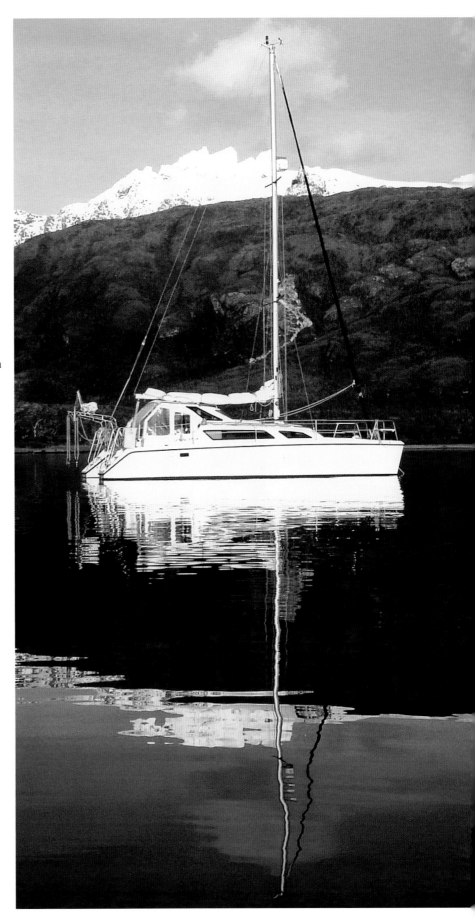

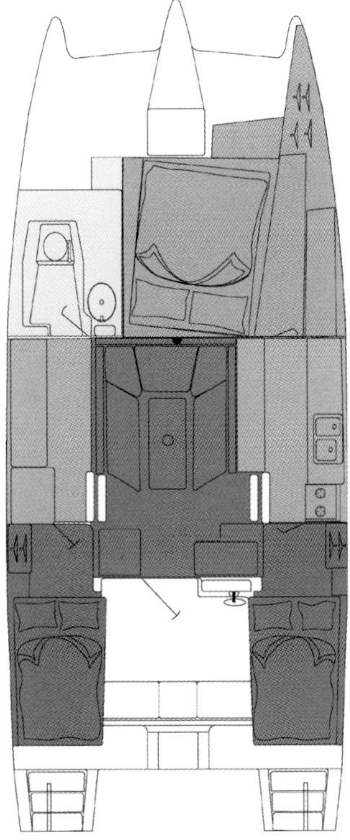

GUNBOAT 49

Specifications

Length .... 48.4'
Beam .... 24.3'
Displacement ..... 22,500 lbs
Draft .... 2' / 7.4'
Mast Height........ 72.2'
Fuel .... 130 gal
Water .... 100 gal

The Gunboat is built in South Africa, out of high-tech aramid composites and introduces a fresh, new concept to performance sailing. The idea of separating the social from the steering cockpit is not a new idea, yet Peter Johnston and his company have taken it one step farther. Low resistance hulls and ultra-low displacement allow 300-mile-per-day runs in ideal conditions, distances which only large racing yachts achieve. Although the interior is not as plush as comparable cruising catamarans', the company uses top-quality fittings and fine woods, tastefully blending the modern with the best of traditional design. Innovative features such as kick-up rudders, centralized sail controls and engines, located midships, make the Gunboat one of the most forward thinking catamarans on the market today.

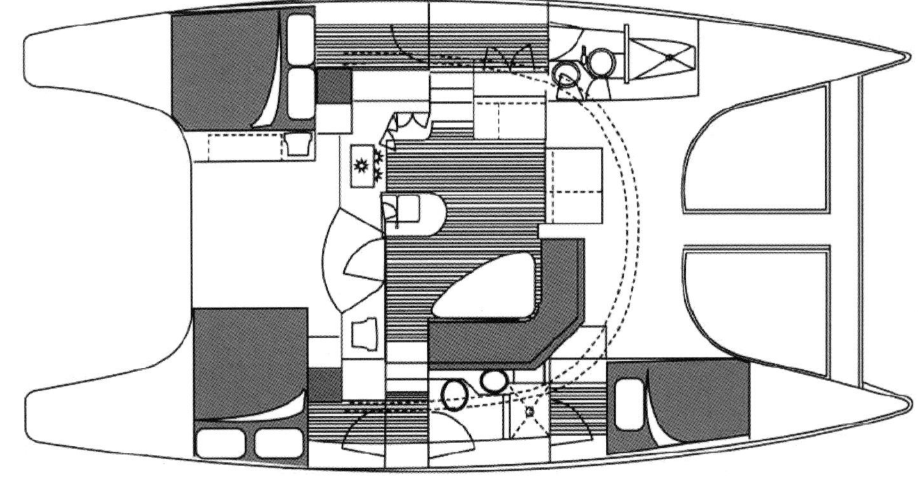

LAGOON 410

Specifications

Length .... 40.5'
Beam .... 23.5'
Displacement ..... 17,400 lbs
Draft .... 3.11'
Mast Height........ 60'
Fuel .... 52 gal
Water .... 103 gal

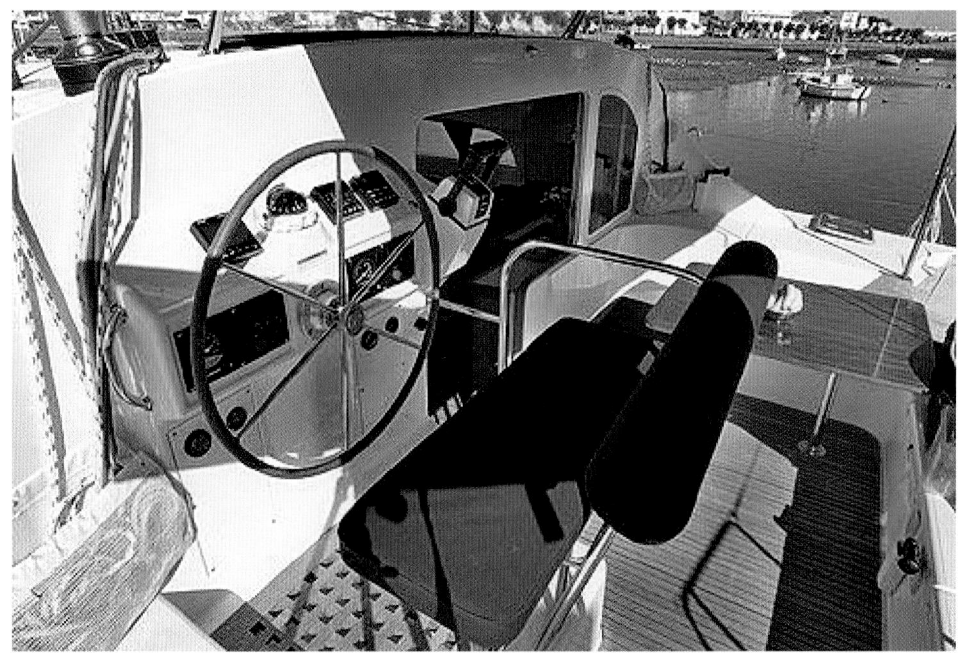

The Lagoon 410 is a popular cruising cat, which through her spacious interior combines comfort with excellent charter potential. Vertical windows surround the saloon, which might not help aerodynamics, yet increase space in the forward part of the bridgedeck. An efficient fractional sail plan facilitates boat handling and her twin-diesel engines allow plenty of maneuverability in tight harbors. The Lagoon 410 features large hull windows and finely finished wood joiner work; all contribute to her liveaboard qualities. Her ample displacement will allow plenty of payload for charter guests and 4 double cabins with en suite heads complement the Lagoon's roomy interior.

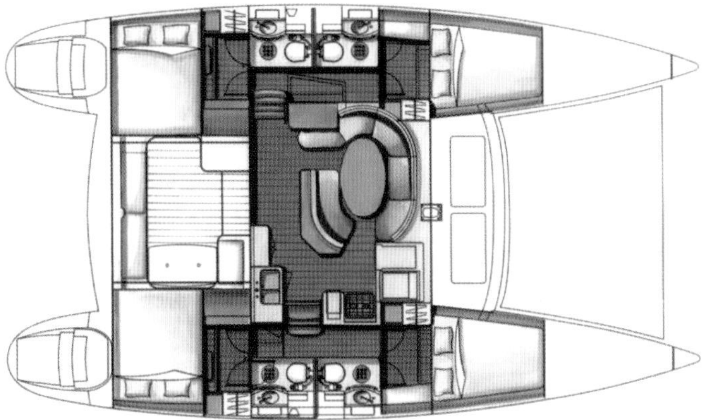

LEOPARD 40

Specifications

Length .... 39.3'
Beam .... 20.1'
Displacement ..... 16,870 lbs
Draft .... 3.9'
Mast Height........ 61.9'
Fuel .... 92 gal
Water................. 206 gal

The Leopard 40 (the charter version is called the Mooring 40) is the newest addition to the popular line of South African catamarans built by Robertson & Caine. Due to her careful construction and standard accommodation features, this catamaran has become sought after by charter companies and cruisers alike. The rigid hardtop spans the entire width of the cockpit and incorporates a sliding section, which allows the helmsman to view the sails from the steering position. Generously proportioned aft-walkways and wide decks make getting about the boat easy. The interior finish features excellent livability with a galley-up design, a spacious saloon area and an aft-facing galley provides the cook with excellent visibility. The Leopard 40 is available with 3 or 4 cabins and a separate study area incorporated into the 3-cabin version.

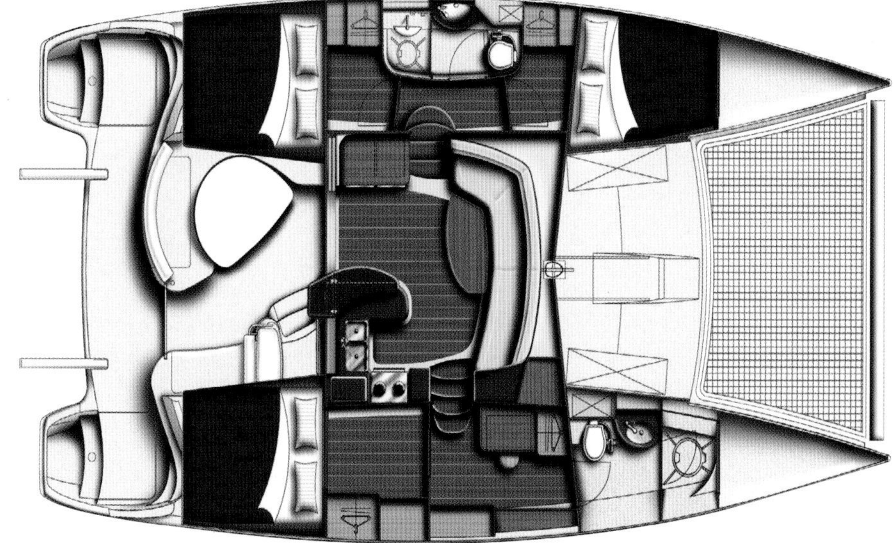

MAINE CAT 41

Specifications

Length .... 41.6'
Beam .... 23'
Displacement ..... 14,000 lbs
Draft .... 3'6" / 7'
Mast Height........ 60'
Fuel .... 92 gal
Water .... 136 gal

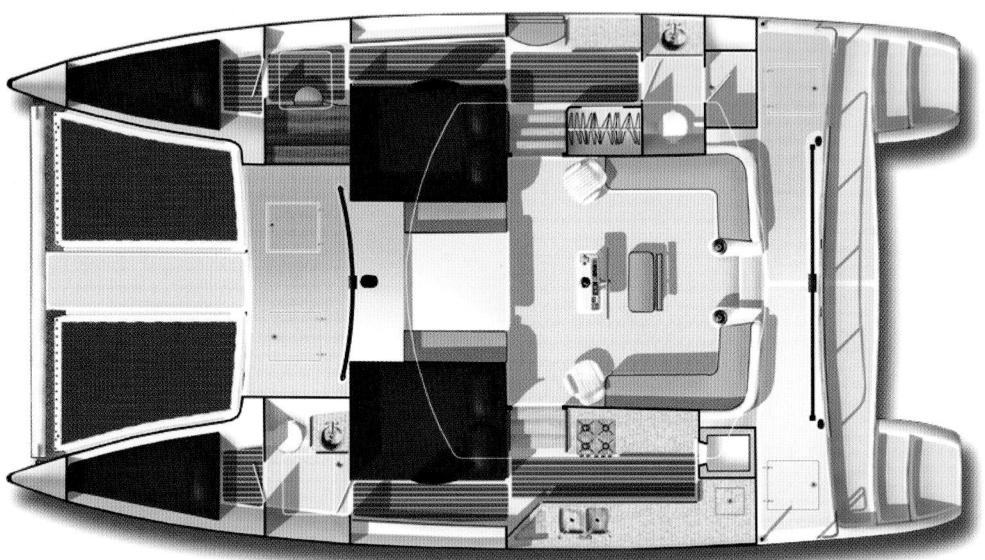

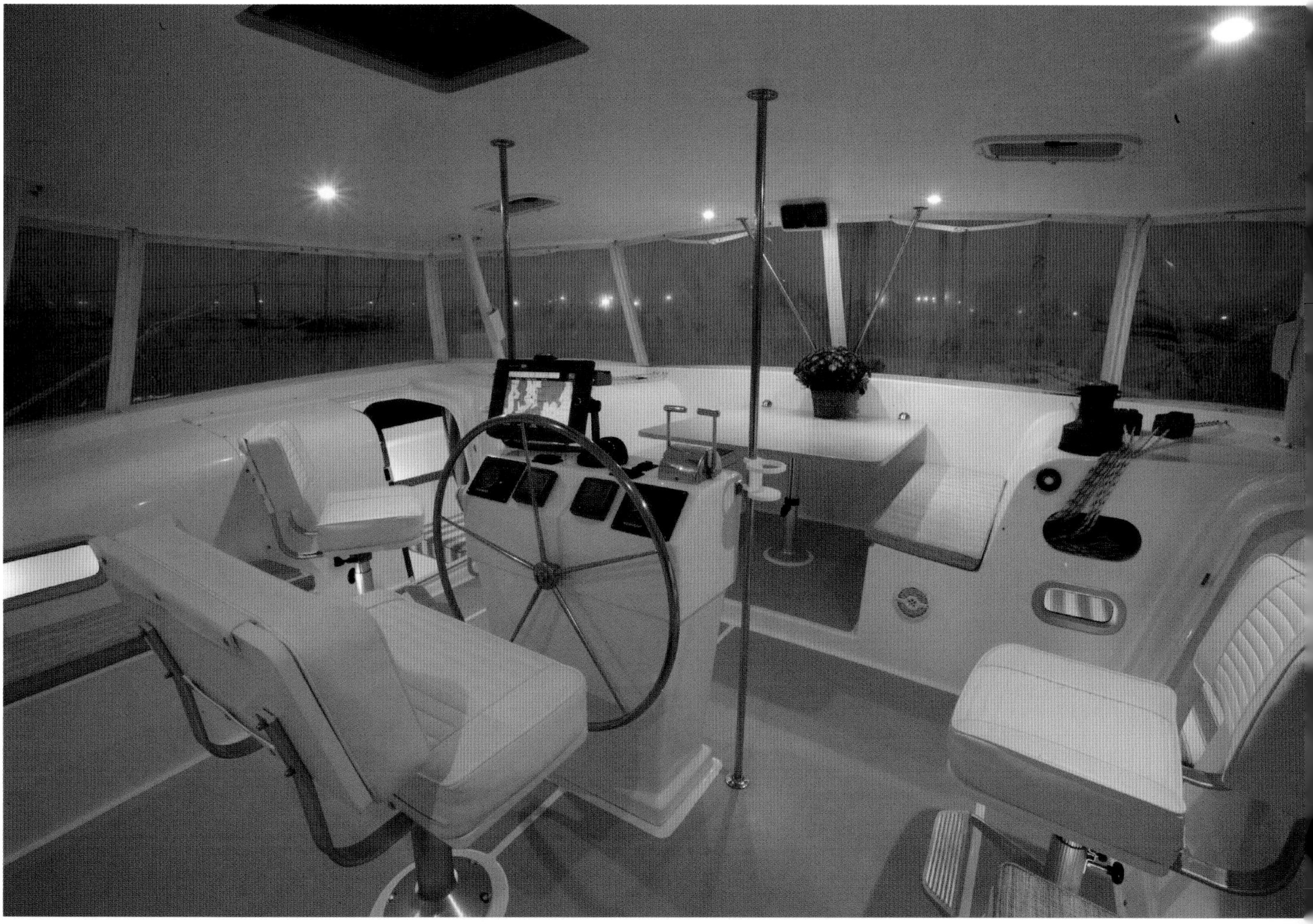

The Maine Cat 41 is a little masterpiece, built in Maine by craftsmen who have also produced the popular Maine Cat 30. The new 41-footer maintains the tradition of an open bridgedeck design, good sailing performance and a practical and exceptionally well-finished interior. This daggerboard-equipped cat can easily be single-handed from a central wheel and navigation station located in the forward part of the cockpit. In inclement weather the entire bridge deck can be converted into an enclosure, via side curtains which quickly attach to the rigid bimini. The Maine Cat 41 has excellent seakeeping abilities, thanks to her high bridgedeck clearance, conservative sail plan and buoyant hulls. This catamaran is an outstanding choice for people looking for a spirited daysailer and safe passage maker.

MANTA 42

Specifications

Length .... 41.8'
Beam .... 21'
Displacement ..... 17,400 lbs
Draft .... 3.8'
Mast Height........ 59.9'
Fuel .... 120 gal
Water .... 100 gal

The Manta 42 is an evolution of the successful 40-footer which established the Florida company at the forefront of the US cruising catamaran market. Perfectly adapted to short-handed sailing, she features a unique camber-spar jib which is self-tacking. Unlike most production multihulls the Manta 42 has a laminated forward crossbeam, which is arched well over the waterline to reduce impacts in heavy seas. A very substantial stainless-steel aft-arch structure is available, which acts as antenna supports and dinghy davits. The Manta 42's solid bimini has integrated solar panels and spans the entire cockpit. Unique features include outside louvers, which keep solar radiation to a minimum and contribute to onboard comfort of this popular catamaran.

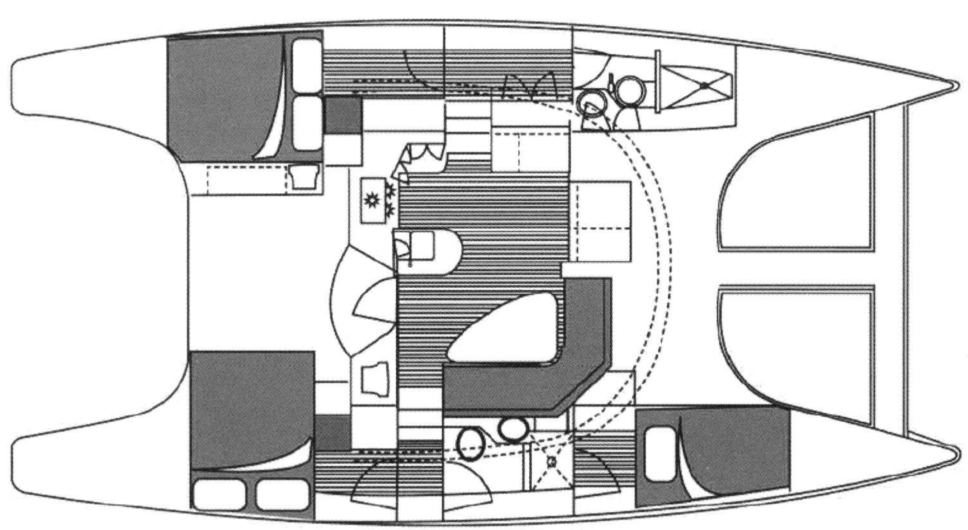

OUTREMER 42

Specifications

Length .... 42.7'
Beam .... 22.4'
Displacement ..... 14,800 lbs
Draft .... 1.9' / 7.9'
Mast Height........ 59.9'
Fuel .... 63 gal
Water .... 115 gal

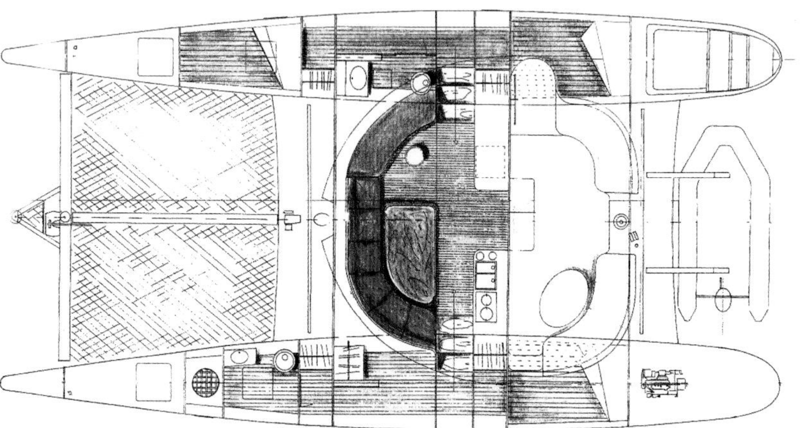

The Outremer line of catamarans belongs to one of the most proven and tested multihulls in the world. More than 160 of these performance-daggerboard cats have been constructed in a period of 25 years by the specialist builders from the south of France. Throughout virtually millions of ocean miles Outremers have demonstrated their seaworthiness and ability to safely sail through the worst weather. Centered weight, high bridgedeck clearance and efficient hulls provide excellent performance under sail or power. The new Outremer 42 is entirely infusion built and will out-rival equivalent length cats in handling and speed. Being able to order a custom interior greatly adds to the nature of these very special catamarans.

PDQ – ANTARES 44

Specifications

Length .... 44'
Beam .... 21.9'
Displacement ..... 22,500 lbs
Draft .... 4'
Mast Height........ 61'
Fuel .... 120 gal
Water................. 150 gal

The Antares 44 is the flagship of PDQ Yachts of Canada. Well known for their popular 32' and 36' models, the Antares combines good sailing characteristics with a spacious, liveaboard interior. Extra volume has been achieved by raising the topsides of the hulls, and although this might create more windage and give the boat a boxy look, the space gained is considerable. As with the earlier vessels the boat features a hard, full-width bimini, which supports the main traveler and twin solar panels. Bridgedeck clearance of 30" at full load and a well-designed hull shape assure seaworthy behavior and good overall performance.

Well finished and with a list of standard options which leave no wish unfulfilled, the Antares 44 is an excellent choice for long-range cruisers who are looking for a quality-built cruising catamaran.

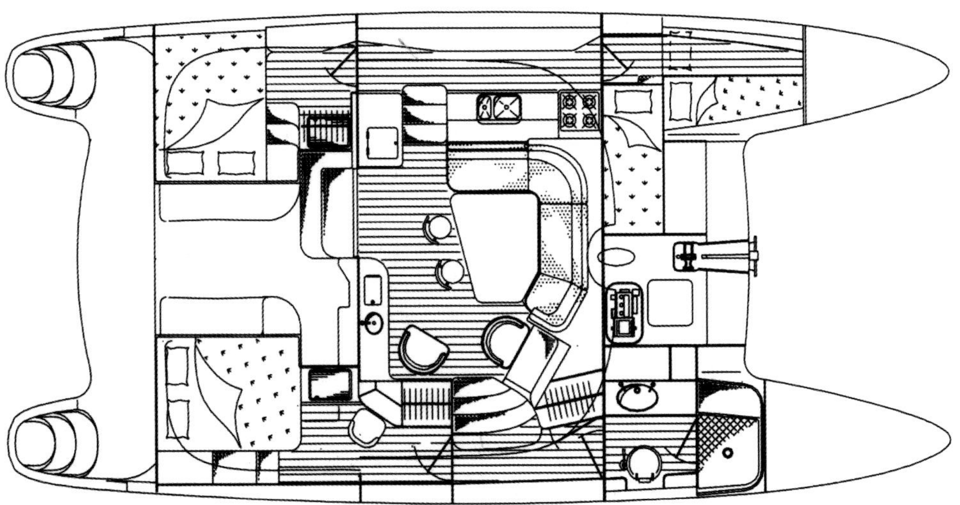

PRIVILÈGE 495

Specifications

Length .... 49.05'
Beam .... 24.05'
Displacement ..... 27,400 lbs
Draft .... 4.4'
Mast Height........ 62.5'
Fuel .... 159 gal
Water................. 185 gal

Like all Privilège yachts, the interior and finish surround the crew in a comfortable and luxurious atmosphere. The trademark for these popular French catamarans is the pronounced nacelle, which extends forward of the saloon and houses either a berth or is used as a large storage locker. Care has to be taken not to overload these compartments as bridgedeck clearance and underway comfort may suffer. Although some manufacturers claim that the sharp V-shape of the nacelle bottom could split through waves, there is very little that can resist continued impact of seas and any conflict between the wing deck and waves should be avoided. Sharply raked saloon windows contribute to the boat's attractive looks and also reduce the vessel's wind resistance. Well known for their stately interiors and good build quality, Privilège catamarans are excellent charter boats and liveaboard cruisers.

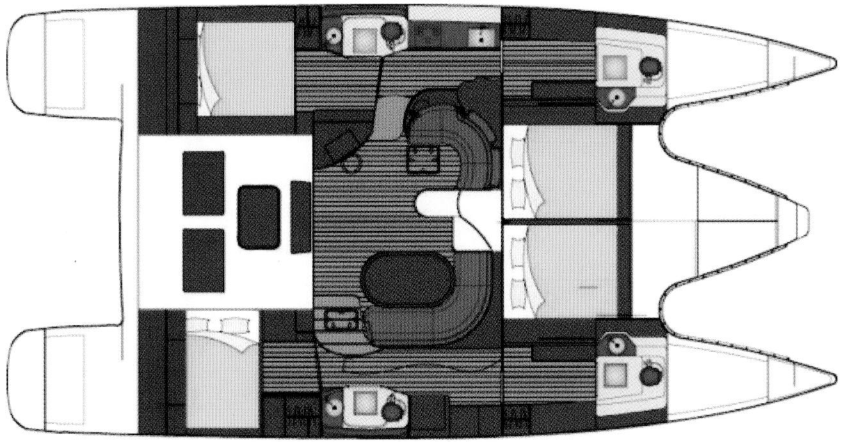

SEAWIND 1160

Specifications

Length .... 38'
Beam .... 21.4'
Displacement ..... 15,400 lbs
Draft .... 3.9'
Mast Height........ 58.7'
Fuel .... 80 gal
Water .... 166 gal

The Seawind 1160 is built in Australia and is the newest addition to the fleet of mid size cruisers from Down Under. She has expanded on the concept of an open floor plan – cockpit/saloon, but also successfully allows the bridge deck to be closed in and secured by an innovative trifold-mechanism door arrangement, which stows the doors into the fiberglass bimini overhead. As a result one gains an unequaled living space, but at the same time enjoys the security of a conventional catamaran layout. The Seawind's accommodations below are well thought out: a queen-sized island bed (unusual for multihulls less than 45') and the availability of a 3- or 4-cabin layout. This performance cruiser also enjoys the ease of a self-tacking jib and a flared hull shape with ample buoyancy. No wonder that the Seawind 1160 is in demand from bareboat rental fleets as well as skippered charter operators.

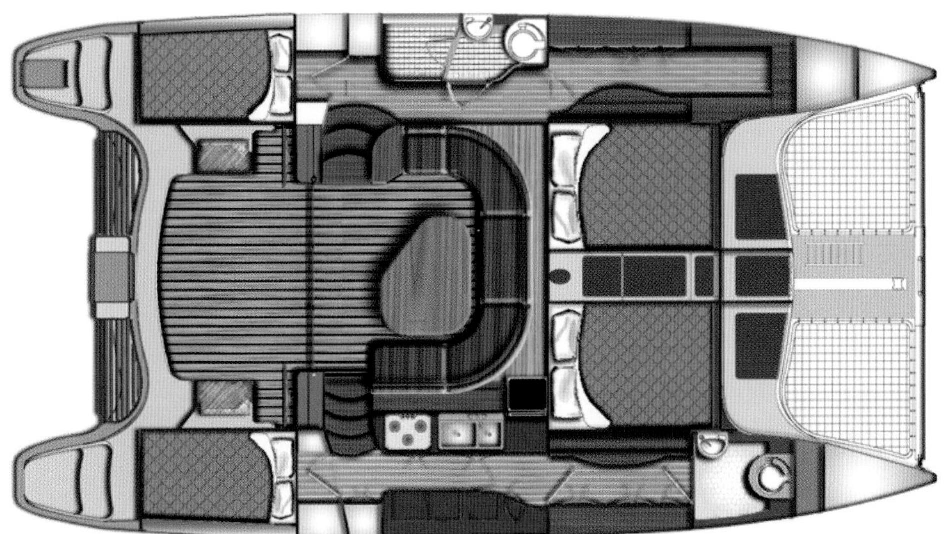

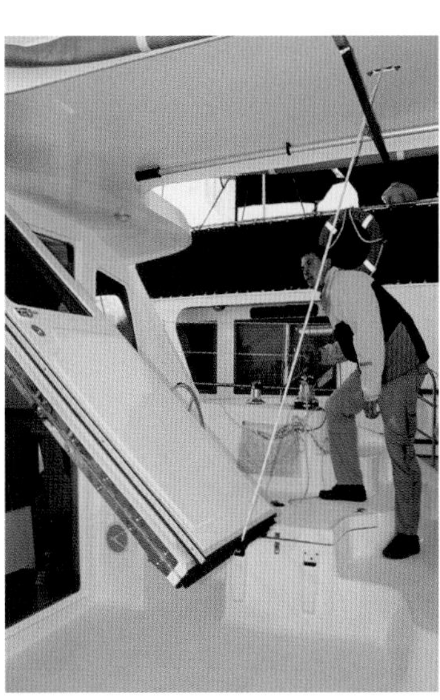

ST FRANCIS 50

Specifications

Length .... 49.05'
Beam .... 24.05'
Displacement ..... 27,400 lbs
Draft .... 4.4'
Mast Height........ 62.5'
Fuel .... 159 gal
Water .... 185 gal

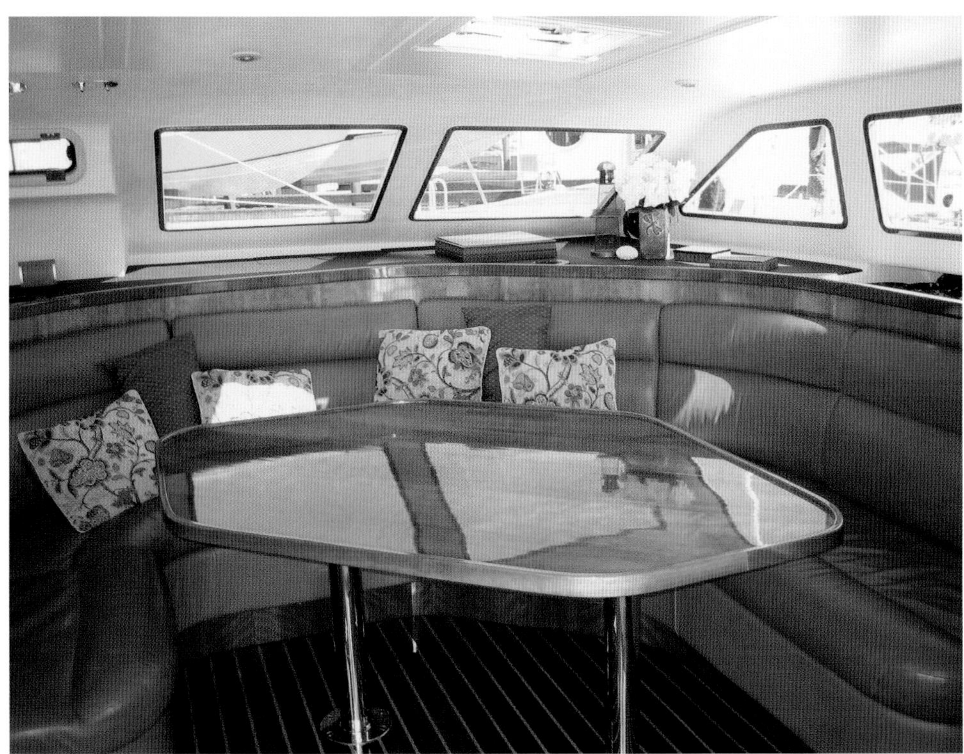

St Francis Marine is one of the oldest boatyards in South Africa that manufactures catamarans, having built the first boat back 1988. Last year the yard celebrated its 50th launch with its new flagship, the St Francis 50, considered a high-quality world cruiser. She features the same attention to detail as her smaller sistership, the popular 44. The yard's innovative thinking in designing basic gear, such as the retractable boarding ladder, self-stowing cockpit gate, multi-functional cockpit table, and lockers, make this boat stand out from the rest. The basic sail-away version is offered with options such as leather upholstery, exotic hardwood joinery work and complete navigation instrumentation. The St Francis 50 is a very well-fitted yacht, offered by a reputable company, which apparently knows what cruisers are looking for.

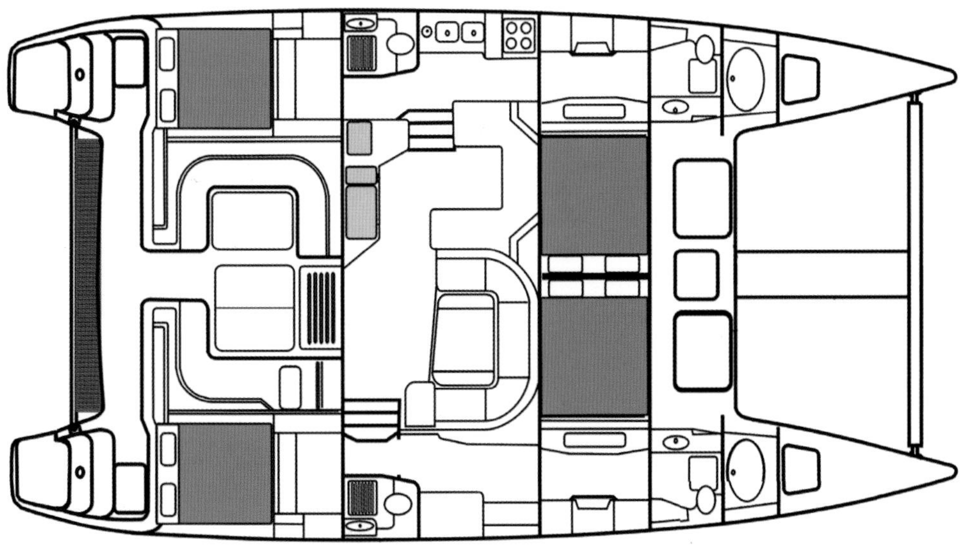

SWITCH 55

Specifications

Length .... 55.9'
Beam .... 25.7'
Displacement ..... 33,200 lbs
Draft .... 3.9' / 8.6'
Mast Height........ 77'
Fuel .... 211 gal
Water................. 116 gal

The new Switch 55 is built in the South of France by Sud Composites and is intended for comfortable bluewater sailing with a small crew. The hulls are molded using vinylester, PVC-sandwich composite for light weight and stiffness, while the interior furniture and bulkheads are made of balsa-sandwich panels with hardwood veneers. Reminiscent of the lines of the older Lagoon 47, she carries a cutter rig and a bowsprit arrangement for the asymmetrical spinnaker or gennaker. This practical sail plan provides the Switch 55 with the power to move well in light airs or under shortened sail in heavy going. The accommodation plan offers a large owner's suite and several roomy guest cabins. This is a boat for customers who want a well-rounded cruising boat, while maintaining their earthly comforts on the open seas.

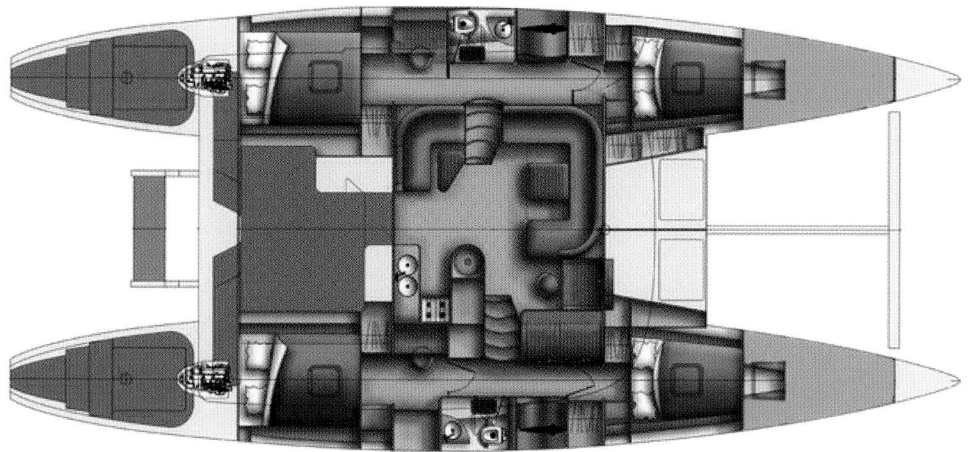

VOYAGE 500

Specifications

Length .... 50'
Beam .... 27'
Displacement ..... 23,200 lbs
Draft .... 3.9'
Mast Height........ 68.4'
Fuel .... 132 gal
Water................. 230 gal

The Voyage 500 design is an evolution of the Norseman 43 that has been around for several years. Built in South Africa, the boat has vacuum-bagged, PVC-cored hulls with watertight compartments forward in both hulls, as is typical for modern cruising catamarans. Displacing 23,200 pounds, the 500 is not the lightest cat in the cruising fleet, but having fairly narrow hulls and a decent sized sailplan, allows the boat to move well, even in light winds. The interior styling of the 500 is clean and futuristic; the owner's version features three double cabins with separate heads plus a small single cabin for crew. The Voyage 500 is one of the beamiest cats on the market with an overall beam-to-length ratio of 58 percent. The new 500 was given 10 inches of expanded beam in the hulls to improve buoyancy, and the bridgedeck was elevated three inches, which has considerably improved wave-slamming while sailing upwind. The main sheet traveler sits on a raised arch over the cockpit that also serves as a base for the bimini.

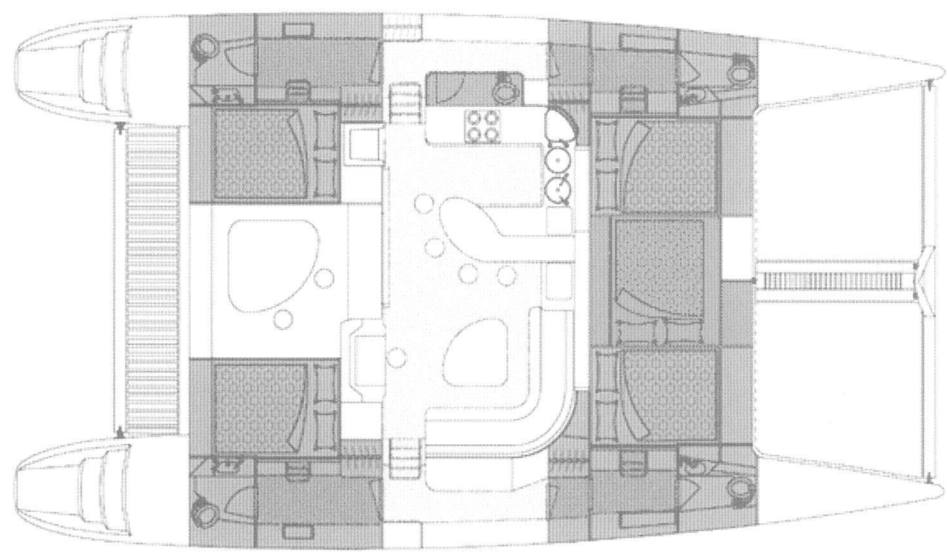

JAGUAR 36

Specifications

Length .... 35.3'
Beam .... 21.3'
Displacement ..... 24,460 lbs
Draft .... 3.3'
Mast Height........ 43.6'
Fuel .... 71 gal
Water .... 71 gal

The Jeff Schionning-designed Jaguar 36 is another highly popular South African cruising cat. In the last years, she has been built in great numbers and has earned her reputation as a good sailer at a reasonable price. The volume in the saloon rivals that of 40-foot multihulls, thanks to her extra-wide beam. As long as care is taken not to overload the boat, the bridgedeck clearance will be adequate for offshore sailing. A fractional sail plan assures that a couple can master the boat from a single helm station, which is located on the port side of the cockpit. The Jaguar is available in various layouts: charter version, 4 cabin plan and owner's version, which is shown below.

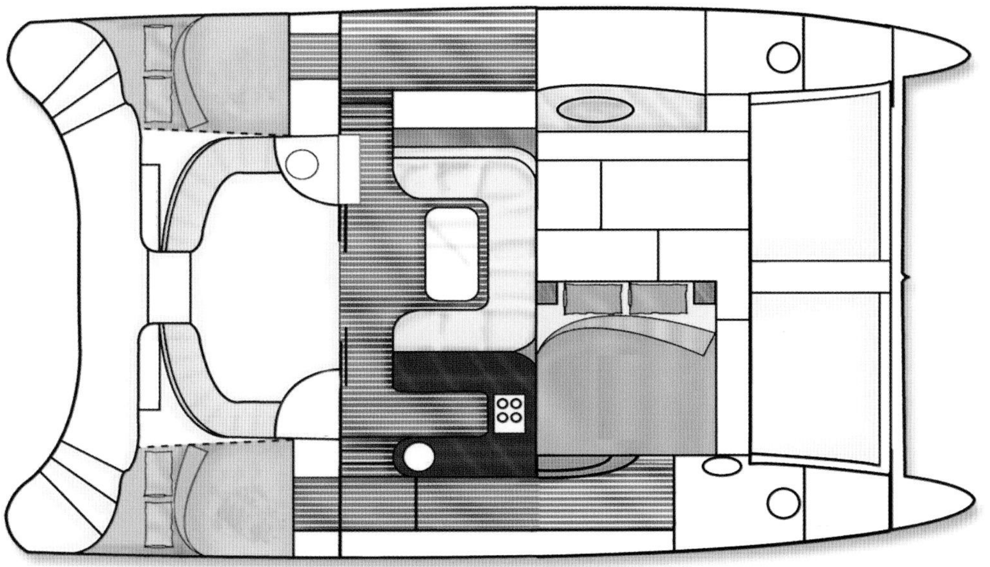

YAPLUKA 70

Specifications

Length .... 73.2'
Beam .... 37'
Displacement ..... 44 T
Draft .... 5.4'
Mast Height........ 98.4'
Fuel .... 1,236 gal
Water .... 1,052 gal

The Yapluka 70 belongs to a select group of extraordinary yachts meticulously built to Bureau Veritas specifications in the North of France. Undoubtedly this aluminum masterpiece represents the highest craftsmanship, design and engineering incorporated into a luxury catamaran. The Yapluka 70's pure lines are beautifully integrated into her trademark bimini, which is a visual continuation of the streamlined saloon-coachhouse. The interior rivals any top class custom furniture builder and is crafted with select exotic woods and designer hardware. The yard works closely with clients to create a one of a kind catamaran to owners' specifications and each boat is a unique reflection of the customer. Yaplukas are renowned for their bulletproof construction, exceptional sailing qualities and high resale value.

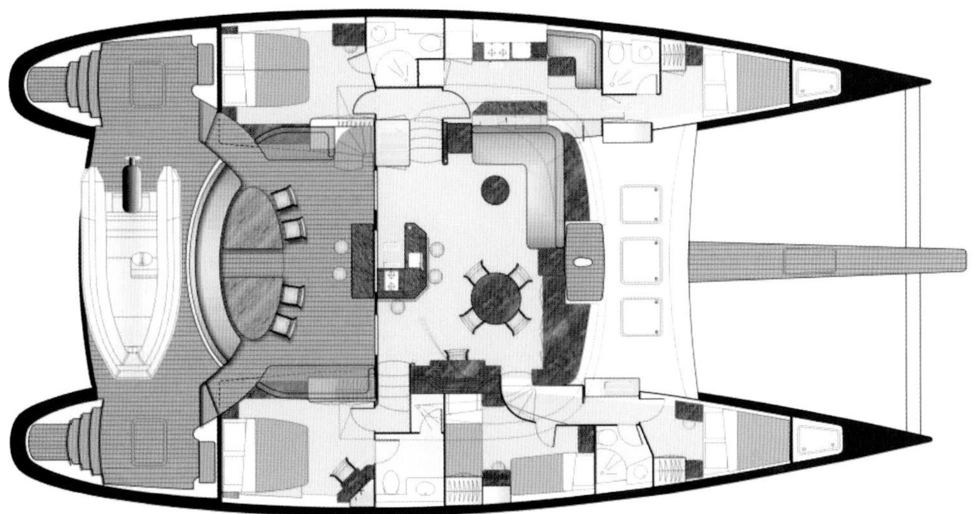

"As for myself, the wonderful sea charmed me from the first."

~ *Joshua Slocum* - Sailing Alone Around the World

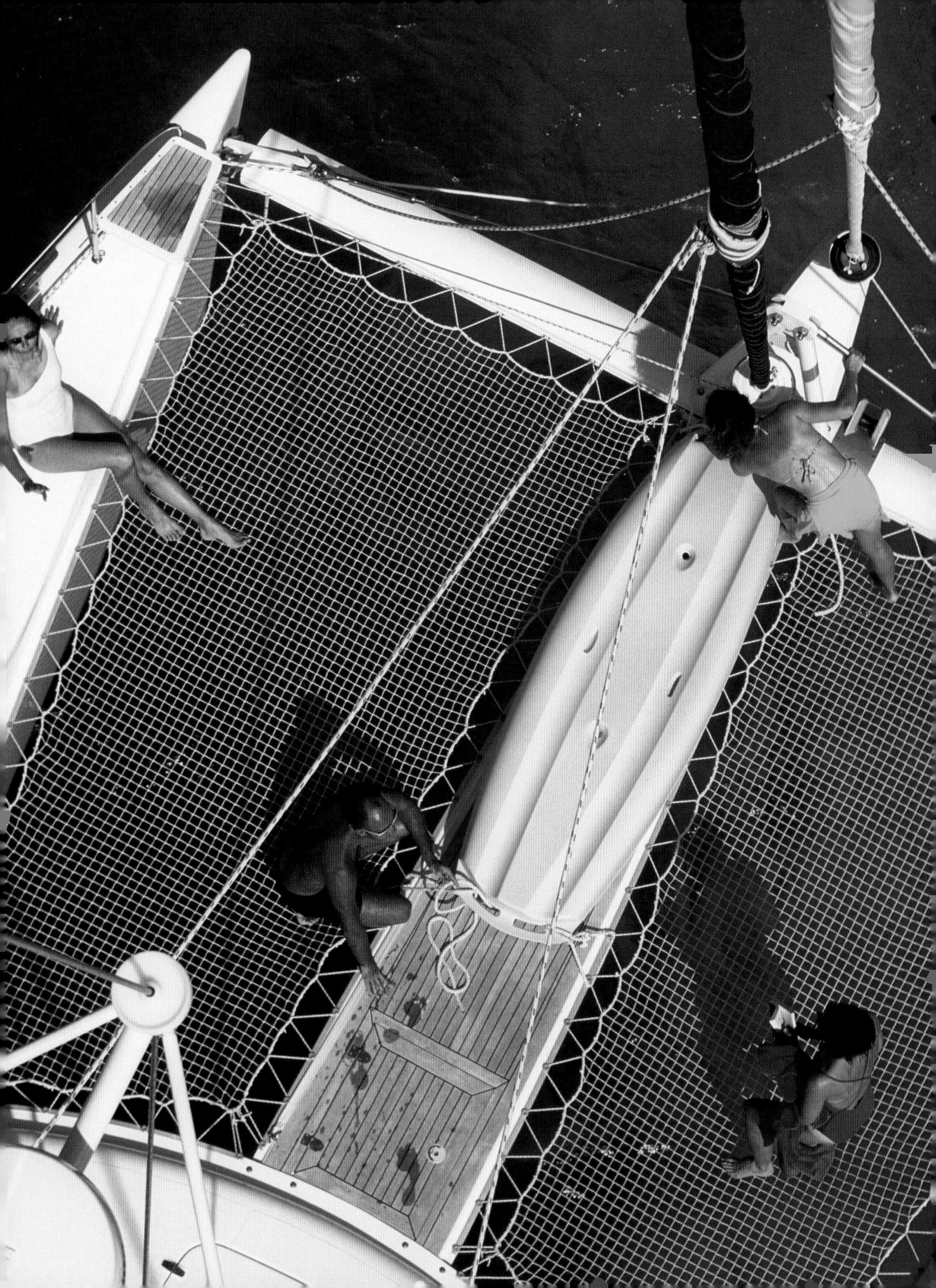

APPENDIXES

A catamaran can sail downwind for days on end; with both gennaker and jib furled, the asymmetric spinnaker is powering the boat towards its destination.

APPENDIX 1

OFFSHORE SURVIVAL GEAR CHECKLIST

This list is excessive and should serve as a guideline only. It is up to each skipper to determine the correct items, depending on intended travel plans, crew and vessel specifics.

Contents should be kept in several tethered, hard-plastic screw-top canisters, 2/3 filled for flotation and well marked with the name of the vessel.

Description	On Boat
150' orange floating signaling strip	
Aloe lotion	
Aluminum Foil	
AM/FM radio (submersible) marked with boat name	
Assorted clothing, hats etc.	
Batteries	
Bible	
Book – Captain's Guide to Liferaft Survival, by Michael Cargal	
Books	
Bucket	
Can opener	
Cash	
Complete major trauma/lacerations medical kit	
Complete minor injuries/burn medical kit	
Copy of boat registration documents	
Cutting boards	
Dish towels	
Dog bowl	
Dry clothes	
Duct tape	
Duplicate credit cards	
Emergency space blankets	
Extra ACR Rapidfix 406 EPIRB with GPS interface	
Extra contact lenses and cleaning solution	
Extra reflective tape	
Feather lures	
Feminine sanitation items	
Filet knife	
Fire extinguisher	
Fishing reel	
Fishing line – 300 lb test	
Fishing supplies	
Flashlight (submersible)	
Fleece blankets	
Fluorescent light sticks (cyalume-type)	
Foul-weather gear	
Freeze-dried food (enough to last 40 days)	
Funnel	
Games	
Gloves	
Graduated drinking cup	
Granola bars	
Handheld flares and gun	
Handheld GPS	
Hard candy	

Hard rubber plugs	
High energy food	
Hooks (large and small saltwater variety)	
Hose clamps (to be used with rubber plugs in fixing life raft leaks)	
Imodium®	
Kite	
Knife and sharpener	
Large-scale paper charts	
Laxative	
Leatherman®	
Life raft repair kit	
Line and polyester ropes	
Medical Kit (bandages, tape, small splints, antiseptic creams, etc.)	
Multi-Vitamins with Iron	
Needle and thread	
Notebooks (waterproof)	
Nylon twine	
Painkillers	
Pan	
Passports (and laminated copies to resist water damage)	
Personal flotation devices (always worn) and flotation cushions	
Pilot charts and navigational tools	
Plastic eating utensils	
Polarized sunglasses (2)	
Polypropylene floating rope - 1/4" x 100 ft	
Propane cooker with gas	
PUR Survivor-06 manual water maker with extra biocide inhibitor	
Rubbing alcohol in sprayer (to subdue fish)	
Sea dye packet	
Seasickness medicine	
Sheet plastic	
Signal mirror	
Sinkers for fishing	
Small gaff (1' length)	
Solar still	
Spare raft pump	
Spear gun with extra tips	
Spinners for fishing	
Sponge	
Stainless steel wire	
Sunscreen	
Survival suits	
Swimming goggles	
Swiss army pocket knife	
Swivels	
Tights (for plankton net)	
Toothbrush	
Tree saw	
VHF Radio (submersible)	
Water containers (2/3 filled) (enough to last 40 days)	
Watertight bag for electronics (zip lock)	
Whistle	
Wind/Waterproof Matches	
Ziploc® bags	

APPENDIX 2

LONG-RANGE CRUISING EQUIPMENT CHECKLIST

Again, this list might seem excessive; however, it mentions items which will be indispensable for long-term cruising.

Description	On Board
Assorted shock chords	
Barbeque	
Barograph	
Binoculars with built in compass	
Blocks, snap shackles, sheaves etc.	
Bosun's chair	
Bottom paint	
Bridle set up for anchor	
Caulking adhesive (3M™ 5200)	
CDs	
Chargers and adaptors	
Cleaners	
Cloths	
Cockpit-mounted serrated knife	
Cordless reversible drill	
Cotter pins and circlips etc.	
Deck brush	
Dinghy anchor	
Dinghy repair kit and foot pump	
Dock cart	
Dock lines	
Drill bits	
Drogue	
Duct tape	
Electrical tape	
Electronic charts	
EPIRB	
Epoxy	
Extra line and rope	
Face mask, respirator	
Fans	
Fenders	
Filters	
Fire extinguishers	
Fish knife	
Fishing gear	
Flare kit	
Flashlights	
Fluids (hydraulic, oil, antifreeze)	
Foghorn or bell	
Foul-weather gear	
Funnels	
Fuses	
Games	
Gelcoat	
Gloves	
Grab bag	
Hand-bearing compass	
Hatch seals	

Head protection	
Home port flag	
Jerry cans for water and fuel	
Kerosene lantern	
Labels	
Lacquer thinner	
Manual bilge pumps	
Manuals	
MOB pole	
Mooring line	
Multimeter	
Music players	
Navigation plotting tools	
Offshore medical kit and doctor contacts	
Outboard repair kit	
Padlock for dinghy	
Painting supplies	
Paper back-up chart	
Personal knives	
PFDs and life jackets (all with strobe and whistle)	
Pilot Charts and Navigational Tools	
Plastic sextant	
Portable electric bilge pump	
Portable vacuum	
Sail repair kit	
Sealants, lubricants and caulking material	
Searchlight	
Shore power cable & adapter plugs	
Sleeping bags	
Snorkel & fins	
Soldering kit	
Spare bulbs	
Spare hose	
Spare impellers and belts	
Stainless fasteners	
Storage boxes	
Sun protection	
Sunglasses	
Super glue	
Survival suit	
Tethers	
Throw rope	
Toilet repair kit	
Toilet snake	
Tool kit	
Various size batteries	
VHF submersible	
Visiting nation flags	
Waterproof safety cases	
Webbing straps	
Winch handles	
Winch maintenance kit and grease	
Wire cutters	
Wooden plugs	
Work gloves	
Ziploc® bags	

APPENDIX 3

GENERAL VESSEL MAINTENANCE

Mast/Boom

Check in particular the possibility of electrolysis of aluminum parts which are in contact with other materials.
Check the horizontal alignment of the spreaders, as they will move every time one adjusts the rig tension.
Sight up the mast and observe a fair curve, which should follow the luff of the mainsail. It should not curve athwartship but rather be uniform in its bend fore and aft.
Regularly inspect the condition of the gooseneck and its surrounding fittings, the mast step and the chainplate including the shroud tensioners. Assure that the pins securing the turnbuckles are safely attached.
Attention and regular inspection should also be undertaken with the forward crossbeam, its attachment pins, the seagull striker and its tension.

Standing Rigging

Adjustment of the standing rigging: consult a specialist who is familiar with the rigging or call upon a mast manufacturer's representative who can perform any adjustments, if necessary.
Adjustment of the rig should be performed after the first sail.
Adjustment of the rig after sailing for the first time in winds higher than 30 knots; thereafter annual adjustments.
Daily visual inspections. The shrouds and side stays should never be slack.
One should make a trip up the mast at least twice a year.
Check all the pins and circlips, especially at the spreaders. All running rigging attachments and exit blocks should be regularly checked for chafe and deterioration.
Note : The majority of marine insurers advise to change the standing rigging every 10 years (or 10,000 nautical miles).

Running Rigging

Flip ropes end-over-end annually.
Change ropes and sheets according to wear – approximately every two years.
Observe the state of the lazy jacks.
Wash sheets, blocks and ball-bearing cars in fresh water at least once per week. If required, lubricate with an appropriate spray.

Sails

All sails (Dacron-Polyester, Spectra, Composites) are sensitive to salt and the ultraviolet rays of the sun. Keep them covered unless sailing.

Rinse as often as possible with fresh water.

Sails should always be protected by a cover or lazy bag when not in use and ideally should be flaked when dry.

Change the chafe guards, in particular at the batten-pockets (annually).

Change the UV covers every 2-3 years as necessary.

Disassemble the jib furling drum before each winter lay-up. Store in a dry place.

Take special care of your jib roller-furling drum. It is well known that in gale conditions furling units can fail, especially if they have been neglected or not serviced regularly. This could cause the jib to unroll unintentionally and tear.

The sails can be cleaned with a stiff brush and fresh water or can be professionally laundered.

Rudders

Check tightness of all fittings of the system, especially at the steering rams.

Check fluid level of the hydraulic reservoir and top off if necessary.

Check the proper function of the rudder angle indicator (annually).

Check especially the feedback control arm of the autopilot and its electric connections.

Assure parallel positions of the rudders. Turn wheel hard to port until it stops. By operating the bypass valve on one of the rudders, manually adjust that rudder to be in exact alignment with the other one. After you have done that, open the rudder's hydraulic circuit again and check for parallel position and proper operation. This maneuver should be done in port and must be performed with the autopilot in the OFF position.

Procedures for Winter Lay-Up

Secure and maintain mooring.

Secure and isolate electric circuit.

Remove all sails from vessel and have them checked and cleaned by a sailmaker.

Arrange bedding and linen in such a way that they are well aerated.

Check that entire vessel is well vented.

Remove and lift floorboards to vent bilges.

Close all gas circuits.

Close 12V circuit (except automatic bilge pumps if you are afloat).

Lubricate all blocks and winches.

Check the antifreeze level in your engines.

Winterize outboard by flushing with fresh water and spraying appropriate machine oil into cylinders.

Store and service the dinghy.
Remove and service life raft (inspect according to manual).
List all repairs to be performed on vessel and organize repairs before the start of the next season.
Empty refrigerator and freezer and leave doors ajar.
Remove all perishable goods from the boat (think of rodents and pests).
Close all valves and thru-hulls.
Fill diesel tanks and close all valves in fuel system.

During Winter

Check mooring ropes against chafe (if afloat).	daily
Check the electrical terminals.	daily
Vent the boat.	weekly
Start engine (1500 rpm for an hour).	weekly
Check the battery charge.	monthly
Check the bilges.	weekly

Check safety system and fire extinguishers.
Renew all permissions, taxes and fees.
Check for updated and active insurance policy.
Check with port authorities for mooring permits.
Have the boat surveyed every three years.
Clean the deck with fresh water and soap.
Cover the boat against snow and rain. It will save you a lot of cleanup in the spring.
Check the function of the valves.
Check the function of the daggerboards.

Spring Procedures

Prepare hauling of the vessel a couple of weeks in advance. Contact boatyard to set up date.

Safety

Check the safety equipment on board.
Check that all payments to the authorities have been made.
Check the expiration date of all the fire-extinguishers.
Check the condition of the ground tackle and the proper operation of the windlass.

Engines

If the engines have been properly serviced and winterized they should start without a problem. A weekly check thereafter will be sufficient. Re-check all fluid levels.

Electricity

If the boat has been properly winterized you will have no problems.
Verify the fluid level in the batteries, use a battery tester and Voltmeter to check their charge.
Check the overall condition of the electrical circuit by testing each appliance for proper function.
Place fresh batteries into all portable devices and test for function.

Electronics

Check all circuits and verify proper function of all systems.

Water

Fill up all reservoirs and tanks.
Check the pressure in each circuit. Purge all circuits and bleed if necessary to remove air.
If water has been sitting in tanks for months, it might be necessary to replace with fresh water.

Make sure all pumps function properly.
Replace all sails and mount them.
Check all running rigging and replace any chafed lines as necessary.
Clean the deck with fresh, soapy water.
Note all events and maintenance records into the Log Book.
Put dinghy and engine back into service. Check rigidity of the davits.
Check that all items on the maintenance list have been performed properly.

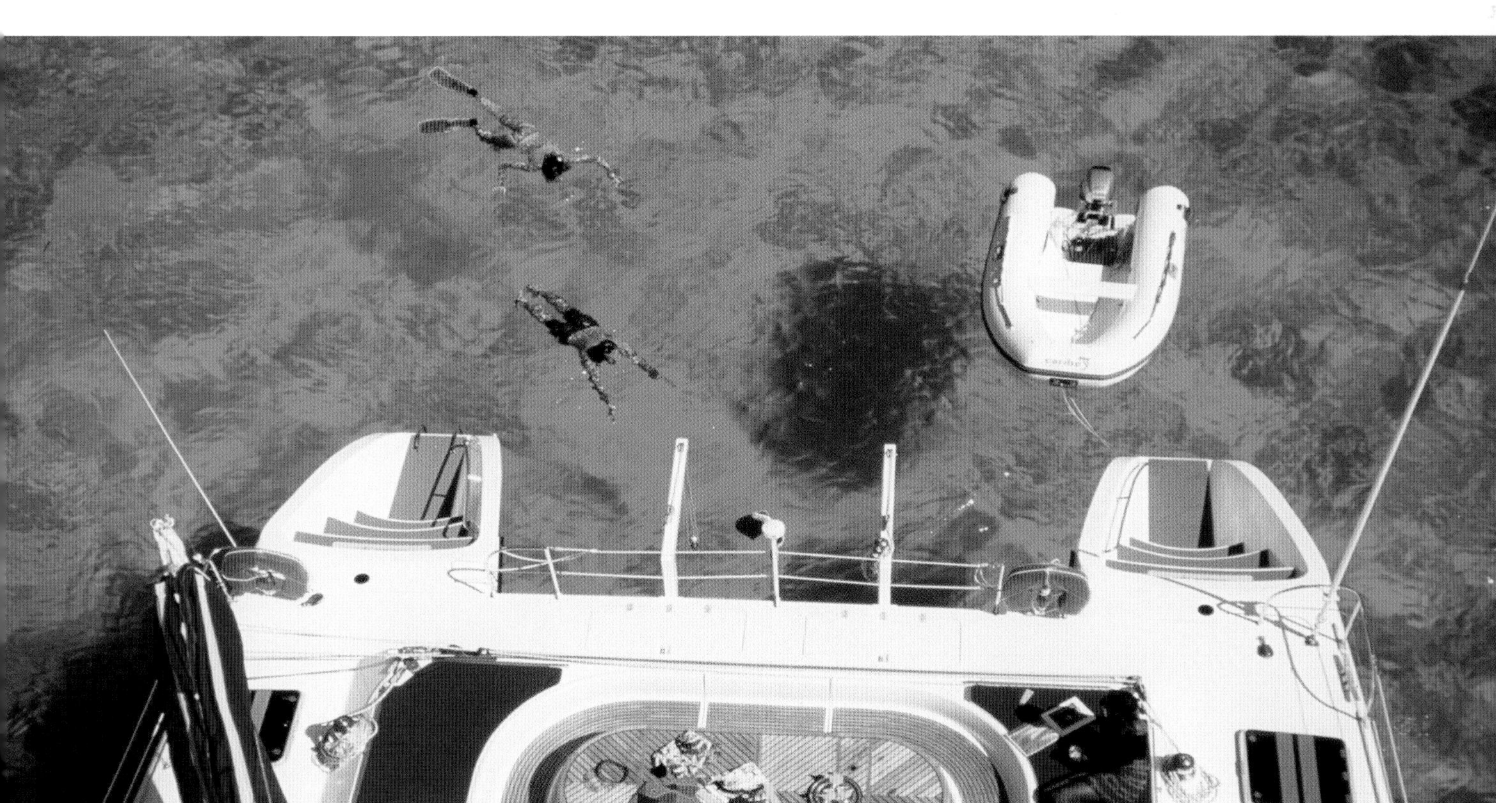

METRIC EQUIVALENTS

Imperial to Metric			Metric to Imperial		
Multiply	By	To Get	Multiply	By	To Get
LENGTH					
Inches	25.4	Millimetres	Millimetres	0.0394	Inches
Inches	2.54	Centimetres	Centimetres	0.3937	Inches
Inches	0.0254	Metres	Metres	39.37	Inches
Feet	30.48	Centimetres	Centimetres	0.0328	Feet
Feet	0.3048	Metres	Metres	3.281	Feet
Yards	0.9144	Metres	Metres	1.094	Yards
Miles	1.609	Kilometres	Kilometres	0.6215	Miles
AREA					
Inches^2	645.16	Millimetres^2	Millimetres^2	0.00155	Inches^2
Inches^2	6.4516	Centimetres^2	Centimetres^2	0.155	Inches^2
Feet^2	929.03	Centimetres^2	Centimetres^2	0.00108	Feet^2
Feet^2	0.0929	Metres^2	Metres^2	10.764	Feet^2
Yards^2	8361.3	Centimetres^2	Centimetres^2	0.00012	Yards^2
Yards^2	0.8361	Metres^2	Metres^2	1.196	Yards^2
Miles^2	2.59	Kilometres^2	Kilometres^2	0.3861	Miles^2
VOLUME					
Inches^3	16.387	Millimetres^3	Millimetres^3	6.1×10^{-5}	Inches^3
Inches^3	16.387	Centimetres^3	Centimetres^3	0.061	Inches^3
Feet^3	0.0283	Metres^3	Metres^3	35.33	Feet^3
Yards^3	0.7646	Metres^3	Metres^3	1.308	Yards^3
ENERGY					
°F	0.556	°C	°C	1.8	°F
°F	0.556 (°F – 32)	°C	°C	1.8 x °C + 32	°F

Adapted with permission from *Boatowner's Illustrated Electrical Handbook*, second edition, by Charlie Wing

GENERAL VESSEL MAINTENANCE

Schedule	Daily	As needed in port/absence	Weekly	Monthly	Yearly	Winter lay-up	Spring	2 years/5 years
Mast and Rigging	check the rigging				adjust rig tension, climb mast, reverse halyards			reverse halyards
Sails	check for chafe	cover them against sun and rain	rinse with fresh water		renew chafe guards	remove jib furler, store sails in dry place, check for damage		change UV cover
Deck Gear	rinse with fresh water			check for proper function	grease winches, windlass, check lifeline, compass	lubricate all fittings	check mooring, windlass	change hatch hinges
Steering Gear			check for any leaks	lubricate parts and change anodes	check rudder angle indicator and autopilot function			
Daggerboards		check uphaul line and jammers			inspect for damage and paint with antifouling	move them up and down in their trunks		
Engines (see owner's manual)	check coolant and oil levels, leakage and pressure		check coolant level	check diesel filters adjust valves	check all hose connections, change impeller and check for fuel leaks	leave all tanks full, start once/week		change saildrive membrane
Electrical Circuit (see owner's manual)		shut down all circuits (except auto. bilge pumps)		clean, tighten and grease battery terminals	spray connections with dehumidifying lubricant	shut down 12V circuit, check shore power and battery charge		
Gas Circuit	immediately shut off in case of leaks	shut down in absence	check gas level in bottles	check valves and appliances for proper function	remove burners and check for dated propane bottles	remove gas bottles and close all gas shut-off valves		
Water Circuit	close on/off switch			check seals for leaks, empty tanks and lubricate valves	check hose connections			
Electronics (see owner's manual)		shut down in case of lightning		check all communications	pay for VHF license and check for proper function	remove all batteries	check all electronics	
Other					pay insurance, check life raft and safety equipment	air out cabin, mattresses, empty fridge and remove perishables, check dinghy	check bilge pumps, sails, rigging, clean deck, mast, note all in logbook	

"The difference between a gale and what has come to be known as a 'survival' storm is that the former, with winds of Force 8, or perhaps 9, the skipper and crew retain control and can take the measures which they think best, where as in a survival gale of Force 10 or over, perhaps gusting to hurricane strength – wind and sea become the masters."

~ *K. Adlard Coles* – Heavy Weather Sailing

APPENDIX 4 BEAUFORT SCALE

Force	Wind speed (kts)	Description	Wave Heights	Sea Conditions
0	0-1	Calm	0'	Sea like a mirror.
1	1-3	Light Air	0-2'	Ripples with the appearance of scales are formed, but without foam crests.
2	4-6	Light Breeze	1-3'	Small wavelets, still short, but more pronounced. Crests have a glassy appearance and do not break.
3	7-10	Gentle Breeze	3-4'	Large wavelets. Crests begin to break. Foam of glassy appearance. Perhaps scattered whitecaps.
4	11-16	Moderate Breeze	4'	Small waves, becoming larger; fairly frequent whitecaps.
5	17-21	Fresh Breeze	6'	Moderate waves, taking a more pronounced long form; many white caps are formed. Chance of some spray.
6	22-27	Strong Breeze	10'	Large waves begin to form; the white foam crests are more extensive everywhere. Probably some spray.
7	28-33	Near Gale	14'	Sea heaps up and white foam from breaking waves begins to be blown in streaks along the direction of the wind.
8	38-40	Gale	18'	Moderately high waves of greater length; edges of crests begin to break into spindrift. The foam is blown in well-marked streaks along the direction of the wind.
9	41-47	Severe Gale	23'	High waves. Dense streaks of foam along the direction of the wind. Crests of waves begin to topple, tumble and roll over. Spray may affect visibility.
10	48-55	Storm	29'	Very high waves with long over-hanging crests. The resulting foam, in great patches, is blown in dense, white streaks along the direction of the wind. On the whole the surface of the sea takes on a white appearance. The 'tumbling' of the sea becomes heavy and shock-like. Visibility affected.
11	56-63	Violent Storm	37'	Exceptionally high waves (small and medium-size ships might be lost to view for a time behind the waves). The sea is completely covered with long, white patches of foam lying along the direction of the wind. Everywhere the edges of the wave crests are blown into froth. Visibility affected.
12	64 +	Hurricane/ Cyclone	45' +	The air is filled with foam and spray. Sea completely white with driving spray; visibility very seriously affected.

APPENDIX 5

PHOTOGRAPHY

Many thanks go to Gilles Martin-Raget and his team, who took the majority of the photographs for this book. It was an honor to share the pages with his work. Gilles is not only considered one of the best marine photographers in the world, but also a top-level sailor. His passion for the sport and the sea is reflected in his stunning photography. Gilles is a much sought-after professional and his art can be viewed either in one of his several galleries, or discovered in his numerous coffee-table books or publications in international magazines.

Gilles Martin-Raget was born on April 9, 1955 in Arles (South of France) where he lived for 20 years before moving to Montpellier and Aix en Provence where he attended University and graduated in Economics. He discovered sailing at the age of 19 during a training session with sailor Marc Linski. His new passion became a permanent hobby and eventually a fulltime job. Improving his crewing skills every year Gilles mainly sailed in the Mediterranean Sea aboard large racing and cruising monohulls, including maxi yachts. After several racing seasons he reached the required level to participate in the prestigious America's Cup on board France 3 at Newport (RI) in 1983 with Bruno Troublé as skipper.

The French team was eliminated during the early stages of what was the first edition of the Louis Vuitton Cup, but Gilles stayed in Newport to cover the historical win of Australia II, working as a journalist for several sailing magazines. Gilles' success began with publications and a cover on Sail Magazine after the Cup was won by a non-American team for the first time ever. This was a memorable moment and Gilles took on photography and journalism as a fulltime job. The America's Cup has since become one of Gilles' specialties, having covered every single edition while working for numerous top sports-media organizations.

Arles, which is located in the beautiful South of France, is known for the famous international photography festival. Living there made it easy for Gilles to always have his camera close by. Amongst the first photos produced were those taken as a teenager of the beautiful landscapes around Arles, such as the vast Camargue, the Alpilles and Luberon. Racing photos then became his passion. Gilles began working for sailing magazines and met his wife, Maguelonne, who is also a yachting journalist. They now enjoy their three children and their home in Marseille.

Gilles has become internationally renowned thanks to his hard work and in-depth knowledge of the marine features he photographs. He is a regular contributor to most of the prominent sailing magazines throughout the world, an author of numerous books on sailing and the official photographer for many top racing sailors, internationally known sponsors and race organizers. Gilles travels nonstop around the world to cover the greatest sailing events, covers reports on cruising destinations and enjoys the privilege to sail on board the most diverse yachts.

Year after year, Gilles has improved his art of the marine world, covering the sea and the shore, as well as every aspect of the maritime environment and sailing. Yet, he always remained faithful to his origins, shooting spectacular landscapes of the beautiful Provence with its vivid traditions and famous *art de vivre*. Two boutiques are located in Saint Rémy de Provence and in Marseille, where the public can admire Gilles' work and purchase photos.

After working many years on his own, Gilles is now surrounded by a small, very efficient and dedicated team that helps him with the production of his images, the boutiques as well as the new services offered to customers. The administration of his web site: www.martin-raget.com was launched in 1998 and fully revised in 2005. The new, more attractive version allows the public to view many more images and order them in a fast, convenient way.

left Photographer extraordinaire Gilles Martin-Raget looking for the next subject from his favorite vantage point.

PHOTO CREDITS

Alliaura: 234, 235
Atelier Outremer: 12, 32, 44, 69, 74, 77, 107, 116, 166, 178, 230, 231
Bailey, Nic: 138
Blubay: 65, 70, 87, 94, 97, 208, 209
Broadblue: 93, 210, 211
Bruneel, Eric: 35, 48
Catana: 68, 212, 213
Classic Cats: 244, 245
Dolphin: 214, 215
Ganem, Joe: 52
Gunboat: 220, 221
Lagoon: 222, 223
Leopard: 224, 225
Maine Cat: 226, 227
Manta: 228, 229
Martin-Raget, Gilles: 2, 6, 11, 13, 15, 17, 22, 26, 27, 29, 33, 34, 38, 39, 41, 42, 45, 51, 54, 57, 59, 63, 64, 66, 73, 80, 81, 83, 85, 86, 88, 89, 90, 98, 101, 103, 105, 109, 110, 133, 134, 146, 147, 149, 162, 165, 169, 173, 174, 177, 181, 183, 185, 193, 199, 202, 205, 216, 217, 249, 259, 265, 267
Multihulls Magazine: 19, 21
PDQ: 232, 233
Performance Cruising: 84, 218, 219
Scape Yachts: 84
Seawind: 236, 237
St Francis: 238, 239
Switch: 240, 241
Tarjan, Gregor: 25, 28, 30, 31, 36, 37, 50, 70, 71, 72, 78, 79, 96, 113, 114, 115, 117, 122, 125, 127, 130, 137, 139, 142, 144, 150, 153, 155, 158, 159, 161, 167, 170, 171, 182, 189, 190, 191, 194, 250, 297
Voyage: 242, 243
White, Chris: 206, 207
Yacht Industries – Yapluka: 55, 58, 60, 61, 62, 95, 129, 131, 187, 201, 246, 247

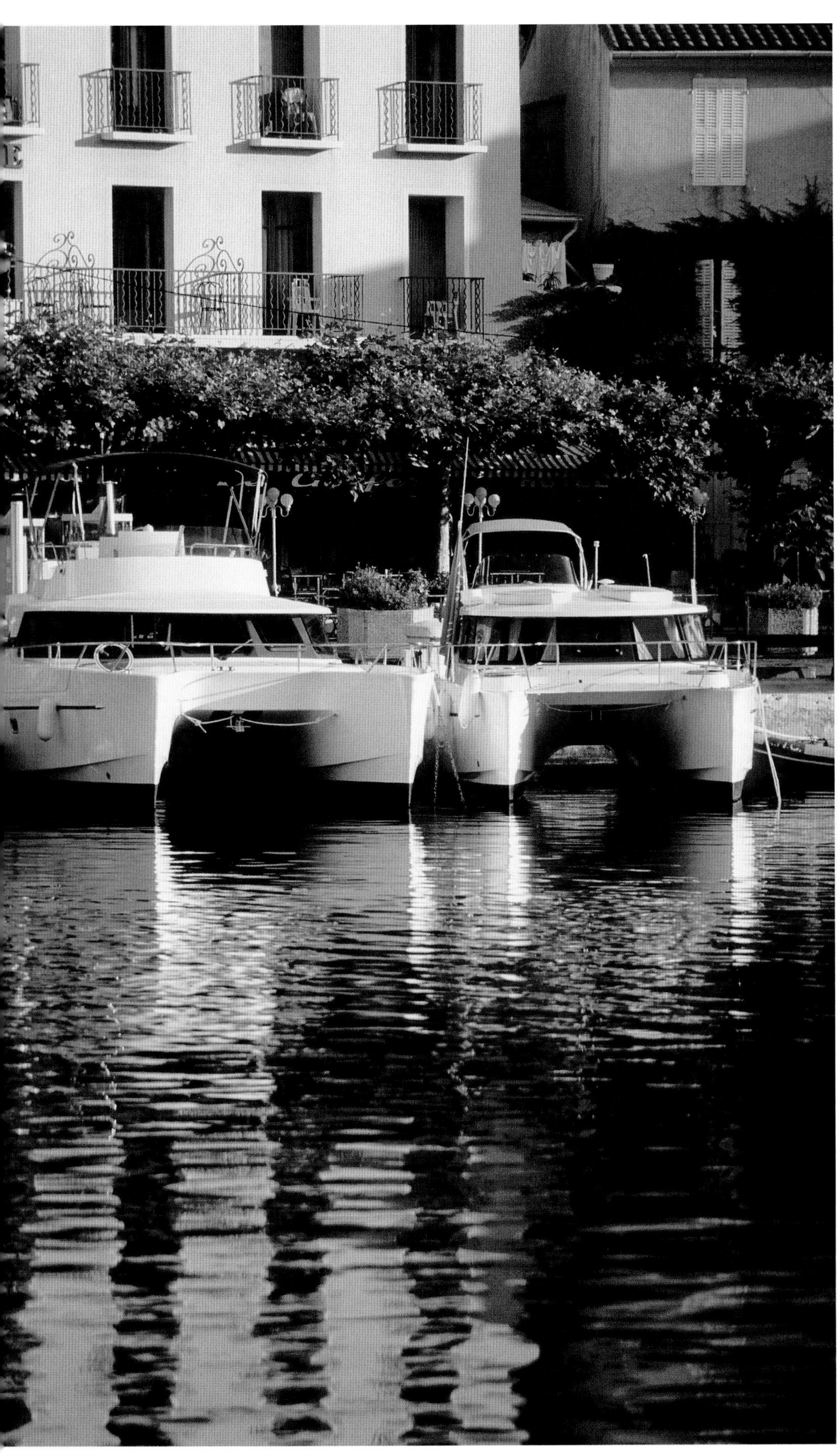

left The next generation of power yachts – fuel-efficient catamarans with a range of 1,000 miles.

BIBLIOGRAPHY & REFERENCES

The field of cruising catamarans is a specialty topic in the world of sailing and readers might have noticed that there aren't many books available on this subject. The following publications, some of them more than 40 years old, have all helped my knowledge and understanding of catamarans and in a sense, all contributed to my book.

A

Alexander, Caroline, *The Endurance,* Alfred A. Knopf, NY, 1999

Amateur Yacht Research Society, *OSTAR 1976 and Multihull Safety,* Berkshire, UK, 1977

Andrews, Jim, *Catamarans for Cruising,* Hollis & Carter, London, UK, 1974

B

Baader, Julian, *Seemanschaft,* Delius Klasing Verlag, Bielefeld, Germany, 1994

Bergreen, Laurence, *Over the Edge of the World,* HarperCollins Publishers, NY, 2003

Bethwaite, Frank, *High Performance Sailing,* International Marine/McGraw Hill, Camden, ME, 1993

Bianchi, Bruno, *The Rules of Sailing Races,* Dodd, Mead & Company, NY, 1970

Brown, Jim, *The Case for the Cruising Trimaran,* Int. Marine Publishing Comp., Camden, ME, 1979

C

Calder, Nigel, *Boatowner's Mechanical and Electrical Manual,* International Marine Publishing Company, Camden, ME, 1996

Callahan, Steven, *Adrift,* Ballantine Books, NY, 1986

Callahan, Steven, *Capsized,* HarperCollins, NY, 1993

Cargal, Michael, *The Captain's Guide to Liferaft Survival,* 1990

Chandler, Roy, *A 30', 6000$ Cruising Catamaran,* Bacon & Freeman Publishers, Orwigsburg, PA,1985

Chichester, Francis Sir, *4000 Meilen in 20 Tagen,* Pietsch Verlag, Stuttgart, Germany, 1980

Chichester, Francis Sir, *The Lonely Sea and the Sky,* Paragon House, NY, 1990

Chiodi, Charles, *The Capsize Bugaboo,* Chiodi Advertising & Publishing Inc., Boston, MA, 1980

Chiodi, Charles, *There Is Always Sunshine Behind the Clouds,* Chiodi Advertising & Publishing Inc., Boston, MA, 2004

Coles, Adlard, *Heavy Weather Sailing,* John de Graff Inc., Clinton Corners, NY, 1981

Cornell, Jimmy, *World Cruising Handbook,* International Marine, 1990

E

Engel, Gerd, *Toern ins Ewige Eis,* Ullstein Verlag, Frankfurt, Germany, 1999

Engel, Gerd, *Weisse Nächte, Schwarzes Meer,* Ullstein, Frankfurt, Germany, 1997

F

Freuchen, Peter, *Book of the Seven Seas,* Julian Messner, NY, 1959

Friedman, Thomas L., *The Lexus and the Olive Tree,* Anchor Book Division, NY, 1999

G

Gelder, Paul, *The Loneliest Race,* Adlard Coles Nautical, London, 1995

Gerr, David, *The Nature of Boats,* International Marine Publishing Company, Camden, ME, 1992

Gibbons, Rod, *The Cruising Catamaran Advantage,* Island Educational Publishing, Manchester, WA, 1988

Gleick, James, *Chaos,* Penguin Books, NY, 1985

Goss, Pete, *Close to the Wind,* Carroll & Graff Publishers, NY, 1999

Gougeon, Meade, *Gougeon Brothers On Boat Construction,* Gougeon Brothers Inc., Bay City, MI, 1990

Greenlaw, Linda, *The Hungry Ocean,* Hyperion, NY, 1993

H

Harvey, Derek, *Multihulls for Cruising and Racing,* International Marine, Camden, ME, 1991

Hausner, Wolfgang, *Atolle und Taifune,* Delius Klasing, Bielefeld, Germany, 1997

Hausner, Wolfgang, *Taboo, Eines Mannes Freiheit,* Delius Klasing, Bielefeld, Germany, 1993

Hausner, Wolfgang, *Taboo 3 Leben auf den Sieben Meeren,* Delius Klasing, Bielefeld, Germany, 1997

Hays, David, Daniel, *My Old Man and the Sea,* Headline Publishing, London, UK, 1995

Henderson, Richard, *Choice Yacht Designs,* International Marine Publishing Company, Camden, ME, 1979

Henderson, Richard, *Singlehanded Sailing,* International Marine, Camden, ME 1992

Heyerdahl, Thor, *Expedition Ra,* Berthelsman, Wien, Austria, 1966

Hiscock, Eric C., *Segeln Ueber die Sieben Meere,* Delius Klasing, Bielefeld, Germany, 1970

Hiscock, Erick C., *Wandering Under Sail,* Oxford University Press, Oxford, UK, 1977

I

Imhoff, Fred, *This is Boat Tuning for Speed,* United Nautical Publishers, Germany, 1975

J

James, Naomi, *Courage at Sea,* Salem House Publishers, Topsfield, MA, 1988

James, Rob, *Multihulls Offshore,* Dodd, Mead & Company, NY, 1984

Jeffrey, Kevin, *Sailors Multihull Guide,* Avalon House Publishing, Belfast, Canada, 2002

Johnson, Peter, *Offshore Manual International,* Dodd, Mead & Company, NY, 1977

Jones, Theodore A., *The Offshore Racer,* Quadrangle, NY Times Book Comp., NY, 1979

Jones, Thomas Firth, *Multihull Voyaging,* Sheridan House, Dobbs Ferry, NY, 1994

Jones, Tristan, *Aka,* Sheridan House, Dobbs Ferry, NY, 1991

K

Kanter, Charles E., *Cruising in Catamarans,* Sailco Press, Key Largo, FL, 2002

Kanter, Charles E., *Cruising on more than One Hull,* Sailco Press, Key Largo, FL, 1992

Kanter, Corinne C., *The Galley K.I.S.S. Cookbook,* Sailco Press, Key Largo, FL, 1987

Kelsall, Derek, *Catamaran Sailing,* The Crossword Press, London, UK, 1992

Kinney, Francis S., *Skene's Elements of Yacht Design,* Dodd, Mead & Company, NY, 1981

Knox-Johnston, Robin, *A World of My Own,* W.W. Norton & Comp., NY, 1970

Kotsch, William J., *Weather for the Mariner,* Naval Institute Press, Annapolis, MD, 1983

Kurtz, Klaus D., *Mehrrumpfboote,* Delius Klasing Verlag, Bielefeld, Germany, 1992

L

Larsen, Paul C., *To the Third Power,* Tilbury House Publishers, Gardiner, ME, 1995

LeSueur, Gavin, *The Line, Not Just a Boat Race,* Cyclone Publishers, Australia, 1995

LeSueur, Gavin Dr., *Multihull Seamanship,* Cyclone Publishers, Victoria, Australia, 1995

Lewis, Cam, Levitt, Michael, *Around the World in Seventy-Nine Days,* Delta Expedition, NY, 1996

Lewis, David, *We, the Navigators,* University of Hawaii Press, Honolulu, HI, 1972

Lewis, Michael, *The New New Thing,* Norton & Company, London, UK, 2000

Lundy, Derek, *Godforsaken Sea,* Anchor Books, Random House, NY, 2000

M

Maloney, Elbert S., *Chapman Piloting: Seamanship & Small Boat Handling,* Hearst Marine Books, NY, 1983

Marchaj, C.A., *Aero-Hydrodynamics of Sailing,* Dodd, Mead & Company, NY, 1979

Marchaj, C.A., *Seaworthiness, The Forgotten Factor,* Adlard Coles Nautical, London, UK, 1986

Mate, Ferenc, *From a Bare Hull,* Albatross Publishing House, Vancouver, BC, Canada, 1983

Maury, Matthew Fontaine, *The Physical Geography of the Sea and its Meteorology,* The Belknap Press of Harvard University, Cambridge, MA, 1963

McMullen, Michael, *Multihull Seamanship,* David McKay Company, NY, 1976

Miranda, Rosalind, *Best of Multihulls, The Book of Cruising,* Chiodi Advertising & Publishing, North Quincy, MA, 1991

Moeller, Jan, Bill, *Living Aboard, The Cruising Sailboat as a Home,* International Marine Publishing Company, Camden, ME, 1977

Moitessier, Bernard, Cape Horn, *The Logical Route,* Sheridan House, Dobbs Ferry, NY, 2003

Moitessier, Bernard, *The Long Way,* Sheridan House, Dobbs Ferry, NY, 1995

Moitessier, Bernard, *Tamata and the Alliance,* Sheridan House, Dobbs Ferry, NY, 1995

Mundle, Rob, *Fatal Storm,* International Marine, Camden, Maine, 2000

N

Nichols, Peter, *Sea Change,* Penguin Books, Middlesex, UK, 1997

Nicholson, Ian, *Boat Data Book,* Nautical Publishing Company Ltd., Lymington, UK, 1978

Norgrove, Ross, *Cruising Rigs and Rigging,* Int. Marine Publishing Comp., Camden, ME, 1982

Novak, Skip, *One Watch at a Time,* W.W. Norton Company, NY, 1988

P

Palmer, David, *The Atlantic Challenge, The Story of Trimaran FT,* Hollis Carter, London, UK, 1977

Perez-Reverte, Arturo, *The Nautical Chart,* A Harvest Book, Harcourt Inc., NY, 2000

Philbrick, Nathaniel, *Sea of Glory,* Penguin Books, London, UK, 2003

Poupon, Philippe, *Segeln mit Multis,* Delius Klasing Verlag, Bielefeld, Germany, 1992

Proctor, Ian, *Sailing Strategy, Wind and Current,* Adlard Coles, London, UK, 1991

R

Richards, Emma, *Around Alone,* McMillan, London, UK, 2004

Ridgway, John, Marie Christine, *Round the World with Ridgway,* Holt Rinehart and Winston, NY, 1978

Rousmaniere, John, *Fastnet, Force 10,* Norton, NY, 1980

Rowe, Nigel, *The Big Blue Marble,* Aurum Press Limited, London, UK, 1995

S

Shane, Victor, *Drag Device Data Base,* Para-Anchors International, Summerland, CA, 1998

Slocum, Joshua Captain, *Sailing Alone Around The World,* Norton, NY, 1984

Smeeton, Miles, *The Sea Was Our Village,* Gray's Publ. Ltd, Sidney, BC, Canada, 1973

Society of Naval Architects and Marine Engineers, *Sailing Yacht Capsize,* Boston, MA, 1983

T

Tabarly, Eric, *Ocean Racing,* W.W. Norton & Company, NY, 1971

Tetley, Nigel, *Victress Round The World,* Nautical Publishing Co., Lymington, UK, 1970

Thomson-Milne, L.M., *Theoretical Aerodynamics,* Dover Publications Inc., NY, 1973

Tomalin, Nicholas & Hall, Ron, *The Strange Last Voyage of Donald Crowhurst,* Stein & Day, NY, 1970

V

Vaitses, Alan H., *Boatbuilding One-Offs in Fiberglass,* International Marine Publishing Company, Camden, ME, 1984

W

Wagner, Rudolf, *Weit Weit Voraus Liegt Antigua,* Ulstein Buch, Frankfurt, Germany, 1991

Walker, Stuart H., *Advanced Racing Tactics,* W.W. Norton Company, NY, 1986

Weld, Phil, *Moxie,* The Bodley Head Ltd., London, UK, 1982

Wharram, James, *Two Girls and a Catamaran,* Abelard – Schuman, London, UK, 1969

Whidden, Tom, *The Art and Science of Sails,* Adlard Coles, London, UK, 1990

White, Chris, *The Cruising Multihull,* International Marine, Camden, ME, 1990

White, Rick, Wells, Mary, *Catamaran Racing for the 90's,* RAM – Press, Key Largo, FL, 1992

White, Rick, Munns, Harry, *Multihull Fundamentals,* International Marine, Camden, ME, 1997

Z

Zimmermann, Tim, *The Race,* NY, 2003

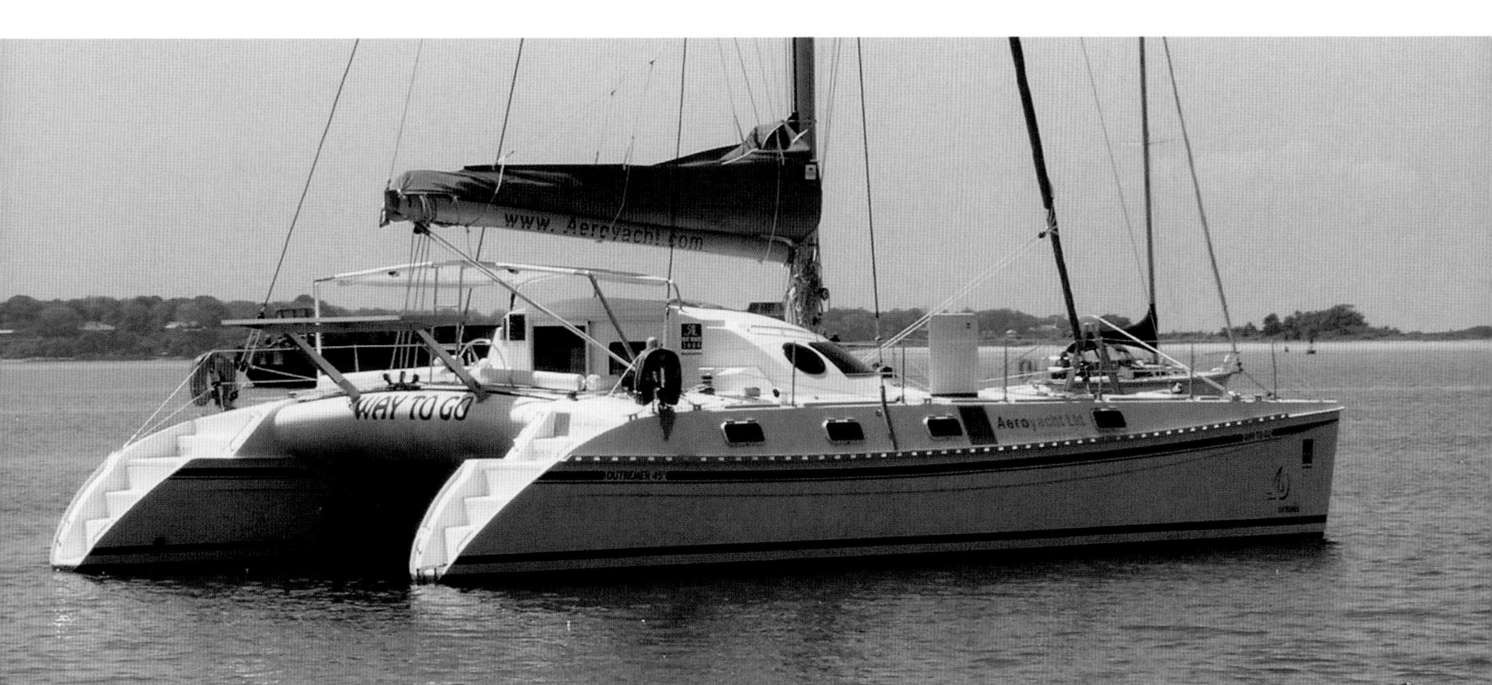

GLOSSARY

A

Abeam
At a right angle to the length of the boat.

Adrift
Floating free with the currents and tide, not under control.

Aft
Toward the stern (rear) of the boat.

Aground
When a boat is in water too shallow for it to float in, i.e.: the boat's bottom is resting on the ground.

Aka
The connecting crossarms between main hull and outboard hull.

Amas
The outboard hulls of a trimaran.

Anchor
(1) a heavy metal object designed in such a way that its weight and shape will help to hold a boat in its position when lowered to the sea bottom on a rode or chain. (2) The act of using an anchor.

Anchorage
A place where a boat anchors, usually an established and marked area.

Anchor locker
A locker used to store the anchor rode and anchor in.

Anchor windlass
A windlass used to assist when raising the anchor.

Anemometer
A device that measures wind velocity.

Apparent Wind
Wind strength and direction which is measured from the moving deck of a boat (vs. True Wind, which is measured from the stationary deck).

Aspect Ratio
The relationship of length of the luff divided by the length of the foot of the sail or the length of a keel divided by its depth.

Astern
Toward the stern of a vessel, or behind the boat.

Athwartships
Lying along the ship's width, at right angles to the vessel's centerline.

Autopilot
A device used to steer a boat automatically, usually electrical, hydraulic or mechanical in nature. A similar mechanism called a self-steering gear may also be used on a sailing vessel.

Auxiliary
A second method of propelling a vessel. On a sailboat this could be an engine.

Aweigh
An anchor raised off the bottom.

B

Backing (wind)
The changing of the wind direction, opposite of veering. Clockwise in the Southern Hemisphere, counter-clockwise in the Northern Hemisphere.

Back splice
A method of weaving the end of a rope to keep it from unraveling.

Backstay
A stay (line or cable) used to support the mast. The backstay runs from the masthead to the stern and helps keep the mast from falling forward.

Back Winded
The state of a sail with the wind pushing on the wrong side of it, causing it to be pushed away from the wind.

Bail
To remove water from a boat, as with a bucket or a pump.

Ballast
Pertains to monohulls. Weight at the bottom of the boat to help keep it stable. Ballast can be placed inside the hull of the boat or externally on a keel.

Bar
A region of shallow water usually made of sand or mud.

Barber Hauler (In-hauler)
A device of lines and blocks which helps pull the jib in or out to provide a better shape.

Bareboat
To charter a boat without a skipper.

Batten
A strip of wood, or composite material, which is inserted into batten pockets of the sail to provide shape and stability to the sail material.

Beach Cat
Small trailerable catamaran, usually 12-20' long (such as the Hobie Cat)

Beam
The widest part of a boat.

Bear Away, Bear Off
To fall off. A boat falls off the wind when it points its bow farther from the eye of the wind. The opposite of heading up.

Beat
To sail on a tack toward the wind.

Beating
Tacking. To sail against the wind by sailing on alternating tacks.

Beaufort Wind Scale
Used to gauge wind speed using observations of the wind's effects on trees and other objects.

Berth
(1) a place for a person to sleep. (2) a place where the ship can be secured. (3) a safe and cautious distance, such as "We gave the shark a wide berth."

Bilge
The lowest part of the hull under the cabin sole.

Bilge Pump
A mechanical, electrical, or manually operated pump used to remove water from the bilge.

Bimini
A cover used to shelter the cockpit from the sun.

Bitter End
The end of a line. Also the end of the anchor rode attached to the boat.

Block
One or more wheels with grooves in them (pulleys) designed to carry a line and change the direction of its travel. A housing around the wheel allows the block to be connected to a spar, or another line. Lines used with a block are known as tackle.

Block and Tackle
A combination of one or more blocks and the associated tackle necessary to give a mechanical advantage. Useful for lifting heavy loads.

Boom
A pole securing the bottom of a sail, allowing more control of the position of a sail.

Bow
The front of the boat.

Bowline
A knot used to make a loop in a line. Easily untied, it is simple and strong. The bowline is used to tie sheets to sails.

Bowsprit
A spar extending forward of the bow of the boat, usually used to attach the tack of a sail to.

Breakers
A wave that approaches shallow water, causing the wave height to exceed the depth of the water it is in, in effect tripping it. The wave changes from a smooth surge in the water to a cresting wave with water tumbling down the front of it.

Bridge deck (Wing deck)
Main structure that spans between the hulls of a catamaran; vulnerable to pounding if engineered too low.

Bridle
Two lines which attach to each bow and hook onto the anchor chain to minimize the boat swinging at anchor.

Broaching
The unplanned turning of a vessel to expose its side to the oncoming waves. In heavy seas this could cause the boat to be knocked down.

Bulkhead
An interior wall in a vessel. Sometimes bulkheads are also watertight, adding to the vessel's safety.

Buoy
A floating device used as a navigational aid by marking channels, hazards and prohibited areas.

C

Capsize
When a boat turns over in the water so that is no longer right side up.

Catamaran
A twin-hulled boat. Catamarans are known for their stability and safety. They have the mobility to plane and are faster than single-hulled boats (monohulls) in some conditions.

Ceiling
The side walls of a cabin (in comparison to the overhead).

Center Line
The imaginary line running from bow to stern along the middle of the boat.

Chainplate
Strong metal plates attached to the sides of the hull to which shrouds are attached.

Chine
The location where the deck joins the hull of the boat.

Chop
Small, steep, disorderly waves.

Cleat
A fitting to which lines can be easily attached.

Clew (of a Sail)
The aft lower corner of the sail where the sheet controls are attached.

Close Hauled
Sailing as close as possible to the wind.

Cockpit
Exterior protected deck space of a boat.

Code Zero
Large gennaker (screacher) type headsail, sheeted as far aft and inboard as possible.

Come About
To tack and change course by turning the bow through the wind.

Compass Course
The course as read on a compass. The compass course adds the magnetic deviation and the magnetic variation to the true course.

Coordinated Universal Time (UTC)
The international time standard. It is the current term for what was commonly referred to as Greenwich Meridian Time (GMT). Zero (0) hours UTC is midnight in Greenwich, England, which lies on the zero longitudinal meridian.

CQR Anchor
Also called a plow anchor – short for coastal quick release anchor. An anchor that is designed to bury itself into the ground by use of its plow shape.

Crossbeam
Any of the three beams of a catamaran which connect the hulls.

Cunningham
Block and tackle system to induce tension on luff of mainsail.

Current
The movement of water, due to tides, river movement and circular currents caused by the motion of the earth.

Cutter
Single mast rig with twin headsails (Yankee and/or staysail).

Cyclone
The generic term for a tropical weather system, including tropical depressions, tropical storms and hurricanes.

D

Daggerboard
A non-pivoting foil which can be lifted or lowered to provide leeway resistance.

Davit
A device that projects beyond the side of the boat to raise objects from the water. Typically a single davit is used on the bow of a vessel to raise an anchor, and a pair are used on the side or stern of the vessel to raise a dinghy.

Dead Ahead
A position directly in front of the vessel.

Dead Ending
Tying off.

Deck Head
The underside of the deck, viewed from below (the ceiling.)

Depth Sounder
An instrument that uses sound waves to measure the distance to the sea floor.

Dinghy, Dink
1) A small boat used to travel from a boat to shore, carrying people or supplies. Also known as a tender.
2) The act of using a dinghy.

Displacement
The weight of a boat measured according to the weight of water it displaces. A boat displaces an amount of water equal to the weight of the boat, so the boat's displacement and weight are identical.

Displacement Speed
Also called hull speed. The theoretical speed that a boat can travel without planing, based on the shape of its hull. This speed is 1.34 times the length of a boat at its waterline. Since most monohull sailboats cannot exceed their hull speed, longer boats are faster.

Distance Made Good
The distance traveled after correction for current, leeway, and other factors that may not have been included in the original distance measurement.

Dolphin Striker
A structure underneath the boat to resist the downward force of the mast.

Douse
To furl or lower a sail.

Downhaul (see Cunningham)

Downwind
In the direction the wind is blowing.

Draft
1) The depth of a boat, measured from the deepest point to the waterline. The water must be at least this depth, or the boat will run aground.
2) A term describing the amount of curvature designed into a sail.

Drogue
Any device that is dragged behind the boat to slow its progress.

E

Ease
To loosen or let out a sail control sheet. (opposite of trimming).

EPIRB
Emergency Position Indicating Radio Beacon. An emergency device that uses a radio signal to alert satellites or passing airplanes to a vessel's position.

Escape Hatch
Emergency hatches set into the sides of the hulls of a catamaran.

F

Fall Off
Also referred to as bear away or bear off. A boat falls off the wind when it points its bow farther from the eye of the wind. The opposite of heading up.

Fat Head (see Square Top Main)

Fathom
Unit of depth measured as 6 feet.

Fender
A cushion hung from the sides of a boat to protect it from rubbing against a dock or another boat.

Fetch
The distance that wind and seas (waves) can travel toward land without being blocked. In areas without obstructions the wind and seas can build to great strength, but in areas such as sheltered coves and harbors the wind and seas can be quite calm.

Fiberglass
A construction method using layers of woven glass mats that are bonded together with glue.

Fin Keel
A keel that is narrower and deeper than a full keel.

Flare
A device that burns to produce a bright light, sometimes colored, usually used to indicate an emergency.

Foil
A wing-like surface below the hull that, when moved through water, lifts the hull out of the water, allowing greater speeds.

Following Sea
Large seas coming from astern.

Footing
Slightly falling off when going to windward on the hypothesis of added speed and higher VMG. The faster the catamaran the more this theory applies.

Fore
Toward the bow (front) of the vessel.

Foresail
A sail placed forward of the mast, such as a jib.

Forestay
A line running from the bow of the boat to the upper part of the mast, designed to pull the mast forward. A forestay that attaches slightly below the top of the mast can be used to help control the bend of the mast. The most forward stay on the boat is also called the headstay.

Fouled (Snafu)
Tangled lines.

Founder
To fill with water and sink.

Fractional Rig
Sail plan in which the jib does not go to the top of the mast height (usually 7/8).

Freeboard
Distance from waterline to deck edge at hull.

Furl
To lower a sail. Sails are sometimes partially furled to reduce the amount of sail area in use without completely lowering the sail. This is usually known as reefing.

G

Gale
A storm with a wind speed between 34 to 40 knots.

Galley
The kitchen area on a boat.

Gelcoat
Pigmented outside layer of a GRP boat

Gennaker (Screacher)
A large genoa-like headsail, usually flown from a soft Spectra luff wire.

Genoa
A large jib that overlaps the mast.

Global Positioning System (GPS)
A system of satellites that allows one's position to be calculated with great accuracy by the use of an electronic receiver.

Gooseneck
A strong metal hinged fitting to secure forward end of boom to mast.

Great Circle Route
A course that is the shortest distance between two points. The center of a great circle is the center of the earth.

Greenwich Meridian Time (GMT)
A time standard that is not affected by time zones or seasons. Now called Coordinated Universal Time (UTC).

Grommet
A ring or eyelet normally used to attach a line, such as on a sail.

Ground Swells
Swells that become shorter and steeper as they approach the shore due to shallow water.

Ground Tackle
The anchor and its rode or chain and any other gear used to hold a boat securely in place.

GRP
Glass Reinforced Plastic (polyester construction method)

Gudgeon
Female part of the rudder hinge mechanism (for transom mount rudders).

Gunkhole
To cruise in and explore shallow waters.

Gybe
Same as jibe.

H

Halyard
A line used to hoist a sail or spar. The tightness of the halyard can affect sail shape.

Hatch
A sliding or hinged opening in the deck, providing people with access to the cabin or space below.

Haul
Pulling on a line.

Haul Out
Remove a boat from the water.

Head
The upper top most section of the sail. The bathroom/toilet of a vessel.

Header
An unfavorable wind shift that forces you to steer lower than your intended course.

Headfoil
A metal extrusion fitted around the forestay and used to secure the luff of the jib by holding its bolt rope in place.

Headsail
Any sail forward of the mast, such as a jib.

Head Seas
Waves coming from the front of the vessel.

Headstay
The most forward forestay. The line from the bow or bowsprit to the top of the mast. This keeps the mast from falling toward the rear of the boat. The headstay is the farthest forward of all the stays on the boat.

Head up
To turn the bow more directly into the eye of the wind. The opposite of falling off.

Heaving To
To slow or stop the forward motion of the boat, such as needed when in heavy seas.

Heavy Seas
When the water has large or breaking waves in stormy conditions.

Heavy Weather
Stormy conditions, including rough, high seas and strong winds.

Heel, Heeling
(1) When a boat tilts away from the wind, caused by wind blowing on the sails and pulling the top of the mast over. Some heeling is normal when under sail. (2) The inboard or lower end of a spar. (3) The lowest point of the keel, rudder, etc.

Helm
The wheel or tiller of a boat.

Helmsman
The person who is steering the boat.

High Tide
The point of a tide when the water is the highest. The opposite of low tide.

Hitch
A knot used to attach a line to a cleat or other object.

Horizon
Where the water and sky or ground and sky appear to intersect.

Hounds
Attachment point of shrouds and forestay on a rotating mast.

Hull
The main structural body of the boat, not including the deck, keel, mast, or cabin. The part that keeps the water out of the boat.

Hull speed
The theoretical speed a boat can travel without planing, based on the shape of its hull. This speed is about 1.34 times the square root of the length of a boat at its waterline. Since most monohull sailboats cannot exceed their hull speed, longer boats are faster.

Hurricane
A strong tropical revolving storm of Force 12 or higher. In the northern hemisphere. hurricanes revolve in a clockwise direction. In the southern hemisphere they revolve counterclockwise and are known as typhoons.

Hydrodynamic
A shape designed to move efficiently through the water.

Hydrofoil
A boat that has foils under its hull onto which it rises to plane across the water surface at high speed.

I

Inboard
(1) toward the center of the boat. (2) an engine that is mounted inside the boat.

Inflatable
A dinghy or raft that can be inflated for use or deflated for easy stowage.

Inmarsat-C
A series of satellites that provide two-way communications.

Irons (in Irons)
Stalling a sailboat head into the wind with no further progress.

J

Jacklines
Safety lines running along the deck used to attach a tether from a safety harness.

Jib
A triangular sail attached to the headstay. A jib that extends aft of the mast is known as a Genoa.

Jibe (also gybe)
To change direction when sailing in such a manner that the stern of the boat passes through the eye of the wind and the boom changes sides. Careful control of the boom and mainsail are required when jibing to prevent a violent motion of the boom when it switches sides.

Jib Sheet
A sheet used to control the position of the jib. The jib has two sheets, and at any time, one is the working sheet and the other is the lazy sheet.

K

Keel
On monohulls, usually ballasted, but never on multihulls. A flat surface built into the bottom of the boat to reduce the leeway caused by the wind pushing against the side of the boat. Usually, a keel also has some ballast to help keep the boat upright and prevent it from heeling too much. There are several types of keels, such as fin keels and full keels.

Knot
(1) a speed of one nautical mile per hour. (2) a method of attaching a rope or line to itself, another line or a fitting.

L

Land Breeze
A wind moving from the land to the water due to temperature changes in the evening.

Lash
To tie something with a line.

Lateral Resistance
To resist being driven sideways by the wind and seas.

Launch
(1) To place a boat in the water; (2) a small boat used to ferry people to and from a larger vessel.

Lazy Jack
A line running from above the mainsail to the boom to aid in the lowering of the sail.

Lazy Sheet
A line attached to a sail but not currently in use. The line currently in use is known as the working sheet. The working and lazy sheets usually change when the boat is tacked.

Leach
The back edge (trailing edge) of the sail.

League
Three nautical miles.

Lee
The direction toward which the wind is blowing. The direction sheltered from the wind.

Lee Helm
Tendency of a boat to turn away from the wind.

Lee Shore
The coast line towards which one is blown in a strong unfavorable wind.

Leeward
The direction away from the wind. Opposite of windward.

Leeway
The sideways movement of a boat away from the wind, usually unwanted. Keels and other devices help prevent a boat from having excessive leeway.

Life Raft
An emergency raft used in case of serious problems to the parent vessel, such as sinking.

Log
A device used to measure the distance traveled through the water. The distance read from a log can be affected by currents, leeway and other factors, so those distances are sometimes corrected to a distance made good.

Longitude
Imaginary lines drawn through the north and south poles on the globe used to measure distance east and west. Greenwich, England, is designated as 0° with other distances being measured in degrees east and west of Greenwich.

Luff
(1) Forward leading edge of a sail; (2) to head into the wind to depower sails.

Lull
Period of lower wind speed.

LWL

Waterline length of a boat.

Lying a Hull

Drifting in heavy seas with all sails lowered and helm locked.

M

Main (Cross) Beam

Crossbeam between the middle section of a catamaran. Usually the mast is stepped on the main beam.

Masthead

Top of the mast.

Messenger

A small line used to pull a heavier line or cable.

Midships

A place on a boat where its beam is the widest.

MOB

Man Overboard.

Monohull

A boat that has only one hull, as opposed to multihull boats.

Moor

To attach a boat to a mooring, dock, post, anchor, etc.

Mooring

A place where a boat can be moored. Usually a buoy marks the location of a firmly set anchor.

Mooring Line

A line used to secure a boat to an anchor, dock, or mooring.

Multihull

A boat with more than one hull. Proas, trimarans and catamarans are all multihulls.

N

Nacelle

Section of the bridgedeck that is lower than the sole.

Nautical Miles

Distance at sea is measured in nautical miles, which are about 6067.12 feet, 1.15 statute miles or exactly 1,852 meters. Nautical miles have the unique property which is that a minute of latitude is equal to one nautical mile (there is a slight error because the earth is not perfectly round). Measurement of speed is done in knots where one knot equals one nautical mile per hour.

Navigation Lights

Lights on a boat help others determine its course, position, and what it is doing. Boats underway should have a red light visible from their port bow, a green light on the starboard bow and a white light at the stern. Other lights are required for vessels under power, fishing, towing, etc.

O

Offshore

Away from land, toward the water.

Off the wind

Sailing with the wind coming from the stern or quarter of the boat.

One-off

Non production, custom built.

Open

A location that is not sheltered from the wind and seas.

Osmosis

Water penetration into the GRP laminate.

Outhaul

A line used to apply tension on the foot of a sail, to maintain proper sail shape.

Outrigger

A flotation device attached to one or both sides of the hull to help prevent capsizing.

Overboard

In the water outside of the vessel.

P

Pad Eye

A loop-shaped fitting used to secure a line to some part of the boat.

Pan-Pan
An urgent radio-announced message regarding the safety of people or property. A mayday call is used when there is an immediate threat to life or property. A pan-pan situation may develop into a mayday situation. Pan-pan and mayday messages have priority on radio channels and should not be interrupted. In the case of a less urgent safety message, the securite signal is used.

Parachute Anchor (Sea Anchor)
A large parachute-shaped device that is used to minimize drift and stop the boat.

PFD
A Personal Flotation Device; a device used to keep a person afloat. Also called a life jacket, life preserver or life vest.

Pinch
Steering a sailboat too close to the eye of the wind, causing the sails to flap.

Pintle
The male part of the hinged fitting of a transom-mounted rudder (opposite of gudgeon).

Pitch
1) A fore and aft rocking motion of a boat.
2) The degree of curvature of a propeller.
3) A material used to seal cracks in wooden planks.

Pitchpole
Capsizing a boat stern over bow.

Pointing
Sailing as close to the wind as possible.

Point of Sail
The position of a sailboat in relation to the wind. A boat with its head into the wind is known as "head to wind" or "in irons." The point of sail with the bow of the boat as close as possible to the wind is called "close-hauled." As the bow moves farther from the wind, the points of sail are called: close reach, beam reach, broad reach and running. The general direction a boat is sailing is known as its tack.

Polar Diagram
A circular diagram showing the speed potential of a boat on various points of sail.

Port
(1) The left side of the boat from the perspective of a person at the stern of the boat and looking toward the bow. The opposite of starboard. (2) A porthole. A window in the side of a boat, usually round or with rounded corners. Sometimes portholes can be opened, sometimes they are fixed shut. Also see hatch. (3) Harbor.

Porthole
A port, a window in the side of a boat, usually round or with rounded corners. Sometimes portholes can be opened, sometimes they are fixed shut.

Port Tack
Sailing with the wind coming over the port rail.

Pound
The action of a boat's bow repeatedly slamming into oncoming waves.

Preventer
A tackle or single line lead forward from the boom to a secure fitting to prevent the boom from gybing or swinging violently when deep reaching or running.

Proa
Two hulled craft with main hull and one outrigger (ama).

Propeller
An object with two or more twisted blades that is designed to propel a vessel through the water when spun rapidly by the boat's engine.

Prop Walk
Sideward force created by a spinning propeller, something that twin engined catamarans are unaffected by.

Pulpit
A sturdy railing around the deck at the bow.

Q

Quarter
The side of a boat aft of the beam. There is both a port quarter and a starboard quarter.

Quartering Sea
A sea which comes over the quarter of the boat.

Quarters
Sleeping areas on the boat.

R

Radar
Radio detection and ranging. An electronic instrument that uses radio waves to find the distance and location of other objects, employed effectively to avoid collisions, particularly in times of poor visibility.

Radio Beacon
A navigational aid that emits radio waves for navigational purposes. The radio beacon's position is known and the direction of the radio beacon can be determined by using a radio direction finder.

Raft
1) A small flat boat, usually inflatable.
2) To moor with more than one boat tied together, usually using only one boat's anchor and rode.

Rail (Bulwark, Gunwale)
The top outside deck edge.

Rake
A measurement of the top of the mast's tilt toward the bow or stern.

Reef
1) To partially lower a sail so that it is not as large, which helps prevent too much sail as the wind increases.
2) A line of rock and coral near the surface of the water.

Reefing Lines
Lines used to pull the reef in the sail.

Reef Points
Strong grommets sewn into luff and leach of sail.

Rhumb Line
A line that passes through all meridians at the same angle. When drawn on a Mercator chart, the Rhumb Line is a straight line. However, the Mercator chart is a distortion of a round globe on a flat surface, so the Rhumb line will be a longer course than a great circle route.

Rig
The mast and its hardware.

Rigging
Cable and lines which support the mast.

Roach
The aft portion of a sail that extends beyond a straight line from clew to the head.

Rocker
A hull characteristic; low in the middle and swept upwards towards the bow and stern section when seen from the side.

Rode
A line or chain attached to an anchor.

Rogue Wave
A freak wave which is much higher than the average seas.

Roll
A side-to-side motion of the boat, usually caused by waves.

Roller Furling
A method of storing a sail, commonly by rolling the jib around the headstay or rolling the mainsail around the boom or on the mast.

Roller Reefing
A system of reefing a sail by partially furling it. Roller furling systems are not necessarily designed to support roller reefing.

Rope
Traditionally a line must be over 1 inch in size to be called a rope.

Round Up
To turn into the wind.

Rudder Post
The post that the rudder is attached to. The wheel or tiller is connected to the rudder post.

Running
1) A point of sail where the boat has the wind coming from aft of the boat.
2) Used to describe a line that has been released and is in motion.

Running Backstay (Runners)
Also known as a runner. An adjustable stay used to control tension on the mast.

S

Safety Harness
A device worn around a person's body that can be attached to the ship to prevent the person from being separated from the ship.

Sail Shape
The shape of a sail, with regard to its efficiency. In high winds, a sail would probably be flatter, in low winds rounder. Other circumstances can cause a sail to twist. Controls such as the outhaul, halyards, sheets and the bend of the main mast all can affect sail shape.

Sail Trim
The position of the sails relative to the wind and desired point of sail. Sails that are not trimmed properly may not operate efficiently. Visible signs of trim are excessive heeling and the flow of air past telltales.

Saloon
The main cabin on the bridge deck of a catamaran.

Scantlings
The engineering data of vessel; results determine the sizes and weights of structures.

Screw
A propeller.

Scope
The ratio between the length of the anchor rode and the depth of the anchor. A scope of 7:1 is usually used, depending on the holding ground. Too little scope can cause the anchor to drag.

Scupper
An opening through the toe rail or gunwale to allow water to drain back into the sea.

Scuttle
To sink a boat.

Sea Anchor
A device designed to bring a boat to a near stop in heavy weather. Typically, a sea anchor is set off the bow of a boat so that the bow points into the wind and rough waves.

Seagull Striker
Rigid reinforcement structure on the forward beam of a catamaran to resist the upward pull of the forestay.

Seamanship
The ability of a person to motor or sail a vessel, including all aspects of its operation.

Secure
To make fast, to stow an object or tie it in place.

Securite
A message transmitted by radio to warn of impending storms, navigational hazards and other potential problems that are not an immediate threat to life or property. Less serious than mayday and pan-pan messages.

Self-Bailing
A boat capable of draining any water from its decks and cockpit by the principle of gravity.

Sextant
A navigational instrument used to determine the vertical position of an object such as the sun, moon or stars, used for celestial navigation.

Shackle
A metal U-shaped connector that attaches to other fittings with the use of a pin that is inserted through the arms of the U.

Shake Out
To remove a reef from a sail.

Sheave
The grooved part of a block through which a line runs.

Sheer
1) The fore-and-aft curvature of the deck.
2) A sudden change of course.

Sheet
A line used to control a sail's trim. The sheets are named after the sail, as in jib sheet and mainsheet.

Shroud
Part of the standing rigging that helps to support the mast by running from the top of the mast to the side of the boat. Sailboats usually have one or more shrouds on each side of the mast.

Sideslip (making leeway)
The tendency of a boat to move sideways in the water instead of along its heading due to the motion of currents or winds.

Singlehand (Shorthanded)
To sail alone without crew.

Skeg
Any flat protrusion on the outside of the hull that is used to support another object, such as the propeller shaft or rudder.

Skin
The outside surface of a boat; often used when describing a fiberglass or other molded hull.

Slamming (Pounding)

Slot
The opening between the jib and the mainsail. Wind passing through this opening increases the pressure difference across the sides of the mainsail, helping to move the boat forward.

Snatch Block
Block that can be opened on one side, allowing it to be placed on a line that is already in use.

Sound
1) To measure the depth of the water.
2) A long wide body of water that connects other large bodies of water.
3) A long, wide ocean inlet.

Sounding
The depth of the water as marked on a chart.

Spinnaker
A very large, lightweight sail used when running or on the point of sail known as a broad reach.

Spinnaker Halyard
A halyard used to raise the spinnaker.

Spinnaker Pole (only on monohulls)
Sometimes called a spinnaker boom. A pole used to extend the foot of the spinnaker beyond the edge of the boat and to secure the corner of the sail.

Splice
The place where two lines are joined together end to end.

Spreaders
Small spars extending toward the sides from one or more places along the mast. The shrouds cross the end of the spreaders, enabling the shrouds to better support the mast.

Spring Lines
Docking lines that help keep a boat from moving fore and aft while docked.

Squall
A sudden intense wind storm of short duration, often accompanied by rain. Squalls often accompany an advancing cold front.

Square Top Main
A type of mainsail which has a large headboard and is quadrilateral to extend sail area.

SSB
A Single sideband radio. A radio used on a boat to transmit for long distances.

Stability (Stiffness)
The ability of a boat to keep from heeling or rolling excessively, and to quickly return upright after heeling.

Stall
1) To stop moving.
2) Air is said to stall when it becomes detached from the surface it is flowing along. Usually air travels smoothly along both sides of a sail, but if the sail is not properly trimmed, the air can leave one of the sides of the sail and begin to stall. Stalled sails are not operating efficiently.

Starboard
The right side of the boat from the perspective of a person at the stern of the boat and looking toward the bow.

Starboard Tack
A sailboat sailing on a tack with the wind coming over the starboard side and the boom on the port side of the boat. If two boats under sail are approaching, the one on port tack must give way to the boat on starboard tack.

Stay (Shroud, Forestay, Backstay)
A wire rope used to support the mast.

Staysail
A triangular sail similar to the jib, set on a stay forward of the mast and aft of the headstay.

Steerage Way
In order for the rudder to be able to properly steer the boat it must be moving through the water. The speed necessary for control is known as steerage way.

Stem
The forward edge of the bow. On a wooden boat the stem is a single timber.

Stepped
1) A mast that is in place.
2) Where the mast is stepped as in keel-stepped or deck-stepped.

Stern
The aft part of a boat. The back of the boat.

Stern Line
Line running from the stern of the boat to a dock when moored.

Stiff (opposite of Tender)
A boat that resists heeling.

Storm Jib
Sometimes called a spitfire. A small jib made out of heavy cloth for use in heavy weather and occasionally brightly colored.

Storm Sails
The storm jib and storm trysail; small sails built from heavy cloth for use during heavy weather.

Storm Trysail
A very strong sail used in stormy weather. It is loose-footed and attached to the mast, but not the boom; this helps prevent boarding waves from damaging the sail or the rigging.

Stow
To put something away.

Surf
(1) The breaking waves and resulting foam near a shore. (2) Sailing beyond hull speed, whereby a portion of the hull is planing.

Swage
A compression method of attaching end fittings for cable.

Swell
Large smooth waves that do not break. Swells are formed by wind action over a long distance.

Swivel
A rotating fitting used to keep a line from tangling.

T

Tack
1) The lower forward corner of a triangular sail.
2) The direction in which a boat is sailing with respect to the wind.
3) To change a boat's direction by bringing the bow through the eye of the wind.

Tacking
1) To change a boat's direction by bringing the bow through the eye of the wind.
2) To tack repeatedly, as when trying to sail to a point upwind of the boat.

Tackle
Lines used with blocks in order to move heavy objects.

Telltale
A small line free to flow in the direction of the breeze. It is attached to sails, stays in the slot, and in other areas, enabling the helmsman and crew to see how the wind is flowing.

Tender
(1) A dinghy. (2) An unstable, tippy boat which heels easily.

Tidal Current
Also called tidal stream. The flow of water caused by the rising and lowering tidal waters.

Tide
The predictable, regular rising and lowering of water in some areas due to the pull of the sun and the moon. Tidal changes can happen approximately every six or 12 hours, depending on the region. To find the time and water levels of different tides, you can use tide tables for your area. The period of high water level is known as high tide, and the period of low water level is known as low tide.

Tiller
An arm attached to the top of the rudder to steer a small boat. If the helmsman wants to steer to starboard, he pushes the tiller to port. Larger boats usually use a wheel instead of a tiller.

Toe Rail
A small rail around the deck. The toe rail may have holes in it for attaching lines or blocks. A larger rail is known as a gunwale.

Tooling
The manufacturing of male plugs or female molds used in composite construction.

Topping Lift
A line which supports the aft end of the boom.

Topsides
The sides of the hull above the waterline and below the deck.

Track
The course a boat travels over ground.

Trade Winds
Winds in certain areas known for their consistent strength and direction. Trade winds are named because of their reliability allowing for planned voyages along the routes favored by those winds.

Traveler
A track with an attached block allowing more controlled adjustment of sail trim, usually for the mainsail or self-tacking jib.

Trim
1) To pull in a line or sail control sheet (opposite of easing).
2) Sail trim.
3) A properly balanced boat that floats evenly on its waterline. Improperly trimmed boats may list or lie with their bow or stern too low in the water.

Trimaran
A boat with a center hull and two smaller outer hulls referred to as amas.

Trip Line
A line attached to the end of an anchor to help free it from the ground.

Trunk (Daggerboard Trunk)
A strong housing in which the daggerboard is lowered and raised.

Turnbuckle
A metal fitting that is turned to tighten or loosen the tension on standing rigging.

U

Under Deck (Bridge Deck)
The underside of a catamaran's wing deck.

Unfurl
To unfold or unroll a sail; the opposite of furl.

Upwind
To windward; to sail in the direction of the eye of the wind.

V

Vang
A block and tackle system that controls the angle of the boom.

Veer (opposite of backing)
A shifting of the wind direction, clockwise in the Northern Hemisphere, counter-clockwise in the Southern Hemisphere.

VHF
1) Very High Frequency radio waves.
2) A radio that transmits in the VHF range; the most common communications radio carried on boats, but its range is limited to "line of sight" between the transmitting and receiving stations.

W

Wake
Waves generated in the water by a moving vessel.

Warps
Heavy mooring lines usually dragged from astern to slow down.

Watch
(1) A division of crew into shifts. (2) The time each watch has duty.

Waterline
The line the water reaches on the hull of a boat. Design waterline is where the waterline was designed to be, load waterline is the waterline when the boat is loaded.

Weather Helm
The tendency of a sailboat to turn into the wind.

Weatherly
The ability of a sailboat to sail close to the wind.

Wheel
One of two methods used to steer a boat. A wheel is turned in the direction that the helmsman wants the boat to move. On smaller boats, a tiller usually is used, and it steers in the opposite manner.

White Caps (White Horses)
Small waves which start to develop at around 20 knots of wind.

Windlass
A mechanical device used to pull in cable or chain, such as an anchor rode.

Windward
In the direction of the wind – opposite of leeward.

Wing Deck
The underside of the bridge deck.

Y

Yacht
A sailboat or powerboat used for pleasure – not a working boat.

Yaw
Swinging off course, usually in heavy seas. The bow moves toward one side of the intended course.

Z

Zephyr
A gentle breeze. The west wind.

Zinc
A sacrificial anode, the least of the noble metals, used to protect other metals from galvanic corrosion.

Zulu (CUT or GMT)
Used to indicated times measured in Coordinated Universal Time – a successor to Greenwich Mean Time. A time standard that is not affected by time zones.

INDEX OF ILLUSTRATIONS AND TABLES

FEATURED CATAMARAN INDEX

INDEX

"Three things in life are free: love, sun and the wind."

~ Josephine Wegdam-Van der Aa